BEYOND THE BLOOD

Also by Marie-Laure Valandro

Camino Walk
Where Inner and Outer Paths Meet

Letters from Florence
Observations on the Inner Art of Travel

Deliverance of the Spellbound God
*An Experiential Journey into Eastern
and Western Meditation Practices*

Touched
*A Painter's Insights into the
Work of Liane Collot d'Herbois*

Wisconsin Hills Farm Stories
Adventures of a Biodynamic Farmer

Nutrition for Enlightened Parenting

Via Podiensis, Path of Power
*A Walk from le Puy, France,
to San Juan de la Peña, Spain*

Beyond *the* Blood

A Celebration of Judaism, Islam, & Christianity

*A Personal Journey Across Foreign Lands and Centuries
with Insights from Spiritual Science*

MARIE-LAURE VALANDRO

Lindisfarne Books | 2015

2015

LINDISFARNE BOOKS
An imprint of Anthroposophic Press / SteinerBooks
610 Main St., Great Barrington, MA 01230
www.steinerbooks.org

Copyright © 2015 by Marie-Laure Valandro.
All rights reserved. No part of this publication may be reproduced, stored in a retrieval system, or transmitted, in any form or by any means, electronic, mechanical, photocopying, recording, or otherwise, without the prior written permission of the publisher.

Cover image copyright © Marie-Laure Valandro
Cover and book design: Jeanne DePrince Bowen

Printed in the United States of America

LIBRARY OF CONGRESS CATALOGING-IN-PUBLICATION DATA IS AVAILABLE

Print ISBN: 978-1-58420-198-4
ebook ISBN: 978-1-58420-199-1

Dedicated to the titanic Spirit of Rudolf Steiner

---

*In memory of my mother,
Paulette Valandro, December 1923 – April 2015*

Contents

Introduction		9
Part I	Egypt ☙ Palestine ☙ Israel ☙ Jordan	17
Part II	Spain: A Walk from Seville to Santiago	109
Part III	Morocco	173
Part IV	Tunisia ☙ Djerba Island ☙ Sahara Desert	189
Part V	Kenya ☙ Tanzania ☙ Zanzibar Island	227
Part VI	Turkey ☙ Patmos	233
Part VII	A Look Into the Past: Iran	285
Part VIII	Poland	295
Part IX	Azerbaijan	315
Part X	Uzbekistan	347
Part XI	Fes, Morocco	405
Bibliography		475

Introduction

This book is meant to wet the appetite of the reader—to awaken an interest in pursuing an understanding of some of the major events in mankind's evolution and perhaps seeing some of the most stunning sites on our Earth. If that happens then I have accomplished my task.

> We have not merely learned something; we have become more alive through what we have learned.
> —Rudolf Steiner, *The Gospel of St. John and Its Relation to the Other Gospels*

> A whole picture of reality can only be acquired by looking beyond the type of blood flowing in a person's veins and instead asking where the soul originates that is only served by this blood.
> —Rudolf Steiner, *Universal Spirituality and Human Physicality: Bridging the Divide*

> "What you think today you'll be tomorrow," does indeed come true. You have to understand that when people have bad, corrupt ways of thinking in one age, the next generation and the next age will have to pay for this physically.
> —Rudolf Steiner, *Original Impulses for the Science of the Spirit*

A very intellectual man went to Jami and asked him to take him as his pupil and give him initiation. Jami looked at him and said, "Have you loved anybody?" This man said, "No, I have not loved." Then Jami said, "Go, and love first. Then come to me and I will show you the way."

—Attar, Sufi poet, AD 1120, in
The Hand of Poetry: Five Mystic Poets of Persia

We need a sphere of spirit and culture firmly rooted in the real world; we need a sphere of spirit and culture in which books are written from life and for life, full of ideas for life and ways and means of living. Especially in the sphere of spirit and culture we must emerge from our libraries and go out into life.

—Rudolf Steiner, *Rudolf Steiner Speaks to the British*

Greater tolerance in regard to religious views has come about in recent times. Modern human beings feel that to hate or persecute those who confess a different faith serves no purpose. In fact, the hatred and intolerance that formerly caused so much blood to flow in the name of religion is no longer understood. This tendency to accept and tolerate will continue for some time, but eventually it will prove too weak, too insipid an attitude for progress....

What is required now is complete mutual understanding, not just tolerance and patience. So far, Christians have tended to take the attitude that, while they do not understand the faith of Muslims or Jewish people, and equally they do not understand Christianity, each one tolerates the other's views. This attitude will prove insufficient. In the future, complete understanding is necessary. Human beings must be able to recognize that their faith has developed within a certain culture and that it determines their thoughts and ideals. But life is shared with people of different cultures and with different views, and these a person must endeavor to understand. The truth should result in more than mere patience and tolerance; it should enable a person to enter with understanding into what the others feel and experience. A person's comprehension of Truth must encompass all faiths.

INTRODUCTION

This is an attitude that is very different from that of mere tolerance. Through spiritual science a person should be able to progress to complete understanding. The followers of particular faiths must realize that they have reached certain aspects of Truth, and that Truth takes on different forms in different souls. This is to be expected and should be no cause for division; rather Truth in all its forms should act as a unifying force. Such an attitude is positive and humane, and brings people together. Also, it is on a higher level than tolerance, and has a greater ennobling effect on the human soul because it is based on insight and love.

—Rudolf Steiner, *Supersensible Knowledge*

When we are reborn, we shall hear the truth spoken in another and a higher form. Truth evolves, as does everything else in the world. It is the form of the divine spirit, but the divine spirit has many forms. If we thoroughly imbue ourselves with this characteristic of truth, we shall acquire a quite different relation to it. We shall say: indeed we live in the truth, but it can take many forms. And we shall then look at modern humanity in a quite different light. We shall not say that we possess absolute truth; we shall say that our fellow men are now at a point where we also once stood. It is our duty to enter into what another person says; we need only make it clear to him that we value him at that stage of truth where he now stands. Everyone has to learn for himself, and thus we shall become tolerant towards every form of truth. We come to a better understanding of things; we do not battle against people but seek to live with them. Modern humanity has cultivated individual freedom. Through this fundamental view of truth, anthroposophy will develop an inner tolerance.

Love is higher than opinion. If people love one another, the most varied opinions can be reconciled. Hence it is deeply significant that in anthroposophy (spiritual science) no religion is attacked and no religion is specially singled out, but all are understood, and so there can be brotherhood because the adherents of the most varied religions understand one another.

This is one of the most important tasks for mankind today and in the future: that people should learn to live together and understand one another.

—Rudolf Steiner, *At the Gates of Spiritual Science*

These words express the reason why I am writing this book: to take a step towards more than tolerance, towards real understanding of the different faiths.

So with these exceptional words, I am beginning a new or rather very old journey into many beautiful areas of our world. This journey which began at my birth has taken me for the last sixty-four years into regions of our Earth where Muslims, Christians, and Jews have lived together in times of peace and in war for thousands of years. I have had intense feelings all of my life towards these three religions. I never really understood where these feelings came from: fascination for the world of the Muslims, love for the Christian churches, and a very limited knowledge of the Jewish faith being born into a Catholic French family (except through intermarriage into the Jewish faith within my mother's family, and of course later with all my American, Canadian, French, and international friends from Jewish background).

At the very beginning of my life the stage was set for my destiny. I was born in the city of Tunis, but conceived in Burgundy, France. Since my mother worked at a government post in Tunis, I was taken care of from birth by a Jewish nanny, and we lived in a very Arab world. My great-aunt on my mother's side who lived also in Tunisia, a former French colony, had married a Mason, and they were very active in the Tunis Masonic lodge which my mother knew nothing about and did not ask questions! All I know is that my Catholic baptism was taken care of by my "Mason" aunt. The stage was set for this newborn to enter the world of three faiths and more, and throughout my life, it has not stopped. I spent my childhood in Burgundy and from ages six through twelve I lived in Morocco and Algeria.

My marriage into a modern Muslim-Persian family has given me a wonderful opportunity (and still does) to experience another way of living, full of warmth, understanding, and love, and of course problems like everywhere else. I shared the lives of this very educated family who showed no racial discrimination of any kind, an acceptance of one another, and respect for a westerner, and for this I am deeply thankful. My mother-in-law was the head mistress of an all-girls school in Tehran, and my father-in-law was a chemist. Living in Iran for many years, I grew to enjoy the

INTRODUCTION

everyday life in the Muslim world until the shariah was imposed on me. Wearing the chador, veiling myself was not part of my upbringing, and it was an impeachment on my personal freedom. I dressed modestly (no shorts, no short sleeves, etc.) for respect of the country's morals, but wearing and covering myself from head to toe was where I drew the limit. I could understand it but could not live with it, so I left Iran in 1985, never to return, after living there off and on for ten years.

Since 2010 these three faiths have had more and more significance in my life as well as in the lives of everyone else around the world whose lives have been turned upside down by political, radical, and religious events so I decided to make pilgrimages to many Muslim spiritual centers, Jewish centers, and of course Christian ones to try and fathom these deeply powerful religions in preparation for this book. I am deeply affected by the hate which surrounds our world between all these faiths and this undertaking is in reaction to these feelings which surround us continuously. Spending the last few years completely engrossed in these matters hopefully will send some thoughts of understanding into the world. These thoughts as we know have an effect. I hope that this small attempt of mine will bring something positive into our world. The journey itself was a journey of love into places where hate and frustration are commonplace, but amidst this confusion the universal human element always shines through. It is the language that I use when I travel. It is this universal element which I wish to share with the reader as I have done in my other journeys. Spiritual science (anthroposophy), as given to the world by Rudolf Steiner at the beginning of the century in thousands of lectures, is my passport towards a deeper understanding and invaluable insights into the worlds of Judaism, Christianity, and Islam.

Four years ago I started this journey by walking across Spain from south to north, from Seville to Santiago, in order to feel the remnants (if any are left!) of a time when the Jews, Muslims, and Christians lived briefly in peace, more than a thousand years ago in southern Spain. I thought it was a great way to begin.

So, this was *my beginning*.

At that time all the religions shared their deeply felt wisdom and knowledge, and worked together. This peaceful period has been the subject of numerous books written by Muslim, Jewish, and Christian scholars. This was *the impulse* which made me start this amazing journey: we need to share one another's wealth of knowledge. Many of the sages, rulers, poets, and religious men and women of the time spoke Arabic, Hebrew, Greek, Latin, and the local languages, and they read one another's sacred books. They had respect for one another's knowledge.

This journey had a will of its own. If I listened closely, I thought I would go to where it was important for me to go. And I *did!*

Starting from Spain, I went on to travel via bus, van, taxi, car, foot, camel, train, plane, and boat through Israel, Palestine, Jordan, Egypt, Morocco, Tunisia, the Sahara Desert, Kenya, Tanzania, Zanzibar, Turkey, Greece, Poland, Uzbekistan, Azerbaijan, and in the past in Afghanistan, Iran, Pakistan, and India. I did not visit these places as a tourist, but as a traveler, alone and always funding my own travels, sometimes with a small group where logistics demanded it so that I am with the people as a human being meeting another, not as a representative of a nation, faith, newspaper, business, or anything for that matter. It is just myself, as a human being wanting to learn and understand the *other* no matter how poor, rich, small, unknown, old, young, uneducated, intelligent, man or woman, Christian, Muslim, or Jew. These words come to mind.

> The tremendous difference from earlier ways will be that human beings and not principles or institutions are the active agent....
>
> The future depends on the existence of people who act in the right way out of their own resources....
>
> If our whole civilization had not fallen into chaos, individuals could not have unfolded freely out of their own resources. They would always have been bound to their environment. The old order must break apart and become chaos. We face great changes in this respect and no one can hope to reform anything in the world except by means of inner development.[*]

---

[*] Steiner, *Original Impulses for the Science of the Spirit*, pp. 96–98.

INTRODUCTION

Intertwined with geographical travels, I will offer other modes of travel, as I have done in the past in my other books. Travels through time, across space, and the inner travels which a knowledge of anthroposophy—given to the world by the seer, scientist Rudolf Steiner—brings to us and makes for a fascinating, deeply felt story about humankind, its descent from heavenly realms, or spiritual worlds, to the Earth, and its very courageous, admirable ascent back towards that invisible land, and God, through the many available paths. The people I meet, all in their own ways, make progress towards the invisible world. That personal journey of individuals, seen in many different forms, is what makes me travel relentlessly around the Earth, and it gives me great joy, but also sufferings, which I will share throughout these pages. My other journeys were complex, but this one is by far the most complex and very relevant to our times of war, dissent, and rebellion in the Arab world, and discontent everywhere else. The task is an impossible one. Sometimes one has to attempt the impossible.

I know my limits as a writer more than anyone else. But I must make the best with what my destiny has given me, or not given me. My work is extremely imperfect, but in that regard, I hope that it is very much alive. To me that is what counts, being *alive* and away from abstraction, and that means embracing imperfections. Something alive is still in the making, still developing, and if it reaches perfection then it is dead. Away from dusty libraries to *life*.

This follows another line of thinking not very well accepted in our culture which celebrates youth, physical youth: the fact that one can grow old but still feel very young. The older I get the more youthful I feel, and I look forward to being much older, unlike most of my contemporaries who hate becoming old and still celebrate the cult of youth.

So in this journey of getting old but feeling youthful and alive, of imperfections but liveliness, I welcome the readers and hope to stir up some unknown forces to help them on their own chosen paths, whatever faith.

Isn't this reason enough to write?

I am not afraid to borrow copiously from writers—recent ones, ancient ones, young, old, male, female, philosophers, historians, poets, doctors, theologians, monks, travelers, etc. They are my teachers, and I am proud to borrow their sacred beautiful words, so that perhaps the reader will be enticed to read more from all of them because their talents far surpass mine!

I must warn the readers that on this journey they will definitely *not* feel comfortable. At times it might feel like, as Rudolf Steiner said, a "tornado-like effect on the soul." They will be thrown into many different situations: backwards, forward in time, moved in circular soul journeys, into geographical hot spots and arduous lands, and into the marvelous paths the spirit takes—whether it is a Jewish, Christian, or Muslim path. The readers will have a chance to experience the intimate writings of many great men of thought and faiths of three religions. Some of the writings will sound obscure and outdated but surprisingly modern, and it is worth it to feel what is behind the writings, what lives within the writings, with an open mind and love for human beings as they try to reach their God. And that is what I take delight in! I hope the reader will, as well.

So again, welcome reader into this very complicated, multifaceted journey into our *common* past, present, and future where you might feel a bit lost, but being a bit lost is a *real* beginning.

Consider these wonderful words by world traveler Ibn Battuta (AD 1100):

> Of the wondrous doings of God Most High is this, That He has created the hearts of mankind with an instinctive desire to seek these sublime sanctuaries, and yearning to present themselves at their illustrious sites, and has given the love of them such power over people's hearts that none alights in them but they seize his whole heart, nor quits them but with grief at separation from them, sorrowing at his far journey away from them, filled with longing for them and purposing to repeat the visitation to them.[*]

---

[*] Ibn Battuta, in Waines, *The Odyssey of Ibn Battuta: Uncommon Tales of a Medieval Adventurer*, p. 35.

Part I

Egypt ✶ Palestine ✶ Israel ✶ Jordan

You can read as much as you like in history books. You will not understand how the people of antiquity developed. You'll read about all kinds of things, wars, and kings, and have chaos and confusion in your minds; for you'll have no idea what it is all about. Religions may also be mentioned, but no one knows where they come from. If you know, however, that the human body consists of physical body, ether body (life forces), astral body (emotions), and "I" (the higher self), and that these were discovered one after the other, depending on the way people looked at life, you find that the Indians (Hindus) discovered the physical body, the Egyptians the ether body, the Babylonians the astral body, and the Jews the I....

The Indians—and many people migrated through there, so that they differ in race—discovered the physical body. The Egyptians, who had to concern themselves a great deal with water (the Nile), discovered the ether, and therefore the ether human being. Among the Babylonians, who took everything they needed for the astral body from other peoples, the priests got the idea of building high towers; they gained knowledge of the stars. And the Jews, who were always on the move—read the stories of Abraham, Moses and so on—were not inclined to venerate anything visible, be it above or below; they found Jahve, the invisible god who created the human I and influenced it....

BEYOND THE BLOOD

A special characteristic of the Indians was that they really looked at the people who lived there as distinct groups, like animal species, and divided them into four castes. Then there was the particular religion the Indians had in earlier times. They saw no difference between the world of the spirit and the world of physical bodies; at the time when this Indian population first evolved in India, no difference was made between spirit and body. A tree would not be differentiated the way many other people did—this is the physical tree, and a spirit lives in it. No such distinction was made. The tree was at the same time a spirit, only a somewhat coarser spirit than a human being or animal. An animal was also not divided into body and soul; it was soul to the ancient Indians, as was the human being.

When an Indian of earliest times asked after the soul—he knew that we inhale, inhale air—then to him the air that is inhaled was the spirit. And he would know: the air is out there; that is the spirit that is all around the Earth. And when this spirit, which is around the whole Earth, began to flow, to waft, he could call spirit that moved everywhere on Earth *Varuna*. But the spirit in him was also Varuna. When there were gales outside Varuna; and inside—also Varuna....

If one goes more deeply into those Indian views, it is interesting to see that the Indians had accurate knowledge of all human organs. It was merely that they saw them as spirit. The human being was made up of many different spirits: lung spirit, stomach spirit, kidney spirit and so on; they would only consider the physical body. With regard to the ancient Indians, therefore, we may say their whole thinking was in terms of the physical body. They saw it as something spiritual....

The Egyptians had the Nile which we may say is really the father who feeds the country. Every July the river rises above its banks, returning to them in October. All an ancient Egyptian would know, therefore, was that the Nile held water; the waters would recede during the cold part of the year and then rise to flood the land again for the benefit of humanity. When the waters receded in October, fertile mud was left behind—the Egyptians do not need to use fertilizer. They would sow their cereal grains and so on in the mud; these would germinate and grow and be harvested before the Nile flooded again. And so the Nile prepared their fields for them year after year. And the Egyptians were deeply conscious of the beneficial nature of water. They gave much thought to water in the world of nature.... Their attention focused on water to an extraordinary degree.... Water has a tremendous influence on the ether body. The Egyptians still had an instinct that enabled them to say: the human being has not only a physical body but also an ether body.... Having discovered the ether body the Egyptians developed the whole of their religion as a religion of the ether body....

The Egyptians whose lands were completely under the influence of the Nile, and who owed everything they were to the Nile, as it were—a situation that makes people aware of the ether—developed a view of the human ether body....

The Egyptians developed geometry because they needed it. They had to establish the position of their fields over and over again, for the Nile would flood everything year after year....

The people of Assyria and the Babylonians lived at some altitude where the air was particularly clear and the stars could have easily been observed. They developed the view of the astral body (*aster* means star).

The Jews, who had to move from place to place in earlier times, and initially had no lasting abode, thought and felt more out of inner human nature. They developed their views of the human I....

The Babylonians developed earthly concern; they had no great interest in earthly things. The fact that the Jews had no great interest in earthly things is evident from the way their real interest lay anywhere except with the world we perceive through the senses....

We thus see the gradual development of human awareness of the physical body, the ether body, the astral body and the I. You see, Jahve actually means "I am the I am." That is the meaning of the word. And if Jahve is worshipped as the greatest god, such recognition of the greatest god clearly points also to the human I.

If we follow the evolution of history in this way, we find that all those peoples essentially gave expression in thoughts and feelings to the way they experienced life. Indians knew a rich, fruitful world of nature, a continual flowering and abundant growth. They really perceived the riches of the physical world and out of this developed their view of the physical body. The Egyptians saw that help came to them only from the Nile, which one can see; they therefore developed the concept of the ether and so on. All those people really developed their views from their life experience....

> This was different with other nations.... Indians knew the natural world from inside; the Egyptians had living experience of ether activity; the Assyrians gained experience of the astral body from the stars; the Jews had living experience of their I. The Greeks were really the first to look at the world outside. The others did not actually look at the world.... The Indians, Egyptians, Babylonians and Jews did not have a real view of the natural world; they did not know much about it because they did not open their eyes to look at it. A view of the natural world developed among the Greeks because they actually looked. And humanity did not really perceive the outside world until the Greeks did so.*

It is helpful to imagine what these statements mean even if one does not accept them. One can work with these insights and see what comes to light!

The Indians discovered the physical body, the Egyptians discovered the etheric body, the Babylonians discovered the astral body, and the Jews discovered the ego. These insights bring much clarity into history and religion as we will see, and I will quote more about these far reaching insights as this journey unfolds. For now, it is like a gigantic puzzle stretching into space and time, just starting with many pieces to be brought in!

To continue, the other picture is man coming down from the spiritual world, still part of the spiritual world and not separated from it, coming slowly down to the Earth.** First he experiences his physical body through India, then his ether body through Egypt, then his feeling, astral body through Babylonia, then finally he closes everything off from the spiritual world and finds his I, Jahve, through the Hebrew nation. We all have been born in these ancient cultures, and we carry the future from our present life and culture, thereby creating our future, a very grave responsibility.

If we picture the development of civilization, like the newborn child who is sleeping much of the time, still in the heavens and not on Earth, then we can understand how we were when we first inhabited the Earth, still

---

* Steiner, *From Beetroot to Buddhism...: Answers to Questions*, pp. 10–12, 14, 16–17, 24–25, 27. For the history of consciousness from a color perspective, see Valandro, *Touched: A Painter's Insights into the Work of Liane Collot d'Herbois*.

** For more on this topic, see Steiner, *An Outline of Esoteric Science*.

dreamy and not aware of our surroundings, still connected to the heavens. Until now, where we have landed on Earth, become complete materialists, atheists, or extremist fanatics in religious beliefs whether Christian, Jewish, or Muslim. We are left to our own devices in the Western world, the most exciting experience! Chaos, as was mentioned before. The heavens do not exist, and God got *lost* or is so far away that this being isn't experienced anymore. Man has been abandoned, immersed in matter, deep within it, with our atomic bombs, cellular biology, the infinitely small, machines, computers, etc. Some choose to hold on to strict rules so as not to get lost in the chaos of modern life, some jump in feet first into the chaos and learn how to swim, many drown under the waves of drugs, sex, fast life, addictions of all kinds. We are struggling with the birth of the Ego, the I. We are still young adults, not fully matured! We have a long way to go, we are hardly walking!

But now let us proceed with the journey to Mount Sinai.

Moses

The is one of the most severe, lifeless, and inhospitable sites that I have ever experienced. I am standing on top of Mount Sinai. The reality of this powerful mountaintop with its little chapel lost in this incredible wilderness is more than my body, soul, and spirit can take. It is simply *too* big, too full of meaning, history, legend, and power for my head to assimilate. A friend does what I should do: he is simply sleeping on the hard stones after the quiet, long hike up Mount Sinai. Perhaps taking a nap would be a better way to experience this ancient center of western man's primordial history. To experience it through sleeping, dreaming would be nice, but I am too much of a thinker to do so, and besides, I am far too excited to sleep. As far as the horizon can reach I see rocky mountains, devoid of life, no trees, simply an endless view of severe mountains with weird shaped peaks. Nothing here speaks of beauty, culture, or majestic views. No, it is simply austere, severe, unforgivable, unbending, unyielding, death. No inner need to walk in these settings. I just sit there on a large rock and gaze at infinity, gaze at what happened in these unsettling surroundings so many thousands of years ago. We are fortunate that the whole area seems empty of people. There are just two

A view from the top of Mount Sinai

of us, and a few locals staying in their little makeshift enclosure within the rocks to serve tea or to give you a place to sleep for the night with plenty of blankets to put up with the intense cold of the night. People come here by the busload from Cairo, or by private car or taxi from Israel. They arrive in the evening and start walking around midnight in order to reach the top and watch the sunrise. That is the custom. We stayed at the monastery inn of Saint Catherine last night and heard great commotion from the many tourists who came to climb this mountain during the night. But we decided to climb during the day, and no one was there which was a welcomed gift. I am not antisocial, but seeing hoards of people climbing up takes away from this very solitary mountain. I wanted to climb it alone, in solitude, silence, and I got my wish. We climbed the whole mountain without anyone in sight. After a few hours of leisurely taking in the wondrous site a few people did show up. We stopped on the way up the cliff to have a drink of tea offered to us by the local Bedouin from the village who tends to the tourists. He was having a nap after working all evening, feeding the cold and hungry climbers during the night. We chatted and he was happy to serve us the warm beverage.

I have seen many incredible, moving sites in my peregrinations but none as severe as this one. In a way, I would call it *Moses* which means "truth." The surroundings speak of Moses, of his awesome task, of the power of God the One, of sacred grounds. The only thought that entered my mind was: *This is the place!* The rest of my thoughts were a jumble of words and feelings befitting the jumble of granite peaks and rocks. I was glad that for some reason I could still come here and hike up to this sacred ground without the interference of wars, dissidence, national disputes, etc.

This site was chosen among the many sacred sites of our Earth, far away from the many Goddesses and Gods of India, away from the fertile Nile with its liveliness, away from the high plateau of Mesopotamia where the Babylonian Towers reach up to the speaking heavens. This is desolate land, a land of stones and jagged rocks where Man is to meet his God in solitude, in loneliness for the birth of the I. "Rock bottom" is a meaningful expression.

One of my favorite writers, Édouard Schuré, writes beautifully about Moses in his famous book, *The Great Initiates*.

> A dark mass of granite stands so bare beneath the splendor of the Sun that one would think it had been furrowed by lightening, and carved by thunder. "This is the summit of Sinai, the Throne of the Elohim," says the children of the desert. Facing it is a lower mountain, the rocks of Serbal, also steep and wild. In its sides are copper mines and caverns. Between the two mountains is a dark valley, a chaos of rocks that the Arab call Horeb, the Ereb of Semitic legend. This valley of desolation is gloomy indeed when night falls upon it along with the shadow of Mount Sinai. It is even more gloomy when the mountain is crowned with a mantle of clouds, from which sinister flashes of light dart forth. Then a terrible wind blows down the narrow valley. It is said here Elohim overthrows those who try to fight Him, casting them into the abyss where torrents of rain pour. The midianites say that here wander the evil ghosts of giants, the *Refaim*, tumbling the rocks upon those who try to climb the sacred cliffs. Popular tradition still has it that sometimes in the flashes of lightening fire the God of Sinai appears in the form of a Medusa head with eagle's wings. Woe to those who see His Face! To see Him is to die.

This is what the nomads related in the evening, sitting in their tents, when the camels and the women were asleep. In reality only the boldest of Jethro's initiates climbed to the cavern of Serval and spent several days there in fasting and prayer. It was a place dedicated from time immemorial to supernatural visions, to Elohim, or to luminous spirits. No priest, no hunter would have consented to lead a pilgrim here.

Fearlessly Moses had climbed up past the ravine of Horeb. Courageously he had crossed the valley of death with its chaos of rocks. Like every human effort, initiation has its phases of humility and pride. In climbing the mountain Moses had reached the summit of pride, for he was approaching the summit of human power. Already he felt himself at one with the Supreme Being. The burning red Sun hung low over the volcanic massive form of Sinai and purple shadows were lying in the valleys below, when Moses found himself before a cavern where a few terebinths protected the entrance. He prepared to enter but suddenly he was blinded by a light that enveloped him. It seemed to him that the Sun burned about him, that the granite mountains had changed into a sea of flames.

At the entrance of the Grotto a blinding light shone upon him. An angel with drawn sword blocked his way. Thunderstruck. Moses fell prone upon the ground. All his pride had been broken. The angel's gaze had pierced him with its light. And then, with that deep sense of things that is awakened in the visionary state, he understood that this being was about to impose serious tasks upon him. He would have liked to escape his mission and creep into the earth like a worm.

But a voice said, "Moses! Moses!" and he answered: "Here am I."

"Come closer; take off your shoes. For the place where you are standing is holy ground!"

Moses hid his face in his hands. He was afraid to look at the angel again, to face his gaze.

And the angel said to him, "You seek Elohim, why do you tremble before me?"

"Who are you?"

"A ray of Elohim, a solar angel, a messenger of the One Who is and Who will be."

"What do you command?"

"You shall say to the children of Israel: the Everlasting, the God of your Fathers, the God of Abraham, the God of Isaac, the God of Jacob sent me to you, to lead you out of the land of Slavery."

"Who am I," asked Moses "that I should lead the Children of Israel out of Egypt?"

"*Go,*" said the angel, "for I shall be with you. I shall put the fire of the Elohim in your heart, and His word upon your lips. For forty years you have been calling upon Him. Your voice has reached Him. Here I seize you in his name! Son of Elohim, you belong to me forever!"

And Moses cried boldly, "Show me Elohim, that I may see His living fire!"

He raised his head. But the sea of flames had vanished; the angel had fled like lightning. The Sun had descended upon the extinguished volcanoes of Sinai; a silence of death spread over the vale of Horeb, and a voice that seemed to roll in the blue, losing itself in infinity, said: "I am, that I am!"...

The importance of the people of Israel in the history of humanity is readily apparent from the very beginning for two reasons. First, it represents monotheism; second, it gave birth to Christianity. But the providential aim of the mission of Israel appears only to one who uncovers the symbols of the Old and New Testaments and perceives that they conceal the entire esoteric tradition of the past, though under a form often altered.... The role of Israel becomes clear when one discovers that these people form the indispensable link between the old and the new cycle, between the East and the West. A result of the monotheistic idea is the unification of humanity under the same God and under a single law....

Moses, the Egyptian initiate and priest of Osiris, was indisputably the organizer of monotheism. Through him this principle, until then hidden beneath the threefold veil of the Mysteries, came out of the depths of the temple and entered the course of history. Moses had the courage to establish the highest principle of initiation as the sole dogma of a national religion, and the prudence to reveal its consequences to only a small number of initiates, while imposing it upon the masses through fear. In so doing, the prophet of Sinai evidently had before him distant vistas that extended far beyond the destinies of his people. The establishment of the universal religion of humankind is the true mission of Israel, which few Jews other than its greatest prophets have understood....

Moses' plan was one of the most extraordinary and courageous that humanity ever conceived. He was to tear a people from the yoke of a nation as powerful as Egypt, to take it to the conquest of a country occupied by hostile and better-armed inhabitants, to lead it for ten, twenty, forty years in the desert, to consume it with thirst, to weaken it with hunger, to torment it like a blood-horse under the arrows of the Hittites and Amalakties, ready to cut it to pieces, to isolate it with its Tabernacle of the Lord in the midst of these idolatrous nations, to impose monotheism upon with a rod of fire and to instill in it such a fear and veneration of this One God that He would become incarnate in its flesh, that he would become its national symbol, the goal of all its aspirations and its reason for being. Such was the amazing work of Moses.*

As I sat there in this desolate rocky mountain, 7,500 feet high above the sea, words were not sufficient but feelings were. The magnitude of the place was beyond logic and I could just stare at the blue sky, and the secrets buried in the mountains.

The end of the day came fast. The young men brought me more tea and I sat in different places—facing north, south, east, and west—to watch this awesome scenery. I felt I was only a small human being here, far too small.

I ran down the mountain because it was getting cold; the mountain was casting its shadow on the path and I wanted to be in the sunlight. Back at the monastery, the quiet abode of the few priests was a welcoming sight. Supper was served to people from Russia, France, Israel, etc., and I went to sleep.

The next day was dedicated to the visit of the monastery. The busloads coming from the Red Sea, full of Russians still dressed in bathing suits, were unloading by the massive doors. Some were told they had to cover up a bit since this is a monastery and men devote their lives to prayer, so perhaps a bit of decency in personal attire was most welcome! The young and pretty Russian girls seemed to be oblivious to it all. They attempted to follow the rules, but soaking up the sunshine was their hard-won pleasure.

---

* Schuré, *The Great Initiates: A Study of the Secret History of Religions*, pp. 152–153, 181–182.

The collection of sacred books and paintings was very special. But I could not see the old illuminated texts in the famous library because I am not a head of state. In any case, what is the use of these books if no one looks at them and reads them? They get lost and gather dust! As usual, I get upset when I can't get access to something because of nonsense rules. I become a bit childish! My anger raises its head.

Christianity is not a religion of the Book! But a religion of the *Word*. So with this in mind, I felt better. Keep your sacred beautiful books, just the few of you living here in this huge monastery. Is this Christian? It should be filled with young and old giving it some sort of life.

And furthermore, I don't need your books. I am meditating on the first fifteen lines of the Gospel of Saint John ("In the beginning was the word...."), and that is far more important than a glimpse at these treasures of the past, no matter how full of gold the pages are! If we do not put them to good use, what of it? Libraries are dead places! The word is buried deep in the layers of dust which have accumulated over thousands of years! And still more to come. Of course they *will* put the holy scriptures into digital storage; that's what one of the highly educated holy monks said. It is only a matter of time. Then they will get stored *forever and ever*, going into the tomb of time.

But there are other means to access ancient knowledge and wisdom!

I decided to hike up on the other side of the monastery to a little oasis-like enclave on the hill above the monastery, looking at Mount Sinai. It had gardens, looked inviting, and had no tall gates.

The gardeners let us in and we admired a profusion of lovely flowers, lots of poppies getting ready to lift their little flower heads to look towards the Sun, many healing plants, and a wonderful vegetable garden. A few small houses which I found out I could have stayed in, some lovely little icons hung up in a tiny chapel, and a place where one could buy a few things made by the local Bedouin women. The Bedouins take care of the area as they have for the last thousand years. There was a parchment in the museum dating from the time of the prophet Muhammad, which says that the prophet respects this religious center and vows to protect it with its own believers, with His signature. This monastery has been in existence for thousands of years, with services held in the name of Christ continuously

Saint Catherine's Monastery at the foot of Mount Sinai in Egypt

and in peace thanks to the protection of the local Bedouin Muslim tribes who respect "the people of the Book."

> Those who have received a revealed scripture are called *ahl al-kitāb*, "the people of the Book," comprising Jews, Christians, Zoroastrians, and Sabians. They should not be killed or converted by force but rather pay a certain tax. By doing so they gain the right to be protected by Muslims and are called *dhimmī*, from *dhimma*, "protection." They are therefore exempt from military service. The pagans, polytheists who have no revealed scripture, have to be fought unless they embrace Islam.*

Peacefully I walked back down, looking at the Saint Catherine Monastery complex in all its awesome beauty, and then took a small taxi to the village itself. I bought some freshly made bread from the local baker, right out of the old oven, and ate some local food at a small café. The people were very hospitable, being used to a few tourists, but most of them do not go down to the village. They come with a tour bus and then leave. I hitched a ride

---

*   Schimmel, *Islam: An Introduction*, p. 70.

back to the monastery, and made arrangement to depart the next day for the Red Sea.

A week before we had arrived here from Israel. At the border with Egypt, we took a taxi run by the local Bedouins. We drove through the desert scenery, sandy, rocky, and the driver stopped at a small, very dusty place by the side of the road. He wanted to take us on a camel trip in the desert for a couple of days so that we could get a feel for the desert. I was tempted, but we decided not to. We had a few more days and did not have the time for the excursion. So they brought us some tea and left us alone while they were talking amongst themselves of other more serious problems! A month later or so, after I had finished my trip into Egypt and gone back to Israel via more buses and a taxi, the area had major problems and it was once again unsafe and illegal to cross the border. They had skirmishes.

The Bedouins had hardened faces from living a very simple, austere life. They know what is important: a bed on the floor, a small samovar in the corner with hot water, a piece of bread, and a few other things. They love to talk sitting on the floor, sipping the delicious beverage. It looked like they had a council, they were old men. They looked old, but the desert weathers their features fast. Their camels were out in the distance, and the women and children were too shy to speak to us. Most of the time I travel alone because then I have access to the women in their surroundings. In this area of Sinai, these men had seen countless wars, skirmishes, and battles in their lifetimes. The big SUV trucks replace the camels as they try to make a living in this very bleak desert land. The wives and children live within tiny, sparse rooms, sleeping on blankets on the floor, cooking outside most of the time, and making do with very little. They are separated from the men and tourists, their heads are covered, and one can see their curious shining eyes and old worn faces accustomed to hardships. How did this separation come about? Males dominating females for thousands of years.

Where is the beginning, or one beginning? There are many beginnings, depending on what time frame we choose! One has to start somewhere. I choose the time of Moses! Of course this is my view!*

---

*   For another perspective, see Valandro, *Letters from Florence: Observations on the Inner Art of Travel.*

Moses started it on a massive scale, with this male versus female business, as did Abraham before him. Here I am going on a bit of a tangent, but a necessary one in this part of the world, and I will come back to the desert!

Going back and forth from Israel to Egypt and then back to Palestine, back to Israel, and within Palestine, going back and forth from the Arab villages to the Israelis' enclaves one gets shoved back and forth between these feelings—veiled, not veiled, covered, not covered. It is tiring on the psyche to have to go back and forth. Walking in Jerusalem was a real challenge for me. Going to Israel was a challenge for me. Why should I go there? I am not a bible enthusiast, not a church-going Christian, so why go there? My Christianity is a more spiritual kind, brought to me by my studies of Anthroposophy. I am more interested in the background of *all* religions, and *how* did we get from there to here—wars, hate, mistrust, misunderstanding, killings, etc. *My* god is better than yours, my Messiah is not here yet, *no* the Messiah is here. Yes he has been here but now we have another prophet!

In the streets of old Jerusalem, some women are covered, some are not. Some are dressed in black clothes and covered up as well with six or more children hanging from their skirts. All the beautiful young women who are in army uniforms look like James Bond's assistants with breasts bursting from within their uniforms, very green tight pants showing their very sexual curves, and a big gun across their shoulders walking along the narrow paths of the covered souk (market). Their hair is beautifully done, and they are wearing makeup, looking like they are going on a date, and trying to keep the peace in that attire! In airports in the United States, I often see women in uniforms, but never the kind of uniforms which are given to the women in the Israeli army. The females in the United States Army are dressed very appropriately, not tight-fitting, relaxed, and show a professional attire suited for their job, which is to serve in the military. Is it on purpose that these sexual uniforms are given to these young women? Everything has a meaning!

Walking along the paths of old Jerusalem was a real *trip*. I never imagined that such a cross-cultural mixture of people could actually survive under these conditions. It is simply *impossible*, yet *it is*. Covered, not covered,

covered, not covered, almost naked under tight clothes—it is one of the most outrageous cities I have ever visited!

This is life in the twentieth century with all its magnificent challenges. The totally modern woman and her totally subjugated sister walking side by side, whether Jewish, Muslim, or Christian.

I took no pictures during my first week so as not to be disturbed from the cacophony of cross-cultural experiences which assaulted my senses perpetually. I wanted a real bath in this impossible, fascinating place. One cannot use one's logic here, it is impossible, there is no logic. It is very befitting for the Birth of Christ, for his Death, and his Resurrection. Throw the intellect out the window! In this very sacred country logic is just thrown out the window. Don't try to understand. Forget it, it just *is*.

It *is* beyond comprehension, one must activate other capacities, which I am trying my hardest to do. So what is it that I am doing here and now, trying to write about these three faiths? Every other moment, I feel like abandoning this totally insane project of mine, letting it go. A woman is born in one family and has to cover herself, while another one is born in another and can run around half naked enjoying her sexual freedom, while another one of the same faith is married off at eighteen or earlier and is expected to have the twelve tribes of Israel children in the hope of one of these blessed children being the next Messiah, and another young woman next door is supposed to be the fourth wife of an old man, some wearing nothing but black or white long skirts, or covered up from head to toe.

These people live side by side—go to work, pray, eat, make love, have children, try to get ahead—and one goes one way, while the other goes the other way. They all have relatives who live on the other side of the Atlantic—New York City, Los Angeles, Chicago—or in Europe, and everyone believes that he or she has the one and only answer to everything.

But I will come back to Jerusalem later on in this tale, I just got sidetracked, overwhelmed with it, which is very easy in this complex, multifaceted journey!

Now back to Moses.

To touch on another mystery about Moses one can turn to Rudolf Steiner's lectures in the book entitled *The Principle of Spiritual Economy*, which the reader will have to study himself as I can only mention a few paragraphs. I just could not omit it even though it is enormously difficult to grasp, so if by reading the reader gets a bit lost, be patient. Moses did not appear out of nothingness, and so it is with the rest of us! In this cycle of lectures, Steiner also mentions that most of us carry a bit of this "special" etheric body and this "special" astral body within ourselves! Earlier I had mentioned that we have four bodies, not just our physical body. We have the etheric body in common with the plant world, the astral body connected to the animal world, our physical body connected to the mineral realm, and our Ego, or "I," which makes us the master of our self—or at least we try!

Here Steiner links Moses with Zarathustra. Zarathustra, the great initiate, was born again and again to bring knowledge and wisdom to man. Moses in a former lifetime was a disciple and special student of Zarathustra, and for the enormous task ahead of him, he had to be prepared by very unusual mysterious happenings. Here we go across time and space, into a different element. We are reborn many times, and certain beings come to help mankind become free.

Here I might lose the interest of some readers, but I must ask for their patience and open minds.

> You must first realize that this reborn disciple of Zarathustra (Moses) possessed his own astral body and ego, and he was now to have the etheric body of Zarathustra woven into his soul. As a small child, he first had to feel how the forces of the etheric body of Zarathustra became active in him, and he had to feel this before the powers of judgment could be activated by his own astral body and before his own ego was able to interfere. So the special event that had to take place was some sort of initiation. The forces of Zarathustra's etheric body had to be awakened in this reborn disciple when he was a very small child, that is before his own individual development could come into play. For this reason, the child was placed in an ark of bulrushes that was then put into the water, so that he was completely cut off from the rest of the world and was unable to interact with it. That is when the forces of Zarathustra's etheric body that had been woven into him germinated and became illuminated.

I am sure that you know by now that this reborn disciple of Zarathustra was none other than Moses. The Biblical story about his abandonment is really a presentation of that profound mystery behind the scenes of the external world dealing with the preservation of Zarathustra's etheric body and its reawakening in Moses. And this is how Hermes and Moses were able to guide the post-Atlantean culture through its recorded stages.

After hearing about these examples of the reincarnation of etheric bodies and of an astral body, we know it is insufficient to speak only of the reincarnation of the ego. Rather, the other members of the human constitution that we have become acquainted with—etheric body and the astral body—can also be reincarnated. It is a principle of spiritual economy that what has once been gained cannot perish, but is preserved and transplanted on the spiritual soil of posterity.*

This is very difficult to follow but I needed to mention it so that the readers, if interested, can read more and start their own path in understanding such mysteries. I am only giving hints about processes that are immensely complex which Steiner's science of the spirit attempts to elucidate. We must start somewhere. We have to learn how to swim sometimes. The great spirit behind Moses is not easily comprehended.

After Mount Sinai, Moses brings his people on the march. The long file of caravans, with tents carried on camels' backs and followed by great herds, prepares to go around the Red Sea. They still number only a few thousand individuals. Later the emigration will grow larger "with all kinds of men," as the Bible says. They will include Canaanites, Edomites, Arabs, Semites of all kinds attracted and fascinated by the desert prophet, who calls them from all directions and shapes them to his liking. The nucleus of his people is formed of the *Beni-Israel*, straightforward people, but obstinate and rebellious. Their *hags* or their leaders have taught them the cult of the One God. This religion constitutes a high patriarchal tradition among them. But in those primitive and violent natures, monotheism is still only a better and

---

* Steiner, *The Principle of Spiritual Economy: In Connection with Questions of Reincarnation: An Aspect of the Spiritual Guidance of Man*, pp. 43–44.

intermittent consciousness. As soon as their evil passions reawaken, the instinct toward polytheism, so natural to human beings, takes the upper hand. Then they fall back into the superstitions, witchcraft, and idolatrous practices of the neighboring peoples of Egypt, and Phonecia. Moses will fight with Draconian laws....

Mighty human beings have known the solitude that creates greatness; but Moses was more alone than others because his principle was more absolute, more transcendent. His God was the male principle *par excellence*. It was pure spirit. In order to inculcate it into human beings, he had to declare war on the feminine principle, on the Goddess Natura, on *Heve*, the eternal feminine, who lives in the heart of the Earth and in the heart of humanity. Unceasingly and mercilessly he had to fight it, not in order to destroy it, but to subdue, to master it. Is it then surprising if nature and woman, between whom reigns a mysterious pact, trembled before him? Is it not so astonishing if they rejoiced at Moses' departure and waited in order to lift their heads until his shadow had ceased to cast on them the feeling of death?*

Here is *one* of the beginnings, the beginning of subjugating women, under the yoke of men's power. Fear of the female, dark forces of sexuality, closeness to the Gods and Goddesses, speaking in the oracles, thereby domination of the male, patriarchy, lasting until these days. We know that it had its function. And now, veiled, unveiled, covered, not covered! Where modern women on one side are trying to get rid of the tyrannical chains of patriarchy, and the other side is trying to keep the forces of the blood within the "tribe" (Judaism) or any tribe. Total paradox! But that is the exciting world of international Jerusalem, Israel, Palestine, and our Earth.

Now back to Jerusalem's cacophony of surreal experiences as I walk in a daze in all the corners of the old city. I walk past the Christian quarters, the Via Dolorosa, and go into the old, very old Church of the sepulchure deep in its subterranean levels. Is this where the eternal feminine is buried? Old stone staircases take you to different little enclaves, up, down, little niches deep within the Earth's bowels. Many women are worshiping in front of an icon of the Madonna lit by tall candles. Candles, flames, light everywhere.

---

* Schuré, *The Great Initiates: A Study of the Secret History of Religions*, pp. 183, 195.

The Al-Aqsa Mosque in Jerusalem

Is this where the eternal feminine is buried, never to see the light of day? Then I leave for a breath of fresh air, back into the paths of the markets, meandering here and there, and I decide to go to the beautiful mosque. I go through the metal detector and here I am in front of this magnificent large space. I can breathe, it is no longer the bowels of the Earth with darkness and candles, but the open sky, the open air, the spacious square, the magnificent mosque attuning my soul with the turquoise domes, and designs which bring some kind of order into my psyche. The suffocating feelings of the church's dark interiors leave me for the feelings of space, clarity, orderliness. The chaos of the Earth is gone, the darkness of the church is gone with its relics, crosses, paintings, Madonnas, sculptures, incense, mysteries, death, blood, nails, sufferings, fervent prayers, richly clothed priests with scepters, tall golden hats, long beards, embroidered tunics, lavish silver and golden cloths, etc. Here in the yard I can breathe in the light, feel the sky. Inside it is quiet, men sway gently, and pray on their rugs, prostrated, facing Mecca. Outside they sit on benches and let the time flow by.

All are praying to God. How creative is mankind in its beliefs is what is the most amazing to me. This intense feeling to reach up there, to escape down here.

Where do I stand in this strange mixture of beliefs, churches, temples, mosques, chapels? I do not choose any of them. I enjoy the immense creativity of all this sacred architecture, the old. But it is too old. I am born under a different star like many of my generation. None of these edifices will satisfy my own search. Practicing the simple words of Saint Paul, "Not I, but Christ in me," is where my temple is. In the deep recess of my soul, when things get overwhelming and my temper rises, where I can't handle injustices, untruths, cruelty, intolerance, my anger, and my weaknesses, I let those words resound within me quietly, and they do the work that I cannot do alone, to let go of my lower instinctual self and allow the higher one to help, which Moses tried to conquer for a *whole nation*!

"Not I, but Christ in me."

A phrase which the Muslims are constantly repeating is one of my favorites: *In shallah!* ("God be willing!" or "As God wills!") Or "Not my will, but let thy will be done!"

If you could forgive that small digression, we are back to the Mount Sinai tale.

After a chaotic drive through desert roads leaving Saint Catherine's Monastery, we arrived in the small tourist city by the Red Sea and found a youth hostel kind of accommodation. The place was a bit of a hippy heaven, not the plush center of tourism of Sharm el-Sheikh farther south where planeloads of Russians come in from cold Russia for rest and relaxation. Here is the backpacker's version. Lots of wonderful restaurants built on the beach and covered by tents, where we sit on countless pillows eating some of the best food you can ever find, with lots and lots of stray cats coming in for snacks (right off of your plate if you are not careful). A good place for shopping, relaxing, and eating after the biblical experience of stones, bare peaks, the desert, and Moses!

We decided to go farther south for a one-day tour into the beach nature park for some swimming and snorkeling. My friend had the wrong visa and could not go to that area, so we said good-bye. I went on for another month of traveling.

Our van, with one less passenger, arrived at the park and I enjoyed the snorkeling, and the sumptuous meal which had been prepared for us by the Bedouins on the local beautiful beach. They had brought everything, and had been cooking all day. We all sat down on the sand covered with a vinyl tablecloth and ate more than we could handle. The place was packed with Russian girls in tiny bikinis; they were oblivious to the looks of the Arab cooks and soldiers. I could not help but tell one of them that it might be considerate to wrap a towel around your copious bosom and bottom while standing in line. The French young men in my party were upset with my comments because they too were enjoying the beauties in their tiny bikinis which could not hold their ample curves. We all laughed!

After a long day out, we all arrived back at the hotel.

Much of my traveling is unplanned. I have my departure date, and that is it. So I spoke to the guides at the hotel and explained what I needed and they found it. I was to take an all night bus from Sharm el-Sheikh to Cairo. Upon arrival we would all go to the museum, then to a boat ride on the Nile with lunch by the Nile with a guide, then a visit to Giza, the pyramids, then a visit to a perfume center, then back on the bus all night for one hundred dollars. I said great, but I would not come back on the all-night bus, but stay in Cairo (my first trip to Cairo and Egypt), so at 10:30 PM a private car took me to Sharm el-Sheikh down south. Quite a long ride, I had not realized how far the city was. Once there the driver could not find the bus. For forty-five minutes we drove around, with phone calls trying to meet up. It was a nightmare. Finally they found each other and I went into the van.

It was full of Russians, and some Irish women who were going for the same thing I was. We drove all night and I didn't get much sleep. In the early morning hours we stopped for breakfast and launched into Cairo's famous city traffic.

One of the thousands of mosques in Cairo

The most stunning aspect of this entrance into the city was the minarets which dotted the city sky line. Mosques were everywhere, by the hundreds. Cairo, the city of thousands of minarets shouting into the sky the name of Allah several times a day, prayers going into the wind. I realized how the country, the city was a real conservative, traditional, very Muslim city. In the West we know of Egypt and the pharaohs and we ignore the rest.

Somehow we arrived at the museum to meet our lady guide but I had to figure out what I was going to do after the end of the day! I had no reservations and no place to go, but not to worry!

The museum is a city unto itself with so much of everything, everywhere, that after a while I became drunken with hieroglyphics, Isis, Golden statues, mummies. You name it, they have it. Not neatly arranged as in our western museums. They have far too much!

EGYPT ⚜ PALESTINE ⚜ ISRAEL ⚜ JORDAN

Pyramids in Giza, with Cairo in the background

The boat ride on the busy Nile was pleasant. We ended at a restaurant on the Nile and the food was superb. The Irish ladies were lots of fun. Mother, sister, and daughters out for two weeks for the trip of their lives that they had saved for, and they enjoyed every minute of it. The red sunburned Russians were also enjoying their time. After the great meal we headed for Giza. I was so surprised to see that it was on the outskirts of a very smoky Cairo. Here are the three monstrous pyramids and we could see the heavy, dirty, polluted air of Cairo in the distance. The Bedouins were assaulting the tourists for camel rides. Looking at the pyramids and seeing the Cairo city silhouette on the horizon did not do anything for putting us into the mood of these former times. A few more centuries and the sand will engulf history. I declined going deep into the pyramids, did not feel like it. A foreboding, or something prevented me from entering into the world of four thousand or more years ago. I felt I would suffocate in there. I like climbing mountains, not going into caves! Then we all packed into the van once again and made our last adventure. We went to a beautiful store selling perfumes made from their plants, flowers, in their gardens and factories in the northern oasis. I have always loved perfumes, and flower oils, so it was great. I bought several scents—rose, lotus, and sandalwood mixtures they sold to major perfume houses in France, etc.—and we drank tea while everyone was busy buying.

But now my predicament needed to be solved so I spoke to the lady guide and asked her if she could help me. She said yes, so after the trip the van let the guide and I off and I took my backpack, said good-bye to the gang, and off they went back for another night on the road. They did not believe that I could travel alone. I said, "Why not?!" We drove around in her car trying to find a place to stay. Well, Cairo being Cairo, we could not find the hotel, and after an hour she suggested I stay at her home with her parents. So I agreed, I had no choice.

We arrived at her parents' little apartment in a large dilapidated building several stories high, surrounded by many of the same, in dirt streets, and a cacophony of donkeys, dogs, people, cars, cats, children, street vendors, and garbage. I walked up the stairs under the watchful eyes of the neighbors. Her mom quickly offered me some food. We chatted while she watched the television, which was permanently turned on. Then, since we were both very tired, she offered me her bed and she slept on the sofa in the small living room. I could not say no. I slept well and we both got up the next day. I chatted with my guide's dad, mom, and brothers for a while and I decided to hire her services as a guide for a few days, showing me the many great Mosques.

The city is enormous and the traffic is impossible, but she was an excellent driver and knew the city well since she is a professional guide. She did not wear the chador. We went to several mosques, she insisted on taking me out to eat in one of her favorite places, then into the big market, or souk, which I love. We went to small cafés, restaurants, rug merchants, and walked into the endless labyrinths of Cairo's famous market which is by the enormous mosques and the large square. I arrived in Cairo, the year of the Arab Spring after the upheaval in Tunisia, when one country after another revolted against the tyranny of their respective countries. It had taken a toll on the Egyptian tourist industry. No one was traveling to the Middle East, except a few of us.

EGYPT ॐ PALESTINE ॐ ISRAEL ॐ JORDAN

One evening we went to the largest mosque in Cairo. The guard let me in after a bit of arguing. He gave me the whole Muslim attire so that I was hidden in several layers of long dresses and a scarf. He looked satisfied and we sat in the beautiful courtyard where everyone was busy getting ready for a talk by one of the great teachers. Many of the corners, niches in the mosque were occupied by devout young men saying their evening prayers totally absorbed in Allah. Other young men were running around setting up speakers, electric line, and so forth, getting ready for Friday prayer which was the next day.

> The architecture of the mosque can be considered the best known, and to a certain degree the best representative artistic expression of Islamic culture.... Under the influence of and often in conjunction with the theological college, *madrasah*, which developed first in the east, the pillared courtyards of the large mosques were later replaced by vast courtyards surrounded by deep niches and porticoes; the facades become large and more monumental; immense gates, often decorated with stalactite work, are typical....
>
> A special area for women, either in the background or on a gallery is usually included in the mosques.
>
> The furnishing of the mosque is extremely simple. In the courtyard one finds a well, a fountain, or a basin for the ablutions. The direction of Mecca is indicated by a small niche, *mihrab*, in the wall.*

In all, this was a very busy time in the mosque, because of the Arab Spring rebellion brewing all over the Islamic world. Egypt is a very large country with many unemployed youth and that spells problems for any country!

Our churches do not have the great religious fervor which Islam brings to its believers, and I wanted to know about the impact of this religious fervor on the future. What does it mean for the world, for the larger world, for the Earth, for evolution to have these prayers sent into the universe, into the cosmos? Those were my questions!

What are the effects of this religious fervor on someone's future life, on his future karma? How does this steady praying several times a day affect the psyche, the life forces, the emotional life of the believers? These were my

---

*   Schimmel, *Islam: An Introduction*, pp. 42–43.

very large questions and the reasons for traveling in these beautiful countries. How does this affect the future, create the future? Why choose to live in a Muslim country? What has driven an individual to experience life in the Muslim world rather than experience life as a Catholic, Protestant, or Orthodox Jew? My search for some answers to these rather unconventional questions is taking me to beautiful places on our Earth, which the West ignores with its know-it-all, dominating, materialistic attitude.

I really do not give much attention to regular history but to these particular larger questions.

In one of Rudolf Steiner's lectures he says that anthroposophists should write travel books because they are the only one who can make sense out of history kings, queens, despots, wars, dates, religions, art, architecture, etc., and I must say that previous to my studying anthroposophy I traveled quite extensively but never really understood what I was seeing. I had not a clue. I was blind when touring Greece, Europe, India, and the Middle East. Only now can I have a glimpse of the tremendous mysteries in the histories of people, continents, centuries, millennia, and in the future.

During our visit of the city, I asked my guide if she could organize a trip on the Nile for me on one of the boats. I said I wanted a cheaper boat, but she insisted that the cheaper boats would give me bad food and I would get sick. She said, "You must go with a good boat." We argued back and forth, and she finally gave me the outrageous price of one thousand dollars for five days on a Nile cruise, with a night train ticket and an airplane ticket back to Sharm el-Sheikh after the cruise, for my return to Israel via bus, taxi, etc.

So the day arrived and she drove me to the train station, late at night, and I handed over the money, in cash, with absolutely nothing in my hand for tickets except the night train ticket to the city on the Nile. I had faith, but I left hoping that I had not been had. She said all would be fine. Someone would pick me up in the morning at the train station and take me to the boat. I am trusting, but this was kind of my limit. She could not give me a ticket, nothing. She only gave me her phone number. Then we said good-bye. She had been a great guide and had helped me throughout the last few days so I said, "OK, deal!" Egyptian style! Travel sometimes is expensive, but at least it is for a good cause.

I have found very often that in the Middle East people do a handshake deal with cash, no banks involved. They trust each other. In the West, we trust the banking system. We can see where that has led us in the last few years of major banking problems which no one understands, not even the bankers, or they understand only too well how to grease their own pockets, a machine that has gone wild. So a handshake is tangible!

The train ride was uneventful except that I had no bed, it was the cheapest ticket. So I slept on the seats and the train attendants made sure no one would bother me!

The early morning arrived and my nose was stuck to the window looking at the slow-moving scenery.

A guide was there to meet me and took me to the boat. Many boats were anchored and not in use, showing the effect of political turmoil on the tourist industry. No one wanted to go on a Nile cruise with religious, political tension in the air. I was brought to my cabin, a beautiful cabin with huge windows overlooking the Nile, a large bathroom, a lovely place. Not the way I am accustomed to traveling!

The dining room was hardly full, some hardy French travelers were there, many Germans, a few Americans here and there, and I was seated with a German couple in their late forties who had given up their job, apartment, sold everything, and decided to take off and see the world. We got along great!

Food was plentiful, sumptuous, conversations flowing, and excitement mounting as our departure approached. We were doing the conventional Nile cruise with stops at the major Egyptian pyramid sites, which I did not really know. I had not had time to look at a map, I had not really entertained the idea of visiting Egypt, but it was so close to Israel I could not resist, so here I was!

As I was not exactly prepared for this part of the trip, seeing these grandiose, colossal centers of man's past where I had lived definitely in former life times was bound to be a memorable experience to add to my personal treasures. I once read that when we die we give all our experiences up to the altar of the Gods, for them to experience. Well, I thought: *They won't be disappointed when I get up there!* The treasures are building up at an amazing rate the older I get. Couldn't it be that the Gods created us so that they could experience it through us because they are stuck in the heavens and can't come down here on Earth? Thereby, it should be our duty to experience as much as possible—a great line of thinking for someone who just simply loves to travel and see the world.

We all settled in our home and the boat left for our leisurely ride down the famous Nile. It was wide and slow moving with many small boats. The rest of the fleet was anchored, waiting for its tourists. As mentioned before, this year the tourists had stayed home waiting for quieter times, and that is one reason why I *traveled* here. This means bread and butter for many Egyptians, one more reason to visit this ancient country.

As we sat on our chairs nonchalantly gazing at the passing scenery, we stepped into another world which had barely changed over the centuries. The villages neatly built on the coast of the Nile, on small hills, farmers working in their fields, tending to their crops, the tall grasses where animals were hiding, birds flying out of the reeds, water buffalo, donkeys with large burdens, minarets standing in the villages, a very peaceful atmosphere. Peasants, farmers maintain the order in the country. It is amazingly green along the shore, but the mountains in the distance are reddish, yellow, and desert-like. Here we can understand this invaluable, great, famous river which brings life to a people. We spent most of the day looking at the peaceful scenery. Then we arrived at our first site. A guide with a car was waiting for me, and he took me to my first grandiose site, still standing in its awesome grandeur. But what did it all mean? It was too complex, too great. Tombs, former Pharaohs, their wives speaking a language I do not understand. I just walked through the very large complex and took in through my skin and eyes the strangeness of it all. I did live in those times, as did everyone else, but that memory has gone. Someday I will recall it, but not now.

Sometimes I meet a new friend, for some reason we get along, and some glimpse of the past comes. Yes, I know this person from Egypt, *I know that*. The rest I cannot recall. It is all strange, how two thousand years from now when we come back to Earth for ever more challenges and we do not remember anything either, we'll look at what is left of great cities, tombs of

A carved relief

the past, and they will mean nothing to us. Skyscrapers lying in desert-like conditions, eaten away by the wind and rain. Will I remember any of it?

Now I certainly don't remember anything at all except one little detail: I wear jewelry. I love beautiful, real stone necklaces of lapis lazuli, or turquoise, or other magnificent stones. I always have. I have designed a large collection of them. In the museum, I love to look at the very old jewels, marvel at their beauty, and think about who wore them, designed them. Here, among the old temples, on the very tall stone frescoes, the women are adorned with jewels as well. Is this feeling a remnant of former times? It could well be. Hints of our past lives come and go. We need to catch their ephemeral touch.

We went back for another festive dinner and another slow boat ride to reach the next destination. Another guide, another taxi ride, and a boat ride to reach a temple built in the middle of the lake. Another awesome site, with just a few tourists. More tall temples, carved reliefs, majestic kings, beautiful women carved into the stones, heads not covered, bodies not covered, yet very chaste, all very much alive. Life carved into the stones—animals, birds, butterflies, bees—full of celebration. A living library carved in stones, living books of the past, standing perfectly mute.

BEYOND THE BLOOD

What has happened to us? Moses came, numbers, weight, measures, letters, intellect, Judaism, monotheism, abstraction—to freedom, and away from life.

How do we go back to life?

Osiris

In the midst of this feverish activity, this glittering life, more than one foreigner seeking the Mysteries, coming from the distant shores of Asia Minor, the Mountains of Thracia, landed in Egypt, attracted by the reputation of its temples. When he arrived in Memphis, he was struck with amazement. Monuments, spectacles, public festivals, all gave him the impression of wealth and grandeur....

But this overwhelming pomp was not what the traveler was seeking. A desire to penetrate the secret of things, a thirst for knowledge, is what brought him from so far away. He had been told that magi and hierophants, in possession of divine science, lived in the sanctuaries of Egypt. He too wanted to fathom the secret of the gods. He had heard a priest of his country speak of the *Book of the Dead*, of its mysterious scroll that as placed beneath mummies' heads like a viaticum, and that related in symbolic form the voyage of the soul after death, according to the priests of Ammon-Ra. With avid curiosity and a certain inner fear mixed with doubt, he had followed this long voyage of the soul into the afterlife, witnessing expiations in a burning region, the purification of its sidereal covering, its encounter with the evil pilot seated in a boat with his head turned aside, and with a good pilot who looks forward. He observed the soul's appearance before the forty-two terrestrial judges, its justification by Toth and finally its entry and transfiguration in the light of Osiris. We can imagine the power of this book, as well as the total revolution that Egyptian initiation sometimes effected upon human minds....

But what truth was there in this disturbing account, in the hieratic pictures, behind which glistened the terrible mysteries of afterlife? "Isis and Osiris know," he was told. But who were these gods about whom one spoke only with one's finger upon one's lips? It was to learn this that the stranger knocked at the door of the great temple of Thebes, or of Memphis.

Servants led him beneath the portico of an inner court, whose great pillars seemed like gigantic lotus supporting the solar ark, the Temple of Osiris, with their strength and purity. The hierophants approached the new arrival. The majesty of his countenance, the tranquility of his face, the mystery of his dark, impenetrable eyes, filled with an inner light, were already enough to disquiet the postulant. That gaze pierced like an awl. The stranger felt that he was facing a man from whom it would be impossible to hide anything. The priest of Osiris questioned the newcomer about the city of his birth, his family and the temple that had instructed him. If in this brief but penetrating examination he was considered unworthy of the Mysteries, a silent but irrevocable gesture pointed to the door. But if the hierophant found in the aspirant the sincere desire for truth, he asked him to follow him. They passed through porticos and inner courts, then through a corridor carved in the rock, open to the sky and bordered with stelae and sphinxes, until they reached a small temple that served as an entrance to the underground crypts. The door was disguised by a life-sized statue of Isis. The goddess, seated in an attitude of meditation and contemplation, held a closed book in her lap. Her face was veiled. Beneath the statue one could read, "No mortal has lifted my veil."

"This is the door to the hidden sanctuary," said the hierophant. "Look at these two columns. The red one represents the ascension of the spirit into the light of Osiris. The black one signifies its captivity in matter, and this fall can continue into annihilation. Whoever approaches our science and teaching risks his life. Madness or death is what the weak or the wicked find; the strong and the good alone find life and immortality. Many reckless ones have entered this door, and have not come out alive. It is an abyss that leads only the fearless to the daylight once again. Therefore, consider carefully what you are about to do, the dangers you will face, and if your courage is not equal to every ordeal, give up the quest. For once this door is closed behind you, you will no longer be able to turn back.

If the stranger persisted in his wish, the hierophant would lead him into the outer court and commend him to the temple servants, with whom he was required to spend a week, obliged to perform the most menial tasks, listening to the hymns and performing ablutions. He is to observe the strictest silence.

When the evening of the ordeals arrived, two neocoros, or assistants, led the candidate for the mysteries to the door of the secret sanctuary. They entered a dark corridor without any visible exit. On the two sides of this dismal room, in the torchlight, the stranger saw a row of statues with human bodies and animals' heads—lions, bulls, birds of prey, and serpents—which seemed to watch the progress while they mocked them. At the end of this sinister passage, which was crossed in complete silence, a mummy and a human skeleton stood opposite each other. And with a silent gesture, the two neocoros showed the novice a hole in the wall in front of him. It was the entrance to a corridor so low that it could be entered only by crawling on hands and knees.

"You can still turn back," said one of the assistants. "The door of the sanctuary is not yet closed. If you do not turn back now, you must continue on your way and cannot return."

"I shall go forward," said the novice, summoning all his courage.*

Every day, the ship lazily followed the curves of the wide Nile. We could feel the life of the river, the busy lives of the villagers. There were small boats carrying food, fodder for goats or sheep, and big loads of reeds which they use for buildings. Life as it had been for thousands of years, undisturbed.

We arrived once more at another colossal site, with more of the same mysterious atmosphere surrounding these ancient sites. The story which I chose, from Édouard Schuré's book *The Great Initiates*, gives the feeling of the inner aspect of these centers of knowledge, these universities of stones which deciphered the long arduous climb of mankind towards the light, the light of Osiris and his consort Isis.

As I walked into the long corridors, small crypts, tombs, and labyrinths of these enormous cities, the carved stones seemed to come alive. So much love went into the carving of these stones. The lovely faces, facing sideways, everything about life was carved into the stones. One of the numerous chambers had all sorts of pharmaceutical recipes for healing carved on the walls, it was like the drugstore carved in stones. The richness of it all was too much, beyond my comprehension, beyond my understanding. Once again, I had entered into the realm of the impossible, impossible to understand.

---

* Schuré, *The Great Initiates: A Study of the Secret History of Religions*, pp. 128–129.

So I took lots of pictures, and many times I sat there looking at a particular scene on the stone and tried to lodge it into my mind. One scene, a tiny one, was showing a woman giving birth to a child in a squatting position, beautifully done, the size of my hand. The gods the size of giants, hundreds of feet tall, with bird heads or other animal heads carved into huge blocks of granite.

Who walked along these sumptuous temples?

The consciousness of the Egyptians was far different from ours. They could still feel life within them, it was not as it is now, where we have abstraction. We see a tree, and we do not feel the tree. We see a flower, and we do not feel the flower unless one has undertaken some meditative path to develop those capacities. The Egyptians knew everything. They knew by instinct the healing powers of plants and places, and they could still feel the power of the animal group souls. They were great healers in these sanctuaries. In other words, they had not completely left the realm of the gods, the world of the spirit. Rudolf Steiner's spiritual research here is helpful because he brings to us memories of previous periods of time. We all know of Atlantis and its wisdom which sank at the bottom of the Atlantic Ocean, but before we had Lemuria which perished before Atlantis in fires and apocalyptic earthquakes in the Pacific area.

> From our studies of the earlier epochs of Earth evolution we can derive that the Egypto-Chaldean period furnished a mirroring in knowledge and experience of what happened in Lemurian time, of what happened on the Earth during and after the departure of the Moon.[*] What people experienced then, they experienced again as a memory in what the Egyptian initiates gave them. The Egyptian initiate himself experienced during his initiation events that which human beings otherwise experience only when they pass through the portal of death....
>
> We have seen that human beings had to descend further and further into the material world, gaining increasing interest in the physical world. In the same proportion, however, the experience in the spiritual world between death and new birth became more pale and shadowy. The livelier that consciousness of the human being became in

---

* For more on this topic, see Steiner, *An Outline of Esoteric Science.*

the physical world, the more they enjoyed being there, the more they discovered the laws of the physical plane, the dimmer their consciousness in the spiritual world became....

Let us look back into the Lemurian period. At that time the etheric was not yet humanlike in its form. In their etheric body human beings were still similar to the animals, and the gods who descended then had to accommodate themselves to the same animal forms in which human beings lived on the Earth. If a being wished to enter into a certain plane, it must fulfill the conditions of that plane. This is also the case here. The divine beings who were connected with the Earth and were on the Earth during the departure of the Sun and Moon (from the Earth), they had to take on a form that was possible at that time, an animal-like form. And since the Egyptian religious views present in a certain way a recapitulation of the Lemurian times, the Egyptian initiate looked upon the gods, Osiris and Isis for example, as having animal-like forms. He still saw the higher gods with animal heads. Therefore from an occult view it was quite correct when such forms were represented with the head of a hawk or a ram in accordance with what the initiates knew. The gods were portrayed in the forms they had when they walked the Earth. The outer images could only resemble what the initiate saw, but they were faithfully reproduced.*

This gives a glimpse, a split-second glimpse, of what stands behind these colossal figures with their eagle head, ram head, etc., which look at us from timeless time, a time when humans did not think as we do today, but felt with their whole body and not their brains.

On another expedition my driver came early and the guide as well. We drove to the Valley of the Dead. A barren valley, deep into the interior, amidst mountain hills. Here the pharaohs had their elaborated tombs carved into the stones, deep in the bowels of the Earth. Dozens of tombs, side by side. Lots of tourists from around the world were here to look at these treasures.

There were so many tombs that I could not go into all of them, so I picked a few, some of them were closed. As I entered these narrow tunnels carved by slave laborers into the mountains, I felt an awe towards such beauty. The

---

* Steiner, *Egyptian Myths and Mysteries*, pp. 154–155, 158.

walls were painted, every inch of the tombs were painted with stories, more than beautiful. I could not take pictures; it was not allowed. It was painful not to take pictures of these masterpieces. The colors were outstanding because they were made of earth tones, crushed stones of lapus, turquoise, magic colors. Scenes from life to accompany the dead on their journey to the other world. After spending time among the tall colossal statues, and carvings, etched stories on walls, etc., it was magical to look at all these paintings. No carvings, no etchings, just the art of painting in the most sumptuous, delicate, outstanding creativity. I was in awe, scene after scene, tomb after tomb, of what had been done so many thousands of years ago. I felt that what we were doing now will never ever reach this stage, it is all downhill. What the Egyptians had accomplished was towering far above mankind.

I was speechless, but very upset. I could take no pictures, not even one. But I could order a book.

The tourists were very quiet as they experienced this feast for the eyes. The preservation of these paintings was superb, and closing some of the tombs part of the time would ensure their survival.

That evening for dinner we were all feeling very lucky to be here and see these remnants of our own history.

Here I will engage the help of the great seer, Rudolf Steiner, from the book of lectures entitled *Egyptian Myths and Mysteries*.

> It will not seem strange that one should look for a connection between widely spread separated periods of time. It is one of our basic convictions that the human soul continually returns, that the experiences between birth and death occur repeatedly for us.... Since these souls that dwell in us today have often been here before, is it not possible that they were also present in ancient Egypt... that the same souls are in us which at that time looked up at the gigantic pyramids and the enigmatic sphinxes?
>
> The answer to this question is, *yes*. Ours souls have beheld the old cultural monuments that they see again today. The same souls that lived then have gone through later periods and have appeared again in our own time. We know that no life remains without fruit; we know that what the soul has gone through in the way of experiences remains

within it and appears in later incarnations as powers, temperament, capacities, and dispositions. Thus the way we look on nature today, the way we take up what our times bring forth, the way we view the world, all this was prepared in ancient Egypt, in the land of the pyramids.[*]

We ended our trip in Karnak and I went around the modern city in a hired horse carriage. He took me for a leisurely ride which I enjoyed thoroughly, including a stop at a major painting shop where I bought beautiful paintings—Osiris, Isis, Horus, etc.—done on papyrus in the old style by modern Egyptian art students. I could take a little something for friends and myself.

Then I walked through the immense temples of Karnak, lost among these gigantic tumbled stones, some erect, some fallen down. Former lakes, the same aura of unfathomable mysteries, lost in the womb of time.

"I shall go forward," said the novice, summoning all his courage.

He was given a little lighted lamp. The neocoros turned around and closed the door to the sanctuary with a loud bang. The novice could no longer hesitate; he had to enter the corridor. Hardly had he eased through by crawling on his knees that he heard a voice at the end of the tunnel, saying, "Fools who covet knowledge and power perish here!" Because of a strange acoustical phenomenon, this sentence was repeated several times by echoes at various points. Nevertheless, he had to move forward; the corridor became wider, but inclined downward sharply. At last the daring traveler would find himself before the shaft that led into a hole. An iron ladder disappeared into the latter; the novice took a chance. As he hung upon the lowest rung of the ladder, his frightened gaze looked downward into a terrifying abyss. His poor naphta lamp that he gripped convulsively in his trembling hand, cast its dim light into endless darkness. What should be done? Above him, impossible to return; below, a drop into the blackness of awful night. In this distress he noticed a crevice on the right. Stretching forward with one hand on the ladder, and his lamp held out with the other, he would see steps. A staircase! Safety! He climbed upward, escaping the abyss. The staircase cut through the rock in the form of a spiral. Finally, the aspirant found himself in front of a bronze grating

---

[*] Steiner, *Egyptian Myths and Mysteries*, p. 9.

leading into a great hall, supported by huge caryatids. On the wall could be seen two rows of symbolic frescoes.

A Magus called a *pastophor*, a guardian of sacred symbols, opened the grating for the novice and welcomed him with a kind smile.*

Later that day, the guide who was taking care of me felt bad because I was still trying to figure out how to get my airplane ticket by calling Cairo. So he took me for a sail on a local faluga sailboat with two of his local friends. I stepped into the little boat, and we headed across the Nile, to the other side of the river to a lovely little oasis with a teahouse, and we walked in a wonderfully rich garden, full of banana trees, and many other plants. He said the locals came here with their kids for a Friday family day. Friday is the Muslims' Sunday. Friday is Venus day (love, beauty, art). Sunday is the day of the *Sun* (*Son* for Christians). The Sabbath is Saturday (after the planet Saturn), the special day for the Jews, where no work is allowed. So we neatly have Friday, Saturday, and Sunday, Muslims, Jews, and Christians.

I chatted with the kids who tried to make a living taking tourists or locals for a sail to this little heaven on the coast of the Big River. The fishermen were working their lines, and boats were gently flowing with the current. It was a living picture of the past. Thousands and thousands of years had developed this life by the river, the great river that ruled all of Egypt. Life, water, Egypt—and something was born from the great river Nile.

> The Egyptians had the Nile which we may say is really the father who feeds the country. Every July the river rises above its banks returning to them in October. All an ancient Egyptian would know, therefore, was that the Nile held water; the waters would recede during the cold part of the year and then rise to flood the land again for the benefit of humanity. When the waters receded in October, fertile mud was left behind—the Egyptians do not need to use fertilizer. They would sow their cereal grains and so on in the mud; these would germinate and grow and be harvested before the Nile flooded again. And so the Nile really prepared their fields for them year after year. And the Egyptians were deeply conscious of the beneficial nature of water.

---

* Schuré, *The Great Initiates: A Study of the Secret History of Religions*, p. 131.

They gave much thought to water in the world of nature. You see, today we admire the skills of engineers who are able to channel the waters. Well the Egyptians were very good at this thousands of years ago! When the Nile rose above its banks and flooded everything, it would of course sometimes also go to places where it should not go. They therefore created a lake, one of the earliest man-made lakes, to control flooding. Egyptians thus controlled nature. With all this, their attention focused on water to an extraordinary degree.

Water has a tremendous influence on the human ether body. The Egyptians still had the instinct that enabled them to say: The human being has not only a physical but also an ether body. This is interesting. You see, over yonder in India were some of the oldest nations; many of them had later migrated via Arabia to Egypt. A kind of old civilization existed in Egypt that had come from India. When the Indians came to Egypt they appreciated the beneficial qualities of water.

Having discovered the ether body the Egyptians developed the whole of their religion as a religion of the ether body.[*]

After my delightful sail, I enjoyed walking around the city and I noticed quite a few older women who were living here in local clothing, shopping. I found out through the horse carriage guide that a lot of older women come here to go out with the younger Egyptian men. He told me that many of these women get taken by these handsome young men. The women spend their money on them, many times marrying them, buying houses, and then they find out that the marriage was not legal, the house is not in their name, or they get abandoned and so forth. A sad story, as the old man was telling me. I thought to myself that perhaps they think I am here for the same reason. I am traveling alone, and I am older! I quickly said that I was married and had two kids and so on, and blurted out that this was not a very good example for their lovely daughters, or mine, for that matter!

But I had not heard of this reverse sex trade or had not paid attention to the sordid details. The men go to the Far East, and the women to the Arab countries, or Africa! I should be careful because I was going to travel for a few years into Muslim countries, all over, and better be prepared than

---

[*] Steiner, *From Beetroot to Buddhism…: Answers to Questions*, p. 12.

pay for my ignorance. But I have traveled widely, and I have become quite proficient at blending into the scenery, so as to disappear, and not calling attention to myself. One way is to just walk past any café full of men, and look straight ahead, making no eye contact with anyone at all, and go where I am supposed to, even though I might not know where that is! The other is to go straight to anyone in one of these public places and say, "I am traveling and looking for this place. Can you tell me where it is?" They know what I want, the mystery is over, and most of the time people are very helpful. That is another way to not get into trouble.

> The trials were not over. When he finished speaking, the *pastophor* opened a door leading to another long, narrow corridor, at the end of which glowed a red-hot furnace. "Why that is death!" exclaimed the novice, looking at his guide fearfully. "My son," said the *pastophor*, "death frightens only weak minds. I once crossed this fire like a bed of roses." And the gate of the hall of secrets closed behind the postulant. Upon approaching the fiery furnace, he saw it reduced to an optical illusion.... A path through the middle allowed him to pass quickly. The *trial by water* followed the *trial by fire*. The aspirant was forced to go through a stagnant black pool, lighted by naphtha flames that flashed up behind him in the room of fire. After this, two assistants led him, still trembling, into a dim grotto where a soft couch could be dimly seen, lighted by the mysterious flickering of a bronze lamp hanging from the vault. He was dried, his body was bathed in exquisite essences, he was dressed in fine linen and was left alone after being told, "Rest and wait for the hierophant."
>
> Weak with fatigue, the novice stretched himself upon the sumptuous bed. After his varied emotions this moment of calm seemed sweet. The sacred paintings he had seen, all those strange faces, the sphinx, the caryatids, again passed before his eyes. But why did one of the paintings keep coming back to him like an hallucination? Again and again he saw arcanum X represented by a wheel suspended on its axis between two columns. On one side sits Hermanubis, genius of good, handsome as a young Ephebe; on the other, Typhon, genius of evil, falls head downward into the abyss. Between the two, on top of the wheel, sits a sphinx holding a sword in its paw.

The tones of lascivious music that seemed to come from outside the grotto, caused this picture to fade. The sounds were light and undefinable, of a sad, penetrating languor. A metallic tinkling reached his ear, mixed with vibrations of the harp and the sounds of a flute, along with panting sighs like a torrid breathing. Wrapped in a dream of fire, the stranger closed his eyes. Upon reopening them, he saw an overwhelming vision of life and infernal seduction a few steps away from his bed. A Nubian woman, clothed in transparent dark-red gauze, a necklace of amulets at her neck, similar to the priestesses of Mylitta, was standing there embracing him with her glance, holding a cup crowned with roses in her left hand. She was of the type whose intense, strong sensuality embodies all the powers of the female animal: high, prominent cheekbones, nostrils dilated, full lips like a delicious ripe fruit. Her dark eyes shone in the dusk. The novice had leapt to his feet in astonishment, not knowing whether he should tremble or rejoice, instinctively crossing his hands over his chest. But the slave moved toward him slowly lowering her eyes. In a low voice she murmured, "Are you afraid of me, noble stranger? I bring you the reward of conquerors, the forgetfulness of troubles, the cup of happiness." The novice hesitated; then as though overcome with lassitude, the Nubian woman sank upon the bed, enveloping the stranger in a pleading look as a humid flame. Woe to him if he did not defy her, if he bent over that mouth, if he became drunk with the heavy perfumes arising from these bronzed shoulders! Once he had touched that hand and had placed his lips upon that cup, he was lost. He turned upon his bed, entwined in a burning grasp.... But after the wild satisfying of his desire, the liquid he had drunk plunged him into a deep sleep. When he awoke, he found himself alone and in anguish. The lamp cast a ghost-like light upon the disordered bed. A man was standing before him; it was the hierophant.

"You were victorious in the first trials. You triumphed over death, fire, and water, but you have not learned to conquer yourself. You who seek the heights of the mind and knowledge succumbed to the first temptation of the senses and fell into the abyss of matter. One who is a slave to the senses lives in darkness. You preferred darkness to light; therefore remain in darkness. I warned you of the dangers to which you were exposing yourself. You saved your life, but you have lost your freedom. You are to remain a slave of the temple, under penalty of death."*

The stay on the boat came to an end, and we said our good-byes. Late that evening I took the airplane to Sharm el-Sheikh. I still had no tickets, none. But I showed up at the airport, and somehow they let me in; how, I do not know! It was full of Russians, of course, going back to their hotels in their beach heaven.

We arrived late at night, and I was fortunate that the whole planeload had to be driven to their various luxury accommodations. I, of course, had found some out-of-the-way cheap place which took a couple of hours to find!

It is called Shark's Bay, a diving club on the oceanfront with little cabanas on top of the mountainous cliffsides, where divers come from everywhere for world-class diving. I wanted to snorkel in the Red Sea, a famous place for lovers of underwater sea life. I had planned on staying for four days before heading up to Israel by bus, and a plane back to Spain and the United States.

It was way past midnight when I settled into my bare room with a common bath house after climbing the steep stairs up the cliff from the beach.

Morning came, and I loved the beautiful little spot, with no luxury at all. Restaurants were by the sea, where one would sit on wooden benches covered with large pillows. I signed up with the diving club, agreed on a price, and was off with a group of French divers. I would snorkel, while they did their scuba diving. The day would be spent on the water with a great cooked lunch included. Different sites for different days, so I could see the coast. I no longer dive, I do not like all the heavy equipment and just enjoy peacefully swimming on top of the water watching the sea life. These French men were avid, serious divers. They had been coming here to dive for thirty years and they loved it. They lived to dive!

The captain of the boat was a handsome Egyptian who had quit being a lawyer and had decided to operate a scuba diving club for foreign tourists. He was very happy with his life, enjoying every minute of it, especially his beautiful, tall, blond, Russian girlfriend!

---

*   Schuré, *The Great Initiates: A Study of the Secret History of Religions*, p. 133.

He spoke at least five languages and now was focusing on Russian. I told him he had better start learning Chinese.

On one of the trips, we went right through a sea of dolphins. I wanted to go and swim with them as they are such beautiful creatures, but the captain refused! He said, "Where there are dolphins, right underneath are the sharks," so I said OK and thanked him.

The other two helpers were wonderful cooks and amiable fellows. Since I knew how to drive a boat, I was at the helm a lot of time while they took a break. The French men were not too happy to see me drive the fast dive boat, but I owned a sailboat for several years and sometimes drive my son's gillnetting boat in Alaska! They thought I did not know what I was doing!

The sea life was abundant, the water was crystal clear, and I was becoming a fish. The gigantic sphinx and colossal statues were slowly drifting away from my mental horizon. It all seemed to disappear into a dream. I wondered if I even went there! But one legend has not disappeared, a legend that is very much alive in our western psyche, but has been transformed—the legend of Isis and Osiris. I have selected long passages because of the nature of the myth which embodies our struggles today.

> Osiris is a god who gradually came to be popular and was universally worshipped in Egypt.... Whatever the ordinary people of Egypt thought about the nature of Osiris, in the *Book of the Dead* we have evidence of a priestly doctrine according to which Osiris was found to be within the human soul....
>
> When the body is given over to the Earth, preserved under earthly conditions, humanity's eternal part enters into the eternal condition that was in the beginning. It appears before Osiris. It stands before him for judgment, surrounded by the forty two judges of the Dead. The destiny of one's eternal being depends upon their verdict. If the soul has confessed its sins, it is deemed to be reconciled with the eternal justice....
>
> In the world of eternal order, one's eternal nature becomes Osiris; after the name of Osiris stands the personal name of the deceased.
>
> "I am the Osiris N. Growing under the blossoms of the fig tree is the name of Osiris N."*

---

*   *Book of the Dead*, ch. 125.

He has "become an Osiris."

Yet being an Osiris is nothing but the final, perfected stage of human life and development. It is clear in this context that even Osiris in his cosmic role as a judge is no more than a man who has attained to the stage of perfected existence....

Osiris in his cosmic form is a unitary being; hence he exists undivided in each human soul. Everyone is an Osiris; yet the unitary Osiris has to be represented as a separate entity. Humanity is looked upon as being still in the process of development, and at the end of the process comes existence as a God.... To be truly human one must already live the most perfect life of an Osiris that is possible under transitory conditions. Human perfection means living like an Osiris—it means undergoing all that Osiris underwent.

It is in this way that the Osiris myth takes on its deeper dimensions of meaning, becoming a paradigm of life for someone who wants to awaken eternal being within him or herself. Osiris is torn to pieces by Typhon; he is killed. The members of his body are cherished and cared for by his consort Isis. After his death, he caused a ray of light to fall upon her and she bore his son Horus, who then takes over the earthly tasks of Osiris; he is the second, still immature Osiris, but he is in the process of becoming an Osiris in the full sense. This true Osiris is to be found in the human soul. For although the soul is to begin with connected to the transitory realm, it is destined to give birth to the eternal. Humanity may therefore be termed the tomb of Osiris; it is our lower nature—Typhon or Set—that has killed him. The love that is present in his soul—Isis—must cherish and care for the members of his corpse, and then the higher nature or eternal soul—Horus—can be born, and in due course rise to the state of "being an Osiris."

This then is the "initiation" practice in Egypt....

If we were able to look inside the temples where the initiatory "transformation into Osiris" took place, we would see that the events enacted there on the human scale were a representation of the cosmogony. Humanity originates from the "Father" and is to bear within it the Son; the actual presence within human beings of the divinity, held captive by a spell, is to be brought to manifestation. The god within is held down by the power of human nature; that lower nature must become a grave, from which the higher nature can rise to new life. The information we possess about the scenarios of initiation makes sense when we understand this. People were subjected to procedures whose character was mysterious, but which intended to "kill" the earthly and awaken something higher....

All the initiates could declare that they had seen hovering before them the prospect of infinity, reaching up to the divine, that they had felt within them also the power of the divine, and had laid to rest in the tomb all that held down that power. The initiate had died to earthly things, and was indeed dead, having died as a lower being and having been in the underworld of the dead—that is with those who had already united with eternity.*

An "Osiris" was the name the initiates of ancient Egypt gave to the manifestations of the Sun's forces within the human being.**

In earlier times, Osiris ruled the Earth, to the blessing of humanity.... Then it was that Typhon, or Set, killed his brother Osiris by inducing him to lay himself down in a chest, which Typhon then closed and committed to the sea. Isis, the sister and wife of Osiris, searched for her brother and husband, and after finding him brought him to Egypt. But the evil Typhon, still striving for the destruction of Osiris, cut him in pieces. Isis gathered the fragments together and buried them in various places. (Various graves of Osiris are still shown in Egypt.) Then Isis bore Horus, who avenged his father on Typhon. Osiris was now again admitted into the world of divine spiritual beings and is no longer active on Earth but he aids humans when they sojourn in the spiritual world between death and a new birth. Therefore in Egypt the path of the dead was called the way to Osiris.***

The so-called "Egyptian Book of the Dead," now restored to us by the diligence of nineteenth-century scholarship, demonstrates the existence

---

*   Steiner, *Christianity as Mystical Fact: And the Mysteries of Antiquity*, pp. 59–62.

** Steiner, *The Sun Mystery and the Mystery of Death and Resurrection: Exoteric and Esoteric Christianity*, p. 126.

*** Steiner, *Egyptian Myths and Mysteries*, p. 91.

among the ancient Egyptians of ideas concerning humanity's eternal existence and communion with the divine, which might be summed up in the words attributed to Empedocles:

> *When, set free from your body, released you rise to the ether,*
> *You become divine, an immortal, escaped from the power of death.*

The days drifted by, we went to faraway coves, small islets, where I swam for hours, drifting with the current and got picked up by the guys hours later. It was a wonderful place but it was time to head back.

On the last day, I packed my backpack, headed for the bus terminal, and bought a ticket to the Israel border which was a day's drive, a beautiful coastal drive. The ladies at the border searched my backpack, and I was in Israel going to the city of Helat for an exorbitant taxi cab ride. The cab driver said arrogantly, "Hey lady, this is not Egypt, things work here." I said, "You are charging me thirty dollars for a two-kilometer drive. You are a thief." Then I left him fuming. I got a bus ticket for a drive to Tel Aviv. The bus was full of vacationers, families with children, lots of soldiers with their guns coming back from duties or going to report for duties, and visitors from the United States; it was quite a crowd. In Tel Aviv I was helped by a lovely couple from Russia and their little one who had emigrated. I did not have a phone to contact some friends in Tel Aviv. They helped, and I could then spend a couple of days with a Tel Aviv family, a writer and inventor in his lovely home, and enjoy a most lively city, a totally different world from Jerusalem. I think Tel Aviv is the *real* Israel, modern, cosmopolitan, and trying to invent itself as a country, because it is very old but yet one of the youngest cities.

Now back to my story in Jerusalem.

I began my journey in Jerusalem, a week before Palm Sunday. I flew from Spain as this was the second leg of this journey. I had crossed Spain on foot from Seville to Santiago, a long walk of seven hundred kilometers in six weeks which was part of this mysterious Muslim, Christian, and Jewish journey with a will of its own!

---

*   Steiner, *Christianity as Mystical Fact: And the Mysteries of Antiquity*, p. 59.

Arriving at the airport was a challenge, I almost turned back, the arrogance of the military police was unbearable!

I took the bus to the center of Jerusalem and went to the famous David gate and followed the directions to my youth hostel. It was in the Christian quarters and was packed with kids, and not-so-young adults, my age. I got a bed in the women's dorm in a small room with eight of us packed in. There were no windows, no ventilation, and one toilet for dozens of us, but that is the reality of cheap travel. Hotels are cost prohibitive. Everyone was from everywhere: Germany, France, Australia, the United States, Spain, etc. It was great to see resilient youth on the road. I put down my pack and went straight outside to meander through the labyrinths of narrow streets in old Jerusalem. It was awesome. I loved the old markets and everything about the old city. I was fortunate that I had many days to discover the city, with no rush. I walked and walked into all the areas. I ate the famous Middle Eastern food, chatted with the Palestinian workers, drank lots of tea, and just simply enjoyed this amalgamation of people, architecture, and ancient sites. It is one of the most beautiful, amazing cities I have experienced.

And as I mentioned earlier, as I walked down the street the profusion of paradoxes was overwhelming, simply overwhelming. How do all these people even live together? It is mind boggling. But sometimes one has to leave the intellect behind and just see what is happening. An older traveler from Spain, with whom I had had a chat since he was staying at the hostel, had been extremely bothered at the border by the show of power of the young male and female soldiers. He had decided then and there: *I am out of here on the next bus!* And so he was! He said, "I simply can't breathe here, it is too dark! Too difficult!" The youthful army with their guns loosely strung on their shoulders is a difficult sight to take in and accept, a show of power, of unlimited power versus the powerlessness of the rest of the population, tourists, Palestinians, etc.

> How can we return to moral life?... The need for an older form of morality has shown itself in the last five years. This lie has been victorious in all peoples and nations. The old Hebrew-Jahve politics have taken such a strong hold on so many peoples, that they would like to believe

EGYPT ❧ PALESTINE ❧ ISRAEL ❧ JORDAN

Soldiers in Jerusalem listening to a young man playing the violin

that long ago in Palestine there was only one united Jewish nation. And so now all peoples want for themselves the kind of political support that the Jews in Palestine were able to get for themselves back then. They would like everything to be as it was; they would like to govern the world in a way that excludes all the annoyances of Christianity.

The content is lacking. In these desires people are clutching at things that actually are void of content. Instead of seeking new sources of morality in new, fruitful, spiritual worldviews, people ask: "What is to be the source of a new morality?" And then they answer: "Having power is an indispensable means for achieving something good in the world; therefore, you should strive to gain the power necessary (if you do not already possess it) for doing good." People would like to have something good to do in the world, and they beautifully advise one another to seek the power to do the good. A second justification for this new ethics is as follows: With the power that you already possess, you can do some good. Therefore, you should always use the power you have for the achievement of the good.

But first you must have some good to do; first you must be able to recognize what is good! The advice that people give is the opposite of what spiritual science must spread throughout the new human civilization. For spiritual science has nothing to do with trying to found something on the basis of having power. You can only found something on the basis of power when you are working with a group of people collectively. When one human being stands before another, it is impossible to found anything on the basis of power; it is only possible to found something on the basis of the things that can develop in the human being, so that the other person has some worth. We all have a worth to discover and to develop within ourselves that will allow us to accomplish something for the sake of humanity; and each of us must simultaneously develop within ourselves a receptivity that allows us to recognize this worth of the other.

This is the only possible means of forming a foundation for the morality of the future: to develop our own individual worth, and to become able to recognize that worth in others. To put this another way: all morality will have to be built on trust!...

I said to some people: "Look at what we do when we walk down the road—some on this side, some on the other. Do we need to have laws in order to avoid bumping into each other? The fact that some people walk on the left and others on the right is simply a demand of existence—a demand that people quite sensibly observe." This is what it means to conduct oneself morally—when the things that lie in the very essence of the human being are truly developed and brought into reality. Without this, there will be no moral code of the future.*

The city is so full of famous everything, that it is even pointless to look up anything. It is all famous, and it all has a meaning. So I just walked endlessly everywhere—one day in that direction, another in the next—and afterwards, read up: *Ah yes, so that is the famous Via Dolorosa, and yes, that is where Christ supposedly died on the cross, and Muhammad came here as well, and so did Abraham.* And so on. Too much for me. Lots of tourists were here in groups from all around the world for the Easter holidays. They knew more than I did about the bible. I actually liked walking around the place not knowing anything. (I do know a few things, I am not that ignorant!) Just feeling the place with its very ancient past, somehow it did not bother

---

* Steiner, *What is Necessary in These Urgent Times*, pp. 38–39.

me at all not to have all this biblical knowledge at my fingertips. I would walk somewhere and experience a small chapel here or a mosque there, or a Jewish site somewhere else, wealthy quarters where the whole of New York City was having a great lunch, fantastic bookstores filled with vacationing New Yorkers buying Yiddish books, and walking in the souks. The wealthy, of course, shop in the malls of Tel Aviv, so I wondered how long these old-fashioned merchants were going to make a living. The smart teenagers of Tel Aviv certainly do not shop here—civilization clashing, big time!

After a few days of walking around the old city, I decided to go out for a trip. I took the bus to the seashore, the Dead Sea, for the day. It was packed with travelers, kids, families. I entered the sea resort and it was full of people enjoying a bath in the heavy salted waters. I heard all the imaginable languages: Jews from Paris, Rome, Madrid, Moscow, New York City, Los Angeles, etc. Palestinian families were bathing in their clothes, Arab women were in their long skirts. I thoroughly enjoyed the water, where one could not drown if one tried. I was very careful not to put my hair and eyes in the water; my eyes would have been stinging for days because of the salt. I gave myself a mud bath like everyone else. The wonderful green mud felt great on my skin—rejuvenation. Everyone had fun in the water. One wished all would get along in life. When it comes to health, beauty, and eating well, religion goes out the window!

All the women—Arab women, westerners, Palestinians, Orthodox and non-Orthodox Jews—were in the store buying beauty remedies, creams, lipsticks, salts, perfumes. In that realm, there is no argument. Perhaps we should build major, enormous *spas*, and *pay people to go there*, side by side—Jews, Muslims, Christians, Armenians, Buddhists, etc. It would be much cheaper than the defense budget; fight with beauty creams instead of bullets! Along with an art scene and a music scene, we would all get along well!

Forget the *peace* agenda of the United Nations; bring in the *health and beauty* agenda. All agree on that point. Massages, creams, mud baths, scents, perfumes, clothes, scarves, ice cream—the international language! (Provided people are not starving.)

The next day, I went on another long bus drive to the fortress up high in the rocky mountains off the Dead Sea, to Masada. It sounded highly biblical, so once again I took the bus and drove through the magnificent, dry scenery of Palestine. The bus let us off at a beautiful hotel complex, and then I walked up from there, a huge plateau high above the Dead Sea. This time the place was very crowded with Jews, mostly from New York City. When I visited, of course, I was totally unaware of its history. Our world is far too complex to know it all; there is only so much one can take in. But this place was just grandiose, and very sorrowful. A mood of doom permeated the ancient city; it was not a happy place. Of course I found out later that in AD 70 many people died here, not wanting to surrender their freedom. The fortress was built by King Herod. One can still see storerooms, cisterns, bathhouses, palaces, synagogues, and rituals baths. Then I took the bus back to the old city. I could easily spend a year in this city, sacred to so many human beings. I can see why numerous Jews from around the world come here and buy or invest in a condo in Palestine, and visit: it is home.

And it is also a fact that after leaving the Muslim world—Egypt in this case—things do work.

Israel is a very modern world, if we could only mix the old and the new and learn from each other.

Abraham

And here the story of Abraham comes to my mind, this patriarch, father of our Western world, father of the Muslims, father of the Christians, and father of the Jews. We are all Abraham's children. Again, the story is not the usual easy story, but unfolds in many ways.

So here we are back to Zarathustra, this great helper of humanity.

> We must realize more and more clearly the fact than an Individuality as great as Zarathustra uses the body as an *instrument*. Even if a Being were to come down to the Earth out of the highest, even the very highest, divine worlds, and were to incarnate in an unsuitable physical organism, such a Being could make use of that body only to the extent to which it was actually capable of being an instrument.... That man's bodily organism is the temple of the soul has long ceased to

be properly understood. We must always remember what has so often been emphasized among us, namely, that the human Ego dwells within three sheaths, each one of which is more ancient than the Ego itself. The Ego is a being of Earth, the youngest of the members of man's nature. The astral body had its beginning on the Old Moon, the etheric or life body on the Old Sun, the physical body on Old Saturn. This means that the physical body is the most highly perfected having four stages of planetary evolution behind it. The physical body has been developed through aeons after aeons until it has become what it is today—this perfect instrument in which the Ego can so unfold that man can be enabled gradually to rise again to the heights of the spirit. If the physical body were as undeveloped as the astral body and the Ego, no evolution on the Earth would be possible for man.

If you realize the full significance of this, the thought of Zarathustra being born from the Hebrew people had to be just what it was, if it was to provide the body for a being as great as Zarathustra. If we bear in mind that ever since the time when he had been the Teacher of the ancient Persian people, this great being had been developing to ever higher stages, we shall understand that for him a bodily instrument had to be provided from a racial stock whose greatness was commensurate with that of his own being.

An instrument had to be created, fit for Zarathustra. Through all the evolutionary periods of Saturn, Sun, Moon, and Earth, have the gods worked at the development of the human physical body. From this we may rightly infer that the more intimate preparation of one particular human body must necessarily have entailed great divine-spiritual labor, in order to produce a human body in the specially constituted form which was to be used at that time by Zarathustra.

To make this possible, the whole history of the ancient Hebrew people had to take the course it did. The Akasha Chronicle reveals that what is set down in the Old Testament conforms entirely with the historical facts. Everything that happened to the ancient Hebrew people had to be directed in such a way that it culminated in the single personality of Jesus of Bethlehem. But to achieve this, very special measures were essential—it was necessary that from the whole of Post-Atlantean civilization, faculties of the highest quality should be extracted, which would enable mankind to develop powers *in place of the old clairvoyant* *gifts*. It was the *Hebrew* people which were chosen for this task, to the end that it might provide a bodily constitution which, right into the most delicate vessels of the brain, was so organized that what we call *knowledge of the world* might evolve, free from the influences of the old clairvoyance—this was to be the mission of the ancient Hebrew people. And in Abraham, the progenitor of this people, such an Individuality was chosen, that out of his bodily constitution, a suitable instrument might be fashioned for the development of reasoned thinking. All previous thinking of any significance was still subject to the influences of the old clairvoyance. But now a personality was chosen because he possessed the brain most capable of withstanding the inrush and coercion of clairvoyant Imaginations and Intuitions and was destined to acquire knowledge of the things of the world purely by the process of reason. This required a specially constituted brain, and the personality chosen because he possessed such a brain, was Abram, or Abraham.*

Here I must take a breather; the story is too big, too complex. One must accept the facts of reincarnation, the facts of high spiritual beings coming to birth after eons of preparation from realms far beyond the common human knowledge. If we can unite in these efforts then it all makes sense. Why are the Orthodox Jews to this day following certain rules of diet, prayers, rituals? Because they are keeping their bodies, minds, and souls pure for higher beings to come into the world. For the Christians, Jesus (or the reincarnated Zarathustra) was born, then Christ into the body prepared for him by Jesus when he was thirty-three years old, his body prepared by these same rules, the rules of the Essenes, followed to this day in some places. The rules are there; the fact that the rules are there is an indication of certain truths, valid truths. Otherwise, why follow these rules?

The men constantly in prayer, their eyes towards God, over sacred scrolls, eating sacred food, wearing sacred clothes, obeying sacred rules so as to live a life of purity, to bring special little beings into the world. We in the West could learn a lot from this sacred approach to life. We have lost

---

*   Steiner, *Deeper Secrets of Human History in the Light of the Gospel of St. Matthew*, pp. 25–28.

our sacredness in these matters, but the Orthodox Jews have not. They are following the rules, to receive a future Messiah which has not come yet!

But for the Christians, Jesus Christ is the Messiah. It is one of the biggest paradoxes in humankind, one which as westerners we must live with. If we are truly Christians we must learn to accept this dilemma. It is thanks to Judaism that we are Christians, and if the Jews still wait for the Messiah, then we must resign ourselves to this turn of events until it resolves itself through destiny and evolution.

We are all born many times. We have been Jews in the past and will be Jews in the future even if we are Christians now. We were Muslims in the past and will be Muslims in the future even though we are Christians now. The world is always changing, and the higher spiritual beings take us where we need to be according to our Karma. Where we have done wrong is where we need to reincarnate, it is called iron necessity. It cannot be changed! If we see history in this light, then it behooves us to develop a kinder approach to life, religions, countries, etc. After death we all go to the same place, but not experiencing the same things. Through knowledge gained by spiritual science we learn that Christ is the biggest helper after death.

In the book of lectures entitled *Life Between Death and Rebirth*, Rudolf Steiner gives us intimate details of life after death. I will only mention one startling fact. Being born into different religions, of course, affects our life after death. If one has had the opportunity to experience the Christ force, love, then it means something different in our sojourn after death into the spiritual world than if we did not. We develop stronger ether bodies, meaning a healthy physical body in the next life. These passages make for difficult reading, but nothing is simple.

> A moral disposition of soul is therefore already of great significance shortly after the period of kamaloca (the short period after death). It also determines destiny for the next Venus period. A different category of ideas also comes into consideration then, ideas a man has evolved during birth and that concern him when he enters the spiritual world. The ideas and conceptions are of a religious character. If religion has been a link between the transitory and the eternal, the life of the soul in the Venus sphere after death is different from what it is if there has

been no such link. Again, whether we are sociable or isolated, hermit-like spirits depends upon whether we were or were not of a religious turn of mind during life on Earth. After death an irreligious soul feels as though enclosed in a capsule, a prison. True, such a soul is aware that there are beings around him, but he feels as though he were in a prison and unable to reach them. Thus, for example, the members of the Monistic Union, inasmuch as with their barren, materialistic ideas they have excluded all religious feeling, will not be united in a community or union after death, but each of them will be confined in his own prison. Naturally, this is not meant as an attack upon the Monistic Union. It is merely a question of making a certain fact intelligible.

In the life on Earth materialistic ideas are an error, a fallacy. In the realm of the spirit they are a reality. Ideas, which here in the physical world merely have the effect of making us shut ourselves off, incarcerate us in the realm of the spirit, make us prisoners of our own astrality. Through our immoral conception of life we deprive ourselves of forces of attraction in the Mercury sphere. Through our irreligious disposition of soul we deprive ourselves of forces of attraction in the Venus sphere. We cannot draw from this sphere the forces we need, which means that in the next incarnation we shall have an astral body that in a certain respect is imperfect.... Why does a feeling of grandeur, of reverent awe, come over us when we look up into the starry heavens? It is because without our knowing it the feeling of our soul's home awakens in us.... Before you came down to Earth to a new incarnation you yourself were in those stars, and out of the stars have come the highest forces that are within you.*

Today was the day to walk up to the Mount of Olives. It was a spectacular sunny day, and I started early. I walked out through the Via Dolorosa, out that big door, and walked down and crossed the small bridge. I went into the Church of the tomb of the Virgin Mary. It is kept by the Armenians and the Greek Orthodox so that there is always a profusion of lit candles. This is the crypt where Mary is buried. I do not know how authentic that is since Mary is supposed to have ended her days in the surrounding mountains of Ephesus in Turkey, where she was taken care of by Saint John.

---

* Steiner, *Life Between Death and Rebirth*, pp. 44–46.

Then I went up to the Garden of Gethsemane, and the gardener let me enter the little garden full of very old trees and gave me a few branches. The place is taken care of by Franciscan brothers. I enjoyed the peaceful atmosphere generated by the old gnarled trees and some lavender growing there.

I went to the Basilica of the Agony, a splendid church, and walked up to the Russian compound, gardens, and church of Mary Magdalene. The nuns were stern; in order to pray in the church one had to wait in line and put on some clothes like in the mosque. It was quiet, full of candles and women praying. The gardens were kept by the nuns and were truly a labor of love.

Then I walked up to the village on top and visited various sites sacred to Christians, Jews, and Muslims. I visited the Dome of the Ascension where a Muslim guardian graciously let me in, then relaxed by a restaurant facing the old city of Jerusalem and had some well-earned food.

I walked back to old Jerusalem and sat on the terrace of the youth hostel which had a beautiful view of the city—mosques, churches, and synagogues all lit up in the evening sky. Meanwhile, an Orthodox Jew by choice was doing his prayer silently facing the city. I had had a chat with him a few days ago. He was from Sweden, and wanted to be an Orthodox Jew and study the Torah, etc., but the Orthodox Jews did not accept him, so he did his own thing. He wrapped himself in his ritualistic ways, put the shawl on his head, and silently moved his body to an unknown rhythm, alone with his God. I silently thanked him for his prayers. I chatted with a motley group of people and then went to my very crowded room. I should have slept on the terrace, but I had no blankets. I slept well until the next day's expedition, my senses not really digesting this incredible city and its treasures, past and present.

> That the path of Abraham's journeyings led westwards from beyond the river Euphrates right up to Cannan, also tallies with what the Akasha Chronicle reveals. Abraham went forth, as the Bible tells us, from Ur in Chaldea. Whereas the aftermath of the ancient, shadowy clairvoyance was still in active operation in Egyptian, as well as in Chaldean-Babylonian civilization, there was chosen from among the Chaldeans an individual who no longer worked by means of these faculties, but *by observing the phenomena of the external world.* This was to be an introduction of that form of culture whose fruits are to this very day

implicit in the whole of the cultural life and civilization of the West. Constructive reasoning and mathematical logic were both introduced through Abraham. Even until far into the Middle Ages he was regarded in a certain sense as the founder of arithmetic. The fundamental trend and character of his thinking led to observation of the world according to the relationships of *measure* and *number*.

A personality so constituted was able, by his very nature, to enter into a living relationship with that Divinity who was to reveal himself through the medium of external phenomena. All other divinities, with the exception of Jehovah, Jahve, proclaimed themselves in the inmost depths of the human soul, and to acquire any knowledge of them man had to awaken in his soul the faculties of Imagination, Inspiration, and Intuition. The men of ancient India gazed at the rising Sun, at the different kingdoms of the Earth, at the processes manifesting in air, and ocean, but regarded all this as the great Illusion, as "Maya," in which they would have found nothing of a divine nature, had they not first acquired knowledge of the divine through inner Imagination, and then afterwards, had proceeded to relate this knowledge to the phenomena of the external world. It must be realized that even Zarathustra could not have taught as he did of the mighty Sun-Being had not Ahura Mazdao in his glory been *inwardly* revealed to him. This is especially apparent in the case of the Egyptian divinities who were first experienced in the inmost depths of the soul and only afterwards related to the things of the external world. All that applies to the Divinities of the pre-Hebraic times must be understood in this way.

Jahve, however, is the Divine Being who gazes down upon men from *outside*, who comes to men from outside, manifesting Himself in wind, and weather. When man penetrates to the relationships of number, measure, and weight inherent in the things of the visible world, he draws near to the God Jahve. In earlier times the process was reversed. Brahma was recognized first, in the inmost depths of the soul and only from that experience did man find his way into the outer world. Jahve is recognized first in the outer world and only afterwards can his reality also be confirmed in man's inmost being. This is the spiritual aspect of what is called in the Bible: Jahve's covenant with Abraham. Abraham was a man who possessed the faculty to grasp and comprehend the nature of Jahve. Abraham's bodily constitution was such that he could recognize Jahve or Jehovah as the God who lives and moves in the outer phenomena of the universe.*

Jerusalem was getting busier with Christian pilgrims pouring in from around the world. That morning it was Palm Sunday and I decided to take part in the procession from Bethphage to Jerusalem. I started walking early in the morning. I walked through the Via Dolorosa and then out that gate down into the Mount of Olives and up the narrow road. I stopped again at Mary's Church for a quick service. The Church was full of Christians and beautiful children dressed in their Sunday clothes holding palms in their hands. I arrived at the top where there was nothing yet. I waited for hours and just watched as people arrived by the thousands—processions of all kinds, people from the four corners of the Earth, children from the Far East singing gospel songs and accompanied by guitars, Chinese, Vietnamese, Koreans, Thais, Africans, African Americans, desert Bedouins in their Bedouins attire with their wives, Europeans, Italian priests and their papal envoy, Russian Orthodox from all over Russia, Armenians, Druzes, Polish pilgrims, Americans from Louisiana, Mexicans, South Americans, etc. It was fully alive, and living proof that something did happen here two thousand years ago. I took lots of pictures of this moving history of Christianity. After the crowd reached a peak, one could not move. The procession was given the OK and we started to walk down. I do not ever take part in a mass procession, but with this one I made an exception. I did not realize that it was so huge. We all moved in unison, and one could not help but feel real love, warmth, understanding from all these people who were not wealthy but had sacrificed much in order to come this far, to this little corner of the world engulfed in massive problems. They all came to celebrate Easter. They went through borders, took long overnight trips on airplanes and buses, to be part of Christianity.

We walked and walked slowly, singing joyfully and enjoying ourselves. On top of the path in various places, Israeli army youngsters stood vigilantly with their guns trying their best to protect the huge crowd. We walked through Palestinians who stood outside looking at the invading

---

* Steiner, *Deeper Secrets of Human History in the Light of the Gospel of St. Matthew*, pp. 28–30.

The Palm Sunday procession and a view of Jerusalem

army of pilgrims from their homes, drinking tea. They did not understand the influx, except that it was invading their homes and they could not get to work, just like the Orthodox Jews walking with their numerous children did not understand what the pilgrims came to do every year, invading *their* territories. The pilgrims distracted everyone from their daily tasks.

We arrived into the city through the Saint Stephan gate, and people went back to their respective hotels to prepare for Holy Week. I went to visit the Church of Saint Anne which was close by. It is supposed to be where Mary was born, and it was the home of Her mother Ann and Father Joachim. It was a lovely church with cared for gardens.

The next day I made an appointment with a local gardener I had met in one of my many visits around Jerusalem and he invited me to visit him at his home in Bethlehem. So I met him along with another young man staying at the hostel who wanted to visit some local Palestinians in their homes. We took a cab and went through check points, went through the awful wall separating Israel with Palestine, and we entered into Muslim country. Extremely poor, lots of young people everywhere, old cars—it looked like a stage of siege. Nothing like Tel Aviv or the surrounding Israeli villages or compounds. We arrived at his home which was right by the barbed-wire wall. We went up on the terrace and he showed me where his family had been shot at by snipers to destroy their hot water heater unit on the roof, a place where his wife hangs up the clothes. It is a real war zone!

He was a very nice, gentle man with eight children. They offered us tea and cookies and the boys and girls were extremely well-behaved and polite. I felt sad about how these people have to live; they can't go anywhere freely. They are sequestered in their own country. It is a shame to have to live life in this manner. I was glad to have seen the awful wall and the way the Palestinians are treated by the Israeli authority. No peace will come out of this except hatred handed down from father to son—not a way to meet the future. We went back on the local bus and were ashamed that in this day and age so much disparity exists between one people and another. We were both very quiet all the way back to Jerusalem, overwhelmed by the massive problems facing this holy city and wondering how long it will last.

> In the things that currently exist in our upbringing and our life, we can experience only the Jahve-consciousness. The Christ-consciousness can be awakened when we believe not only in the evolution of humanity, but also in the transformation that will occur in human beings when they believe that something will develop in them that has nothing to do with the aptitudes and predispositions they received from their ancestors, but rather is a part of them because they each have lived through earlier incarnations in previous earthly periods. At one time, the principle of lineage predominated in human existence and outshone the things that were carried over from earlier incarnations. Now inherited characteristics are less important, and those characteristics that we carry from previous soul incarnations, and not our blood, have become stronger.
>
> This is something that we each can bring to consciousness. And when it truly lives in the consciousness of even one human being, that person will encounter others with a set of feelings entirely different from what is typical nowadays....
>
> If we desire to appeal to individual persons with ethical, with moral impulses, then we cannot simultaneously desire to organize our society on general abstractions; we cannot bring together groups of people like a herd of animals in order to give them some sort of general directive....

BEYOND THE BLOOD

Lions are brought together by virtue of their physical form, as are hyenas, as are dogs; but the direction of human evolution is toward a time in the future when human beings do not organize like a pack of animals according to blood ties or organizational ideals, a time when cooperation of human beings comes out of the powers of each individual.[*]

It was now a matter of deriving from the particular faculties possessed by the individual man Abraham, the mission of a whole people. Abraham's spiritual constitution had to be transmitted to others. But this spiritual constitution is bound up with the physical instrument; whatever is to be brought to outward expression depends upon the physical body being organized in a definite and specific way. In the ancient religions, built up as they were on the foundation of shadowy clairvoyance, the particular formation of various parts of the brain was not of such essential importance. Understanding *Jehovah*, however, was fundamentally bound up with the constitution of the physical brain. Only by way of physical heredity, within a people, linked by *blood-relationship*, could such faculties be transmitted....

Very special measures were necessary for the achievement of this end. Abraham must have descendants who would carry to further stages of development that unique physical organism which until then had been the work of the gods and which had come to its most perfect expression in Abraham. The elaboration of the physical, bodily constitution was now to be taken in hand by man independently and that which for long ages had been the work of the gods be led by man to further stages. A brain capable of understanding Jahve had to be preserved through physical heredity....

Through Abraham's devotion to Jahve was made possible the right development of that which had hitherto been the work of the gods, namely the physical nature of humanity which had come into being out of the universe. As we know, the physical bodily constitution of man on the Earth is connected, according to number, measure and weight with all the laws governing the world of the stars. Out of the world of the stars man is born; in his very being he embodies the laws

---

[*] Steiner, *What is Necessary in These Urgent Times*, pp. 42, 65.

of that world. These laws had, as it were, to be inscribed into the blood flowing down from Abraham through the generations of the ancient Hebrew people....

We can see how this comes to pass. Isaac has two sons, Jacob and Esau. We see how all that is carried by the blood through the generations develops—the blood of the line of Esau having been cut out and the main stream separated from it. Again Jacob has twelve sons, corresponding to the twelve signs of the zodiac through which the Sun passes in the heavens, thus fulfilling the inner principle of the starry laws. Thus the number and measure prevailing in the heavens are factually portrayed to us in the life and descent, through their generations, of the Hebrew people.*

Another amazing insight into the Hebrew nation is this, again looking at the number *twelve*, but this time looking at the time of all the prophets. I am constantly stunned to see the magic of cosmic happenings coming right down to the Earth.

Consider the prophets from Isaiah to Malachi, through Jeremiah, Ezekiel and Daniel and study what it relates of these figures.... It is said they appeared when the voice of God stirred in their souls, enabling them to see in a different way from ordinary men, making it possible for them to make indications as to the future course of the destiny of their people.... We find that the souls of the Hebrew prophets are reincarnations of initiates who had lived in other nations, and who had attained certain stages of initiation. When we trace backward one of these prophets, we arrive at some other people and find an initiated soul who remained a long time with his people. This soul then went through the portal of death and was reincarnated in the Jewish people. If we wish to find the earlier incarnations of the souls of Jeremiah, Isaiah, Daniel and so on, we must seek them among other peoples. Trivially speaking, it is as though there were a gradual assembling of the initiates of other peoples among the Jewish people, where these initiates appear in the form of prophets.... All this emerges, but not always in the harmonious form it had in earlier incarnations, for a soul

---

* Steiner, *Deeper Secrets of Human History in the Light of the Gospel of St. Matthew*, pp. 30–33.

that had been incarnated in a Persian or Egyptian body would first have to accustom itself to the bodily nature of the Jewish people....

Thus we see that the Jewish prophets gave their people many spiritual impulses, which are often disarrayed, but nonetheless grandiose recollections of former incarnations.... Why is this? It is because in fact the whole evolution of humanity had to go through this passageway, so that what was achieved in its parts over the whole world should be brought together in one focal point, to be born again from out of the blood of the people of the Old Testament.... It was in the blood that flowed through this people that the elements of initiation of other peoples were to reincarnate. Like rays of light coming from different sides, streaming in and uniting in the center, the incarnating rays of the various peoples were collected together as in one central point in the blood of the Old Hebrew people. The psychical element of human evolution had once to pass through that experience.*

This beautiful picture of the prophets and their ancient wisdom is a welcomed change from regular history. It makes us realize we are all related through various streams whether in blood, hereditary, or soul-spiritual evolution.

It is also said that the twelve apostles surrounding Christ each also came from twelve different ancient tribes representing all of mankind.**

Easter was approaching and I had made arrangements to tour Palestine and Israel by car on Easter Friday with a friend. I had to leave my quarters, since there was no room. I left old Jerusalem, walked once more through the Via Dolorosa, and walked out through the Damascus Gate which was very busy, a market full of vegetables and many Palestinians were shopping. I found my new hotel but the place had no recollection of my reservation, and I was out in the street during Easter week. So I yelled at them, and stayed on one of the sofas because I had no place to go, and it was their fault!

The place was packed with travelers. The room on the roof had at least one hundred people sleeping on the floor—a real hazard if I ever saw one!

They finally told me I could sleep in the dining room after everyone had finished eating, which was better than nothing. I did not sleep very well, as

---

*   Steiner, *The Gospel of St. Mark*, pp. 26–28.

** For more on this topic, see Steiner, *The Gospel of St. Mark*.

there were five others stranded as I was! Sometimes things go wrong, one must expect this sort of thing when traveling.

The next day, I visited the old garden tomb, which was a delightful place, and I thought more likely to be where Christ was buried. It had enormous grottos, rocks, boulders, and a beautifully kept garden with places to sit and meditate. They had a service while I was there which was very touching.

> But Mary of Magdala stood outside before the tomb and wept. And weeping she bends forward into the tomb and sees two angels in shining white garments sitting there, one at the head and the other at the feet where the body of Jesus had lain. And they say to her, "Woman, why are you weeping?" She answers, "They have taken away my Lord, and I do not know where they have laid him." And saying this, she turned and sees Jesus standing, but is not aware that it is Jesus. And Jesus says to her, "Woman why are you weeping? Whom are you seeking?" He appears to her to be the gardener, and she says to him, "Sir if you have taken him away, tell me where you have laid him, so that I can take him back." Jesus says to her, "Mary!" And again she turns and says to him in Hebrew, "Rabboni"; that means: Master. But Jesus says to her, "Do not touch me, for I have not yet ascended to the Father. Now go to my brothers and say to them: I ascend to the Father who gives existence to me and to you and who lives as a divine power in me and also in you." Then Mary of Magdala goes and tells the disciples the message, "I have seen the Lord and he spoke these words to me."
>
> —John 20:11–18

I stayed in the garden until afternoon enjoying the peace there, unlike the cacophony of Jerusalem which was reaching intense proportion, then I took the bus to the airport, rented a car with a friend, and without further problems was on the road to Galilee, crossing Samaria.

> The main aim of Jesus of Nazareth was to give human beings also an inner nature as they walk about on Earth. The Jews would say that everything came from Jahve. But Jahve only has a major influence until we are born; once a human being is born and walks about on the Earth he does not merely continue in the Jahve impulse. The most important thing Christ Jesus brought into the world was that

human beings are not just like a ball that keeps rolling, continuing the momentum given by Jahve when they were in the womb, but that they have their own inherent nature, their individual nature, for better for worse. This was a tremendous idea at the time.... It was a significant deed when Jesus of Nazareth, pointing first of all to the Sun, not the other stars, said: "Human beings are influenced not only by the Moon but also by the Sun."...

As you know, we distinguish the Jews from the Earth's population. The difference has arisen because the Jews have been brought up in the Moon religion for centuries, refusing in their hearts to accept any other influence. Here we have to consider the particular trait of Judaism if we want to understand the situation. Look where you may, the Jews have a great gift for music and very little talent when it comes to sculpture, painting and the like. The Jews have a great gift for materialism, but little for recognition of the spiritual world because out of the whole world beyond this Earth they venerated only the Moon.... Jewish and Greek nature are complete opposites. The Greeks were mainly concentrating on sculpture and painting and architecture.... The Jews are the musical people, the priest nation where the inner life is essentially developed; and that is due to gifts originally developed in the womb.

This characteristic was very highly developed at the time when Jesus of Nazareth lived. You see, the Jews we meet in Europe today have lived among other nations and acquired things from them. But anyone who is able to judge this can still distinguish the special nature of the Jewish spirit from that of other people. It does not mean they are less good, but there is a difference. How was it with the Jews? It was like this: they concentrated with all their heart and soul on the Moon. Because of this they developed everything connected with the Moon but not with the Sun. The Sun was completely forgotten. And if Jesus of Nazareth had continued in the Jewish way, he could not have taught anything but the Moon religion. But he developed another impulse as life went on, and a direct spiritual influence came to him from the Sun.

You see, because of this he may be said to have been twice-born. All the early eastern religions had this aspect of being twice-born, which has since been forgotten, become merely an item of information. People no longer understand it. Jesus of Nazareth knew a particular moment when he felt: "Now I am born again, as it were; just as in the womb I received my soul through the Moon, so my soul has now been given new life from the Sun." Among initiates, the individual who was Jesus of Nazareth was known as Christ Jesus from that moment. And they would say: "Like other Jews, Jesus of Nazareth has become a human being, a Jew, through the Moon powers; but because he received the Sun influence at a particular moment in his life he was born again as the Christ."*

The beautiful hills were a welcomed sight after the harsh desert mountains of Judae. Soft rolling hills, very Mediterranean, like where I had grown up in Algeria from age nine through twelve. We drove through Samaria, the middle area of the Holy Land, with gentle hills, olive trees, and the Mediterranean feeling of sunshine and leisure as we traveled through the ancient sites. We finally arrived at the Sea of Galilee. We stayed in a lovely monastery-like bed and breakfast with Christian-French caretakers, with a room was overlooking the beautiful lake and a lovely garden in springtime bloom. We walked around the old city with its many restaurants, shops, and vacation homes. There were families strolling. The peace surrounding the lake was magical.

The next morning we drove to Capernaum, a site of many healings and where Jesus met his first disciples, Peter, James, Andrew, John, and Matthew. The ruins bore witness to events which are so powerful that I am left speechless, and as if standing in front of an enormous abyss, between the events and my understanding.

> And they came to the town Capernaum, and as it was a Sabbath he went straight away into the synagogue and taught. And they were taken out of themselves by his teachings, for he taught them like someone in whom a creative power lives, and not like the scribes. And suddenly there was in their synagogue a man with an unclean spirit; he cried out: "What is between us and you, Jesus, you Nazarene? You have come to destroy us. I know who you are, you are the Holy One of God." Then Jesus raised his hand threateningly against him and said: "Be silent and leave him!" And the unclean spirit threw the man this way and that; then it left him with loud shouts and cries. And all were

---

* Steiner, *From Beetroot to Buddhism...: Answers to Questions*, pp. 58–60.

amazed and asked one another, "What is this? A new teaching with creative authority? He commands the unclean spirits and they obey him?" And at once the news about him spread through all the regions surrounding Galilee.

—Mark 1:21–28

What happened here are magical deeds which are befitting of this whole area. I walked to the sea, and rested there, looking at the gentleness of the water, the flowers, plants growing there, and the amazing peacefulness which one could actually touch. I have been in beautiful lake surroundings everywhere on this planet, but this small lake by far had this magical atmosphere which cannot be denied. Then as I walked up the hillside I tried to remain more open to what had occurred here. Jerusalem was so packed with happenings that it was an overdose. Here, at least, it was manageable, which is the reason why I opted *not* to run around and visit everything. Just a few places, so I could meditate and feel the atmosphere.

A real experience from hell to paradise—the death forces of the Dead Sea, the liveliness of the Sea of Galilee, and Samaria in the middle with all its springs and wells.

> The uniqueness and magic of this region, preferred and chosen by destiny, do not originate solely from the events reported by the Gospels. The Holy Land is not just any corner of Asia Minor which, by chance, became the earthly stage of the life of Jesus....
>
> The Holy Land stands out above all other lands and regions of the Earth because of the Jordan fault that leads deeply into the Earth's interior. It is the deepest rift and largest, most conspicuous scar on the face of our Earth. On its path from north to south, having flowed through the Sea of Galilee located two hundred meters below sea level, the River Jordan leads into almost subterranean regions until, four hundred meters below the level of the nearby Mediterranean Sea, it ends in the brine of the Dead Sea. The special character of this depression cannot really be experienced without feeling that we are facing the evolutionary riddle of Earth's origin and primal history, without ultimately sensing that we are standing at a focal point of the drama of planetary development....

> We become aware of a paradisal Sun scenery, a world of life richly infused with etheric forces in the northern province of Galilee. By contrast, in Judea, the southern province, we recognize a lunar landscape of infernal character, a desert of death stripped of life forces. We cannot help but feel that we encounter terrestrial reflections and vestiges of our Earth's primal epochs of evolution in the northern and southern part of western Jordan. Cosmically and topographically, "Paradise" and "Fall" appear to be symbolized to us. It is as if our planet were retaining recollections of a solar and lunar landscape that it had to pass through in primordial times before it could become "Earth" in the actual sense.*

I could not resist and went for an enchanting swim one early morning before leaving the Sea of Galilee. It was very clean, and an old man was fishing. I floated in this healing water, so unlike the Dead Sea which carried my body in its heavy salt. This lake was so alive, the other was completely dead, and the river Jordan connects them both, a strange configuration.

One special place I wanted to hike up was Mount Tabor. We parked the car below and found a path that went straight up the small but steep mountain. The mountain has stood there for thousands of years. We slowly walked up. I had sandals, which was not very efficient, but I managed to reach the top. There was a road, and many came here for picnics up on top. The large monastery church was unfortunately closed!

It was a strange mountain with very green surroundings. One does not know where it came from; some say it is of volcanic origin. The mountain of the transfiguration had more meaning for me than the other stories from Jesus Christ's life. I am a painter, and I have tried to live into this scene as I have painted this momentous event which logic, mind, and intellect refuse to grasp. It can't!

> And he said to them, "Yes I say to you: Among those who are standing here there are some who will not taste death before they have seen the Kingdom of God powerfully breaking through."

---

*   Bock, *The Childhood of Jesus: The Unknown Years*, pp. 11–13.

And after six days Jesus took Peter and James and John aside and took them up with him onto a high mountain to be together, intimately alone. And his appearance was transformed before their eyes, and his garments shone radiantly, a shining white, bright beyond measure, whiter than anyone on Earth would be able to make them. And there appeared to their seeing souls Elijah and Moses, conversing with Jesus. This made Peter say to Jesus, "Master, it is good that we are here; let us build three shelters, one for you, one for Moses, and one for Elijah." But he was unaware of what it was he was saying; for they had been shaken and were deeply awed. Then a cloud formed which overshadowed them, and out of the cloud sounded a voice: "This is my beloved Son, hear him!" And suddenly, as they looked about them, they saw no one any more, only Jesus was with them.

And as they again descended from the mountain he told them to say nothing to anyone about what they had seen, before the Son of Man should have risen from the dead. This saying remained with them and they discussed amongst themselves how this resurrection from the dead was to be understood. And they asked him, "Why do the scribes say that first Elijah must come again?" He answered, "It is right that first Elijah must come again and set everything to rights. That is in accordance with scripture and is the preparation for the coming of the Son of Man who will have to endure many stages of suffering and humiliation. But I say to you: Elijah has already come and men treated him according to their whim as scripture says of him."
—Mark 9:1–13

Being here at this site is one thing and trying to fit in the inner process of this soul-spiritual world event with the actual geographical setting is beyond my capacity. So many mysteries, which will take thousands of years to decipher.

We drove through Galilee towards the Mediterranean Sea to the city of Acre. There we stepped into the Arab world, with a sumptuous lunch, the familiar souks, and a step back of some eight hundred years, during the time of the crusaders and the knights, and the Order of the Knights of Saint John. Walking through these vast, gigantic underground rooms, refactories, kitchens, dormitories, knights halls, tower, cloisters, and hospital, I was ready to see knights in armor, knights having a meal discussing their battles, it was so *real*. Then we walked around the old city, and headed back into Galilee to visit the city of Nazareth. The city is very large and completely out of sync with its history. The giant Basilica of the Annunciation is the largest Christian church in the Middle East, partly financed by the Israeli Government. The large religious paintings inside are some of the most beautifully designed I have witnessed with cooperation from artists around the world to complete it. It is very modern and the city has more than one hundred thousand inhabitants: Muslims, Christians, and Jews.

We drove a few kilometers more into the small foothills to Nain to see the site of the youth of Nain which is one of my favorite stories, but there was nothing much to witness, except a small church, and a small town with kids playing around. But the small event which happened there has had untold significance and effect on our evolution according to the science of the spirit, or anthroposophy.

> Soon afterwards his way led him to the town of Nain. His disciples and a great crowd followed him. And as he approached the gate of the town, see, a dead man was being carried out, the one and only son of his mother who was a widow. And many people from the town went with her, and when the Lord saw her, he was deeply moved, and he said to her, "Do not weep!" And he came up and touched the bier so that the bearers stood still. And he said, "Young man, I say to you, stand up!" And the dead man sat up and began to speak. And he gave him to his mother. Fear took hold of them all, but then they praised the revelation of God and said, "A great prophet has risen among us, God is turning to His people again." These words about him spread through the whole of Judea and all the neighboring regions.
> —Luke 7:11–17

Rudolf Steiner often mentions this youth of Nain because through his spiritual investigations into karma, the young man became one of the greatest helpers of Christianity, Mani, then Parzival. And in this context many secrets are hidden to be fully divulged. The peaceful tiny village at the foot of a hill, within sight of Mount Tabor, hides many mysteries.

Another young man, Lazarus, also underwent an initiation by Christ, and became the disciple whom Jesus loved (John), after his resurrection from death, or the temple sleep. Steiner's research states that he was born again in the twelfth century and became another of the great helpers of humanity, Christian Rosenkreutz.

Two young men, the youth of Nain and Lazarus (John), underwent an initiation by Christ which brought *initiation* rites out of the secret of the temples into the daylight, with untold significance for the further development of mankind: Manicheism, the Grail, the Rosicrucian mysteries and brotherhoods, and now anthroposophy, or spiritual science.

> In a place in Europe... a lodge of a very spiritual nature was formed comprising a council of twelve men who had received into themselves the sum of the spiritual wisdom of olden times and of their own time. Thus we are concerned with twelve men who lived in that dark era, twelve outstanding individualities, who united to help the progress of humanity. None of them could see directly into the spiritual world, but they could awaken to life in themselves memories of what they had experienced through earlier incarnations. And the karma of mankind brought it about that everything that still remained to mankind of the ancient Atlantean epoch was incarnated in seven of these twelve.... Another four could look back into times long past but could look back to the occult vision mankind had acquired in the four post-Atlantean epochs (ancient Indian, Persian, Egyptian-Chaldean-Assyrian, Graeco-Roman).... The twelfth was a man who attained the intellectual wisdom of his time in the highest degree....
>
> The beginning of a new culture was only possible, however, because a thirteenth came to join the twelfth. The thirteenth did not become a scholar in the accepted sense at that time. He was an individuality who had been incarnated at the time of the Mystery of Golgotha (Lazarus). In the incarnation that followed he prepared himself for his mission through humility of soul and through a fervent life devoted to God. He was a great soul, a pious, deeply mystical human being, who had not just acquired these qualities but was born with them. If you imagine a young man who is very pious and who devotes all his time to fervent prayer to God, then you can have a picture of this thirteenth individuality. He grew up entirely under the care and instruction of

the twelve, and he received as much wisdom as each one could give him. He was educated with the greatest care, and every precaution was taken to see that no one other than the twelve exercised an influence on him. He was kept apart from the rest of the world. He was a very delicate child in that incarnation in the thirteenth century, and therefore the education that the twelve bestowed upon him worked right into his physical body. Now the twelve, being deeply devoted to their spiritual tasks and inwardly permeated with Christianity, were conscious that the external Christianity of the Church was only a caricature of Christianity, although in the outside world they were regarded as its enemies. Each individuality worked his way into just one aspect of Christianity. Their endeavour was to unite the various religions into one great whole. They were convinced that the whole of spiritual life was contained in their twelve streams, and each one influenced the pupil to the best of his ability. Their aim was to achieve a synthesis of all the religions, but they knew that this was not to be achieved by means of any theory but only through active spiritual life. And for this a suitable education of the thirteenth was essential....

The wisdom of the twelve reflected in him. It reached the point where the thirteenth refused to eat and wasted away. Then an event occurred that could only happen once in history. It was the kind of event that takes place when the forces of the macrocosm cooperate for the sake of what they can bring to fruition. After a few days the body of the thirteenth became quite transparent, and for days he lay as though dead. The twelve now gathered around him at certain intervals. At these moments all knowledge and wisdom flowed from their lips. While the thirteenth lay as though dead, they let their wisdom flow towards him in short prayer-like formulae.... This situation ended when the soul of the thirteenth awakened like a new soul. He had experienced a great transformation of soul. Within him there now existed something that was like a completely new birth of the twelve streams of wisdom, so that the twelve wise men could also learn something entirely new from the youth.... In the course of a few weeks the thirteenth reproduced all the wisdom he had received from the twelve, but in a new form. This new form was as though given by Christ Himself. What he now revealed to them, the twelve called Christianity, the synthesis of all the religions.... The thirteenth died relatively young, and the twelve then devoted themselves to the task of recording what the thirteenth had revealed to them in imaginations....

The individuality of the thirteenth reincarnated as early as 1350. In this incarnation he lived for over a hundred years. He was brought up in a similar way, in the circle of the pupils and successors of the twelve, but not so secluded as in his previous incarnation. When he was twenty-eight years old he conceived a remarkable ideal. He had to leave Europe and travel. First he went to Damascus, and what Paul had experienced there happened again to him. This event can be described as the fruit of what took place in the previous incarnation. All the forces of the wonderful etheric body of the individuality of the thirteenth century remained intact.... The same highly spiritual etheric body again radiated from the spiritual world into this new incarnation.... This is the individuality of Christian Rosenkreutz. He was the thirteenth in the circle of the twelve... and the pupils of this thirteenth are the successors of the other twelve in the thirteenth century. These are the Rosicrucians.

At that time Christian Rosenkreutz traveled through the whole of the known world. After he had received all the wisdom of the twelve, fructified by the mighty Being of the Christ, it was easy for him to receive all the wisdom of that time in the course of seven years. When, after seven years he returned to Europe, he took the most highly developed pupils and successors of the twelve as his pupils, and then began the actual work of the Rosicrucians....

They wanted to investigate the maya of matter. Just as man has an etheric body, so does the whole macrocosm have an etheric macrocosm, an etheric body. There is a certain point of transition from the coarser to the finer substance. Let us look at the boundary between physical and etheric substance. What lies between the physical and etheric substance is like nothing else in the world. It is neither gold nor silver, lead nor copper. It is something that cannot be compared with any other physical substance, yet it is the essence of them all. It is a substance that is contained in every other physical substance, so that other physical substances can be considered to be modifications of this one substance. To see this substance clairvoyantly was the endeavour of the Rosicrucians. The preparation, the development of such vision they saw to require a heightened activity of the soul's moral forces, which would then enable them to see this substance. They realized that the power for this vision lay in the moral power of the soul. This substance was really seen and discovered by the Rosicrucians. They found that this substance lived in the world in a certain form both in the macrocosm and in man. In the world outside man they revered it as the mighty garment of the macrocosm. They saw it arising in man when there is a harmonious interplay between thinking and willing. They saw the will forces as being not only in man but in the macrocosm also, for instance in thunder and lightening. And they saw the forces of thought on the one hand in man and also outside in the world, in the rainbow, and the rosy light of dawn. The Rosicrucians sought the strength to achieve such harmony of willing and thinking in their own soul in the forces radiating from this etheric body of the thirteenth, Christian Rosenkreutz....

Everything that is made known in the name of anthroposophy is strengthened by the etheric body of Christian Rosenkreutz, and those who make anthroposophy known let themselves be overshadowed by the etheric body, that can work on them both when Christian Rosenkreutz is incarnated and when he is not in incarnation.*

One can read the rest of this fascinating event since I cannot quote the entire book, but can only give the reader the incentive, the enthusiasm to pursue the rest of the story which is still enfolding right now. This is why the little village of Nain had a meaning for myself, as a student of anthroposophy. And why did I mention Lazarus, the disciple whom Jesus loved, along with the youth of Nain?

In my other pilgrimages, I came upon a wonderful little chapel around Lake Constance, the monastery of Richenau in Switzerland, on a small island which was famous in the Middle Ages, not far from Saint Gallen. I happened to see the frescoes inside this little chapel in an art book dedicated to the famous monasteries of Europe. The frescoes were all about the event in Nain, the youth of Nain, and several other healings. So I made a trip to specifically see for myself. I had the very special feeling that this particular area was where perhaps Christian Rosenkreutz was raised. The frescoes are very old and extremely precious. One can go and look for oneself! The little island

---

* Steiner, *Esoteric Christianity and the Mission of Christian Rosenkreutz*, pp. 48–55.

is full of luscious gardens, orchards and has a different climate, a special aura from the surrounding area, a bit of Galilee lightness. I felt that in this secluded atmosphere the young man who became Christian Rosenkreutz was brought up by the circle of twelve. And Steiner never divulged where the place was located. These two young men, the youth of Nain and Lazarus (John), who were both initiated by Christ himself, have had a powerful influence in keeping alive the Mysteries to this day, and far into the future.*

The Christ raised the youth at Nain from the dead, as the most momentous initiation. Then the youth of Nain is reborn to a religious family as Mani and lives in Basra in AD 216. He founded the Manichean religion which was very important for one thousand years from one end of Asia to Europe.** Mani is imprisoned, and dies a martyr in Persia, but not before he sends twelve apostles to spread his teachings. Then his next incarnation is Parzival in the eighth to ninth centuries.***

If we read this poem dating from the earlier centuries, then we can have an inkling of what happened to the youth of Nain, reincarnated as Mani, son of the widow during his initiation by Christ as a youth.

The Mind of the Savior
When I had said these words, with soul a-tremble,
    I beheld the Saviour as he shone before me.
I beheld the sight of all the Helmsmen,
    Who descended with him to array my soul.
I lifted up my eyes toward that direction,
    And saw all deaths were hidden by the Envoy.
All ravages had become remote from me,
    And grievous sickness and the anguish of their distress
The sight of them was hidden, their darkness
    Had fled away. All was divine nature, without peer.
There shone forth Light, elating and lovely

---

*   For more on this topic, see Valandro, *Via Podiensis, Path of Power: A Walk from le Puy, France, to San Juan de la Peña, Spain*.

**   For more on this topic, see Welburn, *Mani, the Angel and the Column of Glory: An Anthology of Manichean Texts*.

***   For more on this topic, see Stein, *The Ninth Century and the Holy Grail*.

EGYPT ❧ PALESTINE ❧ ISRAEL ❧ JORDAN

And full of gladness, pervading all my mind.
In joy unbounded he spoke with me,
    Raising up my soul from deep affliction.
To me he sayeth, Come, spirit! Fear not.
    I am thy Mind, thy glad tidings of hope.
And thou art the... garment of my body,
    Which brought dismay to the Powers of Darkness...
I am thy Light, radiant, primeval,
    Thy Great Mind and complete hope.*

Here is another passage about Mani from the Cologne Mani-Codex.

For we know, brothers, with this arrival of the Paraclete of Truth, how great the magnitude of his wisdom is in relationship to us. We acknowledge that he has received it neither from men, nor from the reading of books, just as our father Mani himself says in the letter which he sent to Edessa. For he says thus: "The Truth and the secrets which I speak about—and the laying on of hands which is in my possession—not from men have I received it nor from fleshy creatures, not even from studies in the Scriptures. But when my most blessed Father, who called me into his Grace, beheld me, since he did not wish me and the rest who are in the world to perish, he felt compassion so that he might extend his well-being to those prepared to be chosen by him from the sects. Then, by his grace, he pulled me from the council of the many who do not recognize the truth and revealed to me his secrets and those of his undefiled Father and of all the cosmos. He disclosed to me how I was before the foundation of the world, and how the groundwork of all the works, both good and evil, was laid and how everything of this aggregation was engendered according to its present boundaries and times."

    He wrote thus again and said in the Gospel of his most holy hope: "I, Mani, an apostle of Jesus Christ through the will of God, the Father of Truth, from whom I was born, who lives and abides forever, existing before all and also abiding after all. All things which are and will be subsist through his power. For from this very one I was begotten; and I am from his will. From him all that is true was revealed to me;

---

*   *Rich Friends of the Light Beings* (canto vi 1–10), in Welburn, *Mani, the Angel and the Column of Glory: An Anthology of Manichean Texts*, p. 141.

and I am from his truth. The truth of ages which he revealed I have seen, and that truth I have disclosed to my fellow travelers; peace I have announced to the children of peace, hope I have proclaimed to the immortal race. The Elect I have chosen and a path to the height I have shown to those who ascend according to this truth. Hope I have proclaimed and this revelation I have revealed. This immortal Gospel I have written, including in it these eminent mysteries, and disclosing in it the greatest works, the greatest and most august forms of the most eminently powerful works. These things which he revealed, I have shown to those who live from the truest vision, which I have beheld, and the most glorious revelation revealed to me.'"*

We can read between the words and read them not as abstract words, but words filled with *power*. Many will ignore these passages, as more words, but one must resist such an attitude, so we can slowly approach these momentous events in the mysteries of our evolution. The stupendous event of the raising from the dead, of the youth of Nain, reborn again in the powerful human being Mani, as a healer, and proclaimer of Christianity in a new form which was enjoyed by people from India, China, North Africa, central Asia, the Middle East, and as far as the heretics in western Europe. The power within the individuality of Mani did not originate from nothing; he was *raised from the dead* as the *youth of Nain*. He went on to incarnate as Mani and Parzival. Here I will only mention a short passage from Walter Johannes Stein just to show the transition from Mani to Parzival.

> After repeated inward efforts to come to an understanding of these facts, the following has resulted. Parzival in his soul's wanderings enters the region of desire. He must pass through this realm. But he must choose a different path from Gawain (adventurous knight).
>
> Gawain stands opposed to evil and fights it. Parzival's way is different. He must connect himself with the Evil and stand on the side of the Evil, but turn all to good. Parzival's is the harder way. I should like to characterize the way that Parzival takes by a picture. The dragon may be fought in two ways. Externally, by actual fight, or from within,

---

* The Cologne Mani-Codex, in Welburn, *Mani, the Angel and the Column of Glory: An Anthology of Manichean Texts*, pp. 56–57.

by allowing oneself to be swallowed by the dragon, and then be free within its organism to unfold the forces which transform it. The latter is a *Manichean idea*. If we wish to fight the Evil, then we shall become evil, for it requires evil means. If, however, we allow the world of light to be swallowed by the world of darkness, then by this means the Dragon of darkness will be illumined from within....

This is the meaning of the Grail: The pure fool does indeed find the Grail, but he is not worthy to possess it; only if he brings the black-white brother, the human brother, with him to the Grail, only then does he become King of the Grail.*

And furthermore, we can say that the youth of Nain, because of his initiation by the Christ, became a leading personality, a being far ahead of humankind in its development, so far ahead that he could bring in a world religion, Manicheism, Parzival and the Holy Grail legend. In the passage just quoted, we can feel a hint of the transformation of Manicheism into modern Parzival, not fighting evil, but bringing the light into the darkness. So far advanced was this individuality that we can say he was thousands of years ahead. In this passage, Rudolf Steiner refers to the far distant stages of development of mankind, far ahead of now where we will have developed an "angel consciousness," which is what the youth of Nain, Mani, and Parzival had.

> On Jupiter (eons of years from now) we will have the same kind of relationship to the spirit self as we do here on Earth to the ego.... We will say: "Our ego has evolved to a certain stage where the spirit self can shine in as though from higher worlds, like a kind of angel being that is other than what we are, can shine in upon us and take possession of us." That is how our spirit self will appear to us. And only on Jupiter will it appear in such a way that it becomes our own true being, like our ego. In such a way does human evolution advance.
>
> Thus in the next, the sixth post-Atlantean cultural epoch, we will feel as though drawn to what shines in upon us. We will not refer to our spirit self as though it were within us, but will say: "I participate in a being who shines in upon me from higher worlds, that leads and

---

*   Stein, *The Ninth Century and the Holy Grail*, pp. 84, 173.

guides me, that has come to be my leader and guide through the grace of higher beings!"

In the future we will speak differently. We will say: "I do not just have my lower nature and my ego, but I have a higher nature which I look up to as something that is part of me in the same way as the bodily sheaths I received in the past."... In the future we will come to know our higher nature as something above us in the same way we now experience our lower nature below us.*

While I stopped at various important Christian sites the reality of what had happened in these sites was sadly beyond my grasp. Perhaps that is the reason why I had never really wanted to see the Holy Land, Palestine, like I had wanted to visit other faraway places. Being here was wonderful because I like to travel and meet people, but being here was not part of my life as a Christian, since I do not go to church or belong to any Christian denominations. Being in the Holy City was not a transforming experience as it can be for Christians who come on pilgrimages. I love the historical, multi-religious city with all its complexities but in my spiritual life it does not have real *meaning*. It is a paradox to me but I think I can understand the complexity of this dilemma. The life of Christ can be lived through in various ways. His life was an *initiation*. It was an initiation that was celebrated in broad daylight. Formerly, initiation was performed within the walls of temples, as we saw in the myth of Osiris, and mystery schools such as the ones in Egypt and various other places in the world. This initiation was to be seen by all.

The initiated person went through a death while still living. Here Christ died on the cross and *was resurrected* three days later. The modern Christian path of initiation which can be followed by modern disciples now follows the life of Christ, which then makes it unnecessary to come to Palestine, to Jerusalem to experience initiation or to join a monastery, or a church, as we did in the old days. Now as modern human beings we can follow the path, while going on with our very active modern lives.

---

*   Steiner, *Esoteric Christianity and the Mission of Christian Rosenkreutz*, pp. 192–193.

The Christian path is accomplished through an awakening of the feelings. There are seven stages of feeling which must be aroused....

1. Washing of the Feet
2. Scourging
3. Crowning with Thorns
4. Crucifixion
5. Mystic Death
6. Burial and Resurrection
7. Ascension

Today it is not possible for all to undertake this path, and so the existence of another method leading to higher worlds has become a necessity. That is the Rosicrucian method....

It has seven stages, though not consecutive....

The seven stages are the following:

1. Study
2. Imaginative Knowledge
3. Inspired Knowledge
4. Preparation of the Philosopher's Stone
5. Correspondence between Macrocosm and Microcosm
6. Living into the Macrocosm
7. Divine Bliss

Study in the Rosicrucian sense is the ability to immerse oneself in the content of thought not taken from the physical reality but from higher worlds....

People often enough think it unnecessary to talk about the different members of the human being (physical body, ether body, astral body, and ego) or the evolution of humanity, or the different planetary evolutions; they would prefer to acquire beautiful feelings rather than study seriously. Nevertheless, however many beautiful feelings one acquires in one's soul, it is impossible to rise into the spiritual worlds by that means alone. Rosicrucian wisdom does not try to arouse the feelings, but through the stupendous facts of the spiritual worlds to let the feelings themselves to begin to resound. The Rosicrucian feels it a kind of impertinence to take people by storm with feelings. He leads them along the path of humanity's evolution in the belief that feelings will then arise of themselves....

Christian schooling is based more on the development of inner feelings. In Rosicrucian schooling all that is spread out in physical reality as the divine nature of the Earth is allowed to work upon us and reverberate in us as feeling. These are two paths that are open to all.*

A great teacher who taught in this same manner, the Rosicrucian way, was Georg Kühlewind from Hungary, a philosopher, scientist, meditation teacher, and spiritual scientist with whom I was privileged to study for several years. He gave instructions throughout Europe, Israel, and the United States. He developed meditation exercises through his research, and a student could, if he or she worked hard enough, have access to what the Rosicrucians discovered: the boundary between the physical and etheric substance, mentioned in the previous passages. In his witty manner, he called it "hot ballooning"! In his books, a student can have access to these exercises. His book *Wilt Thou Be Made Whole?* is a small masterpiece where he concentrates on the healings of Jesus Christ. Michael Lipson is one of his talented students and continues teaching and practicing in this manner. His book *Stairway to Heaven* is also full of simple exercises for the student to follow in this meditative practice. Both of these teachers chose to incarnate in a Jewish body for this lifetime.

> Spiritual healing means that the "one from above" heals the lower part of us, which is the only part that can become sick. It may be a sickness of the body or of the soul (e.g., possession by demons). For healing, the higher being has to be made independent of the lower. The part of the higher being that has connected itself to the "robe" has to be freed from this connection so that the higher self can act on it as if from outside. Even in everyday life we can forget "ourselves," our me-feeling, to a certain extent, as for example in artistic, creative activity or in prayer. To be healed we need a deep, total "self-forgetting," so that we are present only in the heights.

---

* Steiner, *Rosicrucian Wisdom: An Introduction*, pp. 156, 159–161, 167.

EGYPT ֍ PALESTINE ֍ ISRAEL ֍ JORDAN

These spiritual healings were not rare in earlier phases of the evolution of consciousness, and are still possible today in many "non-civilized" regions wherever the *me* is undeveloped. In these cases, the everyday consciousness was and is extinguished through various procedures, similar or identical to the earlier initiation rites that operated through a dislocation of one's awareness. We can describe these processes as very deep examples of self-forgetting. This is how John the Baptist worked, holding the person to be baptized under water to the brink of death (which is why he needed "much water," cf. John 3:23).

The new Christian baptism (with "fire and holy spirit") is a purely inward way, accomplished without the extinction of consciousness, though it does involve a radical transformation of it. Today, a schooling of consciousness begins in everyday awareness and leads continually, without loss of consciousness, to the "forgetting" of the *me*. This new kind of initiation goes along with a new potential in healing: in the healings of the New Testament, the healed person is perfectly awake, consciousness is neither asleep nor extinguished. At first the Lord is present at the healings; later the disciples heal and, after Golgotha, the apostles as well.*

From our wanderings in Galilee, we headed south following the Jordan Valley, to the Jordan-Palestine-Israel border because I wanted to see Petra. On the way we stopped at the momentous site of the Mount of Temptation, and the city of Jericho because that name has always had some meaning for me. When I was about five years old, I remember being at the home of my great-aunt, Tante Lili, and I would be in a large bed while my aunt (her daughter) was reading some novels and gave me a bible to read. I had taught myself to read, and for some reason I must have read some passages with these biblical names, and they stuck in my childish memory. Of course I could not understand anything I was reading; just pictures would come to my child's mind. Jericho was one of those! So I had to see it.

And Jesus left the Jordan valley, his soul filled with the Holy Spirit. And he followed the guidance of the Spirit into the loneliness of the

---

* Kühlewind, *Wilt Thou Be Made Whole? Healing in the Gospels*, p. 40.

desert. There he remained for forty days, during which he had to withstand the temptation by the Adversary.

During this time he took no food at all, and when the days came to an end he felt hunger. Then the Adversary said to him, "If you are the Son of God, speak to this stone so that it becomes bread." But Jesus answered him, "Scripture says:

Man does not live by bread alone."

And the Adversary led him up, showed him all realms of the world in one single moment, and said to him, "I will give you power over everything that you see, the earthly and even the forces beyond the earthly. For the power belongs to me, and I can give it to whom I will. If you will kneel in worship of me, the whole world shall be yours." But Jesus replied, "Scripture says:

Let all your worship be for the divine Lord,

Let your service be for Him alone."

Then he removed him to Jerusalem and set him on the parapet of the Temple and said to him, "If you are the Son of God, throw yourself down from here. For it says in the scriptures that He has commanded His angels to protect you and bear you up on their hands so that not even your foot shall strike against a stone." But Jesus answered him, "Yet it also says:

You shall not make your heavenly Lord become a servant of your arbitrary wishes."

And when the Adversary had put him through temptation, he departed from him to bide his time.

—Luke 4:1–14

The Mount of Temptation was a harsh mountain, with sheer cliffs, a look of severity unlike Mount Sinai, but a very austere and unkindly scenery.

We went up the mountain with a cable and enjoyed the beautiful Russian church carved out of the mountainside where Christ fasted for forty days. The monastery was full of cells within the mountain and had a quiet atmosphere, candles were lit, and many beautiful icons were hung throughout the large chapels. In these settings the monks were praying and keeping their inner adversaries in check!

Men and women being baptized in the Jordan River

I enjoyed the magnificent scenery from the little chapels overlooking the valley of Jericho below, and would have enjoyed staying in one of the rooms available to pilgrims, but I had made no arrangements.

The city of Jericho in Palestine was more successful than the others. There was a large Muslim hotel full of Muslim families enjoying the resort-like hotel. I wish I could have seen more of this kind of normal lifestyle among the Palestinians. We had a wonderful lunch in one of the very busy local restaurants. For the first time, I saw Palestinians families enjoying themselves!

Then we went to the Jordan site picked by very merchant-minded people, to witness where Jesus became Christ through the baptism in the Jordan. People said it was not the real site, but we had gone to the "real" site and it was closed with barbed wires since it was close to the border with Jordan.

The site had dozens of buses at the entrance. Huge restaurants, tourist attractions, shops, and many bathrooms where people could change their clothes for their baptismal white clothes. Then accompanied by their priest, they would receive baptism with enormous outpouring of feelings. Many South American people were ecstatic, and many African old women were totally transformed by the experience. Many had come from the southern

United States and had saved for years for this journey. Some of the women were truly afraid of drowning and had to be taken care of by their friends. Much crying, singing, and general elation went on as the very busy merchants were making lots of shekels, which made this site a circus, but the reality of people's feelings made up for it in some ways!

> Then Jesus came from Galilee to the Jordan to John, to be baptized by him. But John refused and said, "It is I who need to be baptized by you—and you come to me?" Jesus answered him. "Let it be so now. It is good thus, so that we fulfill properly all that destiny requires." Then he consented. When Jesus had received the baptism and was already coming out of the water again, see, the heavens opened and he saw the Spirit of God descending in the form of a dove and hovering over him. And see, a voice spoke out of the heavens:
> "This is my Son whom I love,
> In him will I reveal myself."
> —Matthew 3:13–17

The coming of the Dove, then the temptation—not the other way around. *Armed* with the Spirit, then fight the temptations.

> John baptized with water, with the result that the etheric body was separated for a short time from the physical body. But John the Baptist wanted to be the forerunner of Him "Who baptizes with fire and with the Holy Spirit." The baptism with fire and the spirit came to our Earth through Christ. Now what is the difference between John's baptism with water and Christ's baptism with fire and the spirit?[*]

Here we can keep in mind the initiation of the youth of Nain, and Lazarus-John.

> The procedure of the old initiation was as follows: the candidate first learned comprehensively all that today we are taught by anthroposophy. That was the preparation for the old initiation. Then, all this was directed to a certain culmination which was achieved by having him

---

[*] Steiner, *The Gospel of St. John and Its Relation to the Other Gospels*, pp. 118–119.

lie in a grave for three and a half days, as though dead. When his etheric body was withdrawn and, in his etheric body, he moved about in the spiritual world, he became a witness of this spiritual world. In order that in the sphere of his etheric forces he might behold the spiritual world, thus achieving initiation it was necessary to withdraw the etheric body. Formerly these forces were not available in the normal state of consciousness; the neophyte had to be brought into an abnormal condition. Christ brought this force to the Earth for initiation also; for today, it is possible for man to become clairvoyant without the withdrawal of the etheric body.

When a person attains the maturity to receive so strong an impulse from the Christ, even for a short time, as to affect the circulation of his blood—this Christ influence expressing itself in a special form of circulation, an influence penetrating even the physical principle—then he is in a position to be initiated within the physical body. The Christ-impulse has the power to bring this about. Anyone who can become so profoundly absorbed in what occurred as a result of the Event of Palestine and the Mystery of Golgotha as to live completely in it and to see it objectively, see it so spiritually alive that it acts as a force communicating itself even to his circulation, such a man achieves through this experience the same result that was formerly brought about by the withdrawal of the etheric body.

You see, then, that through the Christ-impulse something has come to Earth which enables the human being to influence the force that causes his blood to pulsate through his body. What is here active is no abnormal event, no submersion in water, but solely the mighty influence of the Christ-Individuality. No physical substance is involved in this baptism—nothing but a spiritual influence; and the ordinary, everyday consciousness undergoes no change. Through the spirit that streams forth as the Christ-impulse something flows into the body, something that can otherwise be induced only by way of psycho-physiological development through fire—an inner fire—expressing itself in the circulation of the blood. John still baptized by submersion with the result that the etheric body withdrew and man could see into the spiritual world. But if a man opens his soul to the Christ-impulse, this impulse acts in such a way that the experiences of the astral body flow over into the etheric body, and clairvoyance results.... The Christ-impulse made it possible for an order of new initiates to come into being.*

But the spirit of John the Baptist who recognized the Christ looms as one of the gigantic figures in this world drama. He steps out, and Christ enters. Here Rudolf Steiner speaks of this momentous happening from another perspective.

> During the baptism by John in the Jordan, the people were plunged into the water. This baptism was not like the usual baptism of today. The baptism of John caused the etheric bodies of the candidates to be loosened and they saw more than they could comprehend with their ordinary powers of understanding. They saw their life in the spirit and the influence of the spirit on this life. They saw also what the Baptist taught, that the old age was fulfilled and that a new age must begin.... They saw that mankind had come to a turning point in evolution.... "Transform your mind, but don't merely turn your gaze backwards as would still be possible. Turn your gaze now to something else, to the God who manifests in the human 'I.'"...
>
> Only when we consider this connection does the spirit of Elijah, which also worked in John the Baptist appear to us in the right light. Then we see that Elijah was the spirit of the old Jewish people. What kind of spirit was this? In a certain respect it was already the spirit of the "I." However it does not appear as the spirit of the individual human being but as the collective folk spirit of the whole people. That which later was to live in each individual man was, so to speak, still in Elijah, the group soul of the ancient Hebrew people. That which was to descend as the individual soul into every individual human breast was at the beginning of the Johannine age still in the supersensible world.... This spirit, hovering over man and man's history, was now about to enter more and more into every bosom. This was the great fact now proclaimed by Elijah-John himself when he said, as he baptized the people, something like the following, "What until now was in the supersensible worlds and worked from these worlds you must now take into your souls as impulses that have come from the kingdom of heaven right into the hearts of men."...

---

*   Ibid., pp. 129–130.

It becomes clear how in this grand figure of the Baptist there is not only his individual personality at work, but something more than a personality which hovers over the individuality like an aura but has an efficacy that transcends it, something alive like an atmosphere among those within whom John the Baptist is working.... It could perhaps be best expressed if we were to say, "John the Baptist perhaps has gone away but what he is as the Elijah-spirit remains and in this Christ can work best. Here He can best pour forth His words, and in that atmosphere that has remained behind, the Elijah-atmosphere, he can best performs His deeds."...

This Elijah soul is at the same time the soul of the Old Testament people, as it enters the Baptist and lives in him. When he was emprisoned and then beheaded by Herod, what happened then to his soul?... His soul left the body and worked on as an aura; and into the domain of this aura Christ Jesus entered. Where then is the soul of Elijah, the soul of John the Baptist?... The soul of John the Baptist, of Elijah, becomes the group soul of the Twelve; it lives, and continues to live in the Twelve.*

John the Baptist reincarnated as Raphael, the great painter of Madonnas. It is said that when Herman Grimm wanted to do a biography of Raphael he had a very difficult time and finally he settled on the title, *Raphael as a World-Power*, thereby revealing the tremendous happenings behind Raphael.**

After spending time witnessing these events, we drove on. I did not want to bathe in the water for the ritual; I would have felt that I was an imposter, a kind of tourist attraction for the Christians! I had done a wonderful impromptu baptism in the mountains of Ecuador by a thundering waterfall with an Indian Shaman and many Christians who were camping there, so I had my own baptism, and also as a Catholic, when I was baptized in Tunis.

We stopped by the side of the road going south to get some vegetables from Palestinian vendors. They told their story of being unable to sell their vegetables in Jerusalem: not allowed. They grew beautiful vegetables but could not sell them; what a world! I think the authorities were afraid that the car or truck bringing the vegetables might be used as weapon. It was very sad.

---

*   Steiner, *The Gospel of St. Mark*, pp. 42–44, 113.
** For more on this topic, see Prokofieff, *Eternal Individuality: Towards a Karmic Biography of Novalis*.

We drove late into the evening, and by 10:00 PM decided to stop. We took a dirt road—it was quite dark—and drove towards the Dead Sea, to what looked like a farm. The owner came out to greet us and we asked him if there was any place to stay. He was a kind jovial fellow, who had lived in Chicago and now operated this farm. He left to make phone calls and to find us a place to stay, for which we were thankful.

Meanwhile, we stayed in the car and saw a few small tractors coming in, operated by people who were of small stature and had scarves over their faces. After five minutes they came down from tractors and the trailers behind and we saw that they were from the Far East, small men and women coming from working in the large plastic-enclosed gardens which they tended. A long day, since it was by now close to 11:00 PM. I thought, *What a world!* The Palestinians have no work, they are not allowed to sell the products of their work, and here the workers are coming from halfway across the world, probably being paid next to nothing, and working very long hours. The farms have very powerful, very deep wells which drain much water from the deep reserve of precious water. How long will that last? Much of the produce such as peppers, herbs, etc., is sent abroad to Europe.

The owner found us a local bed and breakfast just down the road for orthodox families coming from Jerusalem who wanted rest and relaxation from raising very boisterous, numerous children. They said the kids could raise hell here and no one minded!

It was set up like a Bedouin camp and quite fun but we could not sleep all night. The people working there were young Jewish people from Russia who watched Russian films all night!

The owners—a very fit, tan, and handsome Israeli couple in their early forties—told us that during the summer they took off to Argentina, because it was too hot here!

The next morning we were off for a swim in the Red Sea in the town of Eilat and the next adventure to Jordan. We hired a taxi, all the way to Petra.

The walk into the ancient city of Petra was breathless. It costs one hundred dollars for a ticket, which I almost refused to pay, but I accepted it. Jordan is a desert country and they need the funds I presumed.

There were lots of tourists, Jordanians on a holiday, and many beautiful young teens wanting their pictures taken—lovely students full of youth and mischief!

I walked through the red-, purple-, yellow-, golden-, and cream-colored canyon towering way up above my head. Canyons carved by the water and weird geological formations. We walked miles and miles, up and down ancient temples high above in the cliffs, here and there. The Bedouins were still camping with their camels, for rides, and there were many restaurants with food, tea, jewelry, and rugs, all waiting patiently for tourists to visit their tents. I stopped everywhere and thoroughly enjoyed these people whose lives had not changed much after so many centuries. Palestine's neighbor—old tribes, cousins of the Jews—but not the chosen people of Israel.

They are not the chosen people, but Abraham was their relative through his servant wife, Hagar, the Egyptian who gave him his first son, Ishmael. Sarah banished her after she had her own son who was the chosen one. Then Essau was banished as well, while his brother was the chosen one. And all these tribes lived on, the cousins of the chosen ones, next door, to this day.

Ishmael is the other branch of the Semitic people, the Arabs. Through Rudolf Steiner I encountered amazing insights into the people of Ishmael, Abraham's other son by his servant wife, Hagar. It is extremely complex—one needs to go to the lecture cycle itself—but here are a few words:

> In Abraham there had been chosen a man whose constitution was such that at the right time the Christ could be born of his descendants. But this required the development and elaboration of faculties which had been present in Abraham as rudiments only. We must realize that if these rudiments were to be unfolded it was constantly necessary for certain elements to be eliminated. We have already seen how this happened in the case of Joseph, but these were even earlier examples, such as Esau, from whom the Edomites descended, because in him too an ancient heritage had remained. Only such qualities as were compatible with the goal described were to be preserved. This is indicated in a wonderful way—Abraham had two sons: Isaac, the son of Sarah, and Ishmael. The Hebrew nation were the descendants of Isaac. In Abraham, however, there were other qualities as well. If these other

qualities had been transmitted through the Hebrew generations, the right conditions would not have been achieved. Hence this different element must radically thrust away into another line of descendants, into the descendants of Ishmael, the son of Hagar, the Egyptian bondwoman. Therefore two lines of descent go out from Abraham, the one through Isaac, and the other through the outcast Ishmael, who having the blood of an Egyptian in his veins, must have in his constitution elements unfitting for the mission of the Hebrew people.

But now something momentous comes to pass! The task of the Hebrew people was to propagate in the direct line of heredity the qualities that were intrinsically their own, and everything that was of an ancient heritage, ancient wisdom, had to be imparted to them from *without*. Hence, they had to go to Egypt in order to receive what could be given to them there. Moses was able to impart this to his people because he was an Egyptian initiate. But he certainly could not have done so had he possessed wisdom merely in its Egyptian form. It would be erroneous to imagine that the ancient Egyptian wisdom could be simply grafted on to what flowed down from Abraham. This would not have been compatible with the intrinsic character of the Hebrew people and would have produced an abortive form of culture. Moses brought with him to the wisdom he acquired from his Egyptian initiation something of a quite different nature. Hence he could not simply impart to the Israelites what came from the Egyptian initiation. His first real gift to them was made after the revelation on Sinai, and made outside Egypt.

What, then, is the revelation on Sinai? What was vouchsafed to Moses there, and what was it that he imparted to the Israelites? He imparted something that could well be grafted into the stem of his people because it was related to them in a very definite way. In times past the descendants of Ishmael had wandered away from their country and settled in the regions now traversed by Moses and his people. Moses found in the Ishmaelites, among whom there was initiation of a certain kind, those attributes and qualities which had been transmitted to them from Hagar, qualities which were derived through Abraham, but in which were preserved many elements inherited from the ancient past. Out of the revelations that he received from this branch of the Hebrew people, it became possible for Moses to make the revelation of Sinai intelligible to the Israelites. In regard to this there is an ancient Hebrew legend that in Ishmael a shoot of Abraham was cast out of Arabia, that is, into the desert. What sprang from this stock is contained in the teaching of Moses. On Sinai, the ancient Hebrew people received back, again, in the Mosaic Law, what had been cast out from their blood: they received it back *from without.*

Here we also see how in the wonderful mission of the Hebrew people everything had to be *given to them*. Had to be received back at a later stage as a gift. As a gift from without Abraham had, in Isaac, received the whole Hebrew nation. Again, Moses and his people received back from the descendants of Ishmael what had once been thrust out from their midst. During the period of their isolation in the wilderness they had to build up their own constitution, and also receive back as a gift from their God, what they had cast out. So, too, Jacob was in the end reconciled with Esau, thus receiving again what, in Esau, had been cast away....

The whole history of the Hebrew people is full of significant happenings such as these. The *giving of the Law* by Moses is connected with something that springs from the descendants of Hagar, whereas, the Hebrew *blood*, which represents the specific Israelitish faculties, springs from Sarah. Hagar, or Agar in Hebrew is the same as *Sinai*, which means the "stone mountain," the great stone. One might say that Moses received the revelation of the Law from the "great stone"—a material representation of Hagar. The Law given to this Judaic people did not spring from the highest faculties of Abraham, but from Hagar, from Sinai. Those, therefore, who are followers merely of the law as given on Sinai—that is, the Pharisees and the Sadduccees—are exposed to the danger of their development coming to a standstill. They are those who at the Baptism of John will see, not the *lamb*, but the *serpent*.*

The second day we walked up to the other little Petra, by taking a path going up the mountain into another canyon and we ended on a plateau which overlooked the surroundings with more teahouses on the way, more beautiful temples hundreds of feet tall, carved into the sandstone mountains, and shepherds and old men walking around, living in the caves nearby.

---

*   Steiner, *Deeper Secrets of Human History in the Light of the Gospel of St. Matthew*, pp. 66–67.

BEYOND THE BLOOD

We stopped for food at the end of the day, and the local Bedouins gave us some of the leftover food because the tourists had all gone home. They said that they loved to live outside and did not like living in houses. They loved to sleep and eat under the stars, and even though they could live in homes in the village, they preferred the freedom of the desert, or homes insides some of the cavernous rooms carved out of the mountains. They still had their goats, sheep, and camels. They were true people of the desert, the ones that had been cast out of the Hebrew nation. But their gift was just as important as the gift of the chosen people.

We walked back the long way towards the village. It was getting dark, and the Bedouins were packing up.

The next day, we hired another taxi to the border and changed our minds about a camelback expedition into the desert. We drove through a fierce dust storm, which is seen often in these parts of the world. We could not see anything. I am glad we were not on camels in the middle of the desert with this sandstorm!

Then we went off through to the other border, through Israel, then to Egypt and on to Sinai which is where I started the tale.

In this roundabout way, my journey into this part of the world ends.

> Whatever differences in principles of what is right and wrong the various religious faiths may show, no two individuals will ever differ in this one natural principle: that every soul seeks after beauty, and that every virtue, righteousness, good action, is nothing but a glimpse of beauty. When once he or she has made this moral one's own, that person does not need to follow a particular belief or faith or restrict oneself to a particular path. He or she can follow the Hindu way, the Muslim way, the way of any church or faith, provided one treads this royal road: that the whole universe is but an immanence of beauty. We are born with the tendency to admire it in every form, and we should not blind ourselves by being dependent on one particular line of beauty.[*]

---

[*] Khan, *The Art of Being and Becoming*, p. 217.

Part II

Spain: A Walk from Seville to Santiago

TWO MONTHS EARLIER

On a bright and early morning in March, backpack on, I walked by the banks of the Guadalquivir River, crossed the bridge in Seville, Spain, and headed north towards Santiago, 850 kilometers—another long journey—not east to west,* but south to north. I wanted to experience something of what was left behind by the three religions one thousand years ago when they lived for a brief period in some kind of peace. If it was achieved then, why not now?

A dream? Wishful thinking? Or an excuse for another six weeks of walking along pilgrims' paths? Or going back to former lives' wanderings? Perhaps all the above!

On this pilgrimage dedicated to the three faiths, I would make detours from the path by bus and train to visit important cities which were not close to the path, and then come back to it, so I could visit Cordova, Granada, Ávila, Toledo, and Segovia. I just wanted *to be* here, walking the land.

Unlike the other three I completed in the last few years,** this path is a lonely one, I was told. Not many take this path. It was well traveled in the old days; men and women crisscrossed Spain, towards the North, and towards the South, across Gibraltar to Morocco and faraway places. So I

---

* See Valandro, *Camino Walk: Where Inner and Outer Paths Meet.*
** See Valandro, *Via Podiensis, Path of Power: A Walk from le Puy, France, to San Juan de la Peña, Spain.*

can do the same. If it is a lonely path, the better for me to ponder, think, and create as I walk with no disturbances!

I had spent a few days in the beautiful city of Seville, Andalusia, rich in architecture from the Christians, the Moors, and the Jews all intertwined in its own style. I wandered along the streets which were lined with orange trees, flowering bougainvilleas, old horse-drawn carriages for tourists, artists selling beautiful Islamic calligraphy on the streets, great restaurants, cafés, Moorish palaces, cathedrals, museums, fountains, etc. It definitely was a city of mixed blood, and still is. I was on the right track for this new journey. Visitors were from all over the Islamic world, English-Muslim couples from England, families from Saudi Arabia, Israelis, tourists from everywhere, and perhaps a few walking pilgrims which I had not seen yet.

An enormous cathedral dominates the center of Seville flanked by a Moorish minaret, the great tower of Abou Yakoub. The bell tower strangely sits on top, so the call to the faithful Christians sounds from a Moorish tower which used to chant *Allah Akbar!*

The Mudejar Palace was outstanding in its beauty and grandeur, reflecting the Islamic faith. I marveled at the beautifully designed, protected geometric gardens with lavish fountains, the calligraphy on tiles, the intricate work on walls, doors, ceilings, arches, alcoves, the ornate, delicate, lace-like stonework and woodwork, all sacred architecture. The activities during that time involved all of the Mediterranean countries. Workers must have traveled far indeed to work on these sumptuous palaces. Only people living in desert conditions can appreciate gardens, water, and create such masterpieces. Seeing these palatial quarters, after spending much time walking along the Christians path of France with its monasteries and cathedrals, and bible stories carved in stone, to sit amidst these works of sacred Islamic art without the human figure anywhere is an experience on the feeling life and the soul life which one must meditate on and discover.

What does it do to the soul, not to see an Icon of Mary, or Christ on the cross? These do not exist for the Muslims or the Jews. I bathed myself in the loneliness of the surroundings, the crystal-clear forms, the uprightness, the rigorous orderliness. I plunged back to experiences in Isfahan, at the site of the Blue Mosque, and how I felt there, more than thirty-five years ago. The feelings were the same, a feeling of security, protection under the turquoise dome, grandeur of spirit, and expansiveness in the large courtyard. The palaces here were more ornate, extensive. Seville is not in the Desert.

> According to the Islamic perspective, men and women still carry deep within their souls that primordial nature (*al-fitrah*), which attests to Divine Unity and which Islam essentially addresses. For Islam, the human being is an intelligence, which by nature confirms *al-tawhīd*, and to this intelligence is added the will, which needs to be guided by revelation. The function of religion is to remove the veil of the passions, which prevent the intelligence from functioning correctly. Religion is essentially the means for men and women to recollect who they are and to return to the inner primordial nature they still carry deep within themselves.
>
> Human beings must be perfectly passive towards heaven as the servant or slave of God (*'abd Allāh*) and active towards the world around them as God's vicegerent on Earth. To be truly human is to receive in perfect submission from God and to give to creation as the central channel of grace for the created order. Islam rejects completely the Promethean and Titanic conception of human beings as creatures in rebellion against heaven, an idea that has come to largely dominate the western concept of the human state since the Renaissance. In the Islamic perspective, the grandeur of men and women is not in themselves, but in their submission to God, and human grandeur is always judged by the degree of servitude toward God and His Will. Even the power given to human beings to both know and dominate things is legitimate only on the condition that they remember their theomorphic nature according to the *hadīth* "God created man upon His form" and continue to remain subservient to that blinding Divine Reality that is the ontological principle and ultimate goal of return of human beings. All human grandeur causes the Muslim soul to remember that *Allāhu akbar*, "God is greater," and that all grandeur belongs ultimately to Him.*

The feeling of protection, order, calm, and strength penetrates the person's soul as they sit and meditate in these sumptuous Islamic architectural

---

* Nasr, *Islam: Religion, History, and Civilization*, pp. 66–67.

spaces. As was described, one does not wish to rebel in these surroundings, it does not call for such behavior. The space speaks order, finitude.*

Prometheus

As mentioned by scholar Seyyed Hossein Nasr, the Muslim man or woman is not a follower of Prometheus. This statement speaks much for the contemporary human being. If we recall who Prometheus is from the Greek myth:

> Prometheus and his brother, Epimetheus, are the sons of one of the great Titans, called Lapatus. And the Titans are the sons of the oldest of the Greek Gods, Uranus (heavens) and his wife Gaia (Earth)…. Prometheus, therefore, is one of the Titans and a descendant of the sons of Uranus and Gaia, likewise his brother Epimetheus. The youngest of the Titans, Chronos or "Time," usurped the throne from his father Uranus, and was himself dethroned by his son Zeus, and along with other Titans, was cast into Tartarus, or Hades. Only the two brothers, Prometheus and Epimetheus, remained loyal to Zeus.
>
> Zeus, however, wished to destroy the race of man, which had become insolent. Prometheus became the protagonist of man. He pondered how he could himself give man something that would enable him to save himself and make himself independent of the help of Zeus. So, we are told, Prometheus gave man writing and the other arts and, more especially, he instructed him in the use of fire. Through this, however, he drew down the wrath of Zeus upon himself and because of the wrath of Zeus he was chained to the Caucasus and made to languish for a long time of great torment….
>
> It is further recounted how the gods, with Zeus at their head, caused a female statue to be made by Hephaestus, the heavenly smith. This female statue was endowed with all the outward attributes of the man of the fifth great epoch. This female statue was Pandora. She was required to bring gifts to mankind, but in the first place to Epimetheus, the brother of Prometheus. Indeed, Prometheus warned his brother about accepting the gifts, but Epimetheus let himself be persuaded and took the presents. All the gifts were showered upon

---

* For more on this topic, see the section on turquoise in Valandro, *Touched: A Painter's Insights into the Work of Liane Collot d'Herbois*.

mankind. Only one thing was retained—hope. The gifts consisted mostly of plagues and suffering for humanity; only hope was retained in Pandora's box.

Prometheus, therefore, was chained to the Caucasus and a vulture gnawed incessantly at his liver.... We are told that Prometheus can only be set free through the intervention of an initiate....

Prometheus can be interpreted as being the one who thinks in advance, Epimetheus as the one who thinks about things after they have happened. Here you have expressed quite clearly two activities of human thinking in the foresight and hindsight of these two human beings. The one with hindsight is the one who lets the things of the world work upon him and then thinks about them afterwards. A kind of thinking such as this is "kama-manasic" thinking, (earthly consciousness, or intellectual-soul activity). Considered from a certain point of view, this is what this kind of thinking is: letting the world work upon one and thinking about it afterwards. The man of the fifth root race thinks chiefly in the manner of Epimetheus.

But in so far as a man does not merely let the things of his surroundings work upon him but creates something for the future, is an inventor and discoverer, just so far is he a Prometheus, one who thinks ahead. There would never be any inventions made if men were all like Epimetheus. An invention comes about because man is able to create something which was not there previously. First of all the thought is there and then the thought is transformed into reality. This is Promethean thinking. Promethean thinking is the thinking of spiritual thoughts....

Mortal man has to learn to stand on his own two feet during the fifth great epoch. He is represented by Prometheus. Man was the inaugurator of the arts, and above all, of the primal art of the use of fire. Zeus is jealous of him because he is predestined to produce his own initiates, who will take over the leadership in the sixth epoch. Mankind has first to pay for that, however. That is why the first great initiate of humanity must take upon himself the whole of life's suffering.*

---

*   Steiner, *The Temple Legend: Freemasonry and Related Occult Movements*, pp. 36, 38, 40, 45.

I thought it important to mention this popular Greek myth. It brings to mind karma. We have lived on this Earth before, at various times, in various bodies. Some choose to live surrounded by Islamic architecture, some choose to live amidst Buddhist Temples, or Gothic architecture, or the desert skies, and some need to experience an Epimetheus destiny or a Prometheus destiny. One balances the other, so we must go beyond the one who is right, or the one who is wrong. What is right for one is wrong for the other. We must go beyond tolerance, to understanding, and truly understand what is in front of us. For the faithful, when he enters the mosque and prays, he is receiving what he truly needs at this time in his karma. A knowledge of karma is truly the fastest way to understand the paradox of our twenty-first-century life. I keep reminding myself that I was most certainly born a Muslim in another life, and a Jew as well, otherwise I would never be attracted to all these faiths. I have been a believer of Allah, I have been a part of the chosen ones, I am now a Christian believer and in my next life things will change, and we will call by other names what there is now.

It is time to go beyond the blood type of thinking. There is more to us than our genes and ancestry if we are to go beyond tolerance, and acquire real understanding of the other. Georg Kühlewind, whom I mentioned before, had accomplished just that in his lifetime, through much, much suffering. Here are more insights from Rudolf Steiner about these deep mysteries of the blood. What is behind the blood question? If we accept karma, then we accept that we choose a certain body, heredity, blood to suit our needs, so that we can think beyond being born in a certain group, nationality. If we do not accept the laws of karma, then we are still stuck within a small group, nationality. Pondering on these matters as I walk the path will bring much to enlighten some of these mysteries about the Jews, Christians, and Muslims:

> Take a look at everything that plays a role in our society up to this point—we do not owe the existence of these structures to the clarity of our thinking; we owe their existence to the spiritual forces that emanate from our blood itself, which were born out of the old blood ties, the blood relations that once existed. To this day, we still have in our society something that came into our world as a carrying over from those old blood relations, which gave us the principle of

nationalities.... The fact that one person refers to himself as English, another called herself French, another Polish—this is rooted in all of the same things that established connections between human beings built on direct blood ties. The principle of blood relations had a reason for existing throughout the millennia of human evolution, for it was these blood relations that brought humanity together, that formed the foundation of human history.*

For millennia, human beings have instilled the insistence on blood bonds into themselves, and out of sheer inertia they are letting the spirits of darkness take control of these habitual ideas. We therefore see insistence on tribal, national, and racial relationships... and this insistence is considered idealistic when in reality it is an early sign of decline in humanity. Everything based on dominance in the blood principle meant progress as long as it was under the authority of the spirits of light; under the authority of the spirits of darkness it is a sign of decline. The spirits of darkness made special efforts in the past to implant a rebellious feeling of independence in human beings at the time when hereditary traits were passed on in a positive sense by the progressive spirits. In the three ages of human evolution which now follow and will continue until the time of the great catastrophe, the spirits of darkness will make extreme efforts to preserve the old hereditary characteristics and inculcate human beings with the attitudes which result in such preservation; in this way they introduce the necessary signs of decline into human evolution.

Someone who speaks of the ideal of the human race and nation and of tribal membership today is speaking of impulses which are part of the decline of humanity. If anyone now considers them to be progressive ideals to present to humanity, this is an untruth. Nothing is more designed to take humanity into its decline than the propagation of ideals of race, nation, and blood. Nothing is more likely to prevent human progress than proclamations of national ideals belonging to earlier centuries which continue to be preserved by the luciferic and ahrimanic powers. The true ideal must arise from what we find in the world of spirit, not in the blood....

---

* Steiner, *What is Necessary in These Urgent Times*, p. 150.

There are still enough people, even today, who simply do not want to get to the point where they are prepared to accept such universal truths, which are independent of all blood bonds. These are universal human truths because they have not come from the Earth but have been brought down from the spiritual worlds.[*]

The same, seen from another perspective:

All laws, institutions, and social fabric existing at that time (pre-Christian) could ultimately be traced back to initiation. At the pinnacle of the social structure was the great initiator from whom all goals and directions originated. The pupil carried the revealed wisdom out into the world, and those hearing it behaved in harmony with these instructions, arranging social life accordingly, everything depended on that. It was the principle of authority based on truth and wisdom lived out to the greatest extent and in the best way. Only those who were great and wise leaders of humanity were allowed to exercise such authority.

It was important to lift the etheric body out of the physical body in the right way.[**] This was not to be done with just any human being.... A long preparation is required to achieve these things. It depended on the proper mixture of the blood. That is why so much emphasis was put on the generations of priests not mixing with others. Preparations were carried out for centuries so that the proper descendant existed who could one day become a suitable initiate. This was a way of handling the human being on a large scale, in an incredibly mysterious way, in a way that was, in the most beautiful sense of the word, mysterious. In terms of their physical principle, the great initiates were prepared through centuries to achieve their mixture of blood. The entire way of preparation for initiation was the characteristic of pre-Christian initiation, but it could not last forever in the course of human evolution. What was connected with this principle of initiation? It was the ability to observe blood communities. The closer we are to such communities, the more we find this kind of principle.

---

[*] Steiner, *The Fall of the Spirits of Darkness*, pp. 185–186.

[**] For more on this topic, see Valandro, *Deliverance of the Spellbound God: An Experiential Journey into Eastern and Western Meditation Practices*.

During the most ancient times, initiation was based on the principle of blood. But this principle was increasingly broken—from family to family, tribe to tribe, people to people. And then something that will increasingly appear in the future began to happen; all such blood ties began to be broken. For where did the principle of community reside when human beings arose form the womb of God? One could say that it flowed through the blood, and if one wanted to initiate someone, then one had to take the blood into consideration.

Having warm blood allowed the divine soul characteristic to be introduced into the I-being and the divine soul flowed through the blood; "I am he who was, who is, who will be." Precisely the one who speaks as the god Jahve says, "I am he who was, who is, and who will be." And where did he work most powerfully? He worked most powerfully in the blood. And how were people led when they were initiated? They were guided through a special treatment of their blood.... You would see that the astral atmosphere of the Earth is altered fundamentally, abruptly changed in a mighty way with the appearance of Jesus Christ.... Something new entered the Earth's spiritual atmosphere....

You will find the manifestation of this spiritual transformation of planet Earth: all close blood ties are torn, everything that has held people together in small blood communities will be gradually eliminated. The small brotherhoods will be expanded gradually to the great community that is to include all human beings on the Earth. Every human being will say "brother" to every other human being when the human being "leaves mother and father and brother and sister." All that the blood contributed to a kind of group-self, to an I that went beyond the ordinary self, must disappear on Earth. When the Earth is prepared to become a new astral sphere, the fruit will have arrived; all bonds will be broken, and a single great bond will embrace all humankind. Jesus Christ was given the task of giving power to the impulse to found this great bond of community....

Let's consider the raised cross on Golgotha, above all the blood that flows from the wounds. Be clear about what this "blood that flows from the wounds" means for world history. Why does it flow? Why do we speak at all about the flowing blood of Jesus Christ? What established all close communities and held small tribes together? What must lose its significance within these narrow limits if all humankind is to be included in community? Blood. What acts on the I and pulses in it can no longer depend on the blood once humanity has become ripe for community. For this reason, the surplus I-blood, the blood that prevents human beings from expanding their I to a universal I, must flow as self-seeking blood, as egoistic blood from the wounds of Christ. It flows forth. Regard this not as a picture, but as reality. Regard the amount of blood that flowed from Christ's wounds as the amount that had to flow so that blood would lose the tendency to establish narrow communities and thereby acquire the possibility of spreading community over the entire Earth.... The meaning of Christianity lies in dissolving all that is bound to tribes, families, and narrowly delimited communities, on the one hand, and, on the other, in making human beings into separate, unique entities, so that they all experience themselves to be both individuals and members of humanity as a whole. These two aspects exist alongside each other as a polarity. In ancient times human beings experienced themselves as members of a family, members of a tribe. To the extent that blood relationships die out, individual independence will grow and increase.*

The people of ancient times who lived in small tribal communities did not love one another any less than people do today. Indeed, they loved one another more, but their love was more like that of a mother for her child. It was conditioned more by nature. Blood itself was attracted to blood, and the human feeling of belonging together was expressed in that blood attraction. Their progress, however, meant that they began to feel sympathy for another as individuals. In this way smaller groups, families, and communities developed, which in turn were brought together into larger communities. As individuals, however, human beings became increasingly egoistic and self-seeking. We have then, on the one hand, humankind becoming increasingly self-seeking and, on the other hand, the arrival of the unifying influence of Christ.... Only when these two streams have fulfilled themselves will it be possible to manifest a condition on the Earth in which everyone is independent and, at the same time, connected with one another by being permeated with what is termed the Christ Spirit.

---

*   Steiner, *The Christian Mystery: Early Lectures*, pp. 79–81.

SPAIN: A WALK FROM SEVILLE TO SANTIAGO

We must realize that all that is connected with the blood, that originally something was expressed in the blood that was revealed in human feelings and worked within blood relationships to bring about love of family. Then human feelings became increasingly egoistic. Self-seeking entered more and more into the blood. This is the secret of human evolution, that the blood more and more assumed the character of self-seeking. This blood grown egoistic had to be overcome. The excess egoism in human blood was sacrificed, actually flowed in a mystical yet real way from the wounds of Jesus Christ on the cross. Had this blood not flowed, the self-seeking element of human blood would have become greater and greater in the course of evolution. The mystery of Golgotha purified the blood of self-seeking. Through this deep love, human blood was saved from its self-seeking.*

In southern Spain and Portugal, or al-Andalus, as the Muslims have known it, the Umayyad prince 'Abd al-Raḥmān I established the Spanish Umayyad dynasty in 756 with its capital in Cordova, which soon became the largest and most cosmopolitan city in Europe. Thus began a rule of two and a half centuries, during which Spain witnessed incredible cultural achievements in nearly every field and the creation of a social climate in which Muslims, Jews, and Christians lived in peace and harmony to a degree rarely seen in human history. Muslim Spain was the locus of not only a flowering of Islamic culture; the close relationship between the two cultures at the time can be seen in the number of works written by Jewish thinkers, one of the most famous of whom was Maimonides, in Arabic. Spain also became the most important center from which Islamic learning in the sciences, philosophy, and the arts was transmitted to the Christian West and had such a profound effect on later European history. The city of Toledo played a particularly prominent role in this transmission.**

The path I am taking, the *Via de la Plata*, starts from Seville in Andalusia and follows the main cities of Monastero, Zafra, Merida, Caceres, Salamanca, Zamora, Puebla de Sanabria, A Gudina, Laza, Ourense, Castro Dozon, and

---

*   Steiner, *The Christian Mystery: Early Lectures*, p. 95.
** Nasr, *Islam: Religion, History, and Civilization*, p. 126.

BEYOND THE BLOOD

A family of black pigs

Santiago. It crosses arid terrain, orange and olive groves, ranches, mountain passes up to eight-thousand feet in elevation, forests with steep paths, hidden valleys, plateaus, lakes, rivers, streams, and is scarcely populated. It is not a walk for the fainthearted! One reason for starting this first week in March was to beat the hot, horrid weather of southern Spain which comes early. I can walk but cannot handle the very hot temperature, especially climbing with a backpack, and a lack of water supply. The towns are not so close together, and one must carry the water supply and some food.

In the soft early morning I walked the path that led through some flat terrain, before starting into the soft hills, with olive plantations as far as the horizon, forests of cork oak, and much to my surprise, small families of black pigs which feed on acorns and live in these oak-forested hills. I loved looking at their big, intelligent eyes when they stopped their foraging in the dirt by the ancient trees as I walked by. I don't eat ham, but traveling through small villages, that was my diet. Butter, bread, good fat-free slices of ham, and sometimes cheese.

I walked past former fortresses, with storks in huge nests on top of what was left, past very large sheep farms with a few horses. Some of the

Walking the path

paths were devoid of people for entire days but I never felt lonely. I was too enthusiastic about being in nature, new surroundings, new horizons as the map of Spain enfolded and became reality. I would see bright white villages in the distance, or small farms, and the path went on, up and down, sometimes getting lost for a few miles. I never tire of walking long distances, even though after six weeks on the road, I swear I am not doing it again. But here I am!

My back starts hurting and, of course, I start getting rid of stuff. Too many socks, too many T-shirts, too many sweaters. Then I am left with almost nothing, but it is much easier to carry. I can handle up to twenty-four pounds on my back; more is too painful since I am not a big person. So on the first day of walking, after five hours of climbing up and down, I unloaded and left the clothes by the side of the road for someone to take. If I need something I can buy it in the many cheap stores or outdoor markets.

The small villages go by one after another on this long, 850-kilometer path. The many whitewashed villages can be seen from afar through the hills and the forests shining in the distance. The villages are well kept in these areas with cobblestone streets and beautiful doors, and sometimes

A cattle ranch along the path

one gets a glimpse of the inside courtyard with beautiful mosaic floors and walls, the influence of the Arab architecture.

On the first few days I passed by many farmers working in their ranches and chatted with a few. They said that they live in town, and drive here to their fields. Their wives do not like to live out in the country, they prefer the village life. So the men drive out and they go home for lunch and then come back for chores later in the day. Then in the more arid hills, one can still see the shepherds with his herd of sheep and dogs taking them to the hills, or bringing them back at end of the day. It is still part of the scenery.

Sleeping after the first few days on the road is difficult because the body is a bit exhausted, painful back, legs, and muscles. Most of the pilgrims go to bed exhausted, and so did I, sometimes with no energy to eat anything. But morning comes, and we start again, refreshed, ready for the next day. I have slept twelve hours after an exhausting day, but by the end of the first week, the body gets accustomed to the walk and does not rebel, muscles build up, and I actually look forward to a new day on the road. So that after six weeks of being on the road and walking every day, coming home becomes a problem because one is accustomed *now* to using our body for what it is made to do, which is to walk, and *not* walking all day becomes painful! So after returning home I usually walk two to three hours every day to give my body what it needs, until I become a bit more sedentary, and do weekend-long hikes wherever I am living.

In the winter, I am used to skiing at least four hours a day of strenuous downhill, and cross-country for at least three months, so my life is always involving some kind of strenuous exercise, it is a way of life. When I see people's lives and how sedentary they are, and the illnesses which come from such lives, I wish people would start walking, not running!

If you want to start being active, you must start little by little, and build up to it. The body will revolt, and put up every kind of barrier, but you must go on.

When my body is painful from such strenuous activities, I take no pills; I let nature do the healing. If one is used to taking pills for pain, then one does not know what is happening. Put up with the pain, it does disappear! Pain has its use, and makes one stop. If it is too painful, take the afternoon off, and then walk the next day!

After the beautiful hill town of Castilleblanco, I walked through the Park Berrocal nature preserve. Great scents were coming from the lavender, thyme plants which grow avidly, eucalyptus trees, olive trees, and pine trees. Walking in the morning through these magical settings is the reward of putting up with pain, and training the body to do *what I want*, and not vice-versa. The meadows and forest had deer droppings, and climbing to Mount Calvary into the city of Almaden de la Plata there were lots of marbled, pink stones used in the walls along the path. I could see that this continent is indeed very, very old—part of the original, primal Earth. The Roman relics are still to be seen on the path, tall cylindrical columns that were used for calculating distances in the forests. The Romans were here to extract silver out of the wealthy Spanish territories.

Most of the path was deserted, and I had to stay in regular hotels in some towns because it is not really equipped for pilgrims since so few travel on this path. Two Dutch pilgrims were having their picnic and then we walked for part of the way. We came to a small river where we needed to take our shoes off to cross, which we did without any problems. I heard when I was in Santiago, that a week later after our crossing there had been torrential rain for a week, and one had to cross the now-swollen river up to the waist, and one pilgrim stepped barefooted on a broken bottle in the crossing and had to go to the hospital. I need to remember that I must wear sandals when crossing, to avoid such problems.

The soft, rounded, old hills stretched into infinity, sometimes filling my field of vision with beautiful geometric rich brown forms freshly made by the farmers' tractors, fields of legumes planted in red rocky soil, brushes growing here and there, and happy sheep mowing the fresh spring grass. Then a village would announce itself, white, seen from far away, the place to rest, have coffee, buy some lunch, and pass by the empty streets, feeling the loneliness of traveling, passing by other people's lives. A farmer here and there planting his vegetable gardens, an occasional dirty smelly farm tucked away in the hills. The indigo spring skies, sometimes ominous, would drop a few rain showers making the path very muddy.

I walked through these quaint villages one after the other enjoying the scenery, the lonely silence, and peaceful atmosphere.

I arrived in Zafra, a beautiful old medieval city and stayed in the converted monastery in a deluxe room for the pilgrim's price, for two days of rest enjoying this beautiful city. I found a shoe cobbler who beautifully cleaned my beloved hiking boots which had become quite dirty from all that sacred soil! I had a great coffee break in a converted Andalusian palace, a parador in their lovely Moorish courtyard, making believe I was back in time and perhaps caught a glimpse of Hernan Courtez before his departure to the New World to conquer Mexico!

I took the bus early and headed east, through fat hilly mountains for a trip to Cordova and then to Granada for a few days before busing back to the path.

Cordova is a beautiful old city with a colossal graceful mosque built around the ninth century. The mosque features eight hundred columns throughout, meeting everywhere in austere arches—an enormous space to house the believers. It has been transformed into a Christian church loosing all its original charm, just like the Hagia Sophia in Istanbul, a former beautiful Christian church which has become a mosque, likewise losing its former beauty. The artistic work is outstanding, woodwork, tilework, sculpture, and there was an enormous stand encrusted with an inlay of precious stones and ivory for the Koran.

'Abd al-Rahmān I, the Umayyad prince who conquered Spain and defied the Abbasid caliph, was a man of simple taste who waited until the end of his life before deciding to build the mosque which came to be known as the Great Mosque of Cordova. Luxury came in with his grandson, 'Abd al-Rahmān II, who made his Spanish eunuch his Vizier and spent his time with his Persian music master, Ziryab, who had wandered into Spain from the court of Harun al-Rashid. The Umayyad caliph was so delighted with the talents of the young and handsome Ziryab that he would seat him beside him and share meals with him, and listen to hours to his songs.... Ziryab was the very symbol of exhausted effeminacy; and he appeared at a time when the Christians of Cordova, exasperated by the fecklessness of the Arabs, were taunting their conquerors with demands for martyrdom, denying the flesh as the Arabs satiated themselves with the refinements of luxury.

Not all the Christians were prepared to die for their faith. In 850, the priest Alvarez of Cordova reproached the Christians for their preference for Arab speech and Arab books. "They neglect the Bible for the Muhammadan scripture," he said. Arab eloquence, Arab refinement, Arab luxury had conquered Spanish hearts, and they were never to free themselves completely from these toils.

Under the reign of 'Abd al-Rahmān III (912–961) who came to the throne at the age of twenty-three, Cordova reached its greatest heights....

All the Umayyad princes helped to build the Great Mosque at Cordova, which had been built on the grounds of the Visigothic church of San Vicenzo, overlooking the river. This immense and battlemented mosque remains today the chief glory of western Islam.... With its hundreds of columns, its strange horseshoe arches painted with red and white bands surmounted by a higher register of similar arches, its infinitely complicated perspectives along jeweled arcades...

The caliph was also spending huge sums on Cordova itself. It was a large city with half a million inhabitants, with 113,000 houses, three thousand mosques, seventy libraries, and nine hundred public baths. Travelers said you could walk ten miles through the streets of Cordova at night, and always there would be a lamp from one of the houses to light the way.... The arts flourished; the lecture rooms were crowded; embassies came flocking from the four corners of the Earth to see the wonderful city; there was more trade than men had ever known before; and there was peace in the land.*

Its history speaks of former caliphs from the East, of old Jewish settlements from Roman times, of old Visigoths kings, and Christian monarchs. Like many of Andalusia's southern cities, its illustrious past included the harmonious living between three separate and distinctive cultures. Each culture provided their great talents and gifts to make for the making of a high renaissance of Islamic history. The Jews provided their expertise in trading and money management (by collecting taxes, office of treasury, and various posts serving caliphs, kings, and queens), the caliphs provided their expertise in warring, building elegant palaces and mosques, and their great vast empires extending from Mongolia, to India, to Africa, and to France, etc. The caliphs and their courts, their Koranic schools of thought, their expertise in medicine exchanged with the Jewish schools of thought and philosophy, and expert medical knowledge. The Christians likewise benefited from the high degree of development and achievements of these caliphs who had been in power since the rise of Islam. The Christians were still barbaric compared to these highly civilized Arabs and their courts. When one sees the fortresses which dot the European countryside, these bastions, with no windows, no real toilets, and no baths, and one sees the absolute exquisite quarters of the Andalusian palaces and other palaces throughout the Arab world, one understands how much Europe owes to the Muslim culture about cleanliness, respect for the body, great culinary cuisine, spices, perfumes, oils, and a very developed medical system, besides architectural genius, birth of gardens, and fountains. Walking through a city like Toledo, and stepping into a French Middle Ages city like Conques, one is struck by the lightness of the Andalusian cities. Of course they are in

---

* Payne, *The History of Islam*, pp. 212–216.

the south where there is plentiful sunshine, and they appreciate the shade of trees, courtyards, and gardens, but one feels the genius of the Muslim world. The caliphs allowed the people to go on with their own religion and just administered the land, collecting taxes with the help of the Jews as their administrator. The Jews had their own cities, own schools, own judges, their own countries within a country, living a life apart.

Both the caliphs and the Jewish natives provided high degrees of culture. Many original thinkers were educated and born in these famous cities, Toledo, Seville, Granada, Segovia, etc all had their training schools where they exercised the gifted minds of great men. Many of these men were great scholars and studied throughout the great centers of learning throughout the Eastern world. Many famous poets read Hebrew, Arabic, Greek, etc., and had a very high level of human understanding of culture, bringing up questions which we are still dealing with today.

We cannot forget that knowledge travels like human beings and these great minds traveled widely and read widely the great books of antiquity as well. The caliphs had fabulous libraries and acquired immense knowledge, and so did the old sages and experts of the Torah. They also had their famous scrolls and scriptures which they studied dutifully, preserving their ancient knowledge dating back to Solomon, the prophets, the kings, and Egypt. The Christians had their saints, but also their cruel popes and bishops who denied access to the Bible. The Jews and Muslims provided the incentive for change because they read and studied their own sacred works, the Koran and Torah, without prohibiting their people the study of these sacred religious works but actually providing famous schools to do so and gain expertise. The Christians had to leave that domain to the priests only, until the heretics finally decided that they, too, could read the sacred Bible themselves in small enclaves without the priests. So this is another gift of these Muslim and Jewish Communities; one can have access to God and Christ directly, and not through the pope and his representatives.

One example of what might have been experienced by these gifted minds in their respective religious schools is taken from *The Wisdom in the Hebrew Alphabet.*

Just as the "word of God" gave being to the heavens, so it is His word that gives beings to everything. Let us try to understand further what is meant by God's "word." And how do the specific, limited utterances of Creation account for the infinite number of species and objects in the universe?...

The twenty-two sacred letters are profound, primal spiritual forces. They are, in effect, the raw material of Creation. When God combined them into words, phrases, commands, they brought about Creation, translating His will into reality, as it were. There is a divine science in the Hebrew alphabet. *Sefer Yetzirah* ("the Book of Creation"), the early Kabbalistic work ascribed to the patriarch Abraham, describes how the sacred letters were used as the agency of creation. The letters can be ordered in countless combinations, by changing their order within words and interchanging letters in line with the rules of various Kabbalistic letter-systems. Each rearrangement of the same letters results in a new blend of the cosmic spiritual forces represented by the letters....

God's utterance that created heaven also created everything associated with it. The sages and the literature of the Kabbalah teach that there are seven heavens representing distinct spiritual levels. Each has its functions and beings that enable it to perform its missions. And each of those, in ways unknown to us, is a product of the combinations of spiritual forces represented by the letters—in their various arrangements—of the words *Let there be a firmament in the midst of the waters, and let it separate between water and water* (Genesis 1:6).*

Many great leaders told stories illustrating the theme that the letters of the *Aleph-Beis*, when uttered in prayerful sincerity, are like spiritual tools in the hands of God. He combines the letters to form words, with the result that the sincerity of an unlearned but devout person becomes translated into potent prayers....

R' Yitzchak Luria, the Holy *Arizal*, once felt that his prayers during the Days of Awe were particularly efficacious, but the Holy Spirit revealed to him that the prayers of someone else were even more pleasing to God than those of the *Arizal*. The sage longed to meet this great

---

*   Munk, *The Wisdom in the Hebrew Alphabet* (from the overview by Rabbi Nosson Scherman), p. 19.

but unknown *tzaddik* and learn the secret of his greatness. The *Arizal* found him and asked if he was a Torah scholar.

"No," replied the ordinary-looking villager.

"What did you do during the Days of Awe?" asked *Arizal*.

The man replied, "Rabbi, I am unlearned and do not even know the complete *Aleph-Beis*. I know only from *aleph* to *yud*. When I saw everyone praying fervently in the synagogue—something I could not do—I recited the first ten letters of the *Aleph-Beis* and said, 'Please, O Master of the Universe, take my letters and form then into words that will please You.' I repeated this time after time all day long."

The heartfelt prayer of the ignorant villager meant more in heaven than the lofty prayers of the *Arizal*.*

At the same time in another corner of Cordova one would have perhaps seen two very prominent sages having a discussion of the highest spirituality that a human mind can attain. These two men were Muhyiddin Ibn 'Arabî and Ibn Rushd (Averroes), both resided periodically in Cordova. These two Andalusian sages, totally dedicated to scholarship, influenced the Middle Ages more than we assume. Walking along the modern city one is moved to think that these powerful immense thinkers, philosophers, and men of religion lived here. They revived Aristotle, revived much of the former old mysteries of truth.

> The last and most celebrated of the Andalusian philosophers, Ibn Rushd or Averroes, was more influential in the West than in Islam. He was born in Cordova in 1126 to a distinguished family of jurists and received the best education possible in law, theology, philosophy, and medicine. He served as chief judge of religious courts in Seville and Cordova and was court physician in Marrakesh. At the end of his life, because of a change in political climate of Andalusia, he fell from grace and died a lonely figure in Marrakesh in 1198....
>
> Averroes, Ibn Rushd, devoted himself most of all to commenting on the works of Aristotle.... Averroes also wrote certain independent philosophical works such as *Incoherence of the Incoherence* and *On the Harmony of Religions and Philosophy*, in which like other Muslim

---

* Munk, *The Wisdom in the Hebrew Alphabet*, pp. 37–38.

philosophers but in his own way he sought to harmonize reason and revelation by giving each its due as an independent way of reaching the truth.*

Here Rudolf Steiner's lectures on karma gives us insights into these outstanding men of learning and their gifts, bringing another view from across the centuries, into the future, so that more of an understanding can be achieved towards the greatness of these Muslim scholars whose tradition is still alive in the Sufi circles of today, which will be discussed later in this long journey.

> In ancient times it was so indeed, that men could not ascribe to themselves the essence of Intelligence. They ascribed to the inspiration of higher Powers all that they could express in forms of Intelligence. And those who had knowledge of these matters knew that the higher Powers here concerned were the ones who afterwards, in Christian terminology, were designated as the Powers of Michael....
>
> Let us try to gain a vivid idea of how the Cosmic Intelligence had been conceived.... In Spain it was taught by the Moorish scholars and above all by such an individuality as Averroes, that the Intelligence holds sway everywhere. The whole world, the whole cosmos is filled with the all-pervading Intelligence. Human beings down here on Earth have many different properties, but they do not possess a personal intelligence of their own. On the contrary, every time a human being is active on Earth, a drop of Intelligence, a ray of Intelligence proceeds from the universal Intelligence, and descends as it were into the head, into the body of the single human being. So that the human being as he walks about on Earth, shares in the universal Cosmic Intelligence which is common to all. And when he dies, when he passes through the gate of death, the Intelligence that was his returns to the universal Intelligence, flows back again. Thus all the thoughts, conceptions, and ideas which man possesses in the life between birth and death flow back into the common reservoir of the universal Intelligence. One cannot therefore say that the thing of outstanding value in man's soul, namely his Intelligence, is subject to personal immortality. Indeed it was actually taught by the Spanish Moorish scholars that man does not

---

*   Nasr, *Islamic Life and Thought*, p. 74.

possess personal immortality. True, he lives on, but, said these scholars, the most important thing about him during his life is the fact that he can unfold intelligence knowledge, and this does *not* remain with his own being. We cannot therefore say that the intelligent being possesses personal immortality. You see, this was the very point in the fury of the battle which was waged by the Schoolmen of the Dominican Order. It was to maintain and uphold the personal immortality of man. And in that time, such a striving could appear in no other way than it did when the Dominicans declared: Man is personally immortal, and the teaching of Averroes on this subject is *heresy*, absolute heresy. Today we have to put it differently, but for that time one can understand that a man like Averroes in Spain, who did not assume the personal immortality of man, was declared a heretic. Today we have to see the matter in its reality. We have to say: In the sense in which man has become immortal, as to his Spiritual Soul, he has indeed attained immortality—the continuous consciousness of personality after passing through the gate of death—but he has attained this only since the time when the Spiritual Soul took up its abode in earthly man. If therefore we had asked Aristotle or Alexander what were their thoughts about immortality, what would have been their answers? The words of course are not the point. But if, being asked, they had answered in our Christian terminology, they would have said: Our soul is received by Michael, and we live on in the communion of Michael. Or they would have expressed it cosmologically. Above all in a community such as that of Alexander or Aristotle, they would have spoken thus in cosmic terms, and indeed they did speak thus: the soul of man is intelligent on Earth, but this Intelligence is a drop out of the fullness of what Michael pours forth like a rain of Intelligence, flowing out over mankind. This rain proceeds from the Sun, and the Sun receives the human soul back again into its own being. The human soul as it exists between birth and death is rayed down upon the Earth from the Sun. Thus on the Sun they would have looked for the dominion of Michael, and such would have been their answer, cosmologically speaking.

 These conceptions found their way into Asia, returned from Asia and flourished among the Moors in Spain at the very time when Scholastic Philosophy rose up in defense of personal immortality. We must not say with the Schoolmen that this conception was an error, but we must say:

BEYOND THE BLOOD

The evolution of mankind brought with it the individual and personal immortality of man. And it was by the Dominican Schoolmen that this personal immortality was first emphasized, while on the other hand an ancient truth—one that was no longer true for that age in the evolution of the human race—was put forward in the Academies conducted by the Moors of Spain. For we today must be tolerant of our contemporaries. We must be tolerant of those who went on propagating ancient teachings. Such tolerance was not possible at the time.*

The other great sage, Ibn 'Arabî, traveled extensively throughout the Muslim world. He was born in Murcia, and met Averroes in Cordova in 1179 when he was fourteen years old. He was initiated into the Sufi order in Seville at age nineteen and he went on to Tunis, Fes, Seville, Granada, Cordova, Marrakesh, Bougie (Algeria), Tunis, Cairo, Jerusalem, Mecca, Bagdad, Anatolya, Hebron, Cairo, Mecca, Aleppo, Konia, Bagdad, Aleppo, Mecca, Malatya (Anatolya-Turkey), and Damascus, and he died in 1240 at age seventy-five. At age thirty-two, he went to Averroes' funeral in Cordova. In Mecca at age thirty-six he met a beautiful young woman, highly educated and spiritual, who inspired much of his work on love, or mystical poetry, like "The Interpreter of Desires."

Ibn 'Arabî is one of the greatest, most read philosophers and he has been the spiritual father of many great sages throughout the Islamic world. One can see the extensive travels which the sages of Islam and other traditions experienced in their lives. It was a world apart from the wars and rebellions. These outstanding personalities lived a life dedicated to loving life, learning, praying, studying, writing, and teaching, and achieved a high level of accomplishment, Illumination being one of them.

> Here is the most delightful experience one can experience in love. And that is, to a lesser degree, to find oneself in love with love (hubb al-hubb), or occupying oneself with being in love to the point of ignoring the beloved. Layla gave herself to the poet Qays, who was madly in love with her, crying, "Layla, Layla!" He took hold of some ice and put it on his burning heart which melted it instantly. Layla acknowledged his

---

* Steiner, *Karmic Relationships: Esoteric Studies, Volume Three*, pp. 162–165.

presence while he was in this state of mind and said to him: "I am the one whom you asked for, whom you desire, I am your beloved, I am the primal source of your being, I am Layla!" Qays turned around and faced her and said: "Leave me instantly, get out of my sight, because the love that I have for you is so consuming that I have no time for you!"

Such a state is so delicious, delightful, and the most refined that one can experience in the state of being in love....

Our Sufi master... asked once of God to allow him to taste the passion of love but not of love itself.*

More about this great philosopher:

Muhyiddin Muhammad ibn-Ali-al-'Arabî, known as Ibn 'Arabî, was born in Murcia in Andalusia in 1165. His father seems to have been a man in affluent circumstances who spared no pains to give the boy a sound education. At the age of eight he was taken to Seville, where he attended the theological seminary and became a teacher. Men observed a strangeness about him from the beginning. He liked to sing, and often fell into a trance while singing. He seemed to acquire knowledge through sources not available to ordinary mortals, and stories were told of his powers of clairvoyance and telepathy. He said once: "It is especially necessary that men should be the masters of their dreams, so gaining all the fruits which come to those who enter the intermediary world." For two years he lived in a reed hut with Fatima bint al-Waliyya, a female mystic renowned for "having the sight of God in everything in the world." She was nearly a hundred years old, but hale and hearty and Ibn 'Arabî acquired from her a delight in associating with female mystics which never left him. He was thirty-seven when he left Seville and took up his residence in Ceuta. One night he dreamed that he had wedded all the stars and moons in the sky, and when he mentioned the dream to a famous interpreter of dreams, he was told: "Immeasurable bounty will flow upon you." Shortly afterwards, he left Spain, and traveled across North Africa, Egypt, and the Hijaz visiting Baghdad, Aleppo, and Mosul; and settled down in Damascus already famous, praised by many, hated by others for his heretical views, the recipient of many gifts from members of the

---

* Ibn 'Arabî, *Traité de L'Amour*, p. 53 (tr. M-L. Valandro).

princely houses, known for his charities, a quiet, simple man possessed of an inner fire and a ruthless determination to express his beliefs even when they outraged conventional morality and orthodoxy. He never returned to Spain....

According to Ibn 'Arabî, man is the mirror in which God contemplates himself, and woman is the mirror in which man contemplates God. He believed that the most perfect vision of God is enjoyed by those who contemplate Him in a woman. Between human love and divine love there was only a hairbreadth of difference....

He wrote voluminously—altogether 289 books were listed in the catalogue he drew up when he was seventy-three—and he seems to have enjoyed life to the full....

It was with his doctrines on the nature of man that Ibn 'Arabî made his most startling discoveries. God worships man. God and man are necessary to each other; without man, God cannot exist. God's dependence on man is so great that He is like a beggar continuously seeking man's mercy. On behalf of God the whole universe is preserved by the existence of man. When Ibn 'Arabî first announced these claims in Egypt, they were regarded as so heretical that attempts were made to assassinate him....

Man is to God as the pupil is to the eye, since sight is effected through the pupil, and so it is through man that God is able to contemplate his creation and dispense His justice. Man is at once ephemeral and eternal, created in perpetuity and graced with immortality, the Word distinguishing and uniting all things together.*

Ibn 'Arabî still belonged to those individuals who had a connection to the old mysteries because of their soul configuration. Their soul was still capable of finding their ways to the spirit world by going through initiation.

> In earlier times the human being could look up to the world of the stars; and in those ancient times he did that much more intensively than he does today. There he saw many things, and he well knew in those times that man is related to them just as he is related to the plant, animal, and mineral kingdoms on Earth. This is knowledge that has disappeared from the outer world today. Ancient man knew that just

---

* Payne, *The History of Islam*, pp. 233–236.

as he is born out of the kingdom of nature on Earth, something in him is also born out of the extra-tellurian, extra-earthly cosmos. Indeed, it was this connection of the human being to the cosmos beyond the Earth that became known to him when he passed through the "gate of man."... He was led to the "gate of man," where he was to become acquainted with man himself. He came to know in himself what externally he could only gaze at, especially in the world of stars....

When he had grasped the full meaning of being placed there, he no longer considered himself the animal-on-two-legs.... He began to feel himself as belonging to the heavens one can see and also to those one cannot see. He began to consider himself a citizen of the whole world, to feel himself really as microcosm, not merely a little Earth, but a little world. He felt his connection with the planets and fixed stars, that he had been born out of the universe. He felt that his being did not end with his fingertips, the tips of his ears, the tips of his toes, but that it extended beyond his body taken from the Earth, that his being extended through endless spaces and on through these spaces into the realms of the spirit.... The matter of importance in those ancient mysteries was the direct experience.*

Ibn 'Arabî was such an individual and only such an exceptional human being could say:

> Once a puzzled student was invited to have breakfast with him. The student said: "Sir, who is the greatest saint of our time?" Ibn 'Arabî answered sternly: "You should pay more attention to your breakfast." But the student was unable to eat, and begged Ibn 'Arabî to tell him the name of the greatest living saint. There was a momentary pause, and then Ibn 'Arabî smiled and said: "The greatest saint is Shaykh Muhiyuddin Ibn 'Arabî."**

In the eleventh century Umayyad power waned. Spain became divided into small principalities ruled by local princes... making it an easy target for the Berbers of North Africa, especially the religiously fervent

---

*   Steiner, *How Can Mankind Find the Christ Again?*, pp. 58, 61.
** Payne, *The History of Islam*, p. 235.

BEYOND THE BLOOD

and puritanical Almoravids and Almohads who conquered much of Spain in the eleventh and twelfth centuries. But these victories were short-lived. With the power of Muslims considerably weakened, the reconquest by Christians began, marked by the fatal defeat of Muslims in the Battle of Las Navas de Tolosa in 1212. Henceforth, Muslims survived only in the mountainous regions of the south, where the Nasrids ruled and built one of the greatest masterpieces of Islamic art, the Alhambra, in Granada in the thirteenth century. Formal Muslim rule over the Iberian Peninsula came to an end in 1492 with the conquest of Granada by the Christian rulers Isabelle and Ferdinand.*

Here is the same history in different words from Annemarie Schimmel:

> The last Umayyad fled to Andalusia where he founded, in 756, a kingdom which was to produce the finest flowers of Arabic culture in art and poetry. The Spanish-Umayyad kingdom reached its culmination under 'Abd al-Rahmān III (912–961). It continued until 1031, witnessing a unique cultural cooperation between Muslims, Christians, and Jews. After 1031 the country fell to pieces, and Berber groups—the Almohads and the Almoravids—entered the Iberian Peninsula to rule there while the Spanish reconquest increased in strength year by year. The only kingdom able to survive till 1492 was that of the Banu Ahmar in Granada; the Alhambra is the last work of Arabic art in Spain.**

After walking through this famed ancient city of Cordova, I took the bus and drove south to Granada, the pearl of the caliphs. We drove through fat, undulating, round, arid mountains with olive groves, sheep, and small villages. Then the city comes into view in its magnificence with the higher snowy Sierra Nevada mountains in the background. I walked through to the old city, at the foot of the Alhambra, to find a small, colorful youth hostel, and planned my travels for the next few days: palaces covering a whole mountain, old fortresses, the old Jewish quarters of the city, and many wonderful Middle Eastern restaurants held by people from Lebanon,

---

*   Nasr, *Islam: Religion, History, and Civilization*, pp. 126–127.
**   Schimmel, *Islam: An Introduction*, p. 22.

The Alhambra

or Syria or other faraway places. Al-Andalus had not changed, people still came here from faraway Middle Eastern countries to work.

For someone who loves people from all lands, gardens, fountains and magnificent architecture, it was a feast for all my senses!

Tourists were here from all over the world for the same reason: To enjoy one of the most outstanding sites in Spain. The Alhambra was spread over large areas and gave us a true impression of the cultural splendor in which these caliphs lived. They lived a lavish lifestyle, and when it came to an end, the caliph who had to leave his beloved estate said that his heart died, he left his heart in these sumptuous settings. Nothing was spared to achieve these momentous palaces. One can imagine the enormous exchange of human beings coming from Damascus, Egypt, or Anatolya to help build these Islamic residences. Parallel to these architectural accomplishments, we have the spiritual achievements of these great Muslim thinkers. They both go hand in hand.

> The availability of religious freedom in Andalusia created a good climate, and pluralism was a concrete everyday fact lived at all level of human relationships. The relationship between the Muslim and the men and women of the Book were as good in the royal courts as in local fairs, and marketplaces and the fraternities. People met, and held conversations freely, united by the same language, Arabic. The literary gatherings were being held in the Jewish shops as well as in the Muslim courts.*

Here is another passage related to this cooperation between the Jews, Muslims, and Christians:

> Conversion by force was and still is very rare. In fact, in early times conversions were not even deemed desirable because the special taxes on the *dhimmīs* were a boon for the treasury. Conversions for practical purposes however are often mentioned, although non-Muslims were not prohibited from working in any profession. Many of them enjoyed high offices at court: Christians and Jews became highly esteemed physicians, and as financial administrators as well as secretaries they were sought after in the state bureaucracy. Christians had long experience in this field, especially in Egypt and Syria.... One should not forget the numerous Jewish physicians and bankers active in the Middle East—it seems typical of the situation that the Spanish Jews, when driven out of Spain in the wake of the reconquista, should have chosen the Ottoman Empire as their refuge, because the Muslim government protected them as *dhimmīs* and enabled them to continue their professions.**

In this climate, some of the greatest architecture was conceived, created. The great arabesque designs, in tiles, wood, paintings, reflect the perfect poetry addressed to the One God, Allah. A wonderful serenity of "being" overcomes the viewer as he sits in a garden, surrounded

---

*   Talbi, *Ma Religion c'est la Liberté: L'Islam et les Défis de la Contemporanéité* (tr. M-L. Valandro).
** Schimmel, *Islam: An Introduction*, pp. 71–72.

by the beautiful curved doorway, windows.... He might just reach the heights mentioned by this other famous sage and scholar, who opposed Averroes, Al-Ghazâlî (1058–1111). He is one of the greatest Sufis of this epoch.*

You must know, my dear ones, that man was not created as a joke, or casually. Even though man is not made of everlasting substance, he lives forever; even though his body is petty, mean, and earthly, his spirit belongs to the height and is divine. When in the crucible of abstinence, he separates himself from his carnal passions, he reaches the highest and instead of being a slave to luxury, and anger, he is vested with angelical qualities. Upon reaching such a state, he meets his heavenly sphere while contemplating eternal beauty, and never goes back to the delights of the flesh. The spiritual alchemy which provokes such a state within him, like the one which changes base metals into gold, is not easy to discover, nor can it be found in the house of any of the ancient learned ones. In order to explain this alchemical process, in the form in which it works, the author has undertaken this work which is called the alchemy of happiness. God's treasury where such alchemy is to be found, is formed by the hearts of the prophets, and if one finds it in other places, he will remain disappointed, cheated, and in bankruptcy at the day of judgment when he hears the words: "We have removed the veil which covered you and today your image is pure."

God has sent to Earth 24,000 prophets in order to teach man the prescription of this alchemy, and how to purify the hearts of their lower qualities in the crucible of abstinence. This alchemy could be described briefly as a moving away from the earthly world and approaching God. It has four elements:

1. Knowing Oneself
2. Knowing God
3. Knowing the World in its Reality
4. Knowing the Other World in its Reality**

---

*   Al-Gazzali, *La Alquimia de la Felicidad* (tr. M-L. Valandro).
** Ibid., pp. 23–24 (tr. M-L. Valandro).

Al-Ghazâlî is also another great individual, who like Ibn 'Arabî could still undergo the process of initiation available among the Sufis. His biography is full of examples of initiatory experiences.

> Abū-Hāmid al-Ghazālī was born in 1058 at Tus in Khurasan, the son of a spinner of wool, who died when he was young, and he was brought up by a Sufi. Though living in a Sufi environment and practicing spiritual exercises, he seems to have had no taste for mysticism. He had a quick brain and a longing for fame. He was about sixteen when he decided that the quickest route to preferment lay in the law. In religious matters he remained a skeptic but it delighted him to improvise on the subject of the religious laws of Islam before admiring students. He became the most brilliant theologian of his age without the least belief in theology. At thirty-three he was professor of theology at Baghdad, with three hundred students....
> Suddenly he felt a profound revulsion against himself and everything he stood for.
> A door of fear was opened to him, which diverted him from everything else and compelled him to ignore everything but God. For six months from the summer to the winter of 1095, he fought up alone in his rooms, uncertain of everything except his uncertainty. He lost his power of speech, and could no longer give lectures. For a while he was unable to eat, and the doctors despaired of his life, and when he asked them what had happened they answered: The trouble arises from the heart, and from there it has spread through the whole system: the only cures lies in allaying the anxieties of the heart.... Suddenly he gave out that he intended to go on pilgrimage to Mecca, although he had already resolved to become a wandering dervish in Syria.... He went to Damascus and stayed there for two years in complete solitude, sometimes climbing the minaret of a mosque and remaining alone. Then he went to Jerusalem where he spent his days within the Dome of the Rock, and afterwards journeyed to Mecca, only to return to the solitude of Damascus, living on dried bread and dressed in rags. He wrote voluminously but did not publish his writings. His days were spent in the endless contemplation of the glory of God, as he followed the Sufi practices he had learned as a child and then abandoned.

> What he had discovered was something very simple. He had learned with certainty that the mystics walk the road of God; their life was the best life, their character the purest. The learning of scholars was as nothing compared with those who bring illumination from the lamp of "prophetic revelation." The mystics alone can speak with angels and behold the spirits of the prophets; to them come the miraculous graces, and the knowledge of God. Unlike most of the Sufis, he respected the religious ordinances and commented upon them at length.
>
> He spent eleven years in tranquil seclusion in Damascus when he was summoned by the "sultan of my time" to teach at Nishapur. It was a summons he could hardly disobey, and so for a few months he was to be found teaching again in a style so unlike his previous style that his friends no longer recognized him.*

From this brief look into Al-Ghazâlî's life we can see that he belonged to the same great souls as Ibn 'Arabî. His life was nothing but initiation experiences which allowed him to bring down great literary, philosophical, religious, and poetic works. Here I will quote more insights from Rudolf Steiner.

> A modern person would like to undergo initiation, if possible, as something to be done casually somewhere along his life path, something to be done incidentally. He would like to inquire—as people say today—into what leads to knowledge; but in any case, he would not like to experience what the people of old seeking initiation had to experience. To be deeply affected in his whole being by the preparation for knowledge, to become a different man—that he would not like.... The essential preparation for the man of old was this: he had to go through an inner soul-condition that, if characterized by one word, must be called fear. He had to experience to a most intense degree the fear that is always felt by someone who is brought face to face with something wholly unknown to him. In the ancient initiations that was the essential condition: that an individual should have the most intense feeling of facing something that would not be met with anywhere in external life.

---

* Payne, *The History of Islam*, pp. 238–239.

Given all the soul forces the man of today expends upon his external life, this soul-condition would today still never be reached. With the soul forces he likes to use he can eat and drink, he can conform to the social customs of the various classes of society recognized today, he can carry on a business, play the bureaucrat, even become a professor, or a scientist—all that: but with these capacities actually he can know nothing whatever that is real. The conditions of soul in which an individual sought enlightenment in those ancient times was essentially different.

It could have nothing in common with the soul-forces that are serviceable for external life; it had to be derived from entirely different regions of the human being. These regions are always present in man, but he has a terrible fear of using them in any way. In a neophyte they were brought into activity in a direct purposeful way. They are the very part of a human being that is avoided by modern man—by the ordinary, secular man of ancient times too—in which modern man does not want to become involved, and concerning which he likes to have illusions or to be indifferent.... Only what lies in the realm of the soul that man fears in his ordinary external life: only this could be used to attain the desired knowledge. This condition of soul was really experienced in those times, and bravely gone through—a condition in which all the individual felt was fear: fear of something unknown. This fear was to lead him to knowledge. Only through this soul condition was he then brought face to face with what I have characterized as the descent of the human being through the regions of heaven, that is, of the spiritual world, to which he was led up again through the eight stages....

By what the neophyte had now carried into the world from out of himself, he was raised to the consciousness of the fourth stage: he became what was expressed, when carried over and translated into later languages, by the word Christophorus, or Christ-bearer. That was fundamentally the goal of this Mystery initiation: to make the human being a Christ-bearer. Naturally, only a few selected individuals became Christ-bearer. Moreover, they could only become such by first seeking within themselves what was not to be found in the outer world, by then taking back into the outer world what they had found within, and then by uniting themselves with their God. This is the way they became Christ-bearers. They knew they had united themselves in the universe with what is called in the Gospel of Saint John the Logos, or the Word... they had united themselves with That out of which all things were made, and without which not anything was made that was made. Thus in those ancient times the Christ Mystery was separated from man, as it were, by an abyss; and man crossed the abyss by becoming able, through self-knowledge, to go out of himself and to unite himself with his God—to become a bearer of his God.[*]

With these insights we can judge the importance of the lives of such towering figures such as Al-Ghazâlî, Ibn 'Arabî, and so many others in Islam and what they brought to the rest of the world.

To finish my stay in Granada let us read what a very gifted Hebrew poet Solomon ibn Gabirol wrote. He was born in 1021 from a Cordova family, then moved to Granada. He died very young because of poor health, at around age twenty-four. He was too sensitive to face the major difficulties of life. He was fluent in Arabic, and wrote in Arabic as was the customs in those days, until the flight of the Moors when the Hebrews started to write in their own language.

> I am poetry, and poetry is my slave
> For poets and musician I am the harp
> My poems are like the kings' crown
> Garlands on the heads of magnates
> Here you see me, I am eighteen years old
> Furthermore, I understand like an eighty-year-old[**]

Here is another poem by this very gifted young man, with a touch of the fabled city, Granada.

> Come my friend, companion of the enlightened ones,
> Come with me, let's spend the night between the alheñas
> I see that the winter has gone, and we can hear

---

[*] Steiner, *How Can Mankind Find the Christ Again?*, pp. 59–61, 66–67.
[**] Solomon ibn Gabirol, in Sáenz-Badillos and Targarona Borrás, *Poetas Hebreos de Al-Andalus, Siglos X–XII: Antología*, p. 130 (tr. M-L. Valandro).

The row of the swallows, and turtledoves;
Let us sleep under the canopy of the pomegranate, palm trees
The apple tree and various orange trees.
Let us walk under the shade of the grapevine,
With the wish to see radiant faces
In this palace dominating the surroundings
Built with various valuable stones*

I spent a few days walking through Granada's sumptuous setting meeting up with a friend who would join me for a few days of walking on the path. We sat, looking at the sunset from the old fort, gazing far into the distance into the mountains. One thousand years ago or so, this whole area was much more alive than it is now, bustling with building activities and spiritual search for truth within the three faiths.

After thoroughly enjoying Granada, I was ready for the next phase of the walk. We took the bus to Merida and once more went on the path like many of these traveling men and women with just a few things on my back. Perhaps it is reliving the past. Walking seems to be so natural a state to me, leaving everything behind!

We made a brief visit to the well-preserved Roman ruins which speak of another era. Upon leaving the city of Merida, I saw the familiar sight of storks sitting on their nests on old Roman columns which used to be an aqueduct. The path followed some of the old Roman paths, still intact, and old stone bridges large enough for the two-wheeled chariots. There were more shepherds and sheep herds, and a wonderful spring scent of lavender blossoms all along the hills we crossed. The meadows were full of spring flowers, and spring was in full bloom. The heat of the summer was fast approaching.

Crossing one of the lovely whitewashed towns, we bought some welcomed food for a picnic. In these deserted places, the store is a truck which comes daily with provisions. We had everything one needs: prosciutto, bread, tomatoes, cheese, and olives. We walked into the hills and proceeded to have a sumptuous lunch, and a nap for the unaccustomed pilgrim! Wanting to walk the path is one thing, and doing it is another! It does take some training.

---

*   Ibid., p. 130 (tr. M-L. Valandro).

A stork sitting on its nest

The old city of Carceles was having a dressing up in period costumes, and a market-fair. This town has been restored to its former beauty, with old stone homes lovingly rebuilt, and small cobblestone streets. We stayed in a lovely monastery setting by the church and enjoyed walking through the old Jewish quarters which used to be quite large until the expulsion edict of March 31, 1492 which changed the face of Spain.

Leaving Carceles, the scenery changed, and we could see the snow-covered mountains of Extremadura in the distance which we would have to cross in a few days. The forests were gone, and the soft hills were covered with spring flowers, with lakes here and there to feed the sheep herds living in the meadows. The path was lined with beautiful stone walls, and here and there lovely vegetable gardens, along with large farms. The olive trees were still growing, with lavender everywhere in the very stony fields. Lambs were frolicking about when not feeding. The Sun was beginning to heat up the day; I had to go in the shade for a respite. I am a northern climate person, and the intense sunshine slows me down. The hills were becoming bigger and harder to climb, but we finally reached a very modern albergue for pilgrims, with a glorious sunset over a lake. There were more antique Roman paths, higher hills, and a lovely mountainside village for lunch.

We climbed and climbed into the mountains along some very steep paths through a pine forest with some welcomed shade and some more very, very ancient olive trees. More mountainous terrain, and small rivers to cross until we reached the stone-walled city on top of a hill. We stayed in a small hotel and proceeded to visit the old walled town.

We encountered more villages, towns, and churches with lovely painted sculptures of Madonnas, then we climbed again into the mountainous terrain through old forested paths, along ravines, into lovely old farms and meadows, called Puerto de Béjar and La Calzada de Béjar. There was a different microclimate here, with moss on the stone walls, not the arid weather. It is more like Galicia, and temperate. We are in the mountains, still snow covered, and crossing very poor stone villages. The reconstruction has not reached these mountain villages except a few renovated homes. We climb higher into the desolate rocky settings, home to sheep and a few cow farms. A cow herder is bringing his cows and their calves home, while we let him go by. We reached our destination, but no one is around to open the hostel.

The hostel is finally opened. It is a sour-smelling place where I won't get much sleep, but it has one amazing feature: the shower! A very modern shower which took me quite a while to figure out—lots of buttons to turn on. I washed in this sumptuous shower which had blasting music features—classical, rock, jazz, etc.—and different water strength features coming from all sides which I did not really know how to use. Anyway, my companion and I had a roaring laugh. It made up for the rancid, dirty beds we slept in, with a vagrant sleeping next door!

The joy of being on the path!

Several more towns, and we arrived in the towns of Baños de Montemayor and Hervás which also had a large Jewish community in the past.

Meeting all these shepherds along the path, one wonders where they came from. It is said that some Berber shepherds coming from the Atlas Mountains in Morocco came here during the invasion and settled in these lands along with the Christian shepherds. So we have quite a mixture of races living side by side. The Arab invaders themselves were not doing this kind of work, they were the aristocrats. When I see the shepherds there is something about their love of their flocks and their closeness to the land and nature which is very tribal, and still is. They walk into the hills, with a few things to eat, and care for their flocks—ancient rites from many thousands of years ago.

The next day we went on to the lovely albergue of the famous priest, Don Blas, who is well known for his pilgrimages with horses and donkeys around the Camino. He is an unusual priest, goes for his daily biking exercise to keep fit, and has numerous followers in Spain. There we were given a super room built by American donations. The first place where we encountered a few more pilgrims, from Holland, Spain, France, etc.

There was more crossing of enormous ranches with roaming cows and bulls, so I was on guard! Then we headed straight up the mountaintop which was lined with tall, powerful windmills. The town of Salamanca was the next big destination and the end of my friend's stay. I would proceed to Santiago on my own.

We spent the day visiting Salamanca, a very beautiful city which had an illustrious past. Its university rivaled Chartres, Paris. One of its famous students was Saint John of the Cross, the greatest Spanish-Christian mystic. In those centuries, students were flocking to Salamanca from every city and town, seminaries, and convents for its prestigious university, dressed in habits and caps. They wore the white, black habit of the Dominicans, the caps of the Franciscans, the black robes of the clericals, and the white cap of the Carmelites which Juan de Yepes wore.

Juan de Yepes (Saint John of the Cross) was born in 1542 in Fontiveros, near Ávila. He went to a Jesuit college from ages seventeen through twenty-one. He entered the University of Salamanca at twenty-two years old as an artist for a three-year course after taking on the habit of the Carmelite at age twenty-one. He became a priest, met Teresa of Ávila, and then returned to study theology at the University of Salamanca for a year. Five years later, at the request of Teresa of Ávila, he became the confessor at her Convent of the Reincarnation. He died at the age of forty-nine, after being of service in different cities (Granada, Ávila, Segovia, etc.) in convents, priories, writing throughout his life, and being a mentor to many aspirants of the spiritual life, nuns and priests alike.

His book, *Ascent of Mount Carmel*, is a classic in the field of mystical theology. With Saint John of the Cross, we enter into the center of Christian mystical theology, which is how to unite with God.

> In the previous chapter, we said that it is not the will of God that souls should desire to receive anything distinctly, by supernatural means, through visions, locutions, etc. Further, we saw in the same chapter, and deduced from testimonies which were there brought forward from Scriptures, that such communion with God was employed in the Old Law and was lawful; and that not only was it lawful, but God commanded it. And when they used not this opportunity, god reproved them, as is to be seen in Isaias, where God reproves the children of Israel because they desired to go down to Egypt without first enquiring of Him, saying: Ye asked not first at My own mouth what was fitting.... Why, then, in the new law—the law of grace—may it not now be as it was aforetime?
>
> To this it must be replied that the principal reason why in the law of Scripture the enquiries that were made of God were lawful, and why it was fitting that prophets and priests should seek visions and revelations of God, was because at that time faith had no firm foundation, neither was the law of the Gospel established; and thus it was needful that men should enquire of God and that He should speak, whether by words or by visions and revelations or whether by figures and similitudes or by many other ways of expressing His meaning. For all that He answered and spoke and revealed belonged to the mysteries of our faith and things touching it or leading to it. And, since the things of faith are not of man, but come from the mouth of God Himself, God Himself reproved them because they enquired not at His mouth in their affairs, so that He might answer, and might direct their affairs and happenings toward their faith, of which at that time they had no knowledge, because it was not yet founded. But now that the faith is founded in Christ, and, in this era of grace, the law of the Gospel has been made manifest, there is no reason to enquire of Him in that manner, nor for Him to speak or to answer as He did then. For in giving us, as He did, His Son, which is His Word—and he has

no other—He spoke to us all together, once and for all, in this single Word, and He has no occasion to speak further.

And this is the sense of that passage with which Saint Paul begins, when he tries to persuade the Hebrews that they should abandon those first manners and ways of converse with God which are in the law of Moses, and should set their eyes on Christ alone saying: that which God spoke of old in the prophets to our fathers, in sundry ways and diverse manners, He has now, at last, in these days, spoken to us once and for all in the Son. Herein the apostle declares that God has become, as it were, dumb, and has no more to say, since that which he spoke aforetime, in part, to the prophets, He has now spoken altogether in Him, giving us the All, which is His Son.

Wherefore he that would now enquire of God, or seek any vision or revelation, would not only be acting foolishly, but would be committing an offence against God by not setting his eyes altogether upon Christ, and seeking no new thing. And God might answer him after this manner saying: If I have spoken all things to thee in My Word, which is My Son, and I have no other Word, what answer can I now make to thee, or what can I reveal to thee which is greater than this? Set thine eyes on Him alone, for in Him I have spoken and revealed to thee all things, and in Him thou shall find yet more than that which thou askest and desirest. For thou askest locutions and revelations which are the part; but if thou set thine eyes upon Him, thou shall find the whole.*

Spain has a very special, strong Christian aura which cannot be missed. The churches have indescribable treasures reflecting the Christian mysteries through paintings, sculptures, and other sacred works of Christian art. Entering many of the churches and cathedrals such as Salamanca's, one is awakened to the deep mysteries of Christianity. It is alive but highly mysterious, hidden, buried, with an atmosphere of fogginess, of no understanding. Only faith can grasp these mysteries. During Easter week, or Passover, or Christmas, or other sacred holidays, the country becomes alive with these reenactments of deeply Christian mysteries. The churches are full

---

* John of the Cross, *Ascent of Mount Carmel*, pp. 164–165.

of Christ on the cross, Christ's sufferings painted in perfect details—nails, blood, tears. Golgotha is present everywhere. I have not experienced that in other countries in such a deep way. In the East, Russia, the icons are alive, but here the painted sculptures bring in something else. It seems something has incarnated more deeply on this land of Spain than on the other continents—the legend of Parzival and the Grail in Spain.* Why would Saint John of the Cross incarnate here? His name—*of the cross*—is deeply meaningful. Rudolf Steiner mentions that many outstanding individuals are born who carry the etheric or the astral body of Christ, such as Francis of Assisi, Aquinas, Saint Augustine, etc. I believe that Saint John of the Cross and Teresa of Ávila are such individuals.**

Rudolf Steiner's insights into the wounds of Christ on the cross bring much necessary help for meditating on these marvelous, life-like sculptures.

> The secret that was to be revealed to the people through the baptism of John was that the time had now come near when the kingdoms of heaven were to shine right into the ego; they were to approach the ego, the earthly ego.... In ancient times there was something like a disharmony between the way in which the true home of man, the spiritual world, was experienced, and that which, if we wish to describe the old soul nature as "ego" was active in the inner being of man. This human inner self was separated from the spiritual world, and only in exceptional conditions could it be united with it. And when all the might of what was later to become the ego and to live within man, when all the power and the impulses of the ego filled him, for example through initiation, or through remembering experiences of initiation in a former incarnation in a later one—when the power and might of the ego prematurely penetrated into his bodily nature, what happened then? It has always been pointed out that in the pre-Christian era the ego force, too powerful for the human bodily nature, could find its proper place in the body, and broke through what was destined for the ego.

---

* For more on this topic, see Valandro, *Via Podiensis, Path of Power: A Walk from le Puy, France, to San Juan de la Peña, Spain.*

** For more on this topic, see Steiner, *The Principle of Spiritual Economy: In Connection with Questions of Reincarnation: An Aspect of the Spiritual Guidance of Man.*

For this reason those human beings who bear within themselves more of the supersensible world, bearing within themselves in pre-Christian times something of what would in a later age become the ego, such persons split apart their human bodily constitution with this ego force because this force is too strong for the pre-Christian era. This is clearly alluded to, for example in the case of certain individualities during a particular incarnation who possess this ego force in themselves, but this ego can remain within them only because the body is in some ways wounded, or vulnerable, wounded and having a vulnerable spot.... We need only recall the vulnerability of Achilles' heel, or Siegfried, and Oedipus whose bodies split asunder by the force of the ego. These examples of wounds demonstrate to us how only a damaged body is compatible with the greatness of the ego, and the superhuman ego force that is within it....

The passage (Zechariah 12:10) is so formulated that it runs approximately as follows, "A man who unites in himself the full force of egohood, and is confronted with the human body, sees it wounded, pierced through with holes. For the higher ego force which in ancient times could not yet live within the inner self, pierces through, penetrates and makes holes in the body." And because the body is adapted only to the smaller portion and not the whole force of the ego, it is worn down.... In the case of Christ Jesus the full power of the ego entered all at once, and entered with the utmost strength into His bodily being, that this body had to appear not only with a single wound, as was the case with some many individualities who carried a superego, but with five wounds. These were necessary because the Christ-Being, that is, the full ego of man, projected far beyond the bodily form appropriate for those times. It was for this reason that the cross had to be erected on the physical plane of world history, that cross that bore the body of Christ, a human body such as that of man would be if for a moment the whole of man's nature, a large part of which has been lost through the influence of Lucifer and Ahriman, were to live within one single human being....

It is, of course, necessary to reflect and meditate on (these words) for a long time. If anyone should feel it difficult to grasp what has just been said, such a feeling is perfectly justifiable, for it goes without saying that anything that can lead the human soul to a full understanding of the highest most significant event that has ever happened on Earth is bound to be difficult.*

Seeing the blood flow from the wounds on all these sculptures brings another strong image from spiritual science, which is at the heart of my search.

> The people of ancient times who lived in small tribal communities did not love one another any less than people do today. Indeed, they loved one another more, but their love was more like that of a mother for her child. It was more conditioned by nature. Blood itself was attracted to blood, and the human feeling of belonging together was expressed in that blood attraction. Their progress, however, meant that they began to feel sympathy for one another as individuals. In this way, smaller groups, families, and communities developed, which in turn were brought together into larger communities. As individuals, however, human beings became increasingly egoistic and self-seeking. We have then, on the one hand, humankind becoming increasingly self-seeking, and on the other hand, the arrival of the unifying influence of Christ; we have increasing individuation and independence along with the unifying spirit of Christianity. Only when these two streams have fulfilled themselves will it be possible to manifest a condition on the Earth where everyone is independent and at the same time connected with one another by being permeated with what is termed the Christ Spirit.
>
> We must realize that all of this is connected with the blood, that originally something was expressed in the blood that was revealed in human feelings and worked within blood relationships to bring about love of family. Then human feelings became increasingly egoistic. Self-seeking entered more and more into the blood. This is the secret of human evolution, that the blood more and more assumed the character of self-seeking. This blood grown egoistic had to be overcome. The excess egoism in human blood was sacrificed, actually flowed in a mystical yet real way from the wounds of Jesus Christ on the cross. Had this blood not flowed, the self-seeking elements of human blood would have become greater and greater in the course of evolution. The

---

* Steiner, *The Gospel of St. Mark*, pp. 131–132, 134.

Mystery of Golgotha purified the blood of self-seeking. Through this deep love, human blood was saved from its self-seeking.

The cosmic significance of what happened on Golgotha cannot be understood by someone who sees only that a human being hung on a cross and bled because he was pierced by a spear. The deep mystical significance of this process lies in the fact that his blood represented the blood that humankind had to lose for its salvation.[*]

And for the future:

A new tree must grow forth, a tree consisting of the dead wood of the cross; a tree on which the fruit of ancient knowledge will not ripen, but the fruit that can ripen for mankind from the Mystery of Golgotha, which is linked as by a new symbol to the cross on Golgotha. In the place of that scene of world history when the Buddha sat under the Boddhi tree stands the picture of Golgotha where another tree, the tree of the cross, is raised, on which hung the living fruit of the God-man revealing himself, so that from Him may radiate the new knowledge of the fruit of the ever growing tree that will bear fruit for all eternity.[**]

The Rose Cross is a symbol for the Mystery of Golgotha. The cross is the symbol of death, from which roses, the symbol of life, sprout with the blood that flowed from the wounds. If we place this symbol with all its significance before our soul, we will have an unconquerable weapon for use against the power that leads us into temptation. And why? Because Christ, through his death, in the moment when the blood flowed, was united with the astral body of the Earth and brought new life and light. In this astral body he lives as the astral light that shines in the darkness. When we have achieved vision we see into astral light. The rose cross is therefore the symbol for the light that conquers the powers of darkness.[***]

Much more is divulged in these volumes.

---

[*] Steiner, *The Christian Mystery: Early Lectures*, pp. 94–99.
[**] Steiner, *The Gospel of St. Mark*, p. 160.
[***] Steiner, *Esoteric Lessons 1904–1909: From the Esoteric School, Volume One*, p. 375.

Early in the morning, I parted with a friend who headed east to Madrid by train and I walked north of Salamanca through busy roads and traffic. The road was not so pleasant as it followed the busy highway, the worse nightmare, until a few hours later I headed into the soft hills through unmarked paths before getting a bit lost when a family stopped by in their car and put me back on track.

I stopped for lunch in a little deserted bar, and then traveled through the small towns of Aldeseca de Armoria, Calzada de Valduncial, and Cerbo de la Tierra del Vina. I walked through very muddy paths, up and down, then arrived in Villanuiva de Campeon with an inviting pilgrim's sign in Hebrew, Arabic, Spanish, and English. I walked on to San Marcial where I hitched a ride for a few kilometers to Zamora since it was getting dark. I visited the church and a beautiful museum of very large tapestries.

I decided to take the bus to Puebla de Sanabria and skipped 150 kilometers (which were on main roads and not paths) and got ready for the mountains into Galicia and Santiago. I did not want to walk on the main roads with traffic. I love walking but not on heavy traffic roads, it is too dangerous. The bus slowly climbed into the mountains, and we passed a few lonely pilgrims walking on the very busy road.

The town of Sanabria is on top of a mountain, and it had more pilgrims. It is a beautiful village, one by the river, the other up the mountain which is a fortified town dating from the 1220s with a former medieval castle being renovated. Beautiful views overlooking the mountains, with narrow, winding cobblestone streets between the old houses. I walked through the lower village with many renovated stones houses overlooking the great valley below, and the many small stores with local delicacies, herbs, etc.

I started early the next day for the thirty-one kilometers, walking down into the valley, crossing the river on an old bridge and up again into the mountains, up to the Ayto. I walked through the town of Cobreros, then stopped in a lovely village by the Ermita de Guadalupe, and had lunch along with the Portuguese group enjoying the well-renovated village with wonderful architecture. I continued into the mountains, looking more Mediterranean again, climbing steadily up and then down, passing more mountain villages with pastures for cows and sheep.

I stopped for lunch and met the Portuguese gang. It was a relief to be in these deserted villages, away from the busy highways, roads, car traffic, and pollution. Here the path was delightful, but quite strenuous.

More pilgrims are walking here then in the southern route. And this group of seven Portuguese pilgrims keeps crossing my path. They beat me most of the time except in the higher, steeper paths where I always get ahead of them, thanks to my hiking in the Canadian Rockies!

After more wonderful spring paths up and down forests and mountains, along rocky paths, and crossing endless crystal-clear streams, I finally arrived on top of the pass, four to five thousand feet high. We walked on the main road down into the valley reaching Lubian, which is another old renovated village with several albergues for pilgrims. We walked through the old town and chatted with locals who were gardening in their luscious vegetable plots.

I got up early and went on, accompanied by a few deer crossing my path. More mountainous paths, rocky, with beautifully covered granite or white marble stones, and once again Mediterranean landscapes climbing more and more into the mountains with the ever-present, gigantic windmill on top of the pass. In the distance one could see the major highway. I had lunch on top of the pass admiring the scenery, then went down, through more forests, and small meadows where lovely cows were grazing, and masons where renovating old stone houses along the path. We passed more old villages, small farms, and lovely wet meadows with the ever-flowing streams. Thirty or so kilometers later, we arrived in the large modern city of A Gudiña, along a very busy highway with many factories of all kinds.

The next day, I got ready for the very long journey, with cloudy weather, into a very remote part of Spain, again into the mountains, Sierra de Cabrera, forty-one kilometers to the town of Laza. These are soft hills, old mountains, with the view of a lake in the distance. Some villages look abandoned, dilapidated, and extremely poor with a few animals wandering here and there. Past a few villages, going deeper into the mountains with no restaurants, nothing to eat in sight. I took a ride for about ten kilometers since I did not want to be caught in the darkness here.

On top of the mountains I could see faraway villages across the other mountains with views of meadows, gardens, forests, and no one on the path. The scenery was again breathtaking, so walking was a delight as it enfolded kilometer after kilometer. I stopped at a hamlet where a group of older people were chatting and I joined them. They said all their children had to go to the city to work and they only come back on holidays to visit, but in the summer it is busy with people who spend their vacations here.

Finally through more up and down paths, I went down into a rich valley with farms and the village of Laza. The albergue for pilgrims was another three kilometers up from the village which was not so much fun, as I had to go back down to get some food. The deluxe albergue was newly built for the pilgrims, with clean showers and very lovely rooms. I am always thankful for the Spanish people and their welcome of strangers, pilgrims in their small towns and cities. One feels a real Christian atmosphere.

The next day, I started again into the remote regions, climbing, passing more villages, out of the valley. I entered a park-like pine forest of soft mountains, with no human habitation this time. It was arid and rocky. I finally arrived after a few hours of very wild surroundings crossing another plateau, to a lovely, surprising old poor village with signs of welcome in several languages. I was very happy to find a great little old place to eat with several other backpacks at the entrance in this almost abandoned village. The whole Portuguese gang was having lunch and plenty of wine! I joined them without the wine, but great food, and a lively conversation with the owner who had dedicated his life to the pilgrims. Everyone signs a shell, and hangs it up. My name is there along with hundreds of others.

Then I went on through the deserted landscape leaving this very warm, welcoming place, arriving in the town of Vilar de Barrio, in softer hills with more modern villages and farms, a typical Galician landscape. Yellow fields of mustard lined the rocky walled path and there were lovely flowers by the beautiful old homes back in the hills. The villages now had a feature I had never seen before. They had granaries built on wooden stilts and stone constructions by the houses to store food. They were beautifully designed. I went to a lonely church in a local town and admired the sculptures. I loved the painted sculptures, some of them dressed up, looking like mannequins of Mary or saints, which are life size, or they look like wax museum pieces. It is a typical Spanish art which I have never seen in the churches of France.

I finally arrived in the city of Ourense, which is named after the gold found in the local river (*oro* is the Spanish word for gold). I stayed in the very large dormitory rooms for pilgrims in the center of the city. These were the most pilgrims I had seen since I left Seville. This large former Roman city with its typical large avenues was full of older people enjoying the day. Then it was time to climb out of the city, a real climb straight up into the mountains, on a warm day!

The arid planes of the south are gone and Galician mountains, rich forests, and farms are there for the walking pilgrim to enjoy. I loved the city of Cea, with its famous ovens and bread, then I headed for the famous Oseida Monastery, lost in the mountains.

The area was stunning, poor, wooded, with spring flowers, small gardens, old dilapidated housing and miles and miles of lonely paths with no one. After a while, I thought that I was thoroughly lost, but finally arrived and peaked from afar at this enormous, austere, almost windowless cold, lonely fortress of the Oseida Monastery, a real bastion of Catholic Spain. I toured the enormous fortress of faith, and was welcomed by the monks dressed in white and black habits. I decided not to stay in the icy cold, enormous room, and left the monastery. I would have preferred to stay with the monks and have some lively conversation, but no; I am a female, so that's the way it is. Stay in the cold, inhospitable, gargantuan stone room, with no food, no hot tea, nothing!

That's the state of Christianity, established Catholics' Christianity. No wonder there are hardly any souls left in there! Unlike the Greek and Russian Orthodox which are livelier, and more human. How far away are the palaces of the caliphs! What vast distances separates these bastions from the flowery Alhambra!

So I went to the small café facing the large, almost unoccupied bastion and put my backpack on for another few hours of walking.

I climbed steadily through meadows, crossed a stinky farm near Outeiro de Coiras, and finally arrived at Castro Dozon, where I stayed in a hotel.

The next day I was on a lovely rocky path which followed a large stream with amazing old Roman stone bridges. After the town of Silleda, I took public transport to Santiago since I do not enjoy walking along busy roads.

Once in Santiago I took the bus to the old city and went to the first place that looked inviting and not so expensive for a wonderful rest.

I walked to the cathedral and was lucky that we would have a wonderful mass for pilgrims with the large incense burner ceremony. I met some of the other pilgrims who had ended their walks from various places, and I enjoyed the cafés and old sites which I had not seen on my previous visit. Then it was time to take the bus to visit Ávila which had not been on the path.

I stayed in the old city town. I walked around the beautiful fortified medieval city, walking down from the higher ground to reach the Monasterio de la Encarnacion de Carmelitas Descalzas, where Saint Teresa of Ávila had resided. From the monastery one could look up to the higher protected grounds. She chose to live in an unprotected environment, outside the ramparts. She was protected by her life of prayer.

There are lovely gardens, with sculptures and a nice museum. There were a few nuns visiting, and I was allowed to visit the church even though it was closed. The museum was exciting because one could see the old manuscript written by Saint Teresa's hands so many hundreds of years ago. Beautiful, artistic handwriting, staring at me from across the ages. Letters to Saint John of the Cross, letters to many great people of the time, Saint Teresa of Ávila was an outstanding scholar, writer, and humanist way ahead of her time. She started many convents. It was meaningful to see her own writing utensils, books, feathers for writing, and special objects of her private life.

All these roads I walked upon were treaded by these saintly people during all these centuries. It is only now that just a few of us walk these ancient paths; everyone else goes by car and the little town and villages are abandoned. As I walked, alone most of the time, I reminded myself that countless souls had walked searching for knowledge, wisdom, success, home, etc.

Saint John of the Cross met Teresa of Ávila, who had acquired some fame as a saintly woman when he had just finished his studies at the University of Salamanca. Saint John of the Cross became her pupil and her equal, he became interested in her reforms. A lifelong friendship developed and made possible the development of their spiritual work. They were equal in the domain of spiritual attainment. And destiny sometimes has two souls of greatness born within a short distance from each other.

I wish that I could explain, with God's help, the difference between union and rapture, or elevation, or flight of spirit or transportation for they are all one. I mean that these are all different names for the same thing, which, is also called ecstasy. It is much more beneficial than union, its results are much greater, and it has very many other effects as well....

How what is called union takes place, and what it is, I cannot tell. It is explained in *mystical theology*, but I cannot use the proper terms; I cannot understand what *mind* is, or how it differs from *soul*, or *spirit*. They all seem one to me, though the soul sometimes leaps out of itself like a burning fire that has become one whole flame and increases with great force. The flame leaps very high above the fire. Nevertheless it is not a different thing, but the same flame which is in the fire. You Sirs, with your learning will understand this. I cannot be more explicit....

In these raptures, the soul no longer seems to animate the body; its natural heat therefore is felt to diminish and it gradually gets cold, though with a feeling of very great joy and sweetness. Here there is no possibility of resisting, as there is in union, in which we are on our own ground. Against union, resistance is almost always possible though it costs pain and effort. But rapture is, as a rule, irresistible. Before you can be warned by a thought or help yourself in any way, it comes as a quick and violent shock; you see and feel this cloud, or this powerful eagle rising bearing you up on its wings.

You realize, I repeat, and indeed see that you are being carried away you know not where. For although this is delightful, the weakness of our nature makes us afraid at first, and we need a much more determined and courageous spirit than for the previous stage of prayer. Come what may, we must risk everything and leave ourselves in God's hands. We have to go willingly to wherever we are carried, for in fact, we are being born off whether we like it or not....

We have no part in bringing rapture on. Very often there comes an unexpected desire—I do not know what impels it—and with that desire, which permeates the whole soul in a moment, it begins to become so weary that it rises far above itself and above all creation. God then so strips it of everything that, strive though it may, it can find no companion on Earth. Nor, indeed does it wish for one; it would rather die in its solitude; and although God seems at that moment very far from the soul, He sometimes reveals His grandeur to it in the strangest way imaginable. It is a communication made not to comfort the soul, but to show it the reason why it is easy—which is because it is absent from that Good that contains all good things within itself.

In this communication the desire grows, and so does the extreme loneliness in which the soul finds itself, and there comes a distress so subtle and piercing that, placed as it is in this desert, the soul can, I think, say literally with the Royal Prophet: "I watch, and am as a sparrow alone upon the house top.". . . The soul, then, seems to be not in itself but on a house-top or roof, raised above itself and all created things. I think it is far above even its own higher part. . . .

What power the soul has when the Lord raised it to a height from which it looks down on everything and is not enmeshed in it! How ashamed it is of the time when it was so enmeshed! It is indeed amazed at its own blindness, and feels pity for those who are still blind especially if they are men of prayer to whom God is granting consolations. It longs to cry aloud and call their attention to their delusions; and sometimes it actually does so, only to bring down a storm of persecutions on its head. Particularly if the person in question is a woman, it is accused of lacking humility, and of wishing to teach those from whom it should learn. So they condemn it, and not without reason, for they know nothing of the force that impels it. At times it cannot help itself, or refrain from enlightening those whom it loves and wishes to see freed from the prison of this life. . . .

The mind is now used to dwelling upon real truth, that everything else seems to it childish. It laughs to itself at times when it sees serious men—men of prayer and religion—paying great attention to points of honor which it long ago trampled underfoot. They say that prudence and the dignity of their calling requires them to behave in this way, in order that they may be able to do greater good. But the soul knows very well that it would achieve far more in one day by putting the love of God above their dignity than in ten years of prudent care of their authority. So this soul continues to lead a troubled life, and always has its crosses, but it is a life of continuous growth. Those with whom it has most to do keep on thinking that it has reached the summit, but soon they see it raised even higher.*

---

*   Teresa of Ávila, *The Life of Saint Teresa of Ávila By Herself*, pp. 123, 136–137, 139, 145, 151.

Saint Teresa of Ávila came from a wealthy, educated family which had its roots in Judaism.

> One of the most illustrious and influential *conversos* was Teresa of Ávila (1515–1582), the mentor and teacher of Saint John of the Cross and the first woman declared a Doctor of the Church. She was a pioneer of the reform of spirituality in Spain and was especially concerned with women who did not benefit of a good education and were frequently led into unhealthy mystical practices by inept spiritual directors, to receive a proper grounding in religious matters. Hysterical trances, visions, and raptures had nothing to do with holiness, she insisted. Mysticism demanded extreme skill, disciplined concentration, a balanced personality and a cheerful, sensible disposition and must be integrated in a controlled and alert manner with normal life. Like Saint John of the Cross, Teresa was a modernizer and a mystic of genius, yet had she remained within Judaism she would not have had the opportunity to develop this gift, since only men were allowed to practice the Kabbalah. Yet interestingly, her spirituality remained Jewish. In the *Interior Castle* she charts the soul's journey through the seven celestial halls until it reaches God, a scheme which bears a marked resemblance to the Throne Mysticism that flourished in the Jewish world from the first to the twelfth centuries. Teresa was a devout loyal catholic, but she still prayed like a Jew and taught the nuns to do the same.
>
> In Teresa's case, Judaism and Christianity were able to blend fruitfully.*

With Saint Teresa of Ávila and many others, I see that in the future when we understand more about karma and karmic connections, it will be easier to accept the different religions that human beings chose, or are born into.

Teresa was obviously from a very old Jewish family, a wealthy and educated one which had withstood hundreds of years within Judaism until the arrival of Ferdinand and Isabella's army into Granada and when they sent out the Edict of Expulsion in 1499, when the Jews or Muslims had to be baptized, or be deported.

---

* Armstrong, *The Battle for God*, p. 14.

BEYOND THE BLOOD

The important aspect of Teresa's karma, *choice*, leads us to look further than one lifetime. This very gifted woman, as Karen Armstrong mentioned, would have never achieved her destiny had she been born into an Orthodox Jewish family, but her bloodline gave her the amazing possibility which another bloodline would not have. Centuries of devoted rabbinical studies, kabbalah studies, and Judaism within families brought this intensity to her work, which Karen Armstrong mentioned is very Jewish. Before birth, as this being was coming down to the Earth, she *chose* to be born into this Jewish family who had converted to Christianity. It provided her with what she *needed* to accomplish her life's work: her Jewish blood and her devoted life to Christ. In this respect, tolerance can appear. Tolerance towards people's choices. I need to study the Torah for this lifetime, or the Koran, or the Bible, etc. The domain of forcing one or the other on a human being no longer makes any sense when one looks at karma, several lives; this life is only *one*.

We know that musicians cannot make use of a body which does not have a particular structure of the human ear. So a human being coming down into birth has to choose a family which has this ear configuration in order to be a good musician. So human beings will choose such a body to incarnate into, because it provides the correct body, or instrument, for their destiny. If we start thinking along these lines, then perhaps we can appreciate what all these religions have to offer the human being, so that we can get beyond the mindset of "I am right, and you are wrong!"

In all these wonderful scholars which I quote, we can see that the words they choose are the same when they get access to the mountaintop!

Saint Teresa of Ávila, Doctor of the Christian Church, was a Jewess through and through. I love to meditate on such a life nowadays in these times of turmoil.

We will always have human beings being born who are very gifted and who are to bring great gifts to us, and part of our modern life is to recognize them, no matter what instrument they have chosen for their body—Orthodox Jew, Buddhist, Mormon, black, white, man, woman, etc.

This is the real reason for writing this book: to look at some more questions about karma—past, present, and future. And I invite the reader to think about these very important issues in this modern age.

And again and again on this journey I am brought to some of the questions which are most important to me about the blood. What does it mean to have a certain kind of blood? Why are some people holding onto their bloodlines, the purity of the bloodlines, and what happens when they do not?

As we have seen with these three religions, the Christians and the Muslims are not focused on the bloodlines, but on the choice. We choose to say: *I believe in Christ*, or *I believe in one God and Allah is its messenger*. But we do not choose to live within Judaism, we are born into it through the mother.

> The male and female principles cooperate in the propagation of mankind.... Forces that bring about resemblance are inherent in the female principle, while all that reduces it, that creates differences lies with the male principle. When within a folk community, you find a number of faces that resemble each other, you have what derives from the female element; but certain differences are to be seen in the faces enabling you to distinguish the separate individuals, and this results in the male influence. If the influence of the female element alone prevailed you would not be able to tell the individual persons apart; and if only the influence of the male element were in evidence you could never recognize a group of people as belonging to the same stock.... The force in women carries over from generation to generation the factor which otherwise expresses itself in the continuous blood stream.*

As we see, in Judaism there is no choice in the matter. The blood stays within the blood, rather than mixing with every single race in the globe as the Muslims have done more so than the Christians. Here we have more to do with a brotherhood of man, brotherhood, not a bloodline.

What happens to the bloodline when it becomes concentrated, and what happens when it mixes? What does it mean for the future of mankind? I have touched upon this subject on this journey.**

---

*   Steiner, *The Gospel of St. John and Its Relation to the Other Gospels*, p. 189.

** For more on this topic, see Steiner, *The Gospel of St. John and Its Relation to the Other Gospels*.

We saw in the case of Saint Teresa of Ávila that she chose this bloodline, she was a genius in her insight and her business ability which allowed her to begin many monasteries for her young nuns.

These are questions of far-reaching consequences which I meditate on when I travel in all these fabulous places.

The world becomes this incredible landscape of human beings choosing this life, that one, born there, traveled here, married there, changing beliefs, lifestyles, modern man, woman.

Here are more insights from Rudolf Steiner:

> At the beginning of the process of Earth evolution human beings were not so unified. Human souls had come to Earth from a wide variety of different places and honestly did not have much love for one another at first. They only learned love for one another because they were born into bodies that were related to one another by blood.... Back then people were dependent upon blood relationships to build society with one another....
>
> Now ahrimanic and luciferic forces are trying to lead human beings astray by making them build their society solely on the foundations of blood ties, even though the time is now ripe for us all to recognize that all human beings of body, soul, and spirit, that stand before us have come down from the spiritual world, come down out of that spiritual world, having already lived through pre-earthly life, seeking the blood into which they intend to incarnate. And a feeling for this spiritual society must be continually developed....
>
> In pre-Christian times, the idea of reincarnation existed solely as a feeling, for a true knowledge of reincarnation existed prior to the year 1860 BC. After 1860 BC, it was known only as an instinctive feeling throughout Egypt, the near East, and the Greco-Roman areas. Now the time has come, however, when the understanding of a human being as a spiritual being that undergoes a development between death and a new birth will grow into a living feeling, a living knowledge—the time in which one must live fully into an imagination of the more-than-earthly significance of the human soul. For without this imagination the culture of the Earth will die. You cannot take a practical action toward developing into the future unless you are able to have

some perspective on the spiritual significance of the fact that every human being is a spiritual being....

We must learn not only to say: "As parents, we take joy in the birth of a new child; we take joy in the new member of our family that this newborn child is"—rather we must also learn to say: "No, we are only the means by which a spiritual individual, waiting to come into existence on Earth, finds the opportunity to do so!" The aristocratic notions of heirs and family lines, for example, must be seen as antiquated thoughts, and in their place must be brought the recognition of and feeling for the whole of humankind. Aristocrats to this day have the idea that it is their most important task to ensure the continued existence of their race, that the physical human being must have a descendent of the same name. This feeling must be turned on its head, and we must recognize that it is important to have descendents for the benefit of all of humanity, so that certain individuals who want to come down here on Earth may have a body into which they can incarnate.*

However much you prove to me what was wrong with my father, my mother, my grandfather, my grandmother, and so on, I know that as well as what I carry in my hereditary impulses I have a soul which has nothing to do with these hereditary impulses because in the time in which the hereditary, the previous generation was here, this soul was in the spiritual world between death and my present birth. I carry these forces equally in me and we will see whether I will not defeat this "hereditary affliction."**

There is no need to explain that the modern psychological, medical, and educational view is certainly the opposite of the spiritual science view. It is our freedom to go beyond what we have received from the blood! And our freedom to determine our own future.

Here are more stunning, revolutionizing insights into this realm of "soul wanderings" if the one mentioned above is not enough!

---

*   Steiner, *What is Necessary in These Urgent Times*, pp. 150–152.
**   Steiner, *Unifying Humanity Spiritually: Through the Christ Impulse*, p. 132.

BEYOND THE BLOOD

We cannot fully understand modern humankind if we take account only of blood relationships and genetic descent, and fail to consider what souls bring with them from past incarnations—which connects to form a whole with outward heredity, outward upbringing....

The original inhabitants of America, the Native American tribes, had remarkable pantheistic sensibilities, and worshipped the Great Spirit who infuses all things. Their souls were filled with an intense faith in this all pervading Great Spirit.... The majority of western and central Europeana, reaching eastward too—not all of them but a large portion—originate in terms of physical inheritance from medieval ancestors but are inhabited by souls that previously lived in Native American tribes. However paradoxical this sounds, it is true for the majority of Europeans....

On the other hand, the souls who became acquainted with Christianity's first developments, its earliest period, have tended to incarnate in modern times, in the present day specifically, in more eastern regions, in Asia.... If we study the Japanese through spiritual science we find that many of their reincarnated souls formerly lived in Europe during the migration period....

But people in Asia living before and after the Mystery of Golgotha were endowed with a creative power of much greater vitality—albeit also more nebulous—than you find in the Orient today. These people living in Asia then, at least a large number of them, are today incarnated amongst the American population and make up a large portion of it....

We could however speak of "soul wanderings" in another sense, in that souls who populate one part of the globe in one life will, in their next incarnation, choose a quite different geographical location. Thus we find that souls who incarnated in southern lands in the early Christian centuries are now living in a new incarnation in central and eastern Europe, living farther north, but that in the regions too, at the same time, live souls who once inhabited the bodies of Native Americans. In Asia we find souls who lived in Europe during the migration period, and also before and after this. And in America are souls who lived in Asia at the time of the Mystery of Golgotha.*

---

*   Steiner, *Universal Spirituality and Human Physicality: Bridging the Divide*, pp. 111–115.

This brings a new level of understanding, fosters new realms of development, and revolutionizes the way we think in all realms of research. For a small example: Why are the Germans fascinated with the Native Americans? If one looks at certain facts worldwide, one will discover that Rudolf Steiner could be right!

Now to get back to Saint John of the Cross. I will mention one more passage. Saint John of the Cross quotes the Old Testament, he could have been a rabbi or a Sufi, and perhaps he was, in other lifetimes!

> Solomon, being well acquainted both with the evil and with the benefit of which we are speaking, said: "I knew that there was nothing better for man than to rejoice and to do good in his life." By this he meant that, in everything that happens to us, howsoever adverse it be, we should rejoice rather than be disturbed, so that we may not lose a blessing which is greater than any kind of prosperity—namely—tranquility and peace of mind in all things, which, whether they bring adversity or prosperity, we must bear in the same manner.*

Totally enmeshed in the life of Saint John and Saint Teresa of Ávila, I left these sacred grounds for Madrid. I reached Toledo by train and found the youth hostel in the beautiful castle overlooking the muddy Tagus River encircling the southern half and my room faced the stunning view of the impressive Fortress Toledo built on a rocky mountain. The city was designed by the Moors and under its rule for almost four hundred years, and maintains its ancient character.

Toledo has a forbidding aspect. The painting by El Greco has captured this with its dark indigo setting, and bright spring green colors. Here is where Saint John of the Cross was imprisoned after being kidnapped in 1577. He was thirty-five years old, and escaped to the convent of the Carmelites in Toledo in 1578. From his cell, I am sure he created and committed to memory some of the most amazing writings in Christianity. He continued to work as prior, and various other spiritual advisor offices in Granada, Cordova, Segovia, and other cities. He died in 1591.

---

* John of the Cross, *Ascent of Mount Carmel*, p. 225.

When we study his treatises... *Ascent to Mt. Carmel* and *The Dark Night*—we have the impression of a master-mind that has scaled the heights of mystical science and from their summit looks down upon and dominates the plain below and the paths leading upward.... The most obscure phenomena he appears to illumine with one lightning flash of understanding, as though the explanation of them were perfectly natural and easy. His solutions of difficult problems are not timid, questioning, and loaded with exceptions, but clear, definite and virile like the man who proposes them....

How much of all this Saint John of the Cross owed to his studies of scholastic philosophy in the University of Salamanca, it is difficult to say.... Nothing but natural genius could impart the vigor and the clarity which enhance all Saint John of the Cross' arguments and nothing but his own deep and varied experience could have made him what he may well be termed—the greatest psychologist in the history of mysticism....

If Saint John of the Cross is able to climb the greatest heights of mysticism and remain upon them without stumbling or dizziness it is because his feet are invariably well shod with the truths of dogmatic theology. The great mysteries—those of the Trinity, the Creation, the Incarnation, and the Redemption—and such dogmas as those concerning Grace, the gifts of the Spirit, the theological virtues, etc., were to him guide-posts for those who attempted to scale, and to lead others to scale, the symbolic mount of sanctity.*

I spent my time walking around the maze of tiny cobblestone pathways, tiny roads fit more for donkeys than cars. I enjoyed the mixture of people walking around: Muslims, Jews, and Christians. I walked in the many famous churches, synagogues, sapharic museums, and art museums. Toledo is a fabulous city steeped with history where I wouldn't mind spending a month.

To end my stay in this amazing city, I choose some sacred words from Saint John of the Cross. Here he talks about the union with God which can never be experienced through the intellect but through other means. The

---

* John of the Cross, *Ascent of Mount Carmel* (from the introduction by E. Allison Peers), pp. xxxvi–xxxvii.

passages selected reflect this man of great learning and a colossal knowledge of the scriptures. The style is difficult to read for modern man, but it's worth the effort.

> Just so all that the imagination can imagine and the understanding can receive and understand in this life is not, nor can it be, a proximate means of union with God. For, if we speak of natural things, since understanding can understand naught save that which is contained within, and comes under the category of, forms and imaginings of things that are received through the bodily sense, the which things, we have said, cannot serve as means, it can make no use of natural intelligence. And if, we speak of the supernatural (in so far as is possible in this life of our ordinary faculties), the understanding in its bodily prison has no preparation or capacity for receiving the clear knowledge of God; for such knowledge belongs not to this state, and we must either die or remain without receiving it. Wherefore Moses, when he entreated God for this clear knowledge, was told by God that he would be unable to see Him, in these words: "No man shall see Me and remain alive." Wherefore Saint John says: "No man hath seen God at any time, neither aught that is like to Him." And Saint Paul says, with Isaias: "Eye had not seen Him, nor hath ear heard Him, neither hath it entered into the heart of man." And it is for this reason that, as is said in the Acts of the Apostles, Moses, in the bush, durst not consider for as long as God was present; for he knew that his understanding could make no consideration that was fitting concerning God, corresponding to the sense which he had of God's presence. And of Elias, our father, it is said that he covered his face on the Mount in the presence of God—an action signifying the blinding of his understanding, which he wrought there, daring not to lay so base a hand upon that which was so high, and seeing clearly that whatsoever he might consider or understand with any precision would be very far from God and completely unlike Him....
>
> And thus it is that contemplation, whereby the understanding has the loftiest knowledge of God, is called mystical theology, which signifies secret wisdom of God; for it is secret even to the understanding that receives it. For that reason Saint Dionysius calls it ray of darkness. Of this the prophet Baruch says: "There is none that knoweth the way,

nor any that can think its paths." It is clear, then, that the understanding must be blind to all the paths that are open to it in order that it may be united with God. Aristotle says that, even as are the eyes of the bat with regard to the Sun, which is total darkness to it, even so is our understanding to that which is greater light in God, which is total darkness to us. And he says further that, the loftier and clearer are the things of God in themselves, the more completely unknown and obscure are they to us. This likewise the apostle affirms, saying: "The lofty things of God are the least known unto men."*

After this great city, I had to see one more: Segovia, at 3,300 feet tall. It is an hour bus ride northwest of Madrid crossing the Guadarrama mountain range.

Segovia is a city as stunning as Toledo, but without the forboding atmosphere. I walked by the Roman Aqueduct standing almost one hundred feet into the air and then up the many stairs to the famed hill city. One cannot count the many Romanesque churches dating from the twelfth to thirteenth centuries. The Alcázar fortress looked like a fairytale castle from which one wanted to see a queen on horseback and knights emerge as if by magic. Memorable and fascinating were the old apothecary rooms inside the castle which looked like an alchemical laboratory with all the old paraphernalia for research into transforming base material into gold, like in the Prague castles. I thought I might see an old alchemist appear through the door fully occupied in his alchemical research. The guards would not let me take pictures. Why? Who knows?

I had lunch in a small restaurant, walked past former synagogues, walked around the whole city, drank coffee observing the many tourists, climbed up onto towers, and walked down the ramparts into the forest below. I followed the beautiful stream, and climbed up some more to see the famous monasteries facing the city from below, one of which is the Carmelite Convent where Saint John of the Cross is buried. Many famous writers, poets have walked these paths at different times, and centuries. This added to the very peaceful atmosphere.

---

* John of the Cross, *Ascent of Mount Carmel*, pp. 91–92.

A view of the cathedral in Segovia

Here are some more words from Saint John of the Cross. This place seemed to be a very appropriate place for him to rest.

> And it is this that Saint John desired to explain when he said ... He gave power to be sons of God—that is, to be transformed in God—only to those who are born, not of blood—that is, not of natural constitution and temperament—neither of the will of the flesh—that is, of the free will of natural capacity and ability—still less of the will of man.... He gave power to none of these to become sons of God, but only to those that are born of God—that is, to those who, being born again through grace, and dying first of all to everything that is of the old man, are raised above themselves to the supernatural, and receive from God this rebirth and adoption, which transcends all that can be imagined....
>
> In order that both these things may be better understood, let us make a comparison. A ray of sunlight is striking a window. If the window is in any way stained or misty, the Sun's ray will be unable to illumine it and transform it into its own light, totally, as it would if it were clean of all these things, and pure; but it will illumine it to a lesser degree, in proportion as it is less free from those mists and stains; and will do so to a greater degree, in proportion as it is cleaner

Inside the Segovia cathedral

from them, and this will not be because of the Sun's ray, but because of itself; so much so that, it if be wholly pure and clean, the ray of sunlight will transform it and illumine it in such wise that it will itself seem to be a ray and will give the same light as the ray. Although in reality the window has a nature distinct from that of the ray itself, however much it may resemble it, yet we may say that that window is a ray of the Sun, or is light by participation. And the soul is like the window, whereupon is ever beating (or to express it better, wherein is ever dwelling) this Divine Light of the Being of God according to nature, which we have described.*

With this great Spirit, I end my walk in Spain.

---

* Ibid., pp. 77–78.

Part III

Morocco

FIVE MONTHS LATER

I wanted to experience a deeply religious country which was not fundamentalist like Saudi Arabia, which loved and welcomed tourists, so one bright day I flew to Morocco from Paris. And it made sense after my crossing of Spain on foot to travel throughout Morocco. The world's tourists have been flocking to Morocco for many years. The English, Australians, French, Spaniards, Americans, etc., own homes in Morocco and enjoy their peaceful, calm way of life which is ruled by the laws of the Koran, but not imposed, or forced on the population. Their warmth and hospitality is still part of the culture. Crossing from Spain into Morocco is a step into the fabulous world of the past. But the modern world has arrived and the future of this nation depends on how the people will adopt and change the religion–modern life dilemma, especially concerning the youth. I hope that the reader will experience this enchanting side of Morocco! A traditional Muslim country!

I arrived in the city of Marrakesh, southern Morocco, walking into the old city through ancient doors while a porter carried our belongings on a large cart. I decided to join a French adventure group of five to drive and camp out across the mountainous regions of southern Morocco, the famous snow-covered mountains of the Moyen Atlas and Anti Atlas. We would drive through the great valley Ounida, and old Kasbat Ben Adou, we will visit Imdahane, Beni Melal, Midelt, Er Rachidia, Erfoud, Dades, the great Gorges Todra, Tineghir, the Palmeraie (with thousands of date palm trees), Merzouga, Ouarzazate, Tazerakat, Taroudannt, the great dunes, and the land of the Tuareg (also known as "people of the veil" or the "blue people"), by Algeria's border with its great Sahara Desert which stretches thousands of miles all the way to Tunisia, Libya, then on to the coast, the city of Agadir, and Essaouira, the lovely quaint port on the way back to the north and to Marrakesh. I would not have to worry about various problems such as transportation infrastructure. And we would camp out most of the time with our own local cook, driver, and guide. The name of the places will not be clearly mentioned as most of the cities did not have a sign post, and I could not read the Arabic signs fast enough. The guide and driver did not really function with a map! And our planned itinerary was often changed which was unnerving, since I love to look at maps! So basically, we did not know where we were going most of the time! For the duration of the trip it was something like this: *We are somewhere in Morocco, in the mountains, and I will figure out where we were when I get home!*

We had a few days in Marrakesh. The enormous square is always full at night with people from all parts of Morocco, farther south or east, bringing their wares—music, food stalls, all sorts of clothes, carpets, spices, musicians, snake charmers, desert men, etc. I love the markets in the Arab world. I had lived in Rabat for three years in my youth (from six to nine years old) and always have had a love for the food and its people.

The women were dressed in their beautiful djellabahs and scarves in bright, happy colors. The place where we stayed was an old renovated typical ryad (a large traditional home) of North Africa, with enclosed gardens and water fountains, and pillows to sit on as we sipped mint tea. It was a difficult task to find the place as it is located in the medina's tortuous, very narrow streets. We enjoyed the evening and the morning breakfasts, and running around all day in the very busy city, modern and old. Then it was time to leave for our journey. The van came fully equipped with the three guides and the five of us.

We drove east into the mountainous terrain for a few hours. There were no trees, just arid, beige, rocky scenery with winding roads. Then we

A snake charmer in the square

stopped for our first wonderful meal of tagine, couscous, and vegetables and meat cooked on coals—delicious. We all ate together and then went for a walk in a small village to visit a well-known waterfall plummeting from several hundred feet. Caves could be seen in the red cliffs. Shops lined the busy Moroccan tourist attraction. There were flat beds with pillows for tea, and benches for the tagine. Monkeys were frolicking in the local trees and bushes. Later we arrived by a lake and put up our tents, in a place that was not so appetizing and clean! And then went inside the large food tent and had a feast. We all retired to rock-hard bedding, listening to the local drunks fighting in the distance. This was no deluxe trip!

Our driver did his prayers every day. His forehead had the mark of his devotion, a small mark of darker skin where his forehead touches the sacred ground five times a day. He was a very sweet family man and an excellent driver.

> One day, the Devil was strolling nude in the streets of Baghdad. Junaid Baghdadi... came across the Devil and said, "Look at you. Aren't you ashamed?"

"Ashamed of what?"

"Look at all these people around you, the whole city of Baghdad."

"You call them people. They are nothing to me. I can play with them like a man juggling balls. What does bother me is the two people in that mosque over there. I cannot even get close to them. If I got anywhere near that mosque their breath would burn me like fire."

Junaid Baghdadi was curious, so he went to the mosque. There were only two people sitting there, reciting *La illahe illallah*, "There is no God but God." Their faces were covered. One of them lifted the cloth in front of his face and smiled. He was a beautiful young man, very young.... He turned and smiled at the great Sufi sheikh. "Oh Junaid, do you believe whatever the Devil tells you?"*

Morning came with breakfast, Arab style, on the ground covered by a vinyl tablecloth. Then we went to a local city to visit gardens and old ruins. Back on the road for a drive and a wonderful picnic in an oasis where some of us had a nap. Women came by selling their pomegranates on the donkey's large rug pockets. It was sheep shearing season, so all trucks came by full of sheep ready for markets.

We drove on that day through a large forest of cedar of Lebanon trees, heading for the higher famous Atlas Mountains.

We had another sumptuous feast after a wonderful walk up in the woods and forested hills. Dry river beds and a shepherd encampment were nearby.

The next day, the guide took us to a shepherd seasonal settlement a few hours walk away. I enjoyed the morning early walk, among the shepherds and their families living in this very poor rocky mountain setting taking care of their animals. During the winter they go back to their village, and the children stay with the relatives in the lower villages to attend school. The sheep had beautiful double horns and rested happily in the arid, rocky meadows while the dogs watched. Women on donkeys were bringing water in large plastic jugs to their camps, and we walked on to the elder who invited all of us for tea. I spent some time with the ladies cooking in their tent kitchen while they prepared homemade bread and more tea. I felt honored

---

* Ozak, *Love is the Wine: Talks of a Sufi Master in America*, p. 79.

A women and her donkeys transporting water

by their hospitality and they wanted some makeup, lipstick, which I did not have. Then we went on farther to meet the van.

There were more beautiful falls cut into ravines, narrow gorges. This time he chose a desert to camp out. It was late, so we put up our tent and saw some ruins of former caravanserais. Cold morning came with our breakfast and we headed again on the small road, this time through the passes in the Moyen Atlas Mountains where I bought some local honey. The place was full of rosemary plants, but still very arid; there were barely any trees after the cedar forest. More rocky mountains, dry river beds and carved ravines, and a small oasis came into view because there was water. The oasis had plantations of dates and various other fruits and vegetables tended by women and men. We could see the beautiful old village, earth colored and architecturally part of the geography, blending into the earth. I had never seen such lush gardens going for miles in between these high, arid plateaus. There were many abandoned caravanserais going back to the earth. We set up our picnic once again inside the oasis under the shade of the date trees and had our usual feast of tomatoes, cucumbers, onions, bread, tuna, and tea with sweets.

One of our picnics in the shade

We headed more towards the desert by the Algerian border, where there was not much but sand and some brushes. We camped by the dunes and had another wonderful meal under the tent prepared by our talented cook. Evening came, and we were fast asleep, but we had to wake up early to go for a walk in the dunes to catch the sunrise. So we all walked in early morning darkness to witness the sunrise. We climbed tall dune after tall dune, with our heads wrapped in shawls against the wind and sand. I walked barefooted even though it was cold. Then we all waited for that miracle to happen—sunlight—and headed for our hard-earned breakfast. From the distance we could see the village far away, and in the east a few kilometers ahead, was the border with Algeria. Intrepid as I am, I would have loved to hire myself a few camels, and take off into the desert! Algeria is not friendly to the former French colonists, now they prefer the Russians and the Chinese! After the French left, many Algerians went to Russian universities for their diplomas, and now many Chinese are buying up stores and homes in small towns across Algeria. I was told this by an Algerian fellow traveler.

The next day we went to a beautiful, spacious, well-decorated caravanserai and stayed there overnight. It was a comfortable change from sleeping in the tent. At night the local tribal people, the Tuareg, with their indigo turbans, played music for us which we danced to. More wonderful food under the tents, and a lovely tended garden in the middle of the caravanserai.

We headed once more into the desert, but this time it had the color of deep indigo as well as orange, but no trees. More caravanserais with camels used for tourists. It was definitely the world of the Arabs, far from the West.

Two of us decided to go for a camel ride early in the afternoon, just for fun, and the two beasts and their owner came by and picked us up. The camel nonchalantly let us climb onto its back, and there we were for a couple of hours walking in the orange desert sand!

But as the owner of the caravanserai said, now he goes into the desert with his four-wheel-drive vehicles or small, recreational four wheelers which we heard as we were walking in the dunes. Noisy, dirty, but modern!

We watched the sunset and went back to the tents.

The next day brought us to a famous mosque and its lovely mosaic gardens full of date palm trees and other flowers and pools which we visited. The regal mullah walked by as if in a cool breeze from his morning recitations.

> The prophets and saints are like mirrors; just as the mirror shows us the dirt on our faces, so do holy men and women show us our faults.
> An old saying goes, "Clean your face instead of blaming the mirror." But most of us would rather break the mirror than give up our bad habits.
> Ibrahim Ad'ham's teachings opened the eyes of his listeners. They also hold for us today, and for all believers until the Day of Resurrection.*

We walked to the old city, inside very small paths to a cavernous store full of silver everything, for shopping!

We headed more towards inland villages with their lively markets, men drinking tea in the street, and women and children going about their business. Our cook went shopping and we tagged along. Very rich in fruits and vegetables, people are not starving here. Women were buying kitchen wares made of plastic or aluminum. All the women wore the classic manteau

---

* Ibid., p. 23.

and headscarf. Once in a while I could see tribal women wearing colorful dresses, with children in their arms; they were very poor compared to the city dwellers. They live far away in the mountains; we had visited them in the shepherds camp.

We now headed west towards the ocean, going through many rich oases full of date palm trees. The horizon was full of the oases which shows how large they are amidst old, crumbling, beautiful villages which have been abandoned for the more modern buildings sprouting everywhere.

Moroccan life is peaceful, conservative Muslim, family oriented, artistic, and agricultural.

We drove to a canyon, surrounded by very tall cliffs at the foot of which was a hotel which we stayed in. By this time, everyone's back was aching from the tough sleeping conditions under the tent. I was used to it, but some were not!

We walked into the canyon by the river and enjoyed the merchants selling their Berber rugs and scarves to the tourists.

The next day, we drove to an oasis for a walk inside the gardens. The gardens were all well taken care of, with small plots for greens, salad, onions, mint, etc. On the perimeter were pomegranate trees, and, of course, fig trees. There were no figs though, it was too late in the season!

Then we drove through sumptuous, formidable mountains forms—looking like fingers up in the air—dotted with former palaces, caravanserais, and estates owned by former rulers of southern Morocco which were immensely powerful and rich from trades with the south. This was once a well-traveled road used by the rich merchants bringing in gold from Africa—the famous gold trade which some historians say was the reason why this region, all the way up to Spain, Andalusia, became so rich, with sumptuous palaces, cities, and libraries fueled by the gold trade coming from Sudan, Ghana, etc.

Then we had a homestay at some of the local homes. A bed on the floor, a door, and a bath and shower outside. We had our supper in their common room down below. Sharing their homes brought them some needed funds as this area was extremely poor. Numerous children were playing in the dirty streets, many of them with green and blue eyes.

Modern buildings next to an old, crumbling village

Then more driving through old ancient cities, with the approaching snowy Atlas Mountains in the distance. The beautiful old cities from a former age were abandoned by the locals. They had built their own homes close by with modern conveniences: washing machines, bathrooms, hot water, etc. Many of the people living in these areas had worked in Europe and saved their money, and came back for their retirement after doing jobs which Europeans would not do themselves. So when they came back, their wives wanted the same comfort they had in Europe!

The region is so picturesque and it is astounding to see these very large kasbahs and imagine who lived there in their richer days. We walked through these ancient fortress villages made of red bricks towering high on top of hills, and then their gardens, and large oases, and watched the local old women sitting on donkeys, covering their faces, carrying bundles of veggies, greens. Women were bent over gathering some herbs in their fields. The oases are well watered through ducts and canal systems and the olive trees still had their harvest.

It was a very rural, quiet country with abundance, beauty, and serenity. The fields had just been watered and were quite muddy but the plants were happy. There was green everywhere, and when one is surrounded by arid, stony ground, this is paradise. But it is still very poor, and many of the women must bear the weight of poverty, where they must carry water to their homes, have a lack of sanitary luxury, lack of bathrooms, and primal cooking arrangements.

Life seems quite peaceful, away from the midwestern style of agriculture. Here it is manual labor and a few donkeys, so the ground has not been polluted. Farther north where the land is owned by wealthier people—aristocracy, foreigners—the western type of farms such as milking and beef do exist, but here the land does not allow such bad practices as is seen in the North American prairies. Here Moroccans are still tied to their land in a healthy way.

The work of the Moroccan Sufi Ahmad Ibn Idris in the nineteenth century could have helped bring some prosperity.

> (Ahmad Ibn Idris') solution to the disintegration of life in the peripheral Ottoman provinces was to educate people and make them better Muslims. He traveled extensively in North Africa and the Yemen, addressing the people in their own dialect, teaching them how to perform the ritual of communal prayer, and trying to shame them out of immoral practices. This was a grassroots movement. Ibn Idris had no time for Wahhabi methods. (Wahhabism is Saudi Arabia's dominant faith.) In his view, education, not force, was the key. Killing people in the name of religion was obviously wrong. In Algeria, Ahmad al-Tigrani, in Medina, Muhammad ibn Abd al-Karim Sameen, and in Libya, Muhammad ibn Ali al-Sanusi all took their faith directly to the people, bypassing the *ulema*. This was a populist reform; they attacked the religious establishment which they considered to be elitist and out of touch, and unlike Abd al-Wahhab, were not interested in doctrinal purity. Taking people back to the basic cult and rituals and persuading them to live morally would cure the ills of society more effectively than complicated *fiqh*.*

Here are a few words from Ibn Idris' master, Al-Ghazâlî.

---

* Armstrong, *The Battle for God*, pp. 44–45.

This world is like a play or the marketplace for the one who spends his journeys in the other world. It is the place where one stores nourishment for the journey: said more clearly, man acquires here, through his earthly feelings, a certain knowledge of God's works and, through them, of God himself, whose vision will form his future happiness. And it is precisely for this knowledge that man's spirit has come down to this world of water and mud (clay). As long as his feelings accompany him, it is said that he is "of this world"; when that abandons him, and only his essential attributes remain, they say that he has gone "to the other world."

Meanwhile, man in this world needs two things: first, protection and nourishment of his soul; second, the care and food for his body. The proper food for the soul, as we have seen previously, is the knowledge and love of God, and being absorbed in love for other things is ruinous for the soul. The body is, let us say, the mount for the soul and perishes while the soul lives. The soul must take care of the body, the same as the pilgrim must take care of his camel; but if the pilgrim spends all his time taking nourishment and decorating his body, the caravan will leave him behind and he will perish in the desert.*

The Abbasids did not control the western provinces of the Islamic world, which pursued a separate political history. In Morocco, a descendant of Hassan, the grandson of the Prophet, established his own rule among the Berbers with his capital in Fes, which has remained ever since the heart of North African Islam....

In North Africa itself, after the assertion of Fatimid rule, tribal battles continued between those who paid allegiance to the Fatimid caliphate and those who remained faithful to the "Abbasids." In the eleventh century the Sanhaja Berbers, who had spread Islam from Mauritania to the mouth of the Senegal rivers, united to form the al-Murabitun (the Almoravids) with their capital in Marrakesh and united much of North Africa and Spain. They were succeeded by a disciple of the famous Persian theologian and Sufi Al-Ghazâlî. This puritanical movement spread as far east as Tripolitania and survived into the thirteenth century....

---

*   Al-Gazzali, *La Alquimia de la Felicidad*, pp. 57–58 (tr. M-L. Valandro).

BEYOND THE BLOOD

In the sixteenth century, North Africa fell into the hands of the Ottomans, except for Morocco, which has been ruled since the sixteenth century by the *sharīfs*, or descendants of the Prophet, who founded the 'Alawid dynasty.*

All the villages had small mosques with old men sitting by the steps chatting. I never noticed the very loud speakers to announce prayers, perhaps because we were on the road. The call to prayer was never as blatant as it is in Iran where it is blasted everywhere. Here it is more within the rhythm of the people. They go to pray as it is part of their lives, and not something that is imposed or forced. They pray willingly.

For a change in our schedule, we went to the local hammam and then had a massage, with men and women separated. After we were renewed, we stepped into the essential oils pharmacy. It was a delight since I love essential oils and grow many of my own herbs. These were wonderful and, of course, we all bought quite a few mixtures.

They have started an industry from the oil of the tiny nut that grows rampant in Morocco, and they sell the oil—argan oil—for a great price to beauty product manufacturers in Europe.

> One day Ibrahim Ad'ham tried to enter a public bath. The bath attendant stopped him and asked for the entrance fee. He hung his head and admitted he had no money.
>
> The attendant replied, "If you have no money, you can't enter the bath."
>
> Ibrahim Ad'ham cried out and sank to the ground, weeping bitterly. Passersby stopped to comfort him. Someone offered him money so he could get into the public bath.
>
> Ibrahim Ad'ham said: "I'm not weeping because I was refused entrance to the bath. When the bath attendant demanded an admission fee I was reminded of something which led me to weep. If I am not allowed to enter the bath in this world unless I pay the fee, what hope do I have of being allowed to enter Paradise? What will happen to me when they demand, 'What good deeds have you brought? What have

---

* Nasr, *Islam: Religion, History, and Civilization*, pp. 126, 128.

you done worthy of being let into Paradise?' Just as I was kept out of the bath because I could not pay, I will surely be kept out of Paradise if I have no good deeds to my credit. That is why I weep and moan."

As they reflected on their own lives and deeds, all his listeners began to cry with Ibrahim Ad'ham.[*]

After being in the wilderness, the usual tourist shopping!

We made another visit to an ancient city on top of a plateau dominating a large wide river bed called Kashbah Ben Hadou. The views were spectacular and the old living quarters were still lived in. I would have liked to spend a night in this old town full of history. But we went back to our tents, this was a no frill camping trip which this French travel agency is famous for!

I could imagine life here five hundred years ago; it does not seem to change. We went by little garden plots neatly arranged with piles of manure on top which had been carried on a donkey's back, as they had done hundreds of years ago. It is a life from another century. People struggle, and thanks to changes made by the government, electricity is available, roads are built reaching all the far corners of Morocco, and life is very traditional.

After the visit to this beautiful, intact, ancient town we drove to a carpet shop which was part of a cooperative (Association-Iklane). Women work together, and bring their carpets to the cooperative to be sold. It seems to work. The cooperative provides the material for free, then they can pay for the material when they deliver the woven carpets. Of course I bought two of them. It is good for the women; they must make a living. And I truly enjoy these colorful woven masterpieces.

It is delightful to be in a country where the artistic has not been rooted out of their souls. The men and women here are still in contact with creativity. We have lost that in the West, so to plunge oneself in a lifestyle that still makes sense is healing. I toured the whole cooperative compound and was invited to come back and stay in the village in order to gather herbs with the local ladies, and do some dyeing of material. Since I plan on coming back for six weeks to complete this project, I will most definitely visit these very warm, generous people. Of course we all drank plenty of mint tea.

---

[*] Ozak, *Love is the Wine: Talks of a Sufi Master in America*, p. 22.

More shopping in a local market for our supper. Camping in the middle of nowhere for another sumptuous feast and a walk into the hills.

The next day we stopped in a larger town, with a great market. I stopped in a teahouse, and watched the women shop for a few hours. I watched life unfold during a busy weekend, drinking milk coffee while enjoying a group of very old toothless men—dressed all in white—playing some music on stringed instruments that seemed older than they were. Women were buying clothes, dressed in lovely bright djellabahs and shawls.

Then we arrived in Agadir, a city on the coast, and our driver invited us at his home to meet his four children and his wife for a wonderful supper. We felt privileged to be his guests. I went upstairs in his spacious apartment and met his very warm-hearted wife, who did not come down to eat with us. But his children loved their father and showed it.

Then we were off on another long drive along the Atlantic Coast after visiting another oil of argan factory.

We arrived very late at Essaouira, an old famous fishing port. We loved the spacious, old, artistic, grand hotel. It was heaven after days in the tent.

We spent the next day visiting the fisherman's wharf, the markets, the old, sinuous, very busy streets, the many wonderful restaurants, the cafés on terraces overlooking the ocean, the artists with their beautiful paintings (of course I had to have a couple), the woodwork, jewelry, copperwear, and a most amazing used bookstore. I could tell that many amazing people had passed by here over centuries reading ancient texts on all possible subjects. Regretfully, I could not indulge in one of my favorite pastimes: books. In the evening under an enormous tent outside, we were treated to a most wonderful Sufi concert coming from Fes. A few hundred people were in attendance, all of Essaouira, including the whole of the wealthy—the highly educated class who spoke several languages, classical dancers, politicians, and guards. A change from life in the villages of the Atlas Mountains. The town hosts one of the biggest music festivals each year, which I will attend one year when my schedule is not so hectic.

More visits to beautiful traditional gardens, pools with fish, wild plants and flowers, mosques, old cities, old palaces with pools encircled by doors, windows, arabesque tiles, carved wooden doors, sacred arches, scalloped

A father and son working at the tannery

tiles—in turquoise, sky blue, and brown—with designs showing fragments of broken spirit descending into frozen matter, Allah's name on tiles in countless beautiful forms, holy men praying on their sacred rugs and facing Mecca, white-clothed bearded men of the Koran walking smoothly by, etc.

Then we were back to Marrakesh. We went to the tanners' quarters in the old city. It was mesmerizing and shocking to see this heavy, dirty, dangerous work. The sheep and goat skins are driven by the truckload to this area of the souk, and the men start working. It is an elaborate process involving acid baths in large vats to eat away at the skin, clean them, soften them. The men wear rubber boots and gloves, and some are barefoot. They look worn out, like slaves. It is the kind of work that you are born into due to lack of other opportunities, and it is all done by hand. In small hidden corners the men scrub, peel, rub the skin. Then the skins are ready for dyeing—another long process. Then it is sold and we buy the beautiful purses, shoes, etc. I thought differently about my leather bag after seeing this gruesome work.

Then we were back at our beautiful, homey, old ryad, sitting on pillows, looking at the flowing fountain, and sharing our memories. We still had a couple of days to visit the old city, the modern city—gardens, parks, dinner on terraces observing the end of the day, tea, and shopping for gifts, purses, djellabahs, tunics, shawls, necklaces, and stones.

The next day before dawn, with a full Moon shining on the ancient city, we walked through the narrow lanes and ancient door, said good-bye to the still-sleeping city, and took a taxi to the airport for my next journey: Tunisia.

Who Says Words With My Mouth?
All day I think about it, then at night I say it.
Where did I come from, and what am I supposed to be doing?
I have no idea.
My soul is from elsewhere, I'm sure of that,
and I intend to end up there.

This drunkenness began in some other tavern.
When I get back around to that place,
I'll be completely sober. Meanwhile,
I'm like a bird from another continent, sitting in this aviary.
The day is coming when I fly off,
but who is it now in my ear who hears my voice?
Who says words with my mouth?

Who looks out with my eyes? What is the soul?
I cannot stop asking.
If I could taste one sip of an answer,
I could break out of this prison for drunks.
I did not come here of my own accord, and I can't leave that way.
Whoever brought me here will have to take me home.

This poetry. I never know what I'm going to say.
I don't plan it.
When I'm outside the saying of it,
I get very quiet and rarely speak at all.[*]

I left Morocco, but with the intention of returning for a month to finish this long project. I chose Fes, to experience the famous medina, and this ancient spiritual center of Islam. So more to come!

---

[*] Rumi, in Washington (ed.), *Persian Poets*, p. 91.

Part IV

Tunisia ✱ Djerba Island ✱ Sahara Desert

After a crazy journey flying from Casablanca through Paris, with cancelled flights and delays, I finally arrived in the city of Tunis. Instead of flying through Italy, we flew through London!

The flight from Casablanca was on a Moroccan airline and families of Orthodox Jews were flying back to Paris. One of the older bearded members stood in the alley of the plane doing his prayer rituals while we were all trying to get to our seats. But he would not budge. Perhaps I should have knelt down in the alley praying to Mary Mother of God with my rosary, and my neighbor, with his prayer rug facing Mecca doing his prayer to Allah! The family of *man* at prayer! I just had to remind myself that the ancient prayers which this rabbi was reciting were holy words, words of power which were sent into the atmosphere. We need all the help we can get!

The taxi ride left me at the door of the small budget hotel, by the wall of the old city. It was pleasant and business-like. I slept well and got up for my breakfast. I chatted with a new arrival from Saudi Arabia, a midwife who was coming for vacation. She worked to make money there, but did not enjoy the confinement of living in such a stern Muslim country. Even though she was a Muslim, she could not go shopping or anywhere unless she was accompanied by a man. She said she was used to it. No jobs in Tunisia for a midwife! She owned her own house on the seashore.

BEYOND THE BLOOD

My trip in Tunisia is not planned. I will travel alone, by local transport wherever I can depending on bus schedules and my interest, and tour the entire country up to the Algerian border. One part of the journey will include meeting another group of French people on the island of Djerba, by the Libyan border, for a camel expedition into the great Sahara Desert.

I walked around as I usually do, going anywhere, first getting lost in the very old, large city of Tunis, the place of my birth which my parents left when I was six months old. I never visited Tunis.

There weren't many tourists because Tunisia was the spark for the Arab Spring of discontentment throughout the Middle East. Their uprising had happened in the spring, this was the fall and one of the reasons for my being here: to acknowledge people's need for freedom, and the man who lost his life doing it. And to finally get acquainted with the land of my birth.

It was raining. I walked into my very favorite place: the covered souks. It was superb, old, winding, and rich, rivaling any of the souks I have visited—Tehran, Delhi, Istanbul, Marrakesh, Cairo, Jerusalem, etc. I was invited by carpet sellers to visit the rooftops and see the city with minarets everywhere, as well as old carpets owned by famous sheikhs and caliphs. I marveled at the gold, silver, clothes, and shoes. I had tea, of course, and food, and was never bothered despite being a woman traveling alone. When people asked what I was doing, I said I was born here and wanted to see the land of my birth. They all smiled and welcomed me!

I stopped at the beautiful mosque dating from the seventh century, but could not go inside; I had to be happy with the very large empty courtyard. Not so full of colors like the Persian mosques, more the style of the Egyptian mosques in their red brick and whitewashed colors. The women were busy shopping, some in chador, some with scarves, but not the beautiful colors of Morocco. Here we had blacks and greys—dreary hues reminiscent of Tehran—to fit with the approaching winter weather. I did miss those colors.

I visited the old cathedral standing lonely on the main avenue—Avenue Habib Bourguiba—still lined with army tanks, personnel, and barbed wire from the Arab Spring.

The next day I took the metro to Bizerte to visit towns on the Mediterranean shore. Summer palaces, villas, a lovely whitewashed village painted with turquoise doors and windows, looking more like Greece than the Arab world. I spent much time in a traditional old house belonging to the local bey, or king, and wandered in the many gardens and elegant quarters of this small palatial home still kept up in its original state by its owner. It had a superb library.

The mountainous village was breathtaking, and the local merchants were complaining that there was no business. I walked up and down the hilly village and had coffee at a beautiful, deluxe tea restaurant overlooking the sea. Then I went on to famous Carthage again on the local train with its antique city ruins. A taxi offered to take me to several ancient sites set amidst large summer villas, home to the wealthy Tunisians. I walked to the ruins and saw kids going to school, coming from school on the train, all very lively teens.

The ruins are extensive, it is a well-maintained park on a hill overlooking the sea, the Byrsa Hill, from another time.

After getting a feeling for Tunis, I went to the museum which was mostly closed, and then to a wonderful array of French bookstores. In the evening I walked on the "Champs-Élysées" of Tunis along with hundreds of Tunisians enjoying the cafés and shopping; the Arab Spring was gone. A wonderful older man, a teacher, gave me directions to various places and welcomed me to his country. Tunis is a very sophisticated city. Sitting at the local cafés, looking at the men and women enjoying the evening, it was almost Italian—a loud, fun, familial, audacious, cosmopolitan, intellectual, artistic, smoky scene. Not what I would encounter in Tehran or Karachi. Restaurants were full of young women in their Muslim attire, or not, enjoying their evening out. This city is more European since Italy is just up the road. A short boat ride to the north is Sardenia, and a shorter one to the northeast is Sicily.

I had lunch in a very big restaurant on the upper floor with large rooms everywhere, and it was so full that the waiter had a hard time finding me a small table. So there I enjoyed the evening watching the world go by eating some sumptuous food. I watched the age-old ritual of male-female courtship which in the last few years has taken on a different look. Many women were putting on the veil, not by force but by choice—a real puzzle to me when I first noticed the sophistication of this new veil. The women put it on with such care; it stretches on the head, gets pinned on everywhere so that it is smooth, and only one perfect fold is allowed here and there—*meticulous*. So this young lady was sitting next to her man, and she was very young, but sure of her looks and sexuality. The fellow was more of a brute kind of man, but he seemed totally charmed by this veiled beauty; he behaved like a gentleman. The veil was subduing his strong masculinity.

This veil has nothing to do with Islam, or with religiousness. To me it is pure sexual tool, and I was delighted to read one of the latest books published in Tunis by a wonderful, famous, awakened, witty, older woman named Hélé Béji. In her book, *Islam Pride: Derrière le voile*, she writes about this new phenomenon which parallels my own thinking on the matter.

> I grew up in a feminist–Bourguiba–avant-garde environment at the heart of a liberal Muslim family, engaged in its fight against colonialism for an ideal towards a republic. It was not unusual to hear at our house free-thinkers kidding the bigots, women with strong personalities making fun of the devouts, and young ladies being courageous against the rules, feeling their oats. In my own circles, most of the young or old women did not wear the veil.... Our circles included many Jewish and Christian friends who grew up as part of our intimate family, without ever questioning where they came from, that would have been of extremely bad taste....
>
> Recently, during a family wake where, as usual, tradition brings families back together, and in an effusion of chaotic sighs, I met once again one of my cousins, who had been educated as freely as I had been, but she was dressed up like a nun. My blood froze. But I managed to control myself. I said nothing. But within me the cacophony of a great turmoil started. *What!?* Must I shut my mouth? Must I hide what I think? Must I stop thinking even? Perhaps not have the right to think either? I, who could speak freely throughout my whole life without any restraint or censure! Is everything I learned at school of absolutely no use? Now, women who were set free by Bourguiba, this visionary, defending our rights, revolutionary for the equality of the sexes, who tore them away from fear, who broke the timeless chains of long centuries of obeying the masters, now I see them in the streets passing me by, austere, in their poor convent attire. "Oh you, women, alas, pale as church candles..." (Baudelaire) I gasp, my heart aches....

I think about all these women that I knew who had discovered not only their head, but their shoulders, their arms, their beautiful breasts, their legs....

And now, facing these new ashen faces, enveloped in a tight cloth, facing this burly costume reminding me of a funeral tomb song, of mute complaints, where have you gone women, women from ages ago? Is there anything left of your indomitable nature? Have you rebellious souls breathed out your last regrets and resigned yourselves? Don't you have anything to say? Can't you even react? Are you discouraged? Desperate? Have all your rights gone to the grave?...

How did they get there? What are they thinking about? How do they reason? First, we count one, two, three... they are too many.... Then we don't count them anymore, they pass by too quickly: they are every where. "Where do they come from?" says one. "What a waste!" says the next. A third: "What a pity!" And while we are asking ourselves the *whys*, getting angry, worked up, the western media world takes to a phobia, hallucination, etc. And the new Iconic figure, wrapped up in its piety, too numerous to count, and silent, walks forward with softened and unstoppable steps. And we stare, mesmerized! Have we ever seen in history, freed slaves begging for their masters' chains? Have we ever seen the blacks begging for the whites' whip? Have we ever seen the Jews go back to the wandering Jews? Have we ever seen the colonized beg for the return of the colonialists? Have we ever seen the freed prisoner stepping backwards towards the open door of his former prison?

We are all stunned. No more words, no more ideas, no more voice. Who could have predicted that one day a woman, knowing the price that her ancestors paid for their freedom, would go back willingly to wallow in slavery, to veil herself without being forced, and go back on the narrow corridor of life and death designed for her by men? We shudder! It is thoroughly absurd! Who would have thought? Who can accept it? Our sense for what is right is failing us. Women born under sky of freedom, for unknown motives, are going back down into the valley of darkness.

Here are my internal debates, thoughts, the abyss in which I fall whenever my path crosses these new Carmelites.... The veil is not a disease of Islam as such, it is a symptom of the disease of the present world....

> Tired to think, making up my mind to act, I decided to do something unthinkable. I wanted to pull her veil off her head, just a little bit, as a joke. And instinctively I did! My cousin jumped up, fearful of my daring act, with a nervous laugh, half serious, half prudish: "Stop it, it's shameful!" she told me, as if I had done the craziest thing which not only attacked her unsoiled state, but had also compromised my salvation. I must say that I had been malicious, I was tempting the devil.*

This book is a meticulous analysis of the debate about whether *to veil* or *not to veil*. It is a must-read for everyone, especially now. It touches upon very deep truths which go beyond Muslims, into the realm of relationship between man and woman—universal themes. Hélé Béji is often on television and talk shows; she is a very visible member of Tunisian society in Tunis as well as throughout Europe.

I myself lived with the veil from 1983 to 1984 when I went back to Iran for my three-year-old son to meet his father. I *had* to. Putting on this scarf every day was a total inconvenience but it was nothing like what the young women are arming themselves with now. In Iran, because the women are forced to adopt such an outfit, the women transgress. Rebellious, they try to get away with as much as they can. They put it on, but with reluctance—hair shows, the scarf falls off, and the women just throw it back on. It is imposed on them; they have no choice, otherwise they are hassled by the religious authorities—young kids from the village who love to tell others what to do, especially women! But here the phenomena, as Hélé Béji explains, is the opposite: there is no military policing. They have chosen to apply this tight bandage on their heads where absolutely no hair is showing, *nothing*.

It is like a punishment for the male race for their desire. The mothers are raising sons which they think cannot help themselves sexually, weaklings who have no say about their sexual urges. Not a good way for a young man to start his adult life! In Iran, women just laugh at it and men too. They just accept the inevitable that the country has been taken over by a religious government and they must abide and find ways to live with it. Here in many circles, the men don't want their wives covered. They say,

---

* Béji, *Islam Pride: Derrière le Voile*, pp. 13, 14, 16, 28 (tr. M-L. Valandro).

"She did it, it is her choice, I have nothing to do with it!" It is a way to regain their power over the men: *I am hidden, you can't have me, unless you pay.* She becomes an object all over again. In a way, she becomes an object through the back door. Her sister in the West is plastered on walls naked, breasts hanging out, as the dish: *Come and have me.* Here she is hidden, but nevertheless, a dish, an object.

Veil, no veil—we will have this battle for a long time.

This is another one of my reasons for traveling in these fabulous countries where women are taking control of their lives, even though it seems they are going backwards, they are acting. Here in Tunisia, and elsewhere, they are covering themselves, sick of being seen naked all over the media. They are saying: *I am keeping my body to myself, too bad, you can't see it, you can't enjoy it, no one can, <u>not even me</u>!*

There is an enormous revolution throughout the Muslim world, and I am happy to be an observing member in these very important times, from one continent to the other. Nothing and no one is spared!

I did have a lovely meal, and I sat observing all the rituals of courting, courting with the veil between a young woman and her beau. The eyes become extremely important! And so the silent language of desire!

> Whatever you taste of love, in whatever manner, in whatever degree—it is a tiny part of Divine Love. Love between men and women is also part of that Divine Love. But sometimes the beloved becomes a curtain between love and realization of true love. One day that curtain will lift and then the real Beloved, the real goal will appear in all Divine Glory.
>
> What is important is to have this feeling of love in your heart in whatever form and shape. It is also important that you be loved. It is easier to love than to be the beloved. If you have been in love you will certainly reach the Beloved one day.
>
> The gifts of God often come to you from the hands of other human beings, through God's servants. And so, Divine Love also expresses itself between human beings. The sheikhs are the pourers of the wine and the dervish is the glass. Love is the wine. By the hand of the wine

pourer, the glass—the dervish—is filled. This is the short way. Love could be offered to one by other hands. This is the short way.*

The Beloved is everything, the lover is only a veil…
Love desires that His word manifest itself.**

It was time for me to tour the country and head south. I went to the busy bus station which was mobbed because this was the biggest holiday all over the Muslim world, when everyone sacrifices a sheep throughout the Islamic world. Everyone was traveling, especially young women going home from school and university, young families, working men, etc. I finally got on a bus towards the city of Kerouan, famous for its mosques and its illustrious past. We drove south through farmland, not so arid as Morocco had been.

This was the land which had been colonized by the French, including some of my relatives who came from Burgundy. My grandfather worked on farms here in these surroundings but was not a wealthy owner, just supervising and working. My mother was born here as well. Her parents went back to Burgundy when she was small. My grandmother married my grandfather because the man she was in love with sailed away for a year, and she thought he would not come back. But he did come back, and she was already married—tragic. She had fourteen children, my mother being the eldest, and she died at age fifty-seven, of exhaustion. My great-aunts also lived here; one was "directrice" of an all-girls school in Tunis. My mother's family went back and forth from Tunisia, France, Belgium, and Argentina. They were involved in the tapestry industry, and lost everything during World War I.

So it was interesting for me to travel through this new country, and imagine how they lived. It was not an easy life! And after living with a passport stamped with "Born in Tunis," it was nice to see the place. I had been putting up with countless interrogations at airports, borders, etc., about being born in a faraway place which I did not even know! "Born in Tunis, eh? Interesting…" The airport authorities looked as if I were the devil: *How dare*

---

*   Ozak, *Love is the Wine: Talks of a Sufi Master in America*, p. 8.
** Rumi (*Mathnavi I, 30*), in Vitray-Meyerovitch, *Rûmî and Sufism*, p. 102.

I be born in a Muslim country! What was I doing? And so on. Still to this day I have to put up with such interrogations.

In Kerouan I stopped at a local cheap hotel which was empty. I was being watched by the curious eyes of the local men sitting at the café wondering what I was doing here. I walked everywhere—souks, old buildings—and went in for my favorite: the woman's hammam just down the road from the hotel. There I was given a couple of plastic buckets, stripped down to my underwear like everyone else, and started to be scrubbed by a local masseuse. She almost scorched my skin; I was squeaky clean. I had a chat with several ladies of all ages, helped wash children's hair, and was invited to a young woman's home. This is where the news spread. The women were surprised to see a westerner but were warm, inviting, and generous.

The ancient mosque had lovely designs carved within the small beige bricks. It was a spacious mosque, very simple, austere in design, almost as old as Islam they say.

It was prayer time, quiet, noon.

The duty that seems most important for the Muslim's daily life and which has shaped the Islamic world most strongly is the second pillar, ritual prayer, *salāt* (in Persian and Turkish, *namāz*). It has been said that "between faith and unbelief lies the giving up of ritual prayers." The *salāt* is performed five times in twenty-four hours: the hour before sunrise, noon, afternoon, after sunset, and nightfall. The Koran does not mention the number of obligatory prayers, but five prayers seem to have been customary in Muhammad's lifetime. The number was fixed, as the hadīth literature tells us, when Muhammad was pleading with God about the duties of the faithful during his nocturnal journey to heaven. The Koran emphasizes the nightly prayer, *tahajjud*, which, however, was never made a binding duty for believers, but was and still is practiced among the pious and in particular among the mystics.

Every prayer begins with the *niyya*, the formulation of the intention, for instance, to perform the evening prayer with its three cycle or *rak'a*. During one *rak'a* the praying person stands upright, uttering the words *Allāhu akbar*, "God is greater [than anything else]" and the Fātiha. Then one bends from the hips, straightens one's posture, prostrates, sits, and then performs another prostration. In the first two *rak'a*, another chapter or some verses from the Koran are also recited. Each prayer consists of a prescribed number of *rak'a* (daybreak prayer, two; noon, four; afternoon, four; sunset, three; and night prayer, four). The various movements and positions are accompanied by special formulae. At the prayer's end one utters the profession of faith while sitting, as well as a formula of blessings on the Prophet and the believers.

The *salāt* can be extended by reciting long parts of the Koran in the first two *rak'a*; many people also add a lengthy meditation while using the rosary, *tasbīh*, repeating religious formulas or Divine names and invocations. Besides the five required *salāt* there are many recommended *salāts* that can also be performed throughout the day.

When prayer time begins, the muezzin calls from the minaret of the mosque or, in some areas, from its roof. The call to prayer, *adhān*, consists of the profession of faith and some additional short phrases and is sung in long cadences.... Once the *adhān* is over, the believer undertakes the ablution. He or she can perform the prayer alone in any clean place or else in the mosque with the community; in both cases absolute ritual purity is the first condition. After each minor pollution (caused by solid, liquid, or gaseous matters leaving the lower part of the body, as well as sleep or fainting), the minor ablution, *wudū'*, is required: the face, part of the head, the arms to the elbows, the feet to the ankles have to be washed in running water that has not been touched by anyone. The details of the ablutions, elaborated exactly in the course of time, have to be observed minutely, from the intaking of the water in the nostrils to the movement of the fingers when cleansing the ears; each movement should be accompanied by a specific prayer formula. If none of the above-mentioned pollutions occurred between two prayers, one need not perform the ablution. After major pollutions such as sex, menstruation, and childbirth, a full bath, *ghusl*, is required in which no place in the whole body, including the hair, can remain dry. Only then may the prayer be performed and the Koran touched and recited. It is a pious custom to perform *ghusl* before the communal prayer on Friday noon, even though no major pollution exists. In case water cannot be found, one may perform the ablution with sand (*tayammum*)....

The belief in the purifying power of ritual prayer is intense; the Prophet compared it to a stream of water that washes off sins five times a day. The performance of the prayer at the prescribed time constitutes ideally a means of educating Muslims to punctuality, cleanliness, and, since there is no ranking in the mosque, equal participation in the life of the community. Prayer can also lead to ecstatic experiences, and when one observes a praying Muslim who is oblivious to everything around him and seems to have drawn himself, as it were, out of this world to stand humbly before the Lord, one realizes best whence Islam derives its vital strength.*

After the visit to the quiet, peaceful mosque, I stopped by an unusual site. Inside a building, a camel in colorful attire was turning a wheel to bring water from a well—the way it was done hundreds and hundreds of years ago!

The next day, I headed for another old city, Gabes, and had a great lunch among the busy travelers. Then finally I headed to the island of Djerba, another famous tourist place for Europe and Tunisia, which looked more like Greece with beautiful whitewashed homes by the sea. I found a lovely hotel, full of decorated tiles, painted tile scenes which I love, a tiled turquoise pool, restaurant, and wonderful spacious room. Now the holiday was in full bloom. Ready for butchering the sheep. No restaurants were open; it was deserted. A few French tourists were also looking for food and having a hard time finding it; all the shops were closed!

But the locals were having a great feast inside the closed walls.

Passing by the waterfront, the Djerba marina, I saw beautiful large sailing vessels, looking like pirate ships. I bought a ticket for a day outing on the water. We would sail to another little island and cook a tribal picnic on the beach with music, while pretending we had been taken by sea pirates. A few French tourists were there, as well as a very sad Libyan family—a mom, dad, and their five children who had run away from Libya and were living here in Djerba waiting for things to get better. The local Djerbans were talking about the influx of these families who had lost their homes, families, and friends. Many had also gone into Algeria.

Our rambunctious group sailed away, along with the captain and lots of young men dressed as pirates, monkeying around the ship and climbing ropes. About thirty of us sailed away, watching the sailors jumping from

---

*   Schimmel, *Islam: An Introduction*, pp. 39–41.

Waiting for our "pirate ship" to set sail

rope to rope. We sailed by a beautiful group of large pink flamingos walking delicately, elegantly along the shore. Then we went to the shore while the pirates prepared a feast, playing old musical instruments and drums. We swam in the sea, feasted on the copious amount of couscous, lamb, vegetables, tea, and sweets, and then were ready to sail back to Djerba marina.

I visited the old forts dating from way back, and went to another little part of the island to see a beautiful small designer inn that had been renovated by some wealthy people. I invited myself to tea in these lovely sumptuous surroundings and headed back to the city. But a tailor caught my attention. He was sewing a beautiful traditional outfit and said he could make it for me in one hour for a very good price. I said yes and watched him sew a stunning tribal local outfit.

I had a lovely evening on the terrace of my little hotel watching the fantastic colors of the sunset with the mosques, minarets in the skyline.

It was time to change hotels and meet the French group for our Sahara adventure. We met in a luxury hotel and had a great supper. There were ten of us traveling. We would go with the four-wheel-drive SUVs into the desert to meet the camel herders and their beasts for our journey into the big sands!

In the morning we packed our gear, settled into three SUVs filled with baggage, and headed inland. I saw numerous trucks carrying very high stacks of sheepskins; the holiday had been successful. We stopped at a beautiful home carved out of the cliffs, just like thousands of years ago.

We saw their wonderful artistic home with the sheep guts hanging to dry in the sunshine. Nothing gets wasted here, unlike in the West.

Beautiful signs of the fish were painted on the entrance door for good luck. Here it was very dry, just small brushes here and there, desert life, no trees, just mountains, rocks, and people trying to make a living in these amazing dwellings inside the cliffs. We drove farther into the desert, with lone camels crossing here and there or trying to eat something in the vast expansive space with endless blue sky and beige desert. We stopped for lunch at the last town and feasted on more couscous, then headed straight for the desert—no road. Just like that—*no road*. I sat in the front, of course, never wanting to miss *any* of the action, and the driver made it his job to scare me, driving like hell through these no-road territories. We were not far from Syria. The French guys laughed like hell at my fear. That is what I deserved for sitting up front. Then we finally met our camel herders, their nine beasts, and an enormous amount of stuff!

I was very happy to leave the SUV, safe and sound.

The cars left and there we were with our guide who had transformed himself into a man of the desert, new outfit and all, with baggy pants, a long tunic, and a turban on his head. Transformed from a western guide to an Arab sheikh!

But we had a job to do; this was no luxurious trip. First of all, we had to put up two enormous tents, which was no easy matter. I was in the all-girls tent. Then, of course, we had to gather wood, from who knows where, so that we could eat our supper, cooked under the stars. So we got to work.

The group was fun and full of very experienced French travelers, so I was in good company—one couple, six women, and two men.

We had our first meal in the desert. The stars were out, the fire was crackling, and the camel herders sang melodious tunes from the age of the patriarchs in their guttural language. Then we all went to bed after washing with half a cup of water; water was rationed.

The cook making a large flat bread

In the morning everyone was up early, packing the big tents once more, and getting ready for breakfast. The cook had prepared a wonderful galette, a large flat bread—not large but extra, extra large—which he had cooked in the sand on a hot bed of charcoal. He proceeded to take the hot, fuming bread from under the sand, and the herders were busy packing and loading their beasts. Then all of a sudden the long caravan was up and going straight into nowhere, by the star, led by the eldest herder who was seventy-five years old, a tall Arab over six feet five, and three more younger herders and cooks in their fifties. In the distance I had seen the eldest herder doing his prayers, alone, by the dunes. I sat on *my* camel and was ready for the day.

I had not realized that this was not a sit-down-on-the-camel expedition, but a walking one, and I had specifically chosen this trek because it had said "Camel Expedition." Anyway, I argued with the guide and said they needed to get me my own camel so I could sit on it, and not walk. I had done too much walking this year (seven hundred miles in Spain just six months prior to this) and I did not want to walk anymore. I had *no intention* to walk; I needed a rest. And besides, I wanted to *sit on a camel!*

The author sitting on her camel

So they reluctantly let me have my way! The others did not mind; they wanted to walk in the desert.

Besides, I had no walking shoes, just some fashionable ankle boots for riding. The French Parisians made fun of my accoutrements. I must be versatile, since I am traveling across the country. So they said I looked like I was ready for the metro in Paris. We laughed.

I thoroughly enjoyed watching these large beasts with their huge eyes and lazy way—*looking* lazy, that is. They were carrying tents, food, water, blankets, fuel, vegetables, flour, everything. Part of the trip was to live with these beasts of burden and their caretakers, to experience life in the desert. The desert had an enormous impact on the three faiths—Judaism, Christianity, and Islam! One might say they were *born* in the desert. So I just could not write about these religions without *being in the desert*.

The men walked by the one-humped camels, or *dromedaries*, chatting, laughing, and singing in unison. I was almost lulled to sleep. Going with the movement, barefoot, heads wrapped up for the sunshine, the gang walked all day, and the scenery became truly desert—no more brushes of any kind, just sand. We were surviving only because of the camels and their herders.

We stopped for a quick lunch and had a short nap in the shade. The camels rested and then it was time to walk some more after a small episode of screaming and shouting because one of the camels had a sore on his mouth. The old herder dealt with the gruesome affair. Since I lived on a farm for years I was used to animal incidents. Then we were off for another afternoon in the warm sunshine, climbing small dunes, and I sat on my camel. Night came, and our usual supper and sitting around the fire listening to the tambourines and small musical instruments, while some of us danced to the wild tunes under the stars. And time for bed. Some of the people wanted to sleep in the desert under the stars. I declined; the tent was fine for me.

I was becoming in tune to the noise of the desert: silence.

Here is a poem from Hakim Sanai, one of my favorite Persian poets.

The Time Needed
Years are needed before the Sun working on
a Yemeni rock can make a bloodstone.

Months must pass before cotton seed
can provide a seamless shroud.

Days go by before a handful of wool
becomes a halter rope.

Decades it takes a child
to change into a poet.

And civilizations fall and are ploughed under
to grow a garden on the ruins,
the true mystic.[*]

Days went by with the same cycle: pick up the wood for the fire, cook the bread in the sunlight, unload, pack up, eat lunch. The same gestures and relentless sunshine in the day. It was November, winter, and cold at night.

---

[*] Sanai, in Barks (trans.) and Khan, *The Hand of Poetry: Five Mystic Poets of Persia*, p. 29.

Our desert caravan

We all began to enjoy the serenity of desert life, but many of us were starting to be hungry. I did not have to walk, so I was not expending enormous amounts of energy, but the rest of the gang was. We only ate bread, rotten tomatoes, cucumbers, some broth with a couple of potatoes, bread for breakfast with some butter and jam, and that was *it*—no meat, no dates, no almonds, no tea, no sweets, no fruit. This lasted the whole trip. People were starting to complain, but in the middle of nowhere there was nothing we could do, so we went on. The guide had kept most of the money given to him by the French agency to buy food and starved all of us. We did starve; I just let it all go, and thought that I was getting a real experience of living in the desert on nothing except bread, water, and some rotten tomatoes.

This is the way it was thousands of years ago; one was lucky to have water. Anyway, if I had known I would have been glad to buy gorgeous dates, great almonds and walnuts, sweets, some cheese, etc. But we all got our desert caravan experience. The French agency, Nouvelles Frontieres, is not joking when they say to their customers: "We give you the real experience!" Indeed they did! *But we had to pay to starve!*

BEYOND THE BLOOD

Here is a taste of the desert, told by Ibn Battuta, a famous historian, pilgrim, and storyteller who was born in Tangiers in 1325. He left his family at age twenty-two, and did not come back until 1354. His pilgrimages brought him to Mecca several times, and the Persian Steppes, Bukhara, Indus, eastern and western Africa, etc.

He made his living as a judge of religious matters, and during his twenty-five years of travels he acquired wives, children, and riches, but never stopped. He went on to the next stage, leaving wives and belongings behind, and just continued on his journeys and adventures. His tales are not accepted as truth by some historians, but nevertheless he is a master storyteller. If you like wild adventures from centuries past, these tales are remarkable.

> Water, or the lack of it, was the travelers' constant concern, especially as south of Maan on the Syrian border the caravan entered a desert of which it was said, "Whoever enters is lost, whoever exits is born (again)." Farther south, four days were spent at Tabuk making preparations to cross a fearsome wilderness to al-Ula. Large reservoirs made of buffalo skins were filled to water the camels, and smaller water containers and bags made of goat skins were also filled; the ordinary pilgrim was charged a fixed sum for this service. The great caravan pressed on in haste from Tabuk, traveling night and day to pass through the so-called valley of hell and avoid the fate of many who in some years had perished from the hot, venomous wind called the *samun*. Ibn Battuta reports a rock inscription recording one occasion when the wind had dried every water source and the cost of a mouthful of the liquid reached one thousand dinars, the last surviving vendor and buyer both perishing in the act of exchange.[*]

After about a week we reached an oasis. The camels finally had a long, long drink, and we looked forward to more of the same!

We baked more bread and gathered more wood, and some people were now wanting to sit on the other camels and join me. There was plenty of room, and I walked to exercise a bit.

---

[*] Waines, *The Odyssey of Ibn Battuta: Uncommon Tales of a Medieval Adventurer*, p. 34.

TUNISIA ✣ DJERBA ISLAND ✣ SAHARA DESERT

The eldest camel herder

By now we were all experts at packing up, unloading, and walking in the dunes which were growing in size. They were becoming mountains, up and down, and I had to hold on in order not to fall. People would disappear behind dunes and had to be careful not to get lost in these immense sandy mountains. At around 3:00 PM the old herder would stop the caravan and do his prayers, always facing Mecca, while the beasts were having a small rest and we watched, some wishing they had such religious fervor.

I am a creature of the Northern Hemisphere. Surround me with ice, snow, a pair of skis, some food, and water, and I can go on for miles without feeling the worse for wear. But here this is not my element. Sitting on the camel is all I can do in this heat; it takes my energy away. The herders just walk on, eating basically nothing. They are used to it, but we are not. They do not have one bit of fat on their sinuous, tough, strong, lean bodies. Their faces are deeply streaked, lined by the sunlight, wind, and age. Their physiques are beautifully sculpted by the wind, harsh sand, stones, and scarcity of everything. They are happy with little, and I am ashamed of being from the West. We consume most of the Earth's treasures. These people live in small homes made of mud and sticks. They burn twigs to cook, use water parsimoniously, and waste absolutely *nothing*. They have only a few clothes. Yet they are happy, content, and in harmony with desert life. We live to waste and create wars so that we can waste some more. Shameful behavior, when I see here how these people respect their surroundings and use almost nothing to live.

Here are some words from Mohamed Talbi, a wonderful scholar, professor of medieval Islamic history, and one of the original founders of the University of Tunis.

> God knew what the angels did not know: God knew that he could trust man. Of course, we are surrounded by chaos, and without doubt, much blood will still flow. There is still much imbalance, and for our alive, and rebellious conscience this becomes more than ever intolerable to accept. For example, when a nation consumes half the resources of the Earth for herself, there cannot be any community of men, and sooner than later the chaotic imbalance will make the human ship sink....
>
> The bet that God made on man, in front of all of the spiritual beings of stunned creation, must be won by man, by a man endowed with a margin of freedom. Or this human being assailed by injustice and ignorance has the power, the physical power to drown the human ship. He can also destroy himself morally, drown the world with its garbage, and make it unfit for life, and provoke consciously or not more than one calamity. "Corruption came to the Earth, to the sea because men did it himself; in order that God might give man a taste of what man has done; maybe man will come back to God." (Koran 30:41)...
>
> Our civilization, so brilliant and proud, isn't any more than the previous ancient ones, not protected from accidents, deviations, and miscarriages of various forms. It is only by thinking about it and being watchful that we can avoid the same destiny. And for this, it is not enough to accumulate technological know-how. We need to build a world in all due conscience and safety, without being in conflict with others, without being strangers or indifferent to each other. In order to reach this goal, each religion—just like each ideology—must clarify its system of multiple beliefs which characterizes and integrates it. All believers, in this quest for the self without making a break with the Other, whomever he may be, will bring the light of God within. God is always present among us in order to show the good path when we are opened to its message. Let us listen to the Koran: "When my servants

are asking questions about me, tell them. Let them listen to me, and believe in me, so that they find the way." (Koran 2:186)*

The desert has quite a beauty to it. Early in the morning I look for some footprints made by various animals in the sand. There are very delicate traces in the sand which we can follow, reminding me of the traces in the pure snow—minuscule footsteps. So I took lots of pictures of these little steps in the sand, signs of the life we do not see, drawings from nature herself leaving her traces behind in this otherwise inhospitable world.

The desert was the birthplace of Islam, and experiencing the desert can bring an understanding for its absolute purity, bare essential quality, back to basics, primordial quality. It is also where Christ spent forty days and experienced the Temptation, and it is where young Israel went for forty years.

Here are a couple of poems by the famous poet Abd al-Karīm al-Jīlī.

Of Divine Darkness
Divine darkness is the primeval center
Where the beauty of the multiple Suns set.
It is God's self itself.
Through which He is, but from whom he never comes,
So that he never changes.
His symbol is the sleeping state of fire within the stone,
If fire emanates from a stone,
It nevertheless does not live apart from it, in its latent state,
It lives on in its unmanifested state
And its manifestation does not change in any shape
from its former state....

When God reveals himself to His servant through the name Allah, the soul of the servant extinguishes itself, and God takes its place, purifying its temple from the clasps of the nonessentials, and breaking the hold which attaches it to existence; then, He is alone in His essence, and alone in His qualities, knowing neither father or mother.

---

* Talbi, *Ma Religion c'est la Liberté: L'Islam et les Défis de la Contemporanéité*, pp. 105, 107 (tr. M-L. Valandro).

BEYOND THE BLOOD

"Remember God, and God will remember you. Contemplate God, and God will contemplate you!" Then He sings in his new found language.

> My soul attracted me to her, substituting itself within me;
> She took my place, certainly, but where am I now?
> I became her and she is within me;
> Nothing exists within her whom she desires.
> I exist through her and within her. Nothing exists between "us."
> My state within her is in the past, just as it is in the future,
> However I elevated my soul, and she took off the wall;
> I woke from my slumber and left my bed.
> She showed me myself by the eye of essential truth.
>
> It is on the forehead of beauty that I read all the letters.
> I polished my inward beauty, my essence, hers.
> And within these virtues is born within me the Sun of beauty.
> My name is really her name, and the name of her essence is my name.
> And all these attributes come to me naturally.*

Now we will enter into the heart of Islam.

> As far as the eye can see there is only yellow sand, black pebbles, small outcrops of flinty rock, and the dim footprints of the sand foxes. Under the asphalt-blue sky of noonday the rippling sand seems to quiver and change color from bronze to gold and then to a strange yellowish purple. The heat is staggering. It seems to explode out of the earth in blinding waves; and the horizon, like a thick black line scrawled on the rim of the world, seems to dance. When the wind comes from the desert, the heat grows thicker, juicier, an intolerable uproar of heat, striking between the eyes. The never-ending desert is never silent....
>
> In all this desolation of Arabia there are only a few towns. Even today there are places where no one has ever penetrated, virgin still, though the seacoast is encumbered with names.... Eternity is very close to Arabia even in this age of oil wells....
>
> Not all of Arabia is desert: there are lava fields, and mountains nine thousand feet high in southern Asir, and fertile fields in the uplands

---

* Jîlî, *De l'Homme Universel: Extraits du Livre al-Insân al-Kâmil*, pp. 58, 71.

of Najd, and rivers wind along the coastal plains. Yet the desert colors the life of the Arabs; it is inescapable. Here "heaven is as iron and the earth is as brass," insecurity is bred into the very roots of life.

The Arabs, a stern, unyielding people... are a handsome race with close-knit loyalties, agile, querulous, proud of their capacity to survive in an inhospitable land, sullen and secretive, quick to anger and quick to begin a friendship, ferociously brave in battle, and very sensual....

There is majesty in their harsh landscape, and there is majesty in their speech. They are perfectly aware of the infinite complexities and magnificence of their language. "God gave three great things to the world," says the Arab proverb, "the brain to the Franks, the hands to the Chinese, and the tongue to the Arabs."...

Today the Arabs worship stones, and so do all the followers of Muhammad. There is nothing particularly surprising in stone worship. If it is believed that a stone has fallen from the Sun, the Moon, a planet, or a bright star, then the stone becomes the physical embodiment of the mysterious forces which move the universe; and by standing completely naked before such a stone and offering blood sacrifice, the worshipper places himself within the circle of divine power emanating from the stone, and some portion of this power is communicated to him.

Today all the holy stones of Arabia save one have been swept away. The one remaining stone, known as the Black Stone, though it is a dark reddish-brown, was worshipped in Mecca long before the time of Muhammad. No one knows its history and no one has ever tried to determine what kind of stone it is. In pre-Muhammadan times it was believed that the stone had fallen from the Moon and was sacred to the old Moon god Hubal. The stone was enclosed in a small square temple known as the Kaaba which also contained lesser idols....

Muhammad ibn-Abdullah never knew his father, who died before he was born. His mother Amina seems to have been a beautiful sickly woman, unable to care for her only son who was often ill, and it was thought best to remove him from the unhealthy air of Mecca and send him to the highlands. So at the age of two he was placed in the hands of a foster mother, the wife of a poor shepherd of the Banu Sa'd living at Taif, a hill town southeast of Mecca. The boy grew up in poverty, despised by his rich relatives, his inheritance from his father being no more than five camels, a few sheep, and an Abyssinian slave girl called Baraka.

According to a fairly authentic tradition, Halima, his foster mother, observed that even as a boy he was given to fits of abstraction, and there were some who said he bore the seal of God from the beginning. When he was four or five he tended sheep....

He was about ten when his uncle first allowed him to accompany caravans to the north, hiring him out as camelman and guard. Tradition asserts that he was traveling with his uncle in Syria at the age of twelve, when he met a Nestorian monk called Bahira, who hailed him as God's messenger. What is certain is that at an early impressionable age Muhammad showed a predilection for conversing with priests and rabbis when the caravans stopped at the trading posts, and he stored these conversations in his capacious memory....

He was about twenty-five when he attracted the attention of a forty-year-old widow, Khadija, who had lost two husbands and acquired an impressive fortune. She was a warm-hearted handsome woman, who had heard from one of her agents of Muhammad's skill as a camel driver and manager of caravans. She asked to see him, and seemed to have fallen in love with him the moment she set eyes on him....

The man who entered the household of Khadija was sturdy and thickset, of medium height, with heavy shoulders and a thick black curling beard....

He was entirely happy with Khadija, who adored him and gave him six children, four girls and two boys (they died in childhood)....

The storm came suddenly one night, at the hottest time of the year, after a long period of meditating alone in a cave outside of Mecca. No one knows what brought him to the cave. It may have been the memory of the ascetic monks in the Syrian desert who also worshiped God in caves, alone with the Alone. Or perhaps he was influenced by those wandering hermits called *Hanifs*, meaning "those who turned away from idol worship," who emerged about this time from the Najd to proclaim the virtues of solitude and the worship of the One God. It may have been the seed of restlessness communicated to him by the old visionary Waraga who sent him out into the desert to live for weeks on end in silent meditation. What is certain is that the storm broke over his head, and the world was never to be the same again.

As Muhammad told the story of his first revelation, he was lying asleep or in a trance wrapped in his cloak, when he heard a voice saying: "Read!" He answered: "I cannot read." The voice said again: "Read!" He answered: "I do not know how to read." Once more, this time with terrible force, the voice said: "Read!" He answered: "What can I read?" The voice thundered:

Read in the name of your Lord, the creator,
Who created man from a clot of blood!
For he has taught men by the pen
And revealed the mysteries to them!

He was shown a scroll, which seemed to be of silk with letters of fire written on it. He read the words, though he had never read before and when he awoke, he remembered them, for they were "as though written upon his heart." Trembling, he went out of the cave onto the hillside, not knowing what had happened to him, and afraid he must be a *sha'ir* or possessed. Angels had come to him before, leaving him weak and dispirited, but that was long ago in his childhood. He was in such agony of mind that he thought of throwing himself off a precipice, and then he heard a voice from heaven saying: "Oh Muhammad! You are Allah's messenger, and I am Gabriel!" Lifting up his eyes he saw "about two bowshots away" the figure of an angel standing in the sky. He was rooted to the spot, dazzled by the brightness of the angelic eyes, and once more he heard the voice. He turned away, but everywhere he turned he saw the angel standing before him, until at last the angel vanished, and he was alone with the beating of his heart.

Later in the morning, terrified by the visitation, he hurried back to Mecca and told Khadija what he had seen. He was afraid he was going mad, but she reassured him. There is a tradition that she tested the genuineness of the visitation by making Muhammad sit first on her right knee, and then on her left: there was no thunderclap from heaven, and Muhammad was aware of the angelic presences hovering close by. When she began to remove her garments and sit Muhammad on her lap, he thought he saw the angelic presences departing in great haste. Khadija explained that if it had been a visitation of devils, they would have remained around the bed, to watch what happened. "Rejoice," she said, "for truly you have seen a visitor from heaven, and no harm can come to you!" Some time later she asked Waraka, now close to death, and quite blind, about the strange meeting in the cave. The old man answered that the angel who appeared to Muhammad was the same who came to Moses, the son of Amran: there was no doubt that a revelation was at hand.*

The first proclamations preached by Muhammad are dominated by one single thought: the nearing Day of Judgment. The terrible shock caused by the sudden approach of the Hour, the Day of Reckoning, and the resurrection is heralded by breathless short lines in sonorous rhymed prose. Close is this Hour. In a short while it will knock at the door and will stir up from heedlessness those who are embroiled in world affairs and who have forgotten God! Then they will have to face their Lord to give account of their sinful actions. Natural catastrophes will announce the Day of Judgment—earthquakes, fires, eclipses—as described in Sura 81 in unforgettable words.

> *When the Sun shall be darkened,*
> *when the stars shall be thrown down,*
> *when the mountains shall be set moving,*
> *when the pregnant camels shall be neglected,*
> *when the savage beasts shall be mustered,*
> *when the seas shall be set boiling,*
> *when the souls shall be coupled,*
> *when the buried infant shall be asked for what sin she was slain,*
> *when the scrolls shall be unrolled,*
> *when heaven shall be stripped off,*
> *when Hell shall be set blazing,*
> *when Paradise shall be brought nigh,*
> *then shall a soul know what it has produced.*
> (translated by A. J. Arberry)

Muhammad learned that he was not only sent to threaten and blame, but also to bring good tidings: every pious man who lives according to God's order will enter Paradise.**

---

*   Payne, *The History of Islam*, pp. 2, 10, 16.
** Schimmel, *Islam: An Introduction*, pp. 12–13.

Islam as the terminal religion of humanity is also a return to the primordial religion. In its categorical and final formulation of the doctrine of Unity, it returns to the primordial message that bound Adam to God and that defines religions as such. The universality of Islam may be said to issue from this return to the primordial religion....

According to Islam, as in all traditional teachings, men and women did not ascend from lower forms of life, but descended from on high, from a Divine prototype. Therefore, humanity has always been humanity and has always had religion.*

The belief in one God, without partners and without adjunct deities, forms the center of the revelation from an early moment onward. Sura 112 declares:

> *Say: God is One; God the Eternal: He did not beget and is not begotten, and no one is equal to Him.*

This *sura*, which is nowadays used mainly to refute the Christian trinitarian dogma, was probably first directed against the ancient Arab concept of "the daughters of Allah." But the *tauhīd*, the acknowledgment of God's unity, was to remain the heart of Islam, in whichever way it was understood, and the only sin that cannot be forgiven is *shirk*, "associating something with God."

The duty of human beings is to surrender to this unique, omnipotent God, the Merciful, the Compassionate (as He is called at the beginning of every human activity); to surrender from the bottom of one's heart, with one's whole soul and one's entire mind. The word "Islam" means this complete surrender to the Divine will; and the one who practices such surrender is a Muslim (active participle of the fourth stem of the root *s.l.m.*, which has also the connotation of *salām*, "peace").**

From these passages written by outstanding scholars, we see that the primordial, pivotal center of Islam is its unity, *the one God*, and its return to

---

*   Nasr, *Islam: Religion, History, and Civilization*, pp. 6, 35–36.
** Schimmel, *Islam: An Introduction*, p. 14.

the primordial religion of mankind. It looks to the *past*, to what was lost, and how to regain that.

Rudolf Steiner's insights into the unfathomable depth of man's evolution are invaluable.

> You all know that about six hundred years after the founding of Christianity, *Arabism*, inspired by Muhammad, began to spread abroad. In *Arabism*, Muhammad founded a body of doctrine which in a certain sense are at variance with Christianity. To what extent at variance? The concept of the three forms of the Godhead—Father, Son, Spirit—is of the very essence of Christianity. The origin of this lies way back in the Ancient Mysteries in which a man was led through four preparatory stages and then through three higher stages. When he had reached the fifth stage, he came forth as a representative of the Christ; at the seventh and highest stage as a representative of the Father....
>
> It is the *trinity* that makes it possible for the *impulse of freedom* to have its place in the evolution of Christianity. We look upwards to the Father God, seeing in the Father God the spirituality implicit in all those forces of the Universe which go out from the Moon to the Earth existence. All those forces which in Earth existence have to do with the impulses of physical germination—in man, therefore, with propagation—proceed from the Moon. It must, of course always be remembered that the human process of reproduction has its spiritual side. From the pre-earthly existence of spirit and soul we come down to earthly existence, uniting with a physical body. But everything that is responsible for placing the human being, from birth onwards, into earthly life, is a creative act of the Father God, a creative act for the Earth through the Moon forces....
>
> Christ lived in an age when the secrets of the Son—I can do no more than touch upon them here—had been lost, were known only to small circles of men. But because of the experience undergone in His thirtieth year, Christ was able to reveal that He, as the last one to do so, had received the Son-impulse directly from the Cosmos—in the way it must be received if after the thirtieth year a man is to be dependent upon the Sun forces, just as hitherto he was dependent on the Moon forces....

Those who were true knowers in the first Christian centuries were able to say: As well as the Father God there is God the Son, the Christ God. The Father God rules over whatever is predetermined in man because it is born with him and works in him as the forces of Nature. It is upon this principle that the Hebrew religion is based. But by the side of it, Christianity places the power of the Son which during the course of man's life draws into his soul as a creative force, making him free and enabling him to be reborn, realizing that in his earthly life he can become something that was *not* predetermined by the Moon forces at birth. Such was the essential impulse of Christianity in the first centuries of its existence.

Muhammadanism set its face against this impulse in its far-reaching decree: There is no God save the God proclaimed by Muhammad. It is a retrogression to the pre-Christian principle, but clothed in a new form—as was inevitable six hundred years after the founding of Christianity. The God of Nature, the Father God—not a God of freedom by whom men are led on to freedom—was proclaimed as the one and only God. Within Arabism, where Muhammadanism was making headway, this was favorable for a revival and renewal of the fruits of ancient cultures, and such a revival, with the exclusion of Christianity did indeed take place in the Orient, on a magnificent scale. Together with the warlike campaigns of Arabism there spread from East towards the West—in Africa as it were enveloping Christianity—an impulse to revive ancient culture.*

This passage is powerful if one meditates on such important impulses in the evolution of man. These insights bring into focus the dilemma which faces our age: living a life of freedom versus a life that is predestined, and lacks freedom. But much more was brought to the West through Muhammad.

Here seen from yet another perspective of Sun and Moon, Islam and Judaism being a Moon religion, and Christianity, a Sun religion.

One must have the capacity to perceive these two opposite activities in the cosmos: the Moon nature directed toward splintering and scattering, and the quickening, life-giving radiance of the Sun.

---

*   Steiner, *Karmic Relationships: Esoteric Studies, Volume Six*, pp. 36–38.

Through both of these experiences one comes to behold, in what is splintering and crumbling to dust, the world of the Father God, which had to be there until such time as the world changed into the world of God the Son, which basically has its physical source in what is Sun-like in the world. What is of the Moon nature and the Sun nature relate to one another as Father God to Son God....

Christianity is not merely a religion of salvation: the Oriental religion was also that. Christianity is a religion of resurrection, a religion that awakens again to life what would otherwise be nothing but matter crumbling away into nothingness.*

In contrast to Christianity, the spiritual life that is connected with the name of Muhammad expresses itself more in abstraction. In Christianity there are many more direct descriptions of the spiritual world than there are in Muhammadanism. But it has been the destiny of Muhammadanism to absorb much ancient science, much ancient culture. We see how Muhammadanism comes over from Asia and spreads in the wake of Christianity. It is an interesting spectacle. We see the stream of Christianity flowing towards the North, reaching Middle Europe; we see too, how Muhammadanism twines as it were around this Christian stream—across north Africa, Spain, and on into France.

Now it is quite easy to realize that had Christianity alone been at work, European culture would have taken a quite different form. In an outer, political sense it is of course true that Europe repulsed the waves of Muhammadanism—or better said, of Arabism. But anyone who observes the spiritual life of Europe will realize, for example, that our modern way of thinking—the materialistic spirit on the one side and science with its clear-cut, arabesque-like logic on the other—would not have developed had Arabism not worked on, despite its setbacks. From Spain, from France, from Sicily, from North Africa, mighty and potent influences have had their effect upon European thinking, have molded it into forms it would not have assumed had Christianity alone been at work. In our modern science there is verily more Arabism than Christianity!**

---

* Steiner, *Cosmosophy, Volume One*, pp. 32, 35.
** Steiner, *Karmic Relationships: Esoteric Studies, Volume Five*, pp. 44–45.

The camels were displaying some very weird behavior, with their swollen tongues stuck out of the corners of their mouths. The herders laughed and said that they had smelled the local females and were getting excited! We all laughed; they had a great sense of humor. We starved, but we did laugh!

Meanwhile, the old wise herder kept praying several times a day in the thirsty desert which seemed to absorb his prayers as if truly thirsty for the prayers of a serious man of God. I was touched by his infinite simple gestures towards God. The others looked up to him as a man of faith and simplicity. They did not pray. He was the leader in the lost space of the desert, we followed. He was always kind, never getting upset with anything. All the herders belonged to the same desert village, and they all had wives, children and grandchildren except the one herder who was almost seven feet tall. He was an outsider, he said he did not have enough money to have a wife and family.

Our old wise guide will remain forever in my mind. This beautiful figure, bowing in the distance on his rug, atop a golden dune, as the Sun is setting. Has God answered his prayers? I am sure he was happy with his devotions.

Here is a poem by Attar, the great twelfth-century poet from Persia.

The Newborn
Muhammad spoke to his friends
about a newborn baby, "This child
may cry out in its helplessness,
but it doesn't want to go back
to the darkness of the womb.

And so it is with your soul
when it finally leaves the nest
and flies out into the sky
over the wide plain of a new life.
Your soul would not trade that freedom
for the warmth of where it was.

Let loving lead your soul.
Make it a place to retire to,
a kind of monastery cave, a retreat
for the deepest core of being.

Then build a road
from there to God.

Let every action be in harmony with your soul
and its soul-place, but don't parade
those doings down the street
on the end of a stick!

Keep quiet and secret with soul-work.
Don't worry so much about your body.
God sewed that robe. Leave it as it is.

Be more deeply courageous.
Change your soul."*

The next day, all of a sudden, we saw the magic of a large date oasis coming right out of the desert. We all gathered for last minute pictures of our guides, cook, and herders, and we descended from the high plateau into this famous last oasis, at the edge of the desert which had a warm spring and some horses for riding. There for our last meager meal of two tomatoes and rotten bread, we left our herders to pack up, and we drove in the SUVs for another ride across the roadless desert tracks, back to civilization. The camel herders went back to their village, a distance of a few days, with almost no food. They had asked me to go back with them to visit their families, but I declined.

We stopped by the lovely town of Tataouine, famous for its colorful pottery. Being starved I promptly bought my favorite date pastries, tea, and fruit and walked around the old city, full of spices, dried red peppers, dates, and fruit of all kinds. The end of the day came, back to Djerba, and the gang was off back home, except that I had another journey ahead: to go back up to the Mediterranean via the western route north, close to the Algerian border.

I headed southwest and arrived in the town by the edge of the big Sahara Desert, called Tozeur, the site of one of the biggest date oases in North Africa. I certainly was not going to starve here. I took local taxis and buses. I was helped to get from one town to another by very warm-hearted

---

*   Attar, in Barks (trans.) and Khan, *The Hand of Poetry: Five Mystic Poets of Persia*, p. 58.

young people. It was an all day affair where I took private shared taxis, vans, and buses.

I found a wonderful old homey hotel, with the usual beautiful tilework everywhere and settled down to visit this ancient city. It is a very artistic place and many foreigners have come here and renovated old castle-like homes within the old city. It was a delight to walk in and enjoy. Like Morocco this is another world, far away from the West. The market in town had so many different dates to sell. It was a wealthy town thanks to the wealthy land which had miraculously survived the periods of wars, conflicts, etc., protected by its vast distance from civilization.

I walked through the old town—still intact—and looked at beautiful architecture and designs. I came upon a pleasant place where old instruments were everywhere, with pillows and tables ready for musicians and poets. A café culture! I got lost in the alleys discovering one treasure after another—an oil painter's gallery, antique stores, rug shops, tea shops, beautiful pots, etc. A few French tourists were walking around on a tour. The buildings were made of small beige-colored bricks and big ancient wooden doors with nails everywhere, giving access to beautiful old gardens and homes.

I hired a driver with horse and carriage to take me around the very large oasis. So we trotted around the gardens and very large estates within the oasis. Then he stopped and I admired all the fruit trees: lemons, oranges, dates, and persimmons. I chatted with the men way up in the date palm trees cutting enormous branches of dates—a dangerous job. I walked around this profuse, rich oasis.

Coming back we encountered some traffic. The town was hosting an international group of long-distance marathon runners from around Europe. I decided to join them and run. They organize marathons in problem places—this year in Tunisia because of the Arab Spring. They ran in the Sahara Desert, too.

I started the run, wearing my small boots and my purse—not very comfortable. A young lady ran with me. We covered about twelve kilometers, and then I gave up; it was too much. A car picked us up and took us back to town. I walk, I don't run!

Two of the marathon runners

It was fun to run through the large oasis with lots of kids and professional athletes, but I paid for my foolishness: my muscles were not used to running, and my legs hurt for days.

In my walks, next to the old mosque, I found a great hammam and enjoyed the usual scrub and warm conversation with the ladies who were interested in why I was there.

Then it was time to go on farther northwest.

I arrived in a very deserted little town by the Algerian border and luckily found a place to stay. One of the local young men became my guide. He took me walking around the mountains, down a carved canyon with a beautiful flowing river, and showed me a whole village that had been abandoned due to a major flood. They had to relocate the village to where it is now. He invited me to his mother's and sister's home, which I accepted.

We walked back to the village, and his mother prepared lunch and tea which I did not want to accept but could not refuse!

They were very simple folks, but extremely intelligent. He was from a family of several children, all older, in their thirties and forties. I chatted with his older sister who was still single, but she did not mind. One of their brothers was married to a French girl living in France. They shared the little food they had, and showed wonderful hospitality which is nonexistent in the richer Western world. Then I went back to my sparse hotel, ready for the next bus journey farther north.

Streaming
When the path ignites a soul,
there's no remaining in place.

The foot touches ground,
But not for long.

The way where love tells its secret
stays always in motion,
and there is no *you* there, and no reason.

The rider urges his horse to gallop,
and so doing, throws himself
under the flying hooves.

In love-unity there's no old or new.
Everything is nothing.
God alone is.

For lovers the phenomena-veil is very transparent,
and the delicate tracings on it cannot
be explained with language.

Clouds burn off as the Sun rises,
and the love-world floods with light.

But cloud-water can be obscuring,
as well as useful.

BEYOND THE BLOOD

There is an affection that covers the glory,
rather than dissolving into it.

It's a subtle difference,
like the change in Persian
from the word "friendship"
to the word "work."

That happens with just a dot
above or below the third letter.

There is a seeing of the beauty
of union that doesn't actively work
for the inner conversation.

Your hands and feet must move,
as a stream streams, working
as its Self, to get to the ocean.
Then there's no more mention
of the search.

Being famous, or being a disgrace,
who's ahead or behind, these considerations
are rocks and clogged places
that slow you. Be as naked as a wheat grain
out of its husk and sleek as Adam.

Don't ask for anything other
than the presence.

Don't speak of a "you"
apart from That.

A full container cannot be more full.
Be whole, and nothing.*

---

*   Sanai, in Barks (trans.) and Khan, *The Hand of Poetry: Five Mystic Poets of Persia*, pp. 16–17.

The ruins of the theater in the ancient Roman city of Dougga

It took all day, waiting for buses, private cars, changing routes. I finally arrived at my destination, Kef, a lovely city on the hills close to the Algerian border but farther north, again like Greece, whitewashed with turquoise doorways and windows. Cobblestones winding the way up to the fortress from the early days, old closed churches, synagogues being revived, and ruins from the Romans inside the new city. One civilization on top of the other. The mountains looked ominous in the background, winter was approaching with its dark clouds. It was a beautiful city, the middle of Tunisia reflecting its ancient rich cultures and now a thriving youth culture.

After having many conversations with curious young ladies in cafés, restaurants, etc., I headed north to the great Roman ruins of Dougga, a World Heritage Site. I arrived in the city of Teboursouk nearby and found a modern hotel where I retired for the evening after a lonely supper amidst businessmen and foreigners.

I hitched a ride with a local whom I hired because the ruins were ten kilometers outside of town. I enjoyed the whole place by myself under the eyes of the local shepherd up above the cliffs with his herd of sheep and his cap and staff. He came right out of the time of Abraham! The ruins are amazingly preserved and I walked for miles among them. They are set in the heights overlooking a rather rich earth, full of farms and cows in bucolic settings. I thought I was somewhere in southern France!

A great city—gone, disappeared. Ancient olive trees were growing at the bottom of the city. There were pools, former paths, roads for chariots, waterways, temples to all the gods, a theater, homes, mosaic scenes, and the peaceful brown cows enjoying their meal.

I had walked for a couple of hours to return to the town when my driver showed up.

The next day it was time to head north, to catch a flight back to the United States. It had been a long three months on the road. I decided not to stay in the busy city of Tunis, but instead to go to a sea town I had not yet seen, Bizerte, and then take the train to the airport in the morning.

I found a bed and breakfast nearby and went discovering the new town. It was a rainy day, but busy at the marketplace and the port. The fishermen were bringing in their daily catch to the market. I tried to walk into the old city, like in Morocco, but here the locals frowned upon my walking around so I turned back and went into the modern souk instead. I noticed many men wearing the very strict outfits and beards of the fundamentalists, which I had not seen elsewhere except in some teahouses and coffeehouses in the villages next to the Algerian border. They stood out like a sore thumb among the Tunisians. The women were covered. There was an anti-foreign atmosphere which I disliked, but to make up for that, the pastry shops were exquisite, and I had plenty of pastries with tea.

I did some last-minute shopping and ignored the general malaise of the place. Tunis had just had its enormous uprising and people must figure out their own answers. So as representing a foreigner I can understand their misgivings.

The next day, the train ride to the airport was very simple and I had avoided the busy city.

Part V

Kenya ৯ Tanzania ৯ Zanzibar Island

FIVE MONTHS LATER

I had not planned on visiting Africa for this project but I had the opportunity to drive and camp through Kenya and Tanzania on a wildlife expedition, so I decided to include a brief section on this fascinating territory.

We started from Nairobi, worked up to the Masai area, and various lakes along the great rift, which starts in Palestine, Syria. We camped out in the interior, in the great game preserves, by the tribal areas, the great Serangeti park, the great lake Victoria, camped at the foot of Mount Kilimanjaro, and crossed into northern Tanzania, where the Maasai people were still living in an idyllic, beautiful, pastoral setting rarely seen in this world. Their world is still intact because they *do not* want anyone to interfere in their affairs. We were not welcomed to walk, hike, camp out, or visit their incredible markets.

But for this journey I was also interested in the Arab influence along the eastern coast of Africa, so we made a stop at Bagamoyo, just north of Dar es Salaam, which was the terminus for caravans from afar. Bagamoyo, which means "throw off your melancholy," later became the terminus for thousands of slaves. Many of the Africans were sold to slavery to the Arabs, and ended up serving in their harems. They were castrated so as not to father children, unlike the slaves imported to other areas of the world such as the Americas, where their offsprings were sold off—gruesome times. So here we see the heavy Muslim influence, then the Portuguese took over, followed by Oman, and the British and Germans who fought for supremacy.

The Arab trading towns were all along the coast. The trade was gold and ivory to Egypt; slaves, gold, iron, copper, skins, ivory, and copal to Arabia and Persia; slaves and ivory to India; and slaves, ivory, rhinoceros horn, tortoise, and ambergris to China. Imports to Bagamoyo were stoneware, porcelain, and silk from China; spices from the islands of the Pacific; and daggers, swords, ironware, and glass from Persia.

Between 1630 and 1860, about fifteen million enslaved people were shipped all over the Americas, the West Indies, and, of course, everywhere else in the Middle East.

Now Kenya is about 80 percent Christian, 10 percent traditional, and 10 percent Muslim.

Islam was imported as well, but not from the north. It was brought by way of North Africa, through Morocco with Berber, Arab tribes crossing from the Atlas Mountains into the desert of Africa. Many Sufis traveled far and wide to spread the faith in the early centuries far into the depths of western Africa and then moving into the interior. The percentage of Muslims is approximately 90 percent in Mali, 90 percent in Mauretania, 80 percent in Niger, 50 percent in Burkina Faso, and 50 percent in Chad. Sudan is mostly Muslim and, of course, traditional beliefs. As we traveled farther south in Africa, Christianity takes root rather than Islam, but the traditional beliefs are very much present.

Traveling through Tanzania, one begins to notice the Muslim influence with small new mosques in the countryside and many madreses serving the Muslim population, educating the children. Many of the madreses were seen in the distance from the highway. In the villages, the school girls in their beautiful Muslim white uniforms were going to school. So there is a mixture of religions living side by side. The African beautiful textiles and dresses mingled with the sober dark long robes of the hejab, some even have their faces covered.

We took the ferry to the famous Zanzibar Island, which is 99 percent Muslim as opposed to the mainland which is about 35 percent Muslim, 35 percent Christian, and 30 percent traditional beliefs. In architecture and

A small mosque in Tanzania

culture, Zanzibar is a complete change from the mainland. It was as if we had been transported to Egypt. All women wore the hejab, young and old, black. I felt the austerity of the place as if I were living in Saudi Arabia.

The world of Black Africa has been in contact with the Islamic world since the days of the Holy Prophet and possesses some of the oldest living Islamic communities. Yet it is also the area where Islam has been growing the most rapidly during the past century and where some of the newest Islamic communities are to be found. The world of Black African Islam represents bewildering cultural diversity and variety in conformity with the tribal structure of the people of this continent. Yet there is a serenity and contemplative quality in Black African Islam which is found everywhere and unifies African Islam despite all the variety encountered over the vast stretches of this continent where Islam spread.

Besides the small number of Muslims who migrated to Ethiopia in the earliest Islamic period, properly speaking the first Islamic community of Black Africa is without doubt that of the Sudan where the Arabs first conquered the Nubians and then the Funj. The latter, who had migrated northwards, became gradually Islamicised by the Sufis in the fourteenth century. Sudan is, however, the only Black African country where the process of Islamicisation and Arabisation went hand in hand and where today Arabic is the official language....

Another distinct Islamic cultural area with a long Islamic history is that embracing the east coast, including Somaliland and Zanzibar. Mogadishu is said to have been founded by immigrants from Al-Ahsa, and Zanzibar received a major wave of immigration from Shiraz (Iran) and the ports of the Persian Gulf in the early centuries of Islamic history. The region has always preserved a close link with the Arab and the Persian cultural worlds and is also closely associated with the cultural climate of the Indian Ocean. In Somaliland, the role of the nomadic Somalis in the spread of Islam in East Africa is particularly important. By the sixteenth century these nomads had adopted Islam and carried it with them to adjacent regions....

Until the building of roads by Europeans in the nineteenth century, the influence of Islam in East Africa remained confined mostly to the coastal region. It was where in fact that the Swahili language, which is a synthesis of Bantu, Arabic, and Persian came into being. It is today the most important Islamic language of East Africa and plays a major role in the cultural life of the region. But from the nineteenth century onwards Islam has been spreading inland, aided also by the migration of many Indo-Pakistanis who have brought the cultural traits of their homeland as well as Twelve-Imām Shī'ism and Ismā'īlism into the region. Today, while Somaliland, Zanzibar, and Eritrea are predominantly Muslim, there are important Muslim minorities in Uganda, and Tanganyika....

From the point of view of population, the main concentration of Muslims in Africa is to be found not in the east but in West Africa where Islam is also over a thousand years old, having spread there from the ninth century on by traders following the southern route of the Sahara as well as by Sufi saints. Soon major Islamic centers were established south of the Sahara and certain cities such as Timbuktu became prominent centers of religious learning and Arabic scholarship. By the eleventh century several Muslim states were established in West Africa and the people of the region gradually became known to the Arabs as the *takārīr*. The great kingdom of Mali came into being with its most famous ruler Mansa Mūsā (fourteenth century) having gained fame throughout the Arab world.*

The former sheikhs of Oman in the eighteenth century owned the island of Zanzibar and so it is a Muslim island.

With my short introduction to the African continent (three weeks) I was stunned by the liveliness of the people, the youthfulness of the men and women and especially the children's beautiful faces, so eager, and open to everything. Unfortunately that openness has been very much trampled upon. Traveling through these mountains, lakes, savannah, strange formations, one is struck by its very ancient origin. We have here Mother Earth, very old Mother Earth. The color is mostly red, red earth, full of iron, and lakes, and it is so much alive, we can feel the pulse of Africa, its wild pulse, generous pulse. Many parts were extremely fertile, full of banana trees, fruit trees, vegetables, such as yams, cassavas, maize, etc., and I often wondered: *Why are the people up north starving?* They had roads, trucks to deliver goods, and no reason for starvation up north.

Seeing the Arab influence on the Tanzanians, where the beautiful-skinned women were covered, somehow did not fit the continent with its exuberant life forces. I took delight in seeing the great array of colors, and styles, and beautiful brown skins out in the open, rather than the ones who were covered up. There is a certain resignation in the covered women, a lack of freedom, which her uncovered sister did not have. The markets were full of engaged, boisterous laughter from the women selling their wares. On the other hand, the swift, quick, ephemeral walk of the women covered under a long dark coat contrasted with the elegant, natural walk dressed in fantastic shades of earth tones, of her uncovered sister.

Only in India have I seen this wealth of colorful fabric, the colors reflecting the red earth, ochre, indigo, bright orange and yellow, red. The Muslim women in Africa did not adopt the beautifully colored hejabs of the Moroccan women—in hot pink, turquoise, apple green, orange, and all shades in between—but instead the black, somber ones of Saudi Arabia.

---

* Nasr, *Islamic Life and Thought*, pp. 51–53.

This shows resignation in their souls, and the African soul, so full of life, living on a continent that is so lively, but shows much pain under these religious restrictions.

After a few days on the island it was time to go on to the next part of the journey. (I will speak about the African journey and its magic in another project since it is not the subject of this venture.) I flew from Dar es Salaam to Nairobi, then on to Istanbul for the next part of the journey.

Because of the political situation, it is difficult and dangerous to visit Mali or the Sudan, which are Muslim countries, so I declined a journey to those amazing countries. In these regions many of the Sufi sages traveled extensively over centuries and brought Islam to the local population. Perhaps we can compare these Sufis to the Irish monks who brought Christianity to much of Europe many centuries ago!

Part VI

Turkey ৯ Patmos

Rumi

These words of mine are no stones
To pick and throw at passing fancies.
They're yeast-sounds, bread waiting
To be broken whilst they're still fresh.
Leave them overnight and they become
Hard as rusting bolts, not fit for eating.
My verse is harbored in lovers' hearts,
Expose it to the indifferent world
Busy with its traffic and it chokes to death.
Like a fish it swims in the lover's blood,
Land it on the rocks and it gasps for life
Then slowly dies, cold and stiff as an icicle.
You must be rich with metaphors,
Like an ore of gold waiting to be mined
If you are to digest my words
When they're fresh. Know this,
My friend, it's nothing new,
These words are turned to bliss when you
Read them with your own imaginative heart.*

---

* *Divan 981*, in Rumi, *Words of Paradise: Selected Poems of Rumi*, p. 35.

This was my fourth visit to Istanbul. I had driven across Turkey in the 1970s, from Europe on my way to Tehran. A beautiful journey, across many different landscapes, then I had made several journeys by bus to the Mediterranean coastline and to the Greek islands from Iran.

I wanted to visit famous Capadoccia, Konya, the center of Sufism, thanks to Rumi who settled there, and Ephesus. But I would drive, stopping anywhere I wanted and changing the itinerary whenever it suited me. I would also visit the Greek island of Patmos by local ferry, where Saint John dictated the apocalypse to his secretary.

I found my hotel after a bit of walking around with my suitcase getting heavy because of my purchases of paintings and various other sculptures in Kenya and Tanzania. But I made it and met a friend for this journey.

We first went to my very favorite place in the Muslim world, the souk, and Istanbul has one of the most active, energetic markets. Then, of course, to the famous Hagia Sophia Museum, a former church turned into a mosque, and to the historical Blue Mosque which faces the museum. Both of them are symbols of man's glorious past.

The mosaics seen throughout the Hagia Sophia are breathtaking and luminous. The space is enormous, and the dome is an architectural masterpiece.

At the mosque was a show of splendid Islamic contemporary calligraphy from outstanding Islamic artists. The name of God, the sacred prayers drawn in various arabesques, geometrical, flowery forms of different colors were breathtaking in their variety and creativity. They were true works of sacred art.

Tourists were here from all over the world, from the Arabian, Muslim world, from the West, from the former Islamic Republic, from Russia, Georgia, etc. Istanbul is truly a melting pot of the East and West and a place of pilgrimage.

Then we enjoyed the palaces, museums, fantastic food, and beautiful weather. We took boats on the bosphorus, a very busy seaway with ferries taking people north or south, to and from work along the sinuous coastline. The Islamic sites were full of Muslim pilgrims visiting, many from Pakistan, Bangladesh, Persia, Algeria, Uzbekistan, Saudi Arabia, the

The interior of the Hagia Sophia Musesum

The Blue Mosque

Philippines, Indonesia, and the Far East. Most of them were wearing the hejab of their countries, some all covered up, some with regular scarves, some with scarves very perfectly set on their heads like in Tunisia. The men had the clothes of their respective country as well. There I could also see the clothes of the very traditional Muslims, the Pakistani shalva and tunic along with the traditional beards of the fundamentalist Muslims. They showed a certain rigorous, harsh, inflexible, very strict mentality, very angular unforgiving faces, with women following them behind, and absolutely disregarding the foreigner, as if we did not exist. Among these the Turks live their own freer, more western life.

The souk was very rich and busy. The mall does not exist in this area but it does in the richer suburbs.

In the evening, the beautiful colors of the sunset seen from the boat on the sea with the great skyline of the mosques in the distance was quite an unforgettable sight.

Fruit stands, food was plentiful and everyone was enjoying life. The airport was enormous, and one of the biggest cargo shipping centers in the world. At night the gigantic domes of the lit mosques were always within our vision.

Then we picked up our rental car and started the drive towards the south, and arrived for the night in Kutahya, famous for its pottery, after driving through many farming fields devoid of the former shepherds and sheep which I had seen thirty-five years ago.

The next day we stopped for a wonderful breakfast of tomatoes, cucumber, fresh bread, feta cheese, and tea served by a very gracious owner. Not many tourists wander around these cities inside the mainland. He brought us fresh cream which had just been whipped. The food is absolutely incomparable to food in the United States which has been seriously degrading in the last century to the point of being almost unpalatable as well as bad for your health, except in the biodynamic and organic food movements.*

Then we took small roads inland to beautiful geographic formations. People were working in the fields, taking care of animals.

---

* For more on this topic, see Valandro, *Nutrition for Enlightened Parenting*.

We arrived in Konya driving through the busy business center on the outskirts and on to the very old city where the hotel was. A few other foreigners were there as well. Then we headed for the spiritual center of Sufism, the home of Sufi poet Rumi, the famous mosques and mausoleum, the Mevlana Museum. The museum was full of pilgrims coming from everywhere. Many were poor peasants from the working class, unlike the pilgrims in Istanbul who were wealthier, upper class. They were very devout and truly honored to be in this sacred place. We could feel the seriousness of their devoutness, and love for this great poet and figure in Sufism, the great Rumi who is more than a legend and still touches the hearts of Muslims as well as others from various traditions.

I will mention here a beautiful rendering of Rumi from a talk given by Pir-o-Murshid Hazrat Inayat Khan, a master Sufi and musician from India, in California in 1923.

> My subject today is Jalaluddin Rumi, the greatest poet the world has ever known: a poet whose message, in his life and work both, marks a distinct line as a new era, a new step in Sufism, which was the most ancient school of Mystics and Philosophers, and which originated from the ancient mystic school of Egypt. The first and best known initiate of that particular school was Abraham, the father of the three great religions of the world: Judaism, the Christian religion, and the Islamic religion.
>
> Jalaluddin Rumi gave a new life and a new form to the mystical current, and it is from his time that the Sufi mystic culture spread throughout the world. The reason was that he was not only a mystic and dreamer, but he was the most learned man of his time—a great statesman and politician, at the head of the law of his country (like a chief judge). And he had a great reputation among the people as a most learned man: a man of reason, most practical and wide awake; a master of theology....
>
> The story of his life is most wonderful, especially his awakening to the Sufi ideal. Once he was sitting at leisure with his manuscripts. At that time there was no printing, no books, so manuscripts were treasures. And there entered a man in rags. From the appearance of that man anyone would have thought that he was a beggar, a pauper; at the

same time he walked like a king. And instead of a salutation of any sort, the first thing he did was to remove all the manuscripts that were there.

Rumi could not understand a man in rags coming into the house of a leading citizen and throwing away all the manuscripts he had so valued. But he was a great man; he did not allow himself to express his annoyance with this conduct. He was perfectly self-disciplined; only he asked him, "What do you wish to do?" And this man said, "What are you reading? Is it not finished yet? You have been reading all your life and still it is not finished. You are reading in small pages which cannot contain what the book of life is continually revealing, and this has absorbed all your life. What little is left, is that also to be absorbed in this?"

Rumi said: "What is there to think about? What do you wish to point out?"

"I wish to ask you if you have considered what is the purpose of your life. Is this position you occupy just now, this rank and position and fame, is this the purpose? What are you growing to, what are you looking forward to?... And these helpless manuscripts, they are subject to destruction one day. If that is your wisdom, how long will it last?

"Have you looked into the manuscript of your heart? Have you looked into life, to see what life is continually teaching everyone? You have worshipped God—have you talked with Him? Have you seen Him? Have you really known Him? What is the use of your worship? A religion that all your life you have followed, do you know where it came from? What is the source of it? Do you wish to live as everybody in this world is living, not knowing for what they are living? The horses and camels also live and they are busy, but there is no credit in their being busy. The credit of one's occupation is in the virtue of the occupation. Have you thought of the virtue of your occupation, is it reliable? If it is a passing virtue, it is not a reliable virtue."*

In the mausoleum dedicated to Rumi, I did not feel very welcome. I felt out of place, and people felt that I was an intruder and could not possibly understand such a Muslim man as Rumi. Or perhaps, there were such devout feelings from the pilgrims which I, as a westerner, do not show

---

* Barks (trans.) and Khan, *The Hand of Poetry: Five Mystic Poets of Persia*, pp. 64–66.

so openly, and this made a wall between myself and the pilgrims. I am a thinker, and my love of Rumi's poetry is not getting lost in the persona of Rumi, the cult of Rumi. In other words, I do not worship Rumi, like the pilgrims. Thereby, uneasy feelings creep up from the believers who know that I do not worship Rumi. I love his poetry. It was the same thing with my pilgrimage to Santiago: pilgrims were touching various stones to receive something. The dividing line between worship and belief, and thousands of years ago between worshipping idols, or truth, knowledge, the One God. Much resides in between—adulation, idol worship, the golden calf, amulets which satisfy the thirst for religion, for the beyond!

We walked all over the town, the bazaar, and found a lovely cultural café that was not so anti-western. There was a trace of the Sufi environment there which I did not pursue. The young man and the older owner met during the week to play music, Sufi music.

I found out that Konya is also the center of Orthodox Muslims which explains the feeling that came to me from the locals. Konya is the center of Sufism, and the orthodox have entered the field of Sufi spirituality so as not to be forgotten. For many centuries, the orthodox religious circles did not mingle with the freer Sufi circles. I can feel this clash to this day. The cult for Rumi, the great spiritual master, cannot be ignored by the Ayatollahs, the theological fundamentalists, because millions of pilgrims come to pay their respects at the tomb. So it seems they have appropriated the aura of greatness of this very free master. The orthodox fundamentalists are not the freer Sufis and here we thread on very complex ground.

Then we headed towards Cappadocia. We stopped along the way by Catalhuyuk, an enormous archeological site from prehistoric Turkey. The home of many of our own ancestors!

> Everything on Earth is subject to the laws of evolution, and that is especially true for the life of the human soul. The life of the soul in ancient times was different from what it is today. In prehistoric times, thousands of years in the past, the scope of the souls of human beings in Europe, Asia, and Africa was much wider and more comprehensive than that of human beings of our time. To be sure, they did not have the kind of minds that enables us to read or do arithmetic, but

they possessed a primitive clairvoyance and a tremendous memory of which ours cannot have the slightest notion....

To give you an idea of how these prehistoric people perceived the world, let me tell you, for example, that they saw everything surrounded by an aura when they awakened to their day-consciousness. A flower, for instance, appeared to them surrounded by a circle of light similar to that which we see around the light of a street lamp in the evening fog. And during sleep these human beings were able to perceive the soul-spiritual beings in their full reality. Human beings learned gradually to see the contours of objects more clearly, but simultaneously and in direct proportion to their ability to do so, the conscious interaction with the spiritual world and the beings in it decreased; it ceased altogether when the ego became individualized in every single being.*

The dig was a very deep pit, covered by a gigantic dome, and it is the home of the beautiful, many-breasted, bountifully formed Goddess of Fertility. Now in these new surroundings, the Goddess has been defeminized by the patriarchal system, covered up and forced to ignore her natural attributes especially in the orthodox Konya circles. We are a long way from making peace with the female element of humanity, the concept of brotherhood among human beings. Male and female is far off into the future.

Here next to the Goddess' ample, fertile, motherly figure, we have the female who is less than a human being, all covered from head to toe, preferably in black or, like her sister in the West, almost naked, advertising her abundant gifts, especially her full breasts, to men for a price. The mother nursing her child is certainly not advertised!**

On the way to Cappadocia, we stopped at Gümüşler Monastery, one of several hundreds of monasteries still in Turkey. They were all built and carved inside the rocks, and have fantastic murals painted on the rock walls. I had come to spend a week among these treasures of Christian

---

* Steiner, *The Principle of Spiritual Economy: In Connection with Questions of Reincarnation: An Aspect of the Spiritual Guidance of Man*, pp. 56–57.

** For more on this topic, see Valandro, *Letters from Florence: Observations on the Inner Art of Travel*.

The author on a roof terrace overlooking the scenery of Göreme

culture which are being abandoned due to lack of resources and interest from the Muslim culture. These carved monasteries date back to the eleventh and twelfth centuries, and go deep under the ground. This particular one had a most adoring painting of Mary and the Christ-Jesus child. Then we drove on for several hours among the most amazing mountain formations, and we arrived in a fairytale-like city in the middle of the mecca of rock-carved monasteries.

Göreme is the town at the center of these funny, mushroom-like rocks which are carved inside to become habitations, churches, tombs, etc. There are thousands of these very tall chimney rocks which dot the countryside amidst mountainous terrain. It is an astonishing sight.

The numerous carved-rock monasteries are beyond the imagination, especially if one knows that all the walls are painted, and were painted by dedicated monks and artists coming from around the world—from up north in the Russian steppes, or from Italy or Europe, or Jerusalem. Truly a special place to make a pilgrimage to.

We found a lovely youth hostel where the room was on the roof, and the restaurant served food on the terrace, overlooking the magnificent scenery.

Then we walked to the famous UNESCO* site of hundreds of these preserved monasteries. They carved whole mountainsides, and some are not even discovered yet!

And there were thousands of visitors from around the world arriving in tour buses. I felt privileged to be able to come here for several days and walk around the whole area to discover the little villages, the hidden monasteries, the farmers working in their very dusty fields, walks in the canyon, on top of mountains, tea in a little oasis, etc.

One of the evenings we were driven to a Sufi show that had been advertised. So we headed in the dark evening to this special place built in the rock. It was a large, round room. The Sufis came in and performed their beautiful ecstatic dance in front of the audience in their long regal white robes after they ceremoniously dropped their long-sleeved dark coats. The musician played classic tones and they whirled all together in strict choreographed movements.

> Wind instruments especially, like the flute and the *algosa*, express the heart quality, for they are played with the breath, which is the very life. Therefore they kindle the heart's fire.
>
> Instruments stringed with gut have a living effect, for they come from a living creature that once had a heart. Those stringed with wire have a thrilling effect and the instruments of percussion such as the drum have a stimulating and animating effect upon people.
>
> After vocal and instrumental music comes the music of the dance. Motion is the nature of vibration. Every motion contains within itself a thought and a feeling. This art is innate in humans, an infant's first pleasure in life is to amuse itself with the movement of hands and feet; a child on hearing music begins to move. Even beasts and birds express their joy in motion. . . .
>
> The mystics have always looked upon this subject as a sacred art. In the Hebrew scriptures we find David dancing before the Lord. And the gods and goddesses of the Greeks, Egyptians, Buddhists, and Brahmans are represented in different poses, all having a certain meaning and philosophy, relating to the great cosmic dance that is evolution.

---

* The United Nations Educational, Scientific, and Cultural Organization

Even up to the present time among Sufis in the East, dancing takes place at their sacred meetings, called *Sama*, for dancing is the outcome of joy. The dervishes at the *Sama* give an outlet to their ecstasy in *Raqs*, dancing which is regarded with great respect and reverence by those present, and is in itself a sacred ceremony.

The art of dancing has greatly degenerated owing to its misuse. People for the most part dance either for the sake of amusement or for exercise, often abusing the art in their frivolity....

When beauty of movement is taken as the presentation of the divine ideal, then the dance becomes sacred.*

One morning at dawn, in the room on the roof, I heard some familiar hissing sounds, so I went outside to see the sky crowded with hundreds of very large, multi-colored, hot air balloons jam-packed with tourists going over the small town, coming very, very close to the chimney formations and the tall, skinny minaret. I thought: *These people are mad!*

Over on the lower part of the town, I saw one balloon unable to climb up and crash into a building. I learned later that several people got hurt. Tourism! This was a large revenue–making enterprise so everyone and their brothers were in the business. We saw them from the roof, hundreds of trucks, with a trailer carrying the balloon going over to the many take off sites.

We walked all around the town following all kinds of donkey paths, into the interior, discovering oases and small teahouses with women who were making beautiful crocheted necklaces and bracelets, a Russian art, probably imported from Georgia. The women did not have the features of the Muslims but looked more Russian. The Province of Capadoccia touches the province of Galatia on its western border. I had found the name strange, associating it with Galacia, Spain.

> The population of the province of Galatia in the mountainous region of Asia Minor, where Paul had been active during his first journeys and had established congregations, were predominantly of Celtic origin, as shown by the name "Galatian." A few centuries earlier, a movement prompted by the feeling of an impending cosmic twilight had entered

---

*   Khan, *The Music of Life: The Inner Nature and Effects of Sound*, pp. 56–57.

among western European Celts that brought about easterly migrations as far as the region of the Caucasus (Georgia). This is the reason for a widespread Celtic settlement in the interior of Asia Minor.

It is not hard to understand why, particularly in this region, Paul had readily found open ears and hearts. Here he had in fact encountered "Europe" before the call of the Spirit had caused him to take the step from Asia to Europe.... Through their contact with the Christ impulse, the Celtic Galatians strongly sensed the inner contrast in which they lived, surrounded as they were by the orgiastic, ecstatic character of Asia Minor. By becoming Christians, they simultaneously became Celts again in a stricter sense.

The genius of the Celtic culture, which was already drawing to a close, was expressed in the way human social life was organized. For the Celts, the social structure combined an aristocratic principle of leadership with egalitarianism of the religious order or lodge.*

In the enormous maze of carved-rock caves, a guide took us to a small chapel dedicated to Mary, hidden in the hills and abandoned. I stood there mesmerized by the beauty of the site which overlooked a deep canyon valley way down below. Here men of faith prayed, lived, worshiped, painted in the quiet splendor of nature, with angelic murals of the life of Mary on all the walls. We sadly and reluctantly left, letting wind, sunlight, and water destroy the masterpieces of the past. He closed the gates and we walked back to the crowded center of Göreme.

Then we walked on another path north of the town, to a carved church dedicated to Saint Joseph. The old man who was the caretaker, about eighty-five years old, had been a worker in France in his younger days. He enjoyed sharing some of his memories but loved his home, carved in the rocks by the small monastery, with tomatoes planted in large aluminum containers and various potted plants.

Then we went for another very long walk with a local taxi driver who offered his services for a modest price. We walked farther into these strange rock formations and saw that farmers were actually working the beige, chalky

---

* Bock, *Saint Paul: Life, Epistles and Teaching*, p. 228.

Saint Jean Church in Gülşehir

soil with donkeys and hand tools, in between canyons and tall chimney rocks. Some olive trees were surviving in this very dry, tough environment.

Then we drove to a famous monastery farther north in a town called Gülşehir. Saint Jean Church, an amazingly beautiful chapel dedicated to Saint John, was set amidst hills of red earth, carved entirely within the red rocks, with beautiful silver olive trees by the sides. The painted mural scenes inside were breathtaking in their originality, colors, profound subject matter. We were the only visitors! Scenes from the New Testament from top to bottom, a picture book of the Bible, so alive. Childlike paintings still here with us from 1212 or so. Memorable is the scene of the Last Supper with a beautiful large fish in a chalice in the middle of the apostles, painted in red earth, ocher and yellow gold, white, black, and indigo. We spent a few hours in these sumptuous religious, spiritual, sacred settings. I must say this site was my very favorite!

Because I am a painter I had really looked forward to the visits of these carved-rock monasteries, but I was not ready for the richness, the magnificence of it all. Many of the scenes in all these monasteries had been badly disfigured from vandalism and other acts. The Christians themselves destroyed much of the Greek temples in their own religious fanatic fervor in the early Christian centuries. Much was destroyed in this manner by all sides due to man's fanaticism.

I took many pictures of these masterpieces as if to preserve them.

For the next several days we drove to more towns with outstanding monasteries dedicated to Mary, Saint John, and many other Christian apostles, and other carved monasteries in the more distant mountains and hills which were not as well preserved.

Then we headed southwest to visit some famous underground cities—real cities built under the ground beside these outstanding monasteries. They say that these cities have been in use since the Bronze Age because of the peculiar rock formations which make them easy to carve and live in. Various continuous invasions forced the people to live underground, including livestock. Provisions, wells, underground waterways, pools, eating rooms, rooms for servants, cooking, sleeping, even places for camels, etc., several floors underground.

Then I wanted to visit the Ihlara Valley, with a lovely river flowing down in it and both mountainous sides of the flowing river were lined with monasteries, from the ground and up to the top, hundreds of them, several kilometers along this river. Much of the paintings were beyond help, disfigured, and falling apart. Another century or so and they will disappear. The task is too enormous to preserve them, so again I took many pictures. I felt privileged to see something that will be extinct very soon. The disfigurement of the paintings and murals is still going on at a furious pace. It was a very special valley which must have housed thousands of monks, painters, merchants, believers, pilgrims, farmers, artists, etc.

By the river, the locals had set up a lovely restaurant where the women were sitting on the ground making the delicious flat bread. Children and babies were running around, and the Turkish visitors, especially the young ladies, were having fun running around and holding the newborn ducklings. The canyon was enormous. But time was not kind; rockslides were common and one had to be careful walking up in the higher elevation of the canyons to see the monasteries perched up there. There were hundreds and hundreds of cave churches.

The Sufis performing their ecstatic dance in their white robes

Then we headed towards Konya again, with the snowy mountains in the background.

We arrived in Konya to see a performance which we had missed. This was a performance by Sufis which I thought was just for the tourists. I was stunned when we got to the place. It was an ultra-modern indoor stadium seating several thousands of people, and it was packed by the locals. Women, men, children, young and old, running around and going to what was probably the only festive occasion beside the Islamic festivals. It was a very jovial, happy atmosphere—nothing austere—and I thought: *How are these Sufis going to dance this ecstatic religious ceremony with such a circus?*

The announcer came and everyone quieted down. The musicians came, the reader, the master of the ceremony, a mullah, and the Sufis came in their stern outfits and started the ceremony amidst thousands of flashing cameras, which was forbidden but no one listened, including me!

The show of colored light hitting the white whirling robes was breathtaking, and people were spellbound. One could feel how proud they were to be Turks, and home to the great Sufi, Rumi.

It was a master ceremony, and then I understood the importance of Sufism in Turkey!

There was nothing the orthodox fundamentalists could do; the people loved the Sufis and it showed. They came en masse to these performances. The Sufi movement is on the rise and nothing will stop them. It is a wonderful sign of changes within ultra-Orthodox Islam. This is the area where the East and the West can have a conversation and meet. The domain of enlightenment is where men and women will agree and converge. Sufism is the only place where Islam can meet the Christianized west. They have always been dedicated to freedom rather than theological abstract deliberations. I was glad to witness this display by the Sufis and the wonderful, rich, happy reception from the locals. Many young men and women will enter the Sufi practices as a result, and perhaps more women!

Female Sufis are well known in Islam and are venerated, as was the century-old, female saint and Sufi in Andalusia who initiated Ibn 'Arabî and perhaps without whom, he would not have become who he was.

> Music is called a divine or celestial art not only because of its use in religion and devotion and because it is in itself a universal religion, but also because of its fineness in comparison with all other arts and sciences.... Music stands before the soul without producing any impression of this objective world, in either name or form, thus preparing the soul to realize the infinite.
>
> Recognizing this, the Sufi names music *ghiza-e-ruh*, the food of the soul, and he uses it as a source of spiritual perfection. For music fans the fire of the heart, and the flame arising from it illumines the soul. The Sufi derives much more benefit from music in his meditations than from anything else. His devotional and meditative attitude makes him responsive to music, which helps him in his spiritual enfoldment. The consciousness by the help of music first frees itself from the body and then from the mind. This once accomplished, only one step more is needed to attain spiritual perfection.
>
> Sufis in all ages have taken a keen interest in music, in whatever land they may have dwelled; Rumi especially adopted this art.... He listened to the verses of the mystics on love and truth, sung by the *qawwals*, the musicians, to the accompaniment of the flute.

The Sufi visualized the object of his devotion in his mind, which is reflected upon the mirror of his soul. The heart, the factor of feeling, is possessed by everyone, although with everyone it is not a living heart. This heart is made alive by the Sufi who gives an outlet to his intense feelings in tears and sighs. By his so doing the clouds of *jelal*, the power that gathers with his psychic development, fall in tears as drops of rain, and the sky of his heart is clear, allowing the soul to shine. This condition is regarded by Sufis as the sacred ecstasy.

Since the time of Rumi, music has become a part of the devotions of the Mevlevi order of the Sufis. The masses in general, owing to their narrow, orthodox views, have cast out the Sufis and opposed them for their freedom of thought, thus misinterpreting the Prophet's teaching, which prohibited the abuse of music, not music in the real sense of the word. For this reason a language of music was made by Sufis, so that only the initiated could understand the meaning of the songs. Many in the East hear and enjoy these songs without realizing what they really mean....

In one individual there are many fine and small beings hidden: in his blood, in his brain cells, in his skin, and in all planes of his existence. As in the physical being of an individual many small germs are born and nourished which are also living beings, so in his mental plane there are many beings, termed *mukwakkals*, or elementals. These are still finer entities born of man's own thoughts and as the germs live in his physical body so the elementals dwell in his mental sphere. People often imagine that thoughts are without life; he does not see that they are more alive than the physical germs and that they have a birth, childhood, youth, age, and death. They work for man's advantage, or disadvantage according to their nature. The Sufi creates, fashions, and controls them. He drills them and rules them throughout his life; they form his army and carry out his desires. As the germs constitutes man's physical being and the elementals his mental life, so the angels constitute his spiritual existence. These are called *farishtas*....

The Sufi looks upon life as one life, upon all religions as his religion: call him a Christian, and he is that; call him a Muslim or a Hindu, and he is that; call him whatever you like, he does not mind. A Sufi does not think about what people call him. Who calls him Sufi? It is not he. But if he does not call himself something, someone else is sure to find a name for him.... Call yourself what you will—philosophy, theosophy, religion, mysticism—it is only the one thing, it is nothing but the constant longing of the soul of the human being. After experiencing all the different aspects of the life of activity, the longing to attain to that state of peace or calm seems in the end to be the only object that the soul wishes to achieve.[*]

I was glad to have come back through Konya again to enjoy this sacred ceremony with more than a thousand spectators!

As soon as the ceremony began, the women covered their heads and gave their full attention to the mystics. Here was an attempt to be modern, meet the needs of the people, accept the Sufis and their freedom-loving nature.

The modern city of Konya is very much like any European city: shopping malls, sprawling middle-class housing, movie theaters, etc., and very modern mosques dotting the city with their cigarette-like steel minarets pointing at the sky, sometimes with a crescent Moon.

> Taking the Moon, contrasted with the Sun, as the symbol representing the Jahve-religion, we may expect that a similar form of belief, by-passing as it were the Christ Impulse, would emerge later on as a kind of Moon-religion. And this is what actually happened. The old Jahve-religion emerged again after the Christ even, in the religion of the Crescent, carrying earlier impulse into post-Christian times. If you do not take things superficially, the use of the Moon and Crescent as symbols for these two faiths will not be something to smile at, for it is an actual fact that a religion or creed and its symbols are intimately connected.... Beginning in the sixth century AD and exercising a very vigorous influence upon all aspects of development, we have the religion brought by the Arabians from Africa over into Spain: this represents a re-emergence, in a different form, of the Jahve-Moon-religion. The intervening Christ Impulse has been ignored. It is not possible to enumerate all the characteristics brought over with the religion of Muhammad; but it is important to realize that the Christ Impulse is disregarded in the religion of Islam which was actually a kind of revival of Mosaic monotheism. This idea of the One God,

---

[*] Khan, *The Music of Life: The Inner Nature and Effects of Sound*, pp. 58–59, 78, 110.

however, included a good deal derived from other sources, for instance from Egypto-Chaldean religion, which had yielded very exact knowledge of the connection of happenings in the starry heavens with earthly events. Thus the thoughts and ideas current among the Egyptians, Chaldeans, Babylonians, and Assyrians appear again in the religion of Muhammad but pervaded by the One God, Jahve. Speaking scientifically, what we have in Arabism is a kind of gathering-together, a synthesis, of the wisdom-teachings of the priests of Egypt, and Chaldea and the Jahve-religion of the ancient Hebrews.

Everything connected with clairvoyant perception had to be discarded and men were to depend entirely upon reason and intellectual thinking. Hence the concepts belonging to the Egyptian art of healing and to Chaldean astronomy—which in both these people were the outcome of clairvoyance—are to be found in the Arabism of Muhammad in an intellectualized and individualized form. Old concepts that had been current among the Egyptians and Chaldeans were denuded of their visionary, pictorial content and re-cast into abstract forms. They reappeared in the wonderful scientific knowledge possessed by the Arabians who made their way into Europe via Africa and Spain. Whereas Christianity brought an impulse connected essentially with man's life of soul, the greatest impulse given to the human intellect was brought by the Arabians. Without thorough knowledge of the course taken by the evolution of humanity it is impossible to form any idea of how much the world-conception which arose in a new form under the symbol of the Moon, has given mankind. There could be no Kepler, no Galileo, without the impulses brought by Arabism into Europe. For the old mode of thinking appears again, but now denuded of its ancient clairvoyance, when the third cultural epoch (before 750 BC) celebrated its resurrection in our own fifth epoch (after AD 1450) in our own modern astronomy, in our modern science.

Thus the course of evolution is such that on the one hand the Christ impulse penetrates into the European people directly, through Greece and Italy and unites with the influences brought indirectly by the Arabians.

Only through the union of Christianity and Muhammadanism during the important period with which we are dealing, was it possible for our modern culture to come into being.... Thus actually six centuries after the Christ event the renewed Moon-cult of the Arabians appears, expanding and spreading into Europe, and until the thirteenth century enriching the Christian culture which had received its direct impulses by other paths.... We can therefore say that the Sun-and-Moon-symbols merged into each other from the sixth and seventh centuries up to the twelfth and thirteenth centuries—again a period of some six hundred years.[*]

Sufism is the enlivening element in Islam, away from the cold abstract orthodox laws which have driven many Muslim believers into unrest in the Islamic world because of this lack of freedom. Many are taking advantage of this element of lack of freedom to forge their own kingdoms by adopting dictatorships and abusing power, as we can see whenever we open a newspaper.

Saint Paul and Saint John

The next day we drove through beautiful rocky mountains and pine trees, with several mountain passes to the sea. The mountains were still covered with snow, and it looked impassable right to the sea. Turkey is mountainous. These ranges of high mountains go all the way into Kurdistan, Iran, Armenia, and the Caucasus Mountains of Georgia. We stopped along this high road to have some more wonderful homemade bread and tea in glorious settings, admiring a few red poppies unfolding their delicate petals amidst the rocks. As we arrived into the Antalya region we saw the beginning of extensive farming; fruit trees and vegetables were growing in profusion. Then the town of Antalya, East of Tarsus, which we enjoyed along with many Russians coming for the warmth of the sea resorts in their almost-naked outfits, mingling among the more reserved locals.

We drove along the coast to Izmir, or Smyrna. Then we drove to Bodrum and we took the ferry to Patmos with a stop on several other islands before reaching our destination. The ferries were again full of Russian families: children, babies, and grandparents on vacation, hard-working people finally able to travel after decades of suffering. Georgia is just up the road,

---

[*] Steiner, *Background to the Gospel of St. Mark*, pp. 150–152.

and buses are constantly traveling between the two countries if people can't afford the airplanes.

The whole region was where Saint Paul walked tirelessly, and the city of Tarsus, farther west along the coast, is where he grew up.

> Tarsus was both metropolis and port. Here, in the most colorful welter of nations, the world streamed through as nowhere else. Orient and occident, Asia and Europe, came together not only exchanging their goods but also their spiritual life. Above the teeming city, mountains and sea conducted a grandiose dialogue. In the majestic chain of Taurus' snowy summits in the north, rising to almost twelve thousand feet were the Cilician gates, the mountain pass which led from middle and northern Asia to the European orbit of the Mediterranean Sea. Similarly, the lower Syrian mountains in the east formed another pass, the "Syrian Gate," that linked up with Babylonia, Persia, and the more southern Orient. Coming from the Taurus Mountains and pouring into the sea near the city, the roaring Kydnos River carried timber from the high forests for the construction of ships and dwellings.... Tarsus represented one of the focal points in the cultural development of that period....
>
> Paul grew up into the profession of carpet and tent weaving, working as his father's assistant from childhood onward. Until the time of his apostolic journeys, this trade allowed him to offer his services as a completely free gift to the congregations....
>
> Like other metropoles of that time, Tarsus was a gathering place for people from all over the known world. In the surging diversity of colors and voices one important thing was concealed. Like Alexandria, Tarsus was a center of the newly awakened culture of thought. Here, within a culture founded on the Asian soul, saturated with suppressed ecstasy, the philosophers and scholars of this age pursued their ideas and research. And here, seeking the distinguished teachers active in their schools of wisdom, there gathered from all over the world those who wished to find fulfillment in their thirst for knowledge....
>
> Fatefully, young Paul was placed in the midst of the modern cosmopolitan life of culture inasmuch as it had one of its most important centers in Tarsus. In him, the *Jewish*, *Greek*, and *Roman* elements combined in significant union. He was the son of Jewish parents. The

fact that his father maintained a close connection to the order of the Pharisees, and, from early on, was at pains to raise his son according to the orders' rules, educating him to become a member, shows that in his family the Jewish religion was more than a mere matter of descent....

The language in which Paul grew up was Greek.... His whole character and demeanor suggest that, in addition to his Jewish education, he might have attended Greek schools of learning.

Aside from Jewish and Greek culture, the fact that Paul had a full share in the Roman life of his time was to be decisive at a future date. Because he had Roman citizenship, he appealed to the Caesar in Rome as the highest authority in the heresy trial conducted against him, and was then taken there.*

We parked the car in Bodrum, and boarded the ferry with an army of Russian families sailing gently towards the Greek islands. Late afternoon, the small island of Patmos and its marina came into view, as well as a fantastic fortress up on top of this mountainous island with the whitewashed houses, monasteries, and chapels by the sea. I had not been to this island during my previous trips to the Greek islands.

As an old man, Saint John–Lazarus was exiled on this island and it is here that he was inspired and gave the Apocalypse which is one of my regular sacred meditative readings, so being here was meaningful to me, and I had painted this scene many times from my own imagination, in veils, following the Liane Collot d'Herbois painting method. So being here was more special to me than other sacred places. What stands behind this ancient man, John, requires the deepest understanding, simple answers just will not do. It means opening ourselves to other laws than the laws of the Earth, to reincarnation in its most complex forms, as we read earlier about the youth of Nain and Lazarus-John.

The paramount and, at the same time, in regard to humankind's evolution, the most significant example of an initiation by destiny, in which the mystery experiences of ancient times bore fruit for the present, took place in the immediate surroundings of Jesus. The Gospel

---

* Bock, *Saint Paul: Life, Epistles and Teaching*, pp. 50–51, 53–55.

of John tells us of Lazarus' sickness and death and his resurrection by Christ from the tomb at Bethany. Lazarus' illness was not of an ordinary kind; it was certainly not brought about by normal causes. The powerful impressions and shocks that Lazarus, who was none other than the "disciple whom Jesus loved," experienced as a witness of the deeds and destiny of Christ, made it possible for the spirit transformation, undergone in former times and cultures, to arise again in the soul as if centuries and millennia had all at once been erased. The mystery of death and resurrection, which, long ago turned a human being into a messenger of God, suddenly appeared again. And it was not only present because it arose out of the past; now, its most sacred culmination cast its mighty shadow out of the immediate future, for, in only a little while, Christ himself would die and rise again. Lazarus was not placed into a deathlike temple sleep by a hierophant who appeared before him in human form. The destiny which made him a disciple of Christ and a witness to his power, was his true hierophant. He died through the unprecedented enhancement of the Christ will, which, as the "three years" drew to a close, became manifest as if in spiritual light and flame. Then it was Christ himself who took charge of the last act of the initiation drama. Like a hierophant, he stepped up to the tomb at Bethany and brought Lazarus to life again. With this deed, Christ affirmed this special joining of the ancient stream of initiation with what was to be inaugurated through his own dying and resurrection: Lazarus, transformed and having become "John," would bestow on humankind as the fruit of his most sublime awakening and enlightenment the Gospel of John and the Patmos Apocalypse....

We draw close to special destinies, ordained by Providence, wherein there come transformation experiences of which it can be said in a very special sense that, here indeed, somebody has become "a different person." As a protective patron and spiritual helper, a great person allows a still greater one to enter into his being in order to carry out even more perfectly the service which he is supposed to accomplish for humankind.

This law of transformation and elevation of being is exemplified by the destiny of Lazarus. When Christ called Lazarus, resting in the grave of Bethany, back to earthly life, the dead man did not only turn into a different person in the sense of a great enlightenment transforming his consciousness. Henceforth, a different genius dwelled in him: the superhuman, almost angelic ego of John the Baptist that also represented the individuality once incarnate of Elijah. After John's decapitation by Herodias, his genius-like ego had accompanied and overshadowed the paths and deeds of the twelve apostles as their protective group spirit. During the mystery event of Bethany, this ego descended and united itself in a special manner with Lazarus when the latter returned to his bodily sheaths following the call by Christ. It was then that Lazarus turned into John, for, henceforth, like a higher angelic ego, the Elijah-John genius dwelt in him together with his own "I."*

These words are describing unfathomable secrets and mysteries which will take timeless experiential lifetimes to understand.

We were anxious to start walking—after spending a few days driving and a long boat ride—so we left our stuff in our spacious room in a local family bed and breakfast inn. I was delighted to take off my covering-up clothes! Unlike the Russian women, when in a Muslim country I cover up even though it is hot. Here, finally, I could bare my arms, legs, head, and enjoy the sunshine on my skin, without feeling like I was an indecent member of humanity enticing man by my flesh. (I am skinny and sixty-three, but that is beside the point!) The change was so radical after being covered up for days. It was such a relief! I had not realized how much I had to give up to travel in Muslim surroundings.

I could breathe normally. The weight was taken off my head, or shoulders, or somewhere. I felt free! Not a guilty member of the female gender who is forced to behave in an unnatural way, which is natural for our Muslim sisters.

We walked up to the famous cave where Saint John received the Revelations of the Apocalypse, called the Cave of the Apocalypse, which was well cared for and open to the public, with monks performing masses and various other rituals. The smell of incense was strong, with candles lighted permanently. As with so many other very sacred sites, it was larger than life. Living in such a setting was beyond my capacity, my grasp, even though I had painted such religious themes several times.

---

* Bock, *Saint Paul: Life, Epistles and Teaching*, pp. 22–23, 27–28.

The overwhelming power of this little island, in the middle of all the other islands such as Samos, birthplace of Pythagoras, and the father of medicine, Hippocrates, and many others in this vicinity, many sacred happenings occurred which brought great powers of life to mankind. Saint John is for Christians *the* leading figure in esoteric and exoteric Christianity. His becoming Saint John after his initiation as Lazarus brought us the great gift of Saint John's Gospel, and then well into his nineties the great Apocalypse of Saint John, a work which is still a mystery to mankind.

I had not planned on dealing with such awesome mysteries, but being here, I cannot ignore them and just stand there enjoying the stupendous scenery. What lives in the atmosphere has a reality far stronger than the air I breathe. In my twenties I stayed in Samos, Rhodes, Kios, Crete, but never stopped in Patmos. I needed to be sixty-three to be able to *be here*.

The setting was magnificent, overlooking the sea, with olive trees and cypress growing on the hillside.

There was an old monk sitting there selling handmade things and he told us his story. He had been a talented traveling-circus acrobat who could do all sorts of amazing things. Then he had become enlightened and was told to stay in this monastery and devote his life to Saint John, and he had remained here ever since. He was about eighty-five or older. He was full of life despite his advanced age, and seemed perfectly at peace. Then we walked up the steep climb to the fortress and monastery up above, which was of the Greek Orthodox Church.

An elder monk was sitting at the entrance of the beautiful church and chatted with us about his life. Then I entered the dark mysterious church and proceeded to take as many pictures of the murals as possible before being caught, as it was forbidden!

It was full of candles, icons, golden chandeliers, paintings, more candles. It smelled of old antiques which needed some fresh air, the fresh air of anthroposophy to bring some light into all these mysterious places, of God the Father, the Son, the Holy Spirit, saints which no one can follow! It seemed to relish in the keeping of this mysterious atmosphere! Of monks in robes, and fathers with long beards and red, gold, rich clothes, rituals, and no women, just like in the Muslim world. Women are not included in their rites; we are "the other."

Then it was time to rest, but my mind was reeling trying to catch up with these eventful surroundings!

> Into Lazarus the "eternal word" entered, making him in Mystery terms one of the "initiated." The process described is one of initiation.
>
> Let us survey the entire process from this point of view. Lazarus was "loved" by Jesus. But this cannot mean ordinary personal affection—that would conflict with the perspective of the Gospel of Saint John, according to which Jesus is "the Word." Rather Jesus loved Lazarus because he found him sufficiently ripe that he could awaken "the Word" within him. There were already links between Jesus and the family at Bethany; that simply indicates that Jesus had made everything ready in the family for the final act of the drama, the raising of Lazarus. Lazarus was a pupil of Jesus.
>
> He was a pupil of whom Jesus could be absolutely confident that his "raising from the dead" could be achieved. The final act of the initiatory drama consisted in a symbolic enactment, through which the spirit was revealed. It was not just a matter of grasping the principle expressed in the words "Die and become"; it had to be consummated through an inward art. The earthly part, of which in the Mysteries the "higher self" learned to feel ashamed, had to be put off. The earthly self had to "die"—that was the reality behind the outer symbol. The body lay for three days in a comatose state. But that was only the outward expression of the immense changes going on within the life of the initiate. It corresponded to a still more radical crisis on the level of spirit.
>
> This act divides the life of the initiate into two separate parts....
>
> The earthly body, then, has lain dead for three days. New life rises out of death. Life has overcome death, and there can be henceforth a sense of trust in the new life. Lazarus has experienced this, for Jesus prepared him to be raised from the dead. His illness was quite real, yet at the same time symbolic. His illness was in fact an initiation, and leads after three days to the reality of a new life....
>
> The great "miracle" of Lazarus, the transformation of his whole being, places Jesus within the line of traditions from archaic times. Here is the link between Christianity and the Mysteries.

> Lazarus was made an initiate by Christ Jesus himself. Hence he could rise into higher worlds. But he was also the first Christian initiate, initiated by Christ Jesus: hence he was in a position to recognize that the "Word," which had risen to life in him, had taken on personal existence in Christ Jesus. The figure who stood visibly before him as his awakener was identical with the spiritual power that had manifested itself within him.*

The next day, we walked up again to the cave and monastery, spending more time, quietly taking in the atmosphere of this setting. We had a chat with the caretaker who was a jovial monk, and travels regularly around Turkey. While my companion kept the monk busy talking, I sneaked back into the church of the fortress and took more photos of the beautiful icons and murals. The scenery from the top is stunning, overlooking the Mediterranean and the many islands.

Then we walked down through the lovely whitewashed houses on the hill, with its narrow cobblestone path and lots of artfully renovated summer homes for people from England, northern countries, etc. We walked down the mountainside through gardens, enclosures, canyons back to the sea. We stopped at a lovely villa on the way down, following the path, and asked the owner of the house for directions to avoid the cliff. He invited us into his house overlooking the sea, and into his private little chapel which had priceless icons. He was very touched by our friendliness, and with warm emotions and tears in his eyes, he said good-bye. I did not understand why he was so emotional about two tourists coming through his land saying hello. But I was quite touched myself. My intellect did not understand, but my heart did. Perhaps he had lost a child or something and that private chapel was a prayer!

> Part of the inner mission of the universal stream of spirituality is to prepare human beings to become so mature in soul that an ever-increasing number of them will be able to absorb a copy of the Ego-being of Christ Jesus. For this is the course of Christian evolution: first, propagation on the physical plane, then through etheric bodies, and then through

---

* Steiner, *Christianity as Mystical Fact: And the Mysteries of Antiquity*, pp. 82–84.

astral bodies that, by and large, were reincarnated astral bodies of Jesus. Now the time is at hand when the ego-nature of Christ Jesus will increasingly light up in human beings as the innermost essence of their souls. Yes, these imprinted copies of the Christ Jesus individuality are waiting to be taken in by human souls—they are waiting!

And now you see from what depths the universal stream of spiritual science flows into our souls. Spiritual science is not a theory, nor the sum total of concepts given merely for the intellectual enlightenment of human beings; it is a reality, and it intends to offer realities to the human soul. Those who wish to gain spiritual understanding of Christianity and experience it within themselves will strive to make a personal contribution so that either in the present or in a later incarnation a copy of the Christ Jesus individuality can be woven into their own egos. A person who understands the true, inmost essence—the actuality—of the universal stream of spiritual science will prepare himself or herself not just for knowledge, but rather for an encounter with actual reality. You must develop a feeling that we in our world movement (anthroposophy) are not concerned with the mere communication of theories, but rather with *preparing human beings to accept facts*. We are also concerned that human beings receive what is waiting in the spiritual world and what they have the power to receive, provided they prepare themselves for this task in the right way.*

When we arrived at the sea, I had to go and jump in the wonderful clear water of the Mediterranean. We spend the rest of the afternoon in a small fishing village, then headed back up to the town of Patmos, another long walk back on the road. It had many beautiful, well-tended vegetable gardens, olive trees, flower gardens, etc., and more private little chapels built here and there with their own icons and bouquets of flowers.

Then it was time to have a wonderful meal by the sea, watching the Greeks and the few tourists.

In the evening, I wanted to catch the sunset by climbing once more to the top of the island to the western side. It took a while to find the path hidden among the winding roads and homes which were scattered along

---

* Steiner, *The Principle of Spiritual Economy: In Connection with Questions of Reincarnation: An Aspect of the Spiritual Guidance of Man*, pp. 54–55.

the whole mountainside. We passed more ruins from another time and we reached the top right on time to watch the Sun disappear into the quiet sea, a lovely sunset, with some horses running around also enjoying themselves. Then after quite a few miles of wanderings we walked back down, in the twilight, overlooking the wide encircling bay which had been the home of this old man almost a century old, John-Lazarus-Elijah, where the skies opened up and sent him this message from the gods above man, the Apocalypse.

> Christianity rightly understood is the religion of the open heavens; the religion of humankind before whom the curtain has been drawn aside which divides the earthly world of the senses from the sphere of the supersensory. The worship of the old covenant was the religion of the closed heavens. The veil of the holy of holies in Solomon's temple was the central symbol of the Old Testament religion. But in the hour of Golgotha the religious principle of the veiled mystery lost its validity and power. The rending of the veil in the temple was a significant gesture of God, a telling spiritual act.
> The Book of Revelation teaches men to read in the world from which the curtain has been drawn aside.[*]

I did not sleep much that night since there was so much that was alive here. Before retiring we spoke to the owner. He said he had come here from Italy to work, around wartime, and had fallen in love with a Greek woman, and stayed. His daughter was taking care of the bed and breakfast with many rambunctious grandchildren running around.

The next day I wanted to visit the cave again and spend a bit more time there before leaving the island. I took a few pictures without the vigilant eye of the monk (photographs were *strictly forbidden*) and meditated on the profundity of this cave. The walk up to the cave from the town is a peaceful climb amidst olive trees, cypress trees, flowers, and a magnificent view of the sea on a very old path which has seen many pilgrims from around the world. Then we climbed up for another visit to the fortress, taking in the wondrous beauty of the island, and had another chat with the white-bearded, long-haired, old monk. Then we walked back again, deep

---

[*] Bock, *The Apocalypse of Saint John*, p. 11.

in thought about it all, too profound for words, and it was time to take the ferry back to Turkey, after stopping on the island of Kalimnos.

We enjoyed the sailing of the ferry along the coast watching scenes from other centuries go by—fortresses up on the mountaintops, small churches perched on impossible rocks overlooking the sea, chapels in lonely corners of islands, small villages, busy cities, peaceful settings—before rejoining land.

Back on the mainland, we drove to Ephesus where Saint John the Evangelist had lived and taken care of Mary, the mother of Jesus Christ, where Paul and various apostles had made many journeys, and where history is seeped in unfathomable mystery wisdom and knowledge. I had never gone to Ephesus. I needed to reach the age of sixty-three to have enough maturity to *be there*, just like with Patmos. It is too grandiose and my learning is still too little to encompass its illustrious past, like Palestine! One needs other faculties to *be here*, brain-bound thinking is surely not enough!

I must enlist the help of Saint Paul and Saint John! We stayed in the town and proceeded to visit these sacred grounds.

What baffles me is that I was not brought up in a super-religious atmosphere. It was mostly a nonchalant approach to religious education. We did not pray at the table and we did not go to church with our parents. They made my two sisters and I go to church and catechism, and we received the various communions of the Catholic Church, but that was it. There was no talk about Jesus, or Christ, or anything. One might have thought that my parents were atheist, but they were not. On my father's side my grandmother was more in tune with the gypsies, who regularly came and camped on her land. My mother was brought up going to church and she knew the church services by heart in Latin. Her father was a regular church goer and used to sing and play the flute at the local village church. My uncles were altar boys. But in our home, nothing of the sort. No pictures of Mary, or Christ, or anything, which was fine with all of us. It left us free to do whatever we wanted! One of my sisters married and became a Greek-Russian Orthodox, I married a Persian-Muslim, and my fourth sister married a Puerto Rican–Austrian and is a devout Catholic.

Walking through the vast site of the antique city of Ephesus took a couple of days where I was in a sort of daze due to the incredible ancient world which spoke through those stones. There were temples dedicated to goddesses, large amphitheaters, and statues of Diana, Artemis, Eros, etc. The past was mute, we no longer understood what happened in these temples. The only ones to awaken them for us are the initiates, such as Rudolf Steiner in his many lecture cycles where he tried with superhuman efforts to wake us from our deep slumber, and the remarkable writings of the Christian Community priest and scholar, Emil Bock (1895–1959), with his deep studies of the Old Testament, New Testament, Saint Paul, and Saint John.

So as I walked up and down the paved paths, sitting here and there, some scenes from former times started to awaken. The first day we did not see many visitors, but the next day was mobbed with tourists coming from the huge luxury cruise ships docked at the big port of Izmir. Everyone enjoyed this sacred site.

Back in the modern town of Ephesus, we hiked up to the extensive ruins of the old Saint John Cathedral and Saint John's grave. The place has much lightness to it, here and there the smiling faces of poppies growing in between the beautiful old stones, and it was empty. We had the whole large place to ourselves.

At the museum I loved the different statues of Artemis. Something special exuded from one of the statues, as if it were living, a living statue with all of its grape shapes and various symbols of animals, plants, bees, and necklaces of grapes around her neck. I could have stayed quite a few hours looking at her, and various other ones similar to this one.

These statues had a life of their own!

Outside the small museum, even though the whole of Ephesus is a museum, a young couple from Holland was on bicycles; we had passed them on the curvy mountain road. They were traveling around the world and had crossed Persia, China, and India, and were now on their way home. They were full of stories which I am sure will delight their children, and grandchildren, with tales of audacious travels. I wish there were more of such intrepid travelers! They make the best diplomats for the Western world!

We went to the ruins of the Artemision, which was the most important sanctuary of Ephesus. Worshipping has been practiced for thousands of years in this area, but the temple itself dates from around 570 BC.

The next day we drove up the mountain, north of Ephesus, to visit the place where Mary lived with her attendants, and Saint John who lived nearby in Ephesus, taking care of her, as is told in many writings.

The place was again mobbed with many busloads of pilgrims.

The small chapel was full of people, and we refreshed ourselves from the small spring coming out of the mountainside which is said to have miraculous properties. We took a little bottle of it like everyone else. Perhaps it would alleviate my second bout of stomach disorder, amoebic dysentery, caught in Istanbul from a chicken sandwich or a glass of fresh, delicious pomegranate juice!

We headed down the mountain but stopped to hike along the inviting mountain peaks which were bordered by a high, old, fortressed wall. From there the whole valley of ancient Ephesus lay before our eyes, serene and magical, but its history buried in time. A wonderful place to meditate before going on with the journey.

At night, I barely slept! So much had happened here!

Ephesus, Saint John, the Virgin Mary, Diana, Artemis, Isis, Paul, Luke, Pythagoras, Heraclitus, and the constant flow of spiritual travelers going between Egypt and Greece over millennia, not to forget the home of the goddess of fertility a few hundred kilometers inland. This particular place has shaped our Western world, before the cultural-scientific Arabic invasion of a thousand years ago with its heritage, and not to forget the Sufis, Rumi, who also decided to settle not far from here, inland, in Konya.

What was there? It is still full of Mysteries. Saint John and the *Word*, Ephesus and its cult, Rumi and the *Word*, Mary, the *Word* becoming flesh, *Paul* and the Word spread throughout the area through his churches.

Artemis, the virgin-mystery goddess with its grape-shaped forms which appear to be breasts but are not. More like the Queen Bee, a statue which only the prepared could see—married women were not allowed, only virgins! What did the makers of such a statue want to hide from the public? To touch the realm of meaning, pure meaning, like the *Word*, the meaning behind the Word (see Georg Kühlewind's books), and thereby obtain power, *power* over things of this world; to the unprepared this was firearms in the hands of lunatics, like the Roman *Caesars* which still exist, just read the newspapers.

A statue of Artemis at the museum in Ephesus

Ephesus today has buried her treasures, her mysteries, and it is up to us to decipher them, thanks again to the insights of a few initiates such as Rudolf Steiner and others who dedicate their lives to divulging this spiritual knowledge, I just mentioned it before but must constantly remind myself of their legacy and be thankful, otherwise, I certainly would not be doing what I am doing now.

When people speak about the Word today they usually only mean the weak human word, which has so little significance in comparison with the majesty of the universe indicated at the beginning of Saint John's Gospel with the momentous words: "In the beginning was the Word, the Logos, and the Word was with God, and God was the Word." And anyone who reflects on this most significant opening of Saint John's Gospel must ask himself: What does it mean when the Word is placed at the primal beginning of all things? What is actually meant by the Logos, the Word? And what connection does it have with our trivial human words?

Now the name of John is connected with the city of Ephesus, and if someone who is equipped with imaginative perception of the world's history contemplates the momentous words, "In the primal beginning was the Logos, and the Logos was with God, and a God was the Logos," he will be directed time and again, by an inner path, to the ancient Temple of Artemis-Diana at Ephesus... and so it must seem to him that knowledge of the Mysteries of Ephesus will help him to understand the beginning of the Saint John's Gospel.

We find that the instruction given in the Mysteries at Ephesus did indeed begin with drawing attention to the sounds of human speech.... The akashic records reveal again and again how the teacher first of all directed the attention of the pupils to human speech.... The attention of the pupil was first directed to the way in which the word sounds forth from the mouth, he was told over and over again: "Mark well what you feel when the word sounds forth from your mouth!"... Observe how in the words "I am" the upward ascent is felt, while in the "I am not" there is more the feeling of pressing downwards.

Then the attention of the pupil was turned more towards the intimate feeling and experiences connected with the word. He became aware that from the word something like warmth rises up towards the head and this warmth, this fire, intercepts thought....

The pupil was then led into the real secret of speech. This secret is connected with the mystery of the human being. Nowadays this secret of the human being is hidden from scientists inasmuch as science places at the summit of all thought the incredible caricature of truth, the so-called law of conservation of energy and matter.

Within the human being matter is continually being transformed. It does not endure. The air that is pushed out of the throat is transformed in the process alternately into the next higher element, into the element of heat or fire, and again into the element of water, Fire-Water-Fire-Water.*

---

*   Steiner, *Mystery Knowledge and Mystery Centres*, pp. 110–111.

This is just a beginning. Then further, in Rudolf Steiner's *Christianity as Mystical Fact*, Heraclitus of Ephesus (535–475 BC) is spoken about.

> The relationship of Heraclitus of Ephesus to the mysteries is immediately clear from a saying that is handed down about him, to the effect that his thoughts were "an impassable road." Anyone who was not an initiate would find in them nothing but "obscurity and darkness," but they were "brighter than the Sun" to those who approached them in the company of *mystai*. It is said that he deposited his book in the temple of Artemis—indicating that he could be understood only by the initiated. Heraclitus was called "the Obscure," because the key of the Mysteries alone cast light on his views....
>
> > *What people want is not always what is best for them. It is illness that makes health sweet and good; hunger that makes food satisfying; toil that brings rest.*
> >
> > *The sea is the purest and impurest water. For fish it is drinkable and salutary, but for men it is undrinkable and harmful.*
>
> The primary thrust of Heraclitus' thought here is not the perishability of earthly things, but rather the splendor and sublimity of the Eternal.
>
> > *The connectedness of things is a tension between opposites, just as in a bow or a lyre.*
>
> The primal fault of human beings was to fix their thought on changeable things, and so become estranged from the Eternal. Life became a danger to human beings, for all that happens to them comes from life. The sting of this danger is removed, however, once people cease to set an uncritical value on life. They regain their innocence. It is as though they abandon their serious attitude towards life and regain their childhood. The child plays with many things taken seriously by the adult. The Heraclitean thinker resembles the child. "Serious" issues lose their value when viewed from the eternal standpoint; life seems like play. "Eternity," says Heraclitus, "is a child at play. It is the reign of a child." The beginning of error lies in taking too seriously a great deal that does not deserve it.

BEYOND THE BLOOD

God has poured himself out into the world of things. To treat things seriously, apart from God, is to make them into "tombs of the divine." To disport ourselves with them like a child is to turn our serious intent toward rediscovering the underlying divinity, the God who sleeps spellbound in things.

There is a "burning process," a consuming fire, in the vision of the Eternal when it acts upon our customary notions about the world. The spirit dissolves thoughts that derive from the senses, evaporates them, as a destructive fire. It is in this higher sense that Heraclitus considers fire to be the first principle of all things.... For Heraclitus the spirit was vitally active in the ordinary fire. The energy of physical fire works in a higher mode in the human soul, and in its crucible melts sense-perceptions down to draw forth from the vision of the Eternal.*

In this realm we rejoin the Sufis and their dedication to meeting God. Ephesus went up in flames in the fifth century BC, just as Alexander the Great was being born.

> Listen oh listen to my plaintive cry
> Listen to my longing or else I die.
> From the sweet home of my bed I was torn
> So my pain and crucial longing was born.
>
> With so many secrets I sing aloud
> But none sees nor hears in this crowd.
> Oh for a friend to know my burning state
> That our souls may mingle and contemplate.
>
> The flame of Love discourses in me
> The wine of Love so enforces me.
> Do you wish to know the fire, the flow
> Listen my listener then you shall know.**

---

* Steiner, *Christianity as Mystical Fact: And the Mysteries of Antiquity*, pp. 18–20.
** *Mathnavi I, 1*, in Rumi, *Words of Paradise: Selected Poems of Rumi*, p. 41.

"This is thy mother." These words of Christ to John always puzzled me. In Ephesus, more than ever. The site of Artemis-Diana, the Goddess of Purity, *is* the site where Mary-Sophia chose to live out the rest of her days. Her beautiful chapel up in the mountain, not far away from Ephesus, is a quiet center where, according to legend, she retired in her old age.

Myriam-Sophia-Mary was a mystery to me from way back. There was a sentence in French from a prayer which I repeated dutifully when I was going to church in my youth: *le fruit de vos entrailles*, or "the fruit of your inside organs." As a very imaginative child, these words were full of scary images. Then I learned that she was a virgin, and had a child. Well, that was more than I could take. A virgin, and she was a mother. That is when I said good-bye to my Catholic upbringing! Thanks, but no thanks!

This birth mystery always haunted me—as it did for everyone else as well—until my studies in anthroposophy where new insights brought some clarity into this center of chaotic images and incomprehensible ideas, facts, and concepts.

Myriam-Mary, who stood by John, is the being to whom Jesus Christ said, "She is thy Mother." I will not enter into the other great mysteries of the childhood of Jesus.*

Artemis-Diana stands in her purity, chastity, abundance, and Myriam-Mary-Sophia up on the hill is resting and overlooking the whole area, as is the tomb of Saint John, the one whom Jesus loved, overlooking the whole area as well on the opposite side. One looks at the other in death as well, and down below, Artemis-Diana.

Saint John became Mary-Sophia's new son, or Sun.

> The forces of the Father still continue to work in human beings; they are a force bound to the Earth; a planetary force. They work in everything that is on the Earth; thus also in human beings....
>
> If the planetary forces coming from the Father were predominantly active until the Mystery of Golgotha, then from this point of view in time onward the forces of the cosmos, the mother forces, *are* added.... In the Egyptian cultural epoch... the Egyptian mysteries of

---

*   For more on this topic, see Rudolf Steiner's lectures about the Gospels, especially Saint Luke.

the Isis *cultus* were cultivated in their highest perfection. The Egyptians revered the forces of nature that are expressed in all minerals, plants, animals. But the Egyptian soul, full of sadness, full of the deepest sorrow, looked at the human being and said to itself that the human being was not actually conscious of these nature forces, for this reason the human being portrayed Isis as veiled, and it was said that no mortal was ever allowed to lift the veil in order to reach Isis. What does it mean? Nothing more than that the Goddess did not dwell in the physical world, but rather in the astral world, and that only those who have stepped through the portal of death can recognize and know her. No one alive could lift her veil. This means that the effects of the forces of Isis were not available to the living.

And what were these Isis forces? They were the *pure forces of the mother*, which before the Mystery of Golgotha were available to human beings only in the spiritual world: that is, when they had walked through the gate of death....

The Egyptian soul could only look with a foreshadowing perception toward the Mystery of Golgotha through which the pure mother-forces were to become active also for living human beings. Only when Christ Jesus, the fatherless human being, had united completely with the Earth when he crossed the threshold of death, only from this time on can the pure forces of the mother (the forces of the cosmos) work within human beings on the Earth....

The forces of the father, which are from the Earth... work constructively bringing their forces until the thirty-third year. Although if the forces that strive downward, the forces of the mother, are already at work in the human being, the father-forces nevertheless, are stronger until this point in time. If only the forces that strive downward (forces of Christ, mother forces) would predominate in human beings, they would not incarnate on Earth. If, on the other hand, only the forces that strive upward, the planetary forces would predominate, then they would always live on the Earth, then there would be no death....

That which was Isis in the Egyptian mysteries, this holy center of forces, is presented to us in Christianity as the Mary-Sophia of John's Gospel. The union of the rising and descending forces that occurred at the Mystery of Golgotha first made it possible that the human being can now feel the mother-forces between birth and death....

In this time of the father-forces we live life as it is karmically determined by our previous lives. However, from the time that the dying down forces, the mother forces, predominate, we create through these spiritual forces what we will be able to live out only in the next life; that is, the karma of our next lifetime.

The father forces, or the constructive forces, work in us without our involvement; on the other hand, we ourselves must work and strive in the spiritual realm so that the mother forces become conscious within us. We must become conscious of these sublime, lofty forces, for they are the power that flows directly from Christ to us.*

So when Christ tells John to take care of his mother, Mary-Sophia-Isis, it is a great, colossal, impossible responsibility. He is the custodian of "the mother force," the cosmic forces which are made visible through her. He is her guardian, as well as her earthly example of what comes from the cosmos.

Looking at the road map I noticed that many of the seven communities mentioned in Saint Paul's writing, and in the Apocalypse of Saint John, were on the road we were traveling, so I decided to go to all of them. It was, as usual, unplanned! A strong desire to see *all* of these ruins from early Christianity grabbed me and we started this Saint Paul journey, as if by magic.

> The road leading up in a wide curve from the sea to the mountain heights, from the first to the seventh apocalyptic church, repeats the path of humanity. It starts in cities which still live in an age-old heritage of culture and wisdom, and leads into surroundings which, though indeed far removed from the centers of life in these days, yet anticipated the future. In our day something of the *plutonion* principle has spread over the whole of modern civilization. We have had to learn on a large scale how to work with subterranean forces such as gases, electricity, or atomic energy. A kind of glazed crust covers the landscape in which Nature has been thrust back by industry. In Laodacea, a prophetic anticipation of modern conditions may have been at work....

---

* Steiner, *Esoteric Lessons 1910–1912: From the Esoteric School, Volume Two,* pp. 324–326.

> If we try to visualize the path which the old man (Saint John) had to travel from Ephesus, whenever he wished to visit the seven churches, the symbolic pattern of this group become apparent. Ephesus was the city by the sea. A wide bay opened out to far horizons. Today the place has become quiet and insignificant, since the harbour is silted up and the town lies inland. Nevertheless, the great natural arena of ancient Ephesus, lying in a circle around the castle hill, is still clearly discernible. In early Christian times the Sun of Homer still shone over Ephesus as over no other city of the Johannine churches. In the very landscape in which Saint John's Gospel was written, the writings of Homer came into being a thousand years earlier. And the soul of the great populous city was still infused with the Mysteries of the often destroyed, often rebuilt, age-old temple of Artemis-Diana.*

So, we just came upon the sites which were always within a two-hour drive, or half a day. I wished I could have walked, but I did not have the extra month to do so. I will have to walk these paths in the future!

These seven communities started from the sea where we were, up into the high plateau, mountains of Asia minor, making a circle.

From Ephesus and Smyrna (Izmir), which is a very large city with no remains of its past, unlike Ephesus, we went on to Laodicea (near Colossae), Philadelphia, Sardis, Thyatira, and Pergamum.

> Moses had to pioneer the development of wide-awake thinking. His mission of consciousness was symbolized in the journey through the wilderness undertaken by him as the leader of his people since the new stage could only be reached by means of a temporary impoverishment. Paul's mission was the opposite one. With the fire of the heart, he was supposed to enkindle the light of a new vision in the darkened, impoverished thoughts of the head. His apostolic journeys were an image of this task. He did not lead a nation already in existence by virtue of blood ties; instead by carrying the word and power of Christ to all nations, he created a new community based on spiritual kinship....
>
> The seven communities to which Paul's nine congregational letters are addressed remind us of the seven archetypal communities to which

---

*   Bock, *The Apocalypse of Saint John*, pp. 28–30.

the seven letters of the Apocalypse are directed. As closely united circles of human beings, the congregations of Ephesus, Smyrna, Pergamum, Thyatira, Sardis, Philadelphia, and Laodicea existed in an earthly sense in the aged John's sphere of activity. In Revelation, on the other hand these communities become transparent and appear as a scale of evolutionary stages that must be undergone by the spiritual vanguard of humanity. There the inner curve leads first of all from the after-effects of the ancient spirituality, still close to heaven, to the descent and impoverishment of Earth, then up again to a gradual attainment of a new spirituality related to human freedom. Just as the seven physical locations, where the seven Johannine communities had originated, form a line resembling a half-circle, the Ionian coast up to the highlands of Asia Minor, so, too, the spiritual archetypes that become visible in them express a path of stages to be undergone by humanity.*

We toured the Hierapolis of Phrygia (300 BC to AD 200) with its extensive necropolis over a couple of miles on a mountainside; it was on the road to Sardis. Large tombs were everywhere, a beautiful bath complex and pools, tall cedar trees amidst hundreds of tombs with poppies growing profusely in between the enormous slabs of stones. It was a site dedicated to the dead, to death.

Then we toured the strange baths where the salt oozed out of the mountainsides, and has been oozing out and leaving salt deposits for thousands of years. It has forever been a bath complex, and pools go up the high mountainside where the tourists can walk up and bathe in these magical, white, salty settings with warm water continuously dripping down. Nothing grows here; it is a salt-covered mountainside, like the Dead Sea, death. From far away the whole mountainside looks as if it were covered in snow, and shines for miles around.

Not far away from Laodicea and Colossum, Hierapolis was the home of the *Plutonium*, one of the most famous oracles of the ancient world. Here a cave penetrated deep into the interior. A sinister atmosphere, a sense of terror, issued from this subterranean rocky cave. It was known

---

*   Bock, *Saint Paul: Life, Epistles and Teaching*, pp. 9, 225.

that it was filled continually with poisonous gases from the interior of the Earth and that whoever entered it would be asphyxiated. Despite or even because of that very reason, this inferno concealed a sanctuary. It was thought to be the dwelling-place of Pluto, the God of the Underworld. A mysterious rite was performed there by the priests of Cybele. These priests must have made use of an early chemical knowledge whereby they protected themselves from the deadly effects of subterranean gases. Thus, by means of these forces flowing from the interior of the Earth, they succeeded in transporting themselves, like the Pythia at Delphi, into a somnambulistic condition which enabled them to give oracular answers from the gods to the questions of men.... In the country near the cities of Hierapolis, Laodicea, and Colossae, the surface of the Earth is like an inverted stalactite cave. In the past (and still now), hot mineral springs issued here from the interior of the Earth, and trickled over the soil so that through stalactite activity a kind of porcelain or glassy crust was formed. Fantastic, needle-like points of rock deposited and crystallized by the mineral waters rise up from the glassy formation of the ground like the surface of an alien, dead planet. All verdant life is scorched by the death-dealing subterranean breath. Here is a complete contrast to Ephesus. There by the sea, everything was still illumined by the dreams of the gods and echoes of the original paradise harmony with heaven. Here in the interior of Asia Minor the powers of hell tread openly in the daylight bringing death to all living things.[*]

The town below on the other side of the salt mountain is a famous spa center for Turkey, and also a chosen site for weddings. We stayed in a local inn with a wonderful restaurant on the terrace overlooking the dead salt mountainside, several hundred feet high and thick from millennia of dripping.

This wall of salt mountainside reminded me of the Dead Sea in Palestine, and the other side the enchanting area of northern Palestine where it is light.

To reach Laodicea, the second church on our agenda, we had to go farther north, through sinuous mountain roads, and beautiful cities and villages hidden in between mountains. The whole area has suffered major

---

[*] Bock, *The Apocalypse of Saint John*, pp. 28–29.

earthquakes throughout its history and still does. The site dominates the area, high on a plateau strewn with archeological debris, temples, paved ancient roads, amphitheaters, and current digs. It is vast, and took a few hours of wandering through these ancient ruins.

Then driving east this time, through extensive vineyards and farms, we arrived at the site of Saint Jean Church in Philadelphia, which was hidden in the middle of a very busy town. The ancient church site was kept by a pleasant attendant. Only a few old ruins remained in a lovely, multi-colored rose garden, with many cool, tall minarets peeking out in the surroundings.

It was an intriguing, mysterious journey for me to imagine Saint Paul walking through this large country, on foot of course, two thousand years ago, and what stood behind his Herculean effort at spreading Christianity.

> A world view characterized by fear of the threshold, as in the Pharisaic-Jewish view, has to be dualistic in the extreme: God and man, heaven and Earth are completely incommensurable and incompatible. How can the living light of God impinge upon the darkness of earthly man, how can the power of His spirit meet the perishable Earth-substance without the Earth splitting asunder and burning up?
>
> Before the Gates of Damascus, Paul was delivered from the terrifying Messianic paradox. From beyond the threshold, a benevolent helping power approached him, releasing his essential being from terror of the divine and awakening in him the force that he himself would later on call "faith." Through this power, the dividing barrier between this world and the beyond disappeared; he was allowed to take the first step across the threshold. This occurred as he was led forward from the element of vision, which he only knew as visionary lightning, into that of inner hearing.
>
> The accounts that we have of what took place in that noon hour before the gates of Damascus remain incomprehensible and even contradictory unless we cease to imagine in physical-sensory terms what were supersensory events and experiences. Neither the overwhelming powerful light, "brighter than the Sun" (Acts 26:13), which shone round Paul, nor the voice that spoke to him, could be perceived by earthly senses....

Paul heard the light. Notwithstanding all the power of that voice, it was still an inner hearing when he felt himself called by his name twice and when the question broke in upon him which compelled him to become conscious of the essential motives of his persecuting zeal: "Saul, Saul, why do you persecute me?" It was a dawning of awareness in which, simultaneously, the voice of his own conscience sounded. In his own inner being, a voice arose which yet only belonged to him. His whole being trembled with the anxious question of who this higher one was: "Who are you, Lord?" (Acts 9:4f). The intensity and sincerity of the question unlocked the answer which now came forth as hearing became seeing. A figure and a countenance could now be perceived. The divine light-force of the Christ Being appeared in a form that bore human traits. Paul beheld the countenance of the Messiah whom he believed he was serving and realized that this countenance was indeed marked by the consummated human incarnation in the man, Jesus of Nazareth.*

We crossed mountains, large areas of farmland, forests, arid plateaus, and then we reached Sardis.

Sardis, like the other settlements, has been inhabited since the Bronze Age, three thousand to seven thousand years ago. This area is part of the natural corridor leading to the Aegean Sea through the main river Hermus, steadily climbing to Anatolia and its distinct inhabitants, the Lydians.

It was in a beautiful, sumptuous setting, amidst mountain pastures, springs flowing everywhere, and rich farmland surrounded by vineyards, with olive tree plantations in the small valley and forests of pines and cedars on the mountainside. The ruins were extensive, with Artemis temples, amphitheaters, and roads, still standing. I can see why King Croesus was fabulously rich. My mother always said, "Riche comme Cresus!" It was a magical setting, and I would have enjoyed staying there and hiking in the nearby mountains with its shepherd and sheep, and mountain people.

Only now did a mature and complete vision begin to enfold within Paul. The brightness of the Pharisaic vision, which had filled his soul

---

* Bock, *Saint Paul: Life, Epistles and Teaching*, pp. 80–81.

Temple of Artemis ruins in Sardis

with so much terror and restlessness, was superseded and healed. It was as if the Sun had risen to quiet the lightning flashes of a nocturnal thunderstorm. Nonetheless, a profound shock in Paul's soul came with this mighty easing and relaxing of tension. What an appalling error he had succumbed to! What evil he had perpetrated under its fanatical duress! The insight gained as a consequence of the true vision struck him so powerfully that his eyes were blinded.

Then it became clear that he of whom Paul had been so deeply afraid was living benevolence and love itself. The experience of feeling himself touched and permeated, of surrendering himself in faith to the One whose will is nothing but help and redemption, allowed Paul to sense a way out of helplessness of the moment; and this escape would be the beginnings of many paths—leading him towards his worldwide mission. The hate-filled passion of persecution would be transformed into the untiring work of apostolic activity....

Paul felt and again and again expressed it in a radical manner, that through the light of Damascus he had found the path *from Moses to Christ.**

---

* Ibid., pp. 82–83, 86.

Towards Thyatira the road goes farther inland and we arrive at the plateau of Asia Minor. The landscape is more monotonous than at the coastal strip. Life is simpler, and less full of history. No shadow of a gigantic past falls upon it.*

We climbed into the mountains, becoming more desert-like, with some traces of large-surface farming, more olive orchards everywhere, and some pharmaceutical farming of the opium poppy. We arrived in the hill town of Akhisar to see the ruins of Thyateria, another of the famous Saint Paul churches where he preached. The site was more difficult to find, since it was in the middle of a very busy city. We parked and enjoyed the remnants of this church, and stopped in a local café to enjoy some well-earned lunch amidst the busy teenagers who were on their cell phones with friends, in lively conversation.

The area now was full of chicken farming operations on an enormous scale. Miles and miles of them, to meet the demand of the Turkish people and the rest of the Middle East. A merchant told me that Turkey provides food for much of Kuwait, Bahrain, and many other Middle Eastern countries, and former Soviet Muslim republics, because, "We work very hard, and they don't," and he added, "especially the Greeks, who just rest on their laurels from their glorious Hellenic past, and do nothing, then they are jealous because we are a very successful country, but we *work*!"

Much of the cultivated land in Turkey has adopted the American style of farming, bigger is better, thereby polluting their land which is a shame. I saw corn growing, which is not really their crop. But they also have large milk cow parlors copied from the United States to meet the demand of milk and cheese production, and that is the reason why many of the shepherds and their flocks who used to roam in these areas have been banned. They only live in the mountainous regions, and thanks to geography, most of Turkey is mountains, thereby protecting them from these terrible farming practices.

Then we drove again through beautiful mountain settings to Pergamum, not far from the sea. We found a lovely bed and breakfast held by a young

---

*   Bock, *The Apocalypse of Saint John*, p. 28.

The Temple of Trajan at Pergamum

couple in a very old house in the old city. Bergamos is on top of a mountain and we hired a taxi to go up the very steep road leading to the site.

It was a kind of windy, dark winter day which fitted the glorious, stunning setting for Pergamum, an apocalyptic setting, majestic, but not infernal like Mount Sinai or the Laodicean plutonium interior of the Earth hell. The large former temples of all sizes, theaters, columns, paths, spoke of former sacred ceremonies held only for the chosen ones. This passage reminds one of what happened in Bergamos and what was described earlier in the Egyptian initiation.

> All pre-Christian initiation was based on the principle of ecstasy. The extreme and complete form consisted in the neophyte being placed into the deathlike temple sleep, the "mystical death," after undergoing the preparatory instructions and soul trials. The ecstasy lifted the fallen being of man to the divine heights from where, transformed and gifted with higher knowledge, it returned after three days into the bodily sheaths. In the late ages of antiquity when the ancient spiritual vision in humanity had virtually shrunk to intellectual thought, only a certain aspect of the ancient initiation remained in some places, for

instance among the Nazirites and Essenes. After long, ascetic preparation by means of certain baptismal rites with water, the souls were loosened from their bondage to the body so that a certain revival of the ancient clairvoyance occurred. Thus, in this manner as a last shadow of the supersensory world, a half imaginative, allegorical picture element became mixed in with the now abstract thinking. With the baptism carried out by long submersion in the waters of the Jordan, John the Baptist still brought it about that the souls experienced a death-like liberation from the body, even if only for a short time. As a result of their entering the higher worlds, they then brought back an awareness of their own mental darkness and of the approach of a divine light into everyday light....

The transformation that was now brought about in the spiritual life of humanity through the Christ event consisted in the principle of ecstasy being replaced by that of incorporation. The Pauline principle of *"Christ in us"* became operative. The principle of ecstasy was at an end; that of incorporation at a beginning....

With this new beginning, the seed existed for a form of consciousness that does not arrive at its insights outwardly, but comes to them from within.... The principle of incorporation viewed in the Pauline sense, must give birth one day to a new creative thinking that will grasp the world from out of the core of the human being and, because of this, will also penetrate through the outer surface of things into their spiritual essence.*

On majestic heights with sweeping views, the city lay crowded closely round the castle and temple hill. Its temple building gave it a character of concentrated greatness. The little Christian community had to lead their quiet life in an environment of powerful heathen cults.**

On the top of the mountain at Pergamum, the movement of the clouds, the sunlight shining through the clouds, and the sunrays hitting the tall temple columns gave this place a feeling of grandeur, of the supernatural

---

* Bock, *Saint Paul: Life, Epistles and Teaching*, pp. 176–177.
** Bock, *The Apocalypse of Saint John*, p. 28.

forces of nature, of unsurpassed beauty. This site was naturally fitting to receive Saint Paul's powerful words.

Since it was the end of the day, the large ruins were almost emptied of visitors. I climbed everywhere, peeked through rocky small windows into the distant valleys, sat in the amphitheater, climbed tall columns, laid down on large slabs of cold stones, and tried to communicate with the sacred surroundings. From the tall mountains we could see the flooded area below, very large lakes going into the distance. This site, more so than the others, was made to receive the Greek Gods into the harmonious temple spaces built for them. I think there was still a hint of their presence!

This detour into Paul's journey awoke something within me, about the incredible power residing in this apostle. I had done numerous paintings of Saint Paul's Damascus. And now visiting these regions, where he preached and fought his way through insurmountable opposition from all people, awakened in me the colossal Personality who was Paul.

The following words by Rudolf Steiner help:

> During this entire evolution of human consciousness the Creators of old, the Spirits of Form, were active; they revealed themselves to the supersensible consciousness. Now it is no longer the Spirits who are revealed to one who stands within the modern life of spirit: it is the Spirits of Personality.
>
> You may ask, what is the difference? This is shown precisely in initiation science. The modern spiritual scientist is still someone very strange to the popular consciousness, even to the general scientific consciousness, because the latter contains only a spark of Galileism, Copernicanism, and Goetheanism and even that in very elementary form, for it is still commonly dominated by the mode of thought of the ancient seers. It was the Spirits of Form who had furnished the ancient visions, who then brought to life in man the conceptions that were active in the ancient religions and even in Christianity up to the present time. These Spirits of Form, whom we call Creators, manifested themselves, to begin with, in imaginations that arose in man involuntarily. That was their initial mode of revelation; then out of the imaginations grew the conceptions of all the ancient religions.... All those who wanted to reach the supersensible knowledge in the ancient

sense started from imaginations; they had to find their way to the Spirits of Form.

Today the way has to be found to the Spirits of Personality. Here, then is a tremendous difference. For the Spirits of Personality do not give imaginations to whoever wants them: a man must work them out of himself; he must go to meet the Spirit of Personality. It was not necessary to go to meet the Spirits of Form. Formerly a man could be what one may call favored by divine grace, because the Spirits of Form gave him their imaginations in the form of visions. Many still seek this path today, because it is easier—but it is only attainable now in a pathological condition. Mankind has evolved, and what was psychological in earlier times is pathological now. Everything in the nature of visions, everything that depends on involuntary imaginations, is pathological in our time and pushes a man down below his normal level. For the Spirits of Personality will not give him imaginations; he must bring the imaginations to them. And something else occurs today. When you develop, when you elaborate valid imaginations, then you meet the Spirits of Personality on your supersensible path of knowledge, and you find the power to verify your imaginations, to bring them to objectivity for yourself.*

It was not an ecstasy and translation as in the spiritual experiences of the past where the soul departed the body and unfolded spiritual vision in the place of day-dreaming consciousness. The miracle that took place was that the soul remained awake *in* the body—and yet did not find itself in exactly the same relationship to its body as before. It was greater than the body, therefore it was *also* but not *only* outside the body. The principle of translation was replaced by that of *indwelling*. The higher power that came to meet Paul and allowed his soul to grow beyond itself, now indwelt him. And because it was mightier than his soul, it permitted his soul to partake of its own greatness, thus allowing an experience of ascent and intensification. In a classic example, Paul expressed this transition which had significance for all humanity: that henceforth the higher world wishes to reveal itself to the *waking* human being. This is reflected in the two related questions that he

---

*   Steiner, *How Can Mankind Find the Christ Again?*, pp. 94–95.

raised during his description: "Was he in the body? Was he outside the body? I do not know, God Knows." The miracle lay in the fact that both states, which until then had been mutually exclusive, now occurred simultaneously: the soul was in the body and yet outside it.*

Completing this circle of the seven churches was meaningful to me, there was some deep significance to these churches. To actually see them, and see the geography, reminded me of Palestine with the contrast of Judae and Galilee, life and death, as I mentioned earlier. Here again I must borrow from Emil Bock's genius and deep insights.

> The seven churches represent in miniature the great human epochs in the course of history. Echoes of a past still near to heaven and God, as in the ancient Indian culture, create the magic of Ephesus. Smyrna has something of the Old Persian epoch, wherein humanity awoke to the struggle between light and darkness, and gained from it the urge to active work and practical labor. Pergamum, on the soil of the former Trojan lands, echoed the Mycenic-Trojan wisdom, sister of the Egyptian-Chaldaic temple culture. The Presbyter of Ephesus met his own epoch in Thyaria, the central city of the seven. At the middle point of history, Christ descended to his Incarnation on Earth, and the current of Christian life could begin to flow into the historic evolution of humanity. Thus the central city of the seven depicts the time of the apostles, that is, the present time of the Johannine epoch. Traveling deeper into the interior of the country, from the cities of the preservers to those of the precursors, we come last to Sardis, Philadelphia, and Laodicea. Although linked together by contemporary existence, the seven cities and churches conceal within their proximity in space a great succession of stages in time, which anyone who together with the aged John visited the seven churches one after another, would have experienced in their symbolic significance.**

---

*   Bock, *Saint Paul: Life, Epistles and Teaching*, pp. 239–240.
** Bock, *The Apocalypse of Saint John*, p. 30.

To head back to Istanbul, I chose a small mountain road, crossing difficult terrain to see the real Turkey, away from tourists and big-time farming, and it was lovely.

It took forever, but it was worth it. Cows were walking, going up and down the small sinuous roads, going back to their barns. Sheep were in the fields enjoying their grass, or walking by the side of the road. Small farms and villages were plentiful in the rounded mountains and forested hills. The homes were well built with beautiful, red-tiled roofs, and people were very busy working. In the last thirty-five years, Turkey has become a very modern European country with the same standards. They had nothing to envy. It was far from being the poor country I had seen years ago. Its standards of living are, in my opinion, better than Spain. The Turkish people work extremely hard, and they are becoming an example for many of the Muslim countries.

Again as we approached the northern areas we drove through more industrial farming, chickens, cows, beef, on a very large scale.

We took a very tiny road by the sea which was quite challenging to drive but finally arrived in the extensive, large, modern city of Istanbul which is spreading steadily into the surrounding mountainous terrain. It is home to thirteen million people and is still growing!

Part VII

A Look Into the Past: Iran

1975–1984

Since I lived in Iran so long ago, I will only briefly speak about it here. This is a book in itself, as yet unwritten.

I arrived in Tehran on January 2, 1975, joining an army of foreign expats from around the world who earned an enormous amount of money (not me) and drained the coffers of the Iranian people. I was a technical English teacher for the Iranian airforce, working on a base in southern Tehran from 7:00 AM to 1:00 PM, teaching young men from villages around Iran who had joined the airforce to be trained as mechanics for helicopters. The students were wonderful, bright, serious, and respectful. I did not wear the veil, but dressed appropriately. At age twenty-six, I was just a few years older than they were.

The first six months I suffered from headaches due to the high altitude (seven thousand feet), but after becoming acclimatized, making my lungs able to draw more oxygen into my blood, I actually was able later on to go hiking and climbing in much higher elevations (thirteen thousand to eighteen thousand feet) in other parts of the world without any problems.

My reason for choosing Iran, rather than Chad, Africa where I would have taught English at the university, was its mountains and ski area. I love skiing and gladly packed up my ski gear and books and entered another episode in my life. As soon as possible, I got some of my co-workers together and rented a chalet in the middle of the twelve-thousand-foot-high ski resort for the weekends, a three-hour drive from Tehran.

After teaching all week, we drove in vans up the very steep, unpaved road to Dizeen, sometimes being stuck after major avalanches. But it was fabulous skiing, partying, and endless activities with friends from around the world, and, of course, Iranians.

When ski season was over, I would spend my Fridays (our Sundays) going to the bazaar, looking at carpets, drinking tea, chatting with Turkomans who came from way up north and lived in small homes in the southern part of Tehran, taking carpets home to enjoy them, buying copperware, eating caviar. I thoroughly enjoyed my new life in this new ancient world. I felt as if I were home, which might have been correct, if one knows about reincarnation!

A favorite activity for Persians, young and old, is to hike up the mountains to twelve thousand feet north of Tehran, drinking tea in the teahouses which lined the path at the bottom on the way up. Below, the river flowed, and families were nonchalantly lying on wooden beds covered with carpet eating delicious ābgusht, food, listening to the magical sounds of the water running on the rocks, where tall walnut trees grew. So I did a lot of early morning hiking.

During other long weekends, I went to surrounding cities: Kashan, famous for its rose gardens; Ghom and Karaj, villages around the mountains; then farther south, to my favorite city of Isfahan, with its most spectacular mosque; Shiraz, to visit Hafiz' tomb; Persepolis; then to the north to Meshad; cities on the north coast of the Caspian Sea, etc.

Persia does not give up its secrets so easily; one must go in private gardens surrounded by mud walls, small oases hidden in the hills, small villages tucked away in valleys. There we can get a touch of the real Persia, a fragrance of its attraction which was the ground for the birth of its dozens of poets living nine hundred years ago.

> The development of poetry in Persia occurred at a time when there was a great conflict between the orthodox and the freethinkers. At that time the law of the nation was a religious law and no one was

at liberty to express his free thought, that might be in conflict with religious ideas. There were great thinkers such as Firdawsi, Fariduddin Attar, Rumi, Sa'adi, Hafiz, Jami, Omar Khayyam, who were not only poets but who were poetry itself. They were living in another world, although they appeared to be on Earth. Their outlook on life, their keen sight were different from those of everyone else. The words that arose from their hearts were not brought forth with effort; they were natural flames rising up out of the heart. These words remain as flames enlightening souls of all times, whatever souls they have touched.

Sufism has been the wisdom of these poets. There has never been a poet of note in Persia who was not a Sufi, and every one of them has added a certain aspect to the Sufi ideas. But they took great care not to affront the minds of the orthodox people. Therefore a new terminology had to be invented in Persian poetry; the poets had to use words such as "wine," "bowl," "beloved," and "rose," words that would not offend the orthodox mind and would yet at the same time serve as symbolical expressions to explain the divine law.*

There was a time when a deep thinker and a free thinker had great difficulties in expressing his thoughts, and that time has not altogether ceased.... At that time, anyone who expressed his thought freely about life and its hidden law—about soul, God, creation, and manifestation—met with great difficulty.

The difficulty was that the religious authorities of all kinds governed, and under the religious reign the principles of the exoteric religion reigned. And therefore those who attained by the esoteric side of philosophy always had difficulty in telling it to the people. Many were persecuted; they were stoned, they were flayed, they were put to death. All sorts of punishments were inflicted upon them, and in this way the progress of humanity was retarded. Today we do not see this. At the same time, the limited attitude of the human mind on religious and philosophical questions is to be found in all ages.

The Sufis, who found by the help of meditation the source of knowledge in their own hearts, for them it was very difficult to give to the world in plain words what little they could explain of the truth....

---

*   Khan, *The Music of Life: The Inner Nature and Effects of Sound*, p. 332.

Hafiz found a way of expressing the experience of his soul and his philosophies in verse. For the soul enjoys expressing itself in verse because the soul itself is music, and when it is experiencing the realization of divine truth the tendency of the soul is to express itself in poetry. Hafiz therefore expressed his soul in poetry. And what poetry! Poetry full of light and shade, line and color, and poetry full of feeling....

The Persian language is considered in the East the most delicious language, a language which stands supreme to all Eastern languages in poetry....

The mission of Hafiz was to express, to a fanatically inclined religious world, the presence of God, which is not to be found only in heaven, but to be found here on Earth.

Very often religious belief in God and in the hereafter has kept man sleeping, waiting for that hour and that day to come when he will be face to face with his Lord, and he is certain that that day will not come before he is dead. And therefore he awaits his death in the hope that in the hereafter he will see God, for heaven alone is the place where God is to be found, there is no other place where God will be found. And that there is only a certain place which is a sacred place of worship, that is, the church, and that anywhere else God was not be found.

The mission of Hafiz was to take away this idea and to make man conscious of the heaven by his side, and to tell man that all he expects in the hereafter as a reward, could be had here, if he lived a fuller life.[*]

Here is a poem by Hafiz:

The Gifts
The margin of a stream, the willow's shade,
A mind inclined to song, a mistress sweet,
A cup-bearer whose cheek outshines the rose,
A friend upon whose heart thy heart laid:
Oh happy-starred! Let not thine hours fleet
Unvalued; may each minute as it goes
Lay tribute of enjoyment at thy feet,
That thou may'st live and know thy life is sweet.

---

[*] Barks (trans.) and Khan, *The Hand of Poetry: Five Mystic Poets of Persia*, pp. 136–138.

Let every one upon whose heart desire
For a fair face lies like a burden sore,
That all his hopes may reach their goal unchecked,
Throw branches of wild rue upon his fire.
My soul is like a bride, with a rich store
Of maiden thoughts and jeweled fancies decked,
And in Time's gallery I yet may meet
Some picture meant for me, some image sweet.

Give thanks for nights spent in good company,
And take the gifts a tranquil mind may bring;
No heart is dark when the kind Moon doth shine,
And grass-grown river-banks are fair to see.
The saki's radiant eyes, God favoring,
Are like a wine-cup brimming o'er with wine,
And him my drunken sense goes out to greet,
For even the pain he leaves behind is sweet.

Hafiz, thy life has sped untouched by care,
With me towards the tavern turn thy feet!
The fairest robbers thou'lt encounter there,
And they will teach thee what to learn is sweet.*

On a longer vacation, I took the bus to Afghanistan to visit friends in Kabul and back, quite a trip!

Other vacations were in the other direction, to Turkey, and the Greek islands, or a short airplane ride to Pakistan, and India, for hiking in Nepal.

And one year, an audacious drive with a car from Dijon, France to Tehran via Italy, Greece, and Turkey. Then later by bus via Herat, Afghanistan, and another bus, the famed "Magic Bus," to Kandahar, Kabul, Kyber Pass, Amritsar, Lahore, Pakistan, Bombay, and all the way to Goa, in southern India, for Christmas. I was twenty-eight years old.

There was no reason for me to ever go back to the West. France did not appeal to me, and neither did the United States. I was very happy here learning Persian, reading the Persian poets, and having fun.

---

*   Hafiz, in Washington (ed.), *Persian Poets*, p. 212.

Then the revolution happened. The language company folded, but I stayed because of my love affair with an Iranian medical student. I lived in the mountains at the ski area for the winter, when it was deserted during the whole ordeal. I had my books and typewriter, and I wrote while a mess was happening in Tehran. One morning I remember on a walk I saw the religious police destroy all the liquor they found in the luxury hotel, and smash the bottles on the stone wall of the hotel's basement. But I was quite oblivious to it all, preferring to focus on poets, philosophy, religious studies, Bhuddism, masters, etc. I do not know what the villagers thought I was doing all day, alone. They never bothered me! Since I am not easily scared, I didn't have the usual fear that people have until I headed back into Tehran and the thought crossed my mind that perhaps I should be a *bit* concerned since I had to cover up, and saw for myself the road blocks by teenage boys with guns. It was serious, and I was living in sin, unmarried, a foreigner, and a Christian, but I just observed the happenings.

Since foreigners had left, many international schools lacked teachers, and so I taught in a French lycée for the spring and headed back to the United States for the summer and fall. Then before the closure of the airport I arrived again back in Tehran, and Khomeini entered Tehran as well. I spent the winter teaching again and became pregnant, so I had to go back to the United States for my son to be born, since I was not married.

Two years later, I came back to Iran for my son to meet his dad, and stayed in the Northern city, on the Caspian Sea for the summer. I then headed back to Tehran, where I taught again until the next June. At this point I left Iran, never to return.

So my idyllic stay in this fabulous country ended on a sour note. I had gone to school to study Farsi and learn the Arabic script, and I was very much interested in its poets and wanted to read them in the original, but time and destiny had other plans!

Perhaps it was a reliving into my past, touching upon former lives in these fabulous settings? I felt totally at home even though my body is a western one—totally a western, blond, small product of northern European genes! But in my soul I am much more at home in Persia, or the Middle

East, or India for that matter, except for the wearing of the hejab, *that* I cannot accept, only temporarily.

What I loved was the people, their warmth, hospitality, customs, and the amazing, magic country. I spent much time hiking in the mountains of northern Tehran while the revolution was at its peak. Youthful movement university students would climb up the mountains in large numbers in order to meet and discuss major issues facing them, like being thrown into prison for their revolutionary activities. They would sit on top of Mount Elborg and talk quietly in groups, away from the watchful eyes of spies, averting me since I was a foreigner. When the United States Embassy was taken over, I drove around like everyone else to see what was going on, which was nothing except for a few people out front—nothing like in the news.

I loved the food, especially the abundance of fruits, vegetables, and nuts. Little trucks drove around the large city, transporting their stuff to local markets and villages, filled to almost unbelievable heights with melons of all kinds, oranges, etc.

During the holy Iranian holiday, I was perplexed by the cult to Hussein. At the time I did not know anything about the Sunni-Shia relationship. So during the holy day when Iranians took to the street to flagellate themselves until blood came, and walked around the city by the hundreds, it was quite a sight. My students tried to explain it to me, being sure to emphasize the bloody aspect to see my reaction, which was no reaction! Just listening skills. During those days, it was the only time I felt out of place, uncomfortable, and a feeling of *this is not my home*. The city had a thick atmosphere of a "beside itself," or "out of one's self" mood. I stayed home, looked out the window, and listened to the cries as they walked down my street. It reached the proportion of being out of oneself, a trance and a real reliving of the sufferings of the past, being kept alive every year. One could feel the working up of the crowd, and an element of extremism, of no control, of not knowing what would happen next during this religious fervor.

I had never experienced this mood in Morocco or Algeria, so it was a puzzling experience which did not fit with the Iranians that I knew. They had not divulged this mysterious aspect of their religiousness. It can be compared to Easter in Spain or Jerusalem, but much bloodier. Here the faithful wanted to *feel the pain*, the more the better, and enter into another world. The world of the saints, and their adoration, worshiping of these saints, going into ecstasy through pain.

I did not feel comfortable because I could feel that any small incident could push the crowd to massive hysteria, uncontrollable hysteria. So most foreigners stayed home, and waited for the holy day to end to pursue a regular life.

Persia is not an Arab nation and its past invariably comes to the surface in many ways. The celebration of Noruz, rite of springs, the sumptuous, gargantuan parties with mountains of food, the love of the oasis, running water, sleeping on terraces, garden parties hidden among tall mud walls, sleeping on rolled blankets with black tea for breakfast, and cherry jam and bread overlooking the mountains in people's simple homes, kabab on rice for lunch, disregard for attending the mosque among *most* Iranians, outrageous parties at home, riding on the kings' horses in northern Tehran, sacrificing a sheep in a home way out in the desert for a party of seventy, following dirt paths for hours, a poet's lunch given by his French wife to expats in Garden of Eden–like settings, etc.

The Persian say they are proud of their heritage. They say: *We don't fight the invaders, we just include them in our life, and we go on. We are not a fighting people.* And it is true, they have not invaded any country, unlike their neighbors, Iraq, Russia, etc.

From the very beginning I began studying more about the country—its history, customs, religion, pre-Islamic past of Zoroastrians, fire worship, Mazdean past, Mani, illustrious kings and caliphs, tales from *One Thousand and One Nights*, and the famous Persian poetry in French and English. Tehran had great French, English, and international bookstores! Studying took most of my time, until I left my Iranian family and my husband joined me seven months later in the United States in 1985 for another life.

Nevertheless, Iran, Persia, this very ancient land has given me the greatest gifts: a son, a daughter, and two grandchildren. They look just like their Persian forefathers, even the little ones, and for that I am so ever grateful!

A LOOK INTO THE PAST: IRAN

Here is another poem by Hafiz:

The Substance You Taste
The sky-wheel turns us into dawn
and fills creation again with color.

Let it be our weakness, this thirst-love
for the world, the Sun coming up
like red-gold being poured!

The potter's wheel moves,
and shapes change quickly.

Let the jar I am becoming
turn to a wine cup.
Fill me with your love
for being awake.

I'm no hypocrite renunciate.
Call me this delicious substance
you taste when you create new beauty.

Be strong, Hafiz!
Work here inside time,
where we fail, catch hold
again, and climb.*

My stay in Iran has probably been the reason for pursuing this present journey, perhaps to try and understand my past—my other incarnations, that is! Or what is this love affair with the Muslim, Christian, and Jewish worlds? Things left undone from the past? Not understood? Or perhaps a strong desire to solve something for the future?

> From the perspective of a spiritual world view, it could be said, "All of these souls who are incarnated in the East—in that region we refer to as the East—they will seek to incarnate during their next lifetime in

---

* Hafiz, in Barks (trans.) and Khan, *The Hand of Poetry: Five Mystic Poets of Persia*, p. 152.

the West. The western people will seek to reincarnate during their next lifetime more toward the East. Those in the middle will need to seek a means of building a bridge between the two."*

The reader has noticed that this section is extremely short and, as I mentioned in the beginning, what is missing will be the subject of another project still in the making. The Iranian Islamic gnosis is an extremely wealthy, rich, and misunderstood tradition and it is beyond the scope of this journey to speak about it. So it will be left untouched except for a few comments by a wonderful French historian of this century, Déodat Roché, which he gave at a conference in Carcassonne on November 22, 1961.

> How are we going to ascend to the Divine world? We have met three great mystery schools of spiritual science.... One of these schools is the one dealing with Iranian Islamic gnosis which Professor Henry Corbin (the Sorbonne and the University of Tehran) has deeply researched and presented to the world. Through his many years of arduous research we have access to the Zoroastrian roots of the mysteries and religions of the West. The other is anthroposophy, which offers a wisdom and a spiritual science designed for the modern age. Anthroposophy allows us to understand the Manichean doctrines as well as deeply understand all the sciences and arts. Finally, the White Brotherhood of Bulgaria, with members like the Manicheans, try to build new communities which prefigure and prepare in advance our future civilization.... None of these great mystery schools are dogmatic and should be mistaken with organized religions of any sort.**

For a small aperçu, Christopher Bamford's introduction to *The Voyage and the Messenger**** by Henry Corbin is a beginning in this complex journey.

---

*   Steiner, *What is Necessary in These Urgent Times*, p. 162.
** Roché, *Les Cathares, Précurseurs des Temps Modernes: Extrait des Cahiers d'Etudes Cathares*, p. 20 (tr. M-L. Valandro).
*** Corbin, *The Voyage and the Messenger: Iran and Philosophy*.

Part VIII

Poland

SIX MONTHS LATER

As usual, I had not planned on visiting Poland, but I had my euro-train pass, and some free time before crossing the Atlantic, so I could not resist touring central Europe. It was not part of this journey, but as it turns out, it is. My journeys have a will of their own sometimes which I must respect. I was supposed to have spent the fall in Fes, Morocco, but I was not inwardly ready to do so. I had more work to do on myself, and it was not as simple as restudying the Arabic script. So I delayed Fes for a year and was in central Europe instead.

I took the train from Berlin after visiting their outstanding museum. I arrived in Warsaw on the first of November, the day of the dead, which was another coincidence. This is the most celebrated holy day in Poland. No one was around. They were *all* at the cemetery. Through the train window, I had seen people dressed in black, carrying enormous flower bouquets at the cemetery in several towns we were crossing.

The train station in Warsaw was in the center and near gigantic buildings not yet renovated, which stood out like sore thumbs from the Soviet period—bulky, enormous, cold buildings. Warsaw was basically destroyed during the war, and the Poles have undergone enormous sufferings; they have had their share of heavy burdens on their shoulders.

This statement by Rudolf Steiner gives some insights into the problems facing our world:

> You will no doubt have heard that certain people are over and over again proclaiming to the world that democracy must spread to the whole civilized world. Salvation lies in making the whole of humanity democratic; everything will have to be smashed to pieces so that democracy may spread to the world. Well, if people go on to accept ideas presented to them as they are, with wholesale acceptance of the term democracy, their idea of democracy will be like the definition of the human being which I gave you: a human being is a creature with two legs and without feathers: a plucked cockerel. The people, who are glorifying democracy today know about as much about it as someone who is shown a plucked cockerel knows about the human being. Concepts are taken for reality, and as a result illusion may take the place of reality where human life is concerned by lulling people to sleep with concepts. They believe the fruits of their endeavors will be that every individual will be able to express their will in the different democratic institutions, and they fail to see that these institutions are such that it is always just a few people who pull the wires, while the rest are pulled along. They are persuaded, however, that they are part of democracy and so they do not notice the strings. Those individuals will find it all the easier to do the pulling if the others all believe that they are doing it themselves, instead of being pulled along. If is quite easy to lull people to sleep with abstract concepts and make them believe the opposite of what is really true.
>
> It is interesting to note that in 1910 someone wrote that large-scale capitalism had succeeded in making democracy into the most marvelous, flexible, and effective tool for exploiting the whole population. Financiers were usually imagined to be the enemies of democracy, the individual concerned wrote, but this was a fundamental error. On the contrary, they run democracy and encourage it, for it provides a screen behind which they can hide their method of exploitation, and they find it their best defense against any objections which the populace may raise.
>
> For once, therefore, a man woke up and saw that what mattered was not to proclaim democracy but to see the full reality, not to follow slogans, but to see things as they are. This would be particularly

important today, for people would then realize that the events which reign with such blood and terror over the whole of humanity are guided and directed from just a few centers. People will never realize this if they persist in the delusion that nation is fighting nation, and allow European and American Press to lull them to sleep over the kinds of relations that are said to exist between nations. Everything said about antagonism and opposition between nations only exists to cast a veil over the true reasons.... And the man who woke up and wrote these statements in 1910 also presented some highly unwelcome accounts in his book. He produced a list of fifty-five individuals who are the real rulers and exploiters of France. This list can be found in Francis Delaisi's *La Democratie et les Financiers*, written in 1910; the same man has also written *La Guerre qui vient* (the coming war).... The book contains impulses which allow one to see through much of what we should see through today, and also to cut through much of the fog which is made to wash over our human brains today.*

Back at the hostel, because of the holy day, there was no food, restaurants were closed, and there was nothing I could do but wait until the next day to eat!

It was a dismal, cold, rainy, windy day. The next day, I walked all over the very large city which reminded me a bit of the colossal Russian cities. It had been totally rebuilt, including the palace. The next day the Poles were out, enjoying the sunny day, the markets, the vendors bundled up in warm clothes.

I took the train to Krakaw which was the old city, where the famous pope was from. The train journey crossed many small farms, forests, and poor areas. The train station in Krakaw was packed because it was also a mall. Everyone was shopping and it took me a while to find the exit. Finally I entered the old city through a beautiful gate and found a lovely inexpensive hotel.

The old city is beautiful to walk in, and it was very busy with visiting tourists, and a lot of priests visiting or teaching in the various seminaries. It looked like rest and relaxation for the international jet-setting Catholic

---

* Steiner, *The Fall of the Spirits of Darkness*, pp. 222–224.

Young seminary students in their black robes

priests, and a lot of black-robed young men for those seminaries which one encounters everywhere in the city. The churches are plentiful, and full of believers, unlike in other Catholic countries. The Sunday services were full in the various churches which I peeked into. The Poles are serious Catholics, next door to the serious Russian Orthodox, probably the only two countries which are still taking religion seriously. Everywhere else traditional religion is no longer a part of life; yoga, exercise, sports, traveling, adventures, and workaholism are taking the lead (I won't mention the negative activities), except for the far right wing religious, orthodox fanatics from all faiths who are still grabbing some people's attention for various reasons. There are lots of books written about this phenomena.

I felt sorry for these young men entering the priesthood. No one can have a normal life when ignoring half the population, except for some very unusual, gifted, selfless priests or nuns, such as the former pope. I walked through his apartment, and it did have a feeling of sanctity. He was very dedicated to the cult of the Mother of God, the Black Madonna, the Lady of Jasna Góra, The Queen of Poland.

One could feel this purity of purpose, and purity of life, which made him a loving pope, loved by his people in return. The Poles seem to be very sturdy on their feet and in their soul, one can't move them so easily, so Catholicism is very much a part of the landscape, and of the psyche of the Poles.

World War II devastated the country, the Russian period as well. We can still see the ravages of centuries of painful sufferings and shameful destruction. I could not help but be shaken by the sturdiness and strength of the Poles. Would I be able to sustain this kind of strength in the face of so much suffering?

> The tragedy of the whole modern machinery of civilization lies in the unrecognized fact that man in his true nature is not fully within his thinking. The brain thinks, not the spirit. The content of consciousness, assimilated through sense perceptions and absorbed intellectually, is brought increasingly closer to the ideal of the machine. Is it any wonder that man's perception penetrates only to the external phenomena? Not until man in his true nature, his spiritual self, becomes the subject of thinking, can he expect the true spiritual essence of the world to become apparent to his perception. Man presumes to think; in reality an It is thinking through him, but a cold, impersonal It, not a higher, divine one. The unavoidable consequence of this is that like his thoughts man finally no longer has any control over things. With apocalyptic intensity, our age is teaching us what has become of the ancient Holy Spirit: an unholy, soulless spirit, a demon.
>
> Eventually, the fruit of the Christian impulse will have to be that people become creative in thinking and perceiving by courageously learning to draw from the spring of the new Holy Spirit, not merely in regard to their existence but also their consciousness. Then, permeated with true Spirit from within, he will find the way to sanctify what he had desecrated and profaned.
>
> *Pistis* (faith) can also be translated as "courage." The modern spirit of research considers itself to be courageous and daring. Yet it is actually being driven—often with manic recklessness—by the lure of ultimate mechanical perfection. But "faith in the machine" in any form is only a camouflage for the lack of faith in an inwardly creative thinking. This had made human souls cowardly and weak. Through intensifying

their outer activity, people conceal from themselves the paralysis and failure of inner activity. They are not even willing to notice the frightening loss of inner tranquility and ability to concentrate which, after all, are the precondition for inner freedom and creativity, be it ever so humble. The deluded belief that intellectual industry is inner activity is especially fatal. It is merely the I-form tied to the physical body, particularly the brain which engages in such industry. The proper self of man, the spiritual I, is not involved.[*]

Walking past some of my favorite older churches, listening to street musicians, watching families with little children, I was disturbed to see vans parked on the main busy street, with advertisements. This place, that place, Auschwitz, hiking in the mountains, etc. I was stunned by this lack of respect considering the history of this hellish place. Due to my ignorance, I thought Auschwitz was in Germany; I did not know that it was just around the corner from here. Many people were visiting the place from hell, and then perhaps visiting other places not so hellish! Like a spa!

Is this the way we should behave towards a major center of evil? Visiting it like any other place? Today let us visit the former concentration camp, the next day let us go to Our Lady of Jasna Góra, or let us go hiking. What kind of mentality is that? I was upset all day about that kind of attitude. Was I the only one feeling this way?

A dear teacher of mine whom I have mentioned several times, Georg Kühlewind, who passed away in 2006, was a great meditation teacher, scientist, and spiritual scientist. He survived two concentration camps, where he was thrown in at a very young age, and when he used to teach a few of us he would be adamant about certain things. One of them was that it is absolutely useless to try to make some sense of evil. Evil does not make sense! He said that all the documentaries on the camps, all the writing, all the efforts to try and understand are totally useless, because they make us focus on evil! He also said that because of that hellish experience he went beyond race, religion, he got rid of all his baggage, to become more universally human, a true Christian. I call it "beyond the blood"!

---

[*]   Bock, *Saint Paul: Life, Epistles and Teaching*, pp. 355–356.

We need to focus on goodness, not evil, so *focus* on making sure this does not happen again, focus on the positive. Focus on passing laws which curb the states' power, which Germany has instituted, other countries have not! Power through arms will never bring peace, but more wars.

Focus on treating other people, the way one would like to be treated, which is not what is happening these days. The real Christianity has not arrived yet!

Christ's words: "Do unto others as you would have them do unto you."

I am reminded of a story told to me by my son, about one of his classes in ethics at Maine Maritime Academy where the professor was teaching a room of future engineers. The students watched a film where the engineers, dressed in suits and ties and briefcases, were going to a meeting to discuss new designs for the enormous gas chambers to be used in various concentration camps during World War II! In suits and ties, black hats and brief cases, very capable businessmen. Then, of course, they went home to their families!

The moral of the story is this: my son refused the very substantial amount of money he was offered to get his doctoral degree in nuclear engineering, as well as a lucrative summer job to design some turbines or other wonderful technological new toys for killing.

He decided to go fishing instead!

How many young men actually think about what it is they are doing to earn money?

This is where we need to bring feelings, not just intellect. Cold, abstract, head, and no *heart*.

> In the schools of the ancient East that served simultaneously as art institutes and religious centers, individuals did not merely learn or apply their intellectual abilities to research. In the Eastern mystery centers, it went without saying that people embedded in ordinary life could not follow the path of the mysteries of existence. Before being allowed to approach these mysteries, students had to completely transform their inner constitution through rigorous inner self-discipline. They had to transform themselves into different beings fit to receive mystery knowledge. The ancient East cultivated a means of cognition based on rich, concrete soul-spiritual activity. Eastern mystery activity

spread to Europe, where it became increasingly filtered down into dialectics, logic, and mere intelligence in ancient Greece, and later into the intellectualism of modern civilization.

Without a complete inner view of these facts, we cannot make sense of the various currents in modern culture or their assets and liabilities, nor can we achieve fruitful perceptions of modern humanity's needs. It is time to take an uncompromising look at our spiritual history and recognize the spiritual worlds in which we are embedded. Having traced the line of development from the "imported" spiritual life of the East through Greece and into our modern intellectualism, we must now look at *how* this evolution occurred. It was possible only because it was linked to a natural facet of the human constitution: namely, heredity or blood relationships. We must base any study of the evolution of human cognition on insight into the full scope of the influence of blood relationships. In the ancient times that produced the precursors of our modern cognitive processes, perception and knowledge were bound to heredity and appeared in different forms in different races, ethnic groups, and other groups of people related by blood. The esoteric training of students admitted to the mystery schools had to be adapted to their bloodlines and inherited gifts and temperaments which provided the natural basis for cultivating spiritual cognition.

If we are aware of the real evolutionary history of humankind, we will discover that in the Western civilized world, the ties binding human mental activity to blood ties were severed abruptly around the middle of the fourteenth century, when they began to be replaced by factors that can never be inherited.... This connection gradually loosened until it ceased to mean anything at all to humankind around the middle of the fifteenth century, when the intellectual element began to predominate in all normal, outer manifestations of spirituality. Since that time, our mental activity is no longer bound to heredity or blood relationship. Today, even the pettiest philosophizers must admit that intellectual ideas no longer have anything to do with the fact of blood kinship, which played a major role in ancient spirituality.

The highly attenuated, purely intellectual mental life that has evolved since the mid-1400s has taught us to become independent of the merely natural element, but it has distanced us from everything once considered essential to being human. A unique and even tragic feature has entered humankind's evolution. We have risen to a level of experience that is independent of natural, elemental forces, but these experiences no longer allow us to understand ourselves. In ancient, blood-bound spirituality, inner insight naturally included knowledge of the essential nature of the human being. Now, however, we have risen to an abstract level of spirituality that experiences great scientific triumphs but is incapable of exploring human nature....

After three or four hundred years, intellectual development has culminated and the modern civilized world is full of the results of intense intellectual research. We find a great variety of ideas, but they have all become too abstract, too remote from life, to transform into impulses for action. Today, when humankind's social and other problems become acute, our souls seem to have fallen into collective sleep that does not allow us to acknowledge that we are sliding down a slippery slope. The need for more profound inner forces that can inspire action is becoming urgent. Instead, we hear abstract religious preaching that bears no relationship to real life, reminding us of the old folksong: "Sleep, Michael, sleep, in the garden goes the sheep, in the garden goes a little priest, leading you to heaven, sleep, Michael, sleep!" We have lost any connection between perceiving the natural world outside us, which has become a purely intellectual process, and perceiving the essential nature of the human being, which was formerly a natural part of ancient, blood-based spiritual cognition....

In time, if our western intellectual life becomes materialistic, our ability to act will be completely paralyzed....

It was both necessary and right for humanity to spend three or four centuries developing the independent intellect. We achieved a certain freedom from natural constraints, but the resulting intellectualism must now be re-imbued with soul and spirit—with knowledge that informs and inspires human actions....

By cultivating an all-embracing Goethean approach, anthroposophical science aspires to a form of spirit cognition that can serve as the foundation for energetic action. That is the only way to help our world. Although intellectual knowledge is also acquired through inner effort, it applies at best only to technology, that is, to the non-human world. Impulses derived from spiritual knowledge, however, can guide our public life, which has grown so difficult, in the direction of recovery.

> Perhaps these claims of spiritual science deserve greater consideration in view of the infinite human suffering caused by failed so-called social movements such as Leninism, Trotskyism, and the like, which are nothing more than intellectual poison. For four hundred years, intellectualism helped to free human beings to be individuals, but it served this useful purpose only as long as it did not attack old social forms. As soon as pure intellectualism seeks to transform society, its horrendous toxic effects become increasingly evident. It is a terrible illusion to believe that we can afford to look on world events dispassionately. These toxic effects are still in their early stages, and recovery can come only from spirit. Spirit cognition must become the basis of social renewal.*

I had to quote this very long passage because Rudolf Steiner foretold the atrocities which were to come into being from the cold, intellectual, materialistic, soulless world. No one was listening! As he pointed out, everyone was asleep! Their will was paralyzed!

I declined to visit the former concentration camp, a place where demons have control! The human beings who lost their lives not so long ago are part of my psyche. When they exited this world through such atrocious inhumane deeds, I was waiting for a body to come down to Earth! I witnessed their massive exiting from the spiritual world as I was waiting to come down.

That is why when such atrocities are being perpetrated around the world, I must, in my own small way, try to become more human by becoming a master of my own self, and not be led by my weaknesses (elementary beings, evil forces). Georg Kühlewind devoted his life to teaching students how to become the master of one's self, or "I," thereby meeting evil at its root, within each of us, and not with an *out there, they did it* attitude.

This journey is part of my attempt to become more human, and meet the other.

> Among archaic peoples, demons were (and are) familiar as negative spiritual beings alongside good spirits (angels). Modern peoples no longer have the experiences described in the New Testament, but we

---

* Steiner, *Freedom of Thought and Societal Forces: Implementing the Demands of Modern Society*, pp. 101–104.

can very well notice independent "forces," processes, and impulses in our own souls. These forces may arise in our consciousness without, or even against, our conscious will, and mislead us into actions that, if we think them through clearly, we do not intend doing, but against which we are incapable of marshalling sufficient resistance. Such independent elements in the soul reveal themselves at various levels, with various potencies. In any exercises of concentration, such as concentrating on a man-made object, we can almost always experience distractions (associations); they are the mildest, weakest independent elements, though they can be very disruptive to the exercise. More serious are obsessive thoughts and compulsions, which we today recognize as pathological; lesser compulsions are common and often unconscious. In our time, independent elements such as these are included within the everyday sense of self, and are generally considered part of the personality. That is, although equipped with a certain independence, they are at least perceived, even temporally tolerated, often also fought against. The situation is more difficult when the everyday self identifies with one or more independent elements and can no longer distinguish between them and its own nature.

In earlier times when the everyday I (which consists in free forces of attention outside the I-body) was far less strongly developed, the separate, unconscious forms were much more independent of the human center, for this center was weaker, less self-aware, and allowed itself to be determined more by forces from above and below, feeling itself compelled by these forces. This kind of experience was very clearly described by Saint Paul. We read, for example, in Romans 7:15–20:

> *For that which I do I understand not: for what I would, that do I not; but what I hate, that do I. If then I do that which I would not, I consent unto the law that it is good. Now then it is no more I that do it, but sin that dwelleth in me. For I know that in me (that is, in my flesh) dwelleth no good thing: for to will is present with me; but how to perform that which is good I find not. For the good that I would I do not: but the evil which I would not, that I do. Now if I do that I would not, it is no more I that do it, but sin that dwelleth in me.*

We have an insight here into what is called sin, since it has such independence that it arises against human will; and it lives in the "flesh."

So the "forgiveness of sins" acquires a special meaning: it is equivalent to the momentary purging of these independent elements. Neither the good nor the evil independent elements are ascribed to the human center: instead, either God or sin affects the soul....

At least since Freud, we know that unconscious forms seem equipped with a certain "intelligence" that helps them prevail. This trait gives them a kind of being, as if they were conscious or at least instinctive entities—even with a goal-directed slyness about them.*

But we do not stop at this insight. In the far, far future, human beings will have shed their lower selves. What made up our lower selves, evil spirits, will become in turn another race, below that of man. Nothing is ever wasted in the evolution of mankind. A very powerful painting for me is the washing of the feet. What we become, our perfection, is built upon the lower kingdoms. This picture creates a balance when we have a tendency to think too much of ourselves. It keeps us humble to know that who we are is at the cost of someone else!

As we shed our lower impulses, like a snake, they do not get lost, they become another race! Which in turn will be helped.

These thoughts are sobering and difficult to assimilate.

After walking throughout the whole city, it was time to visit the famous site of the Queen of Poland, Lady of Jasna Góra, which had been my intention for visiting Poland all along.

These words are written on the sign which welcomes the public to Jasna Góra:

> Jasna Góra (Bright Mountain) is a spiritual capital of Poland. Here, in front of the Holy Picture of Mother of God called "The Black Madonna," generations of Poles did entrust her with their fates and the fate of Poland as well, believing and recognizing the Lady of Jasna Góra as the Queen of Poland. The cult of Miraculous Picture of God's Mother was supported by Polish sovereigns from its beginning in the sixteenth century. Later in the eighteenth century or earlier, the cult

---

* Kühlewind, *Wilt Thou Be Made Whole? Healing in the Gospels*, pp. 55–57.

crossed borders of Poland and first spread out in other European countries, then in other parts of the world. At present Jasna Góra is one of the most important pilgrimage centers for Christians. About four million people from eighty countries come here and visit the sanctuary each year.

The complex of the basilica and the Pauline monastery has both religious and historical significance.*

I took the bus, and drove through the countryside. The very tall chimney of atomic power dotted the countryside on the way to the city. Whole cities right next to the fuming, steaming, gargantuan chimneys, supplying energy to Poland.

I arrived in a very busy city and decided to stay at the monastery which housed pilgrims coming by the thousands every year to pay respect to Our Lady of Jasna Góra.

The monastery was an enormous compound, like a citadel or fortress, with huge cathedrals, monasteries, chapels, a museum, gardens, and a very large complex on top of a hill dominating the busy city.

Priests were numerous, and many more seminarians were walking around going to their classes. They were everywhere, this must have been a huge training center, bigger than Krakow. The building housing the pilgrims was very modern and efficiently run. I had my own lovely room amidst hundreds of other rooms which were filled with many visiting priests, bishops, etc., from all around the world.

I walked up to the large monastery complex and was ready to witness the opening of the special chapel where the Beloved Icon of the Virgin Mary was housed. The place was packed, and very devout. After waiting for quite a while, the ceremony started!

Music sounded from the sound system, and the grilled, iron gate that covered the icon was lifted by some mechanical means. The priests were in the back talking as this ceremony was happening. Then they saw that I was looking at them chatting, and they closed the door!

---

* For more about other Black Madonna sites, see Valandro, *Via Podiensis, Path of Power: A Walk from le Puy, France, to San Juan de la Peña, Spain.*

The Jasna Góra Monastery

They were chatting while the crowd, devout and fervently praying, was busy contemplating this icon which the pope adored and worshipped. This icon, the Virgin Mary, is worshipped as the representative of a whole country. The symbol of a whole country! Is the dollar sign our symbol in the Western world?

It reminded me of the Russian men and women who stand very often in front of a beautiful icon of the Virgin Mary with total devotion, attention, and love. The same depth of soul which is almost non-existent in our Western world on the other side of the Atlantic, except with our Mexican and South American religious family whose devotion to Mary Mother of God is alive and well.

> In creation's primal beginning, the Father bestowed on mankind a spirituality that was sacred because it was still divine, not yet human. After the Fall, humanity increasingly obscured and used up this sustenance, and by the time of Christ clear signals of its exhaustion had become evident. It was then that the Father, who in the beginning had sent the Spirit, sent the Son....

A multitude of flowers and oil candles at the local cemetery

In the East, the ancient sustenance of God-given spirituality was not as exhausted, as it was in the West. As ardently as the eastern Christians loved the Resurrected One, so they correspondingly failed to sense the necessity for a new wellspring of spirituality, since they were still rich.*

To put it bluntly, the Eastern Christians still have some fuel, they are not running on nothing, or less than nothing as we are in the West. The Father is still all powerful, and Christ the brother of mankind has not arrived! As is the case everywhere else.

After visiting the monastery compounds, one early morning I decided to go to the large local cemetery. I walked down from the hill, through the cold, sunny, sleepy morning to the large enclosed cemetery. It was acres and acres of flowers and oil candles arranged on top of massive tombstones, crosses, statues, and large alleys with tall trees lining the avenues with many benches for the relatives and visitors to pray. The Sun was beginning to shine on the rich slab of granite stones, covered with offerings. I was

---

* Bock, *Saint Paul: Life, Epistles and Teaching*, p. 353.

stunned by the beauty of the cemetery, the serenity of the place, especially a few days after the first of November, which had celebrated the day of the dead. It was so beautifully kept and loved that I felt I received another insight into the very sturdy, loving, large soul of the Poles. *They* do not forget their dead. The dead are part of the life in Poland, they are not forgotten. None are forgotten.

> When Christians of the Middle Ages—and even Christians of more recent centuries—turned their thoughts in prayer to the dead who had been related or known to them, their prayers and feelings bore them up toward the souls of the dead with much greater power than today. It was far easier in the past for souls of the dead to feel warmed by the breath of love flowing from those who looked up or sent their thoughts upward to them in prayer....
>
> Again, the dead are cut off more drastically from the living in the present age than they were a comparatively short time ago, which makes it more difficult for them to perceive what stirs in the souls of those left behind. This is part of humanity's evolution, but that evolution must also lead to rediscovering the connection, the real communion between the living and the dead....
>
> There is something else that will make an even stronger appeal for communication between the dead and the living. The souls of those who have died need nourishment in a certain sense—not, of course, the kind needed by human beings on Earth, but spirit and soul nourishment. On the Earth, we must have cornfields where grain for physical sustenance ripens; likewise, the souls of the dead must have "cornfields" from which to gather the sustenance they need between death and a new birth. The clairvoyant eye sees that cornfields for the souls of the dead are in fact the souls of sleeping human beings. One who experiences this for the first time in the spirit world is not only surprised but deeply shattered to see how the souls living between death and a new birth hurry, so to speak, toward the souls of the sleeping human beings, seeking their thoughts and ideas. *Such thoughts are food for the souls of the dead—nourishment they need.*
>
> When we go to sleep at night, the ideas and thoughts that have passed through our consciousness in our waking hours come to life as living beings. The souls of the dead approach and share those ideas,

> feeling nourished as they perceive them. Clairvoyant vision can see the dead as, night after night, they make their way toward the sleeping human beings left behind on Earth (especially blood relations, but also friends), seeking refreshment and nourishment from the thoughts and the ideas carried into sleep. And it is a shattering experience to see that they often find nothing, because in the sleep state there is a great difference between one kind of thought and another.
>
> If we are caught up all day in thoughts related to material life, with the mind directed only toward what is happening in the physical world and what may be accomplished there, and if we have no thought for the spiritual worlds before going to sleep, but, in fact, often take ourselves into those worlds by means quite other than such thoughts, then we have no nourishment to offer the dead....
>
> In ancient times, when a certain spirituality pervaded the souls of human beings, religious communities and blood relatives were where help was sought after death. But the power of blood relationship has diminished and must be replaced by cultivation of the spiritual life.*

Poland still had a community which included the dead in their life. Being in this cemetery soothed my soul after the upheaval that I felt in Krakow. I walked peacefully for many of the early hours before heading back up the hill.

This country still takes religion seriously and perhaps for the future it has immense meaning. On their large and strong shoulders, might the Poles and the Russians take on the responsibility of keeping Christ alive in their hearts, thereby making sure we have *a future*? The mainstream in the West is certainly not doing it! Do we leave the weight on their shoulders?

> What would have happened to mankind if the Christ event had not taken place?... We learned that in very old times civilization rested upon a form of love closely linked with tribal relationship, with consanguinity. Those related by blood loved each other. And we saw how in the course of human evolution this bond was increasingly torn....

---

*   Steiner, *Staying Connected: How to Continue Your Relationships with Those Who Have Died*, pp. 59–60, 62, 64.

While in most ancient epochs marriage was always consummated within one and the same tribe, you will find that during Roman dominion—and that is the time of the Christ Event—the custom of endogamy was increasingly ignored, that a great variety of peoples were thrown together as a result of the Roman expeditions, and that the "close marriage" had very largely to give way to exogamy, the "distant marriage." It was necessary for blood ties to lose their strength in the evolution of mankind because men were destined to take their stand upon their own ego.

Assuming, now, that Christ had not come to provide new forces, to replace the old love engendered by blood ties with a new spiritual love, what would have happened? In that case love, the factor that brings men together, would gradually have vanished from the face of the Earth. The love that unites men would have perished in man's nature. Without the Christ the human race would have lived to see the dying out of love of one person for another. Men would have been driven into their own segregated individualities. Looked at only from the point of view of external science, these things do not disclose the profound truths underlying them. If you were to examine—not chemically, but by the means at the disposal of spiritual research—the blood of the present-day man and compare it with that of the people who lived several thousand years before the appearance of Christ, you would find that it had changed, had taken on a character tending to make it less and less a vehicle capable of bearing love. Imagine, in ancient times, a man of insight who could see deep into the course of human development, who could foretell what would come to pass should only the one antiquated tendency persist without the intervention of the Christ event: how would the course of future evolution present itself to an initiate of that sort? What images would he have had to evoke in the human soul to indicate what would happen in the future if love in the soul, the Christ love, failed to replace the love arising from blood ties in the same measure as the latter disappeared? He had to say: if men become ever more isolated, more hardened in their own ego; if the lines separating souls become ever more marked so that souls understand each other less and less, then men of the outer world will fall increasingly into discord, and contention, and the dissension of all against all will usurp the place of love on Earth.

And this is indeed what would have ensued if evolution had proceeded on the basis of blood relationship *without* the intervention of Christ. All men would inevitably have been involved in the conflict of all against all which will come to pass in any case, but only for those who have not become imbued in the right way with the Christ principle. That is what a prophetic seer beheld as an end of the *Earth* evolution, and well could it fill his soul with terror: souls no longer understand each other, hence, they must rage, soul against soul....

In the outer sense world men can eliminate the antagonistic attitude arising from their differences of opinion, feelings, and actions only by combating and adjusting within themselves all that would otherwise flow out into the external world. No one is going to quarrel with a different opinion in the soul of another, if he establishes harmony among the various principles of his being. He will confront the outer world as one who loves, not as one who quarrels. It is all a matter of diverting the conflict from the outer world to the inner man. The forces holding sway in human nature must battle each other within man.*

And to help us in this battle, we have the work of Georg Kühlewind, as mentioned before, a survivor of the worst atrocities this century has ever had, who dedicated his life's work to this inner battleground. The true inner Jihad which Muslim brothers speak about, not the distorted, outside one adopted by the extreme fundamentalists.

And thus ends my unplanned trip to Poland.

---

* Steiner, *The Gospel of St. John and Its Relation to the Other Gospels*, pp. 206–207, 209.

Part IX

Azerbaijan

FIVE MONTHS LATER

Zarathustra

My Turkish airline flight left Chicago, and twelve hours later I was in Istanbul once again. I spent a day enjoying one of my favorite cities and met a friend to accompany me. The next day, we took a flight to Baku, Azerbaijan for three weeks of wandering around the country. When I mentioned to some very educated friends where I was heading this time, their reaction was: *Where? What's over there? Why?*

Well, dear friends, there is plenty!

Being a former Soviet republic, it was not easy to get a visa and prepare a trip. The Soviet apparatus has not disappeared, unfortunately! So I had to hire a driver and a car, and give the "authorities" my whereabouts, meaning the travel agency would organize my stay. Not what I would have liked, but I had no choice, and it was expensive! Of course, I dictated to them what I wanted, which included visits to faraway valleys in the Caucasian Mountains, for hiking and staying with villagers, ancient Zoroastrian sites, main cities, old sites, old Christian Albanian churches, mosques, etc., and whatever else they wanted to include. In the end they did a great job! Much more than I expected!

BEYOND THE BLOOD

The guide came to meet us at the airport and drove us to our hotel located in the old, walled-in city with its cobblestone paths, narrow alleys, fifteenth century palace of Persian kings, old mosques, old towers, hammams, and quaint restaurants, surrounded by a very rich, modern Baku with its extensive, modern, flashy skyscrapers on the horizon.

I chose to visit Azerbaijan because of its Zoroastrian history; Rudolf Steiner dedicated hundreds of lectures to Zarathustra when speaking about the evolution of humanity. I have mentioned Zarathustra's name many times on this journey.

Baku is very rich in oil which is under the Caspian Sea and seeps out of the ground by the shore. The burning fire is caused by the gases which escape the ground seeped in oil and gas and, of course, it ignites. All along the shore around Baku is where the Zoroastrians established one of their temples where pilgrims still worship and visit, as they did thousands of years ago. They come from as far away as Bombay, India, home of the Parsis. So I had to experience such an illustrious country.

The burning fire is not far, north of Baku. *Baku* means "bad wind" in Persian (one interpretation).

So our driver picked us up in the morning and we started on our journey around the city.

We toured the famous Ateshgah fire temple which is being modernized to accommodate the pilgrims and to acknowledge the importance of its famous past, the birthplace of Zarathustra. It had a courtyard, a little temple where the eternal flame was burning (thanks to piped-in gas), and several little rooms in the rectangular buildings with several very basic scenes of Zoroastrian worship featuring the black- and white-clothed human beings, for light and dark, powers of good and evil, Ahura Mazdao (god of light and goodness) and Ahriman (god of darkness and evil).

Other countries claim *their* land to be the birthplace of Zarathustra and they are all correct, since Zarathustra had many consecutive former lives, as we all do! Zarathustra was reborn many times, thirteen to be specific, starting from around 5000 BC to AD 1. Andrew Welburn's intensive research into this fascinating prophet, wise man, and great initiate is described in *The Book with Fourteen Seals*.

AZERBAIJAN

Zoroastrianism is the oldest of the revealed creed religions, and it has probably had more influence on mankind, directly and indirectly, than any other single faith. In its own right it was the state religion of three great Iranian empires, which flourished almost continually from 600 BC to AD 7 and dominated much of the Near and Middle East. Iran's power and wealth lent it immense prestige, and some of its leading doctrines were adopted by Judaism, Christianity, and Islam as well as a host of Gnostic faiths, while in the East it had some influence on the development of northern Buddhism.*

Rudolf Steiner's lecture cycles have brought the importance of Zoroaster into the light. Andrew Welburn's thorough and masterful research has shed light on the incarnations of Zoroaster-Zarathustra.

Here is the cycle of Zarathustra's former incarnations:

Zarathustra (eastern Iran, now Uzbekistan-Afghanistan region)
Zal (northern Iran, Elburz mountain region)
Faridun (Parthia, now Turkmenistan-Uzbekistan, 5000 BC to 3000 BC)
Menyelek (Ethiopia, 1000 BC)
Vahagn (Armenia, eighth century BC)
Skanda (India)
Nabu-Apla-Usur (Babylon, seventh century BC)
Zaratas (Babylon, sixth century BC)
Zoroaster of Proconnesus (island northeast of Istanbul, fifth century BC)
Nekhnebef (Egypt, fourth century BC)
Gayomart (Media-Azerbaijan 3rd century BC)
Nechepso (Egypt, second century BC)
Jesus (Palestine, AD 1)**

The first three incarnations of Zarathustra are concentrated in the Iranian plateau and mountains of the north, both in the east and west, and the eleventh incarnation returns to Azerbaijan, in the third century AD.

---

* Boyce, *Zoroastrians: Their Religious Beliefs and Practices*, p. 1.
** Welburn, *The Book with Fourteen Seals: The Prophet Zarathustra and the Christ-Revelation*, pp. 188, 192.

BEYOND THE BLOOD

I wanted to explore some of these regions because such a pivotal figure in humanity's evolution and history leaves behind traces of its illustrious past, even though it was thousands of years ago. Through my studying the work of Rudolf Steiner, I have learned that Zarathustra is one of the leading initiates in our evolutionary history, as mentioned earlier by Mary Boyce. All the religions owe something to the Zarathustra spirit-being, the illuminator, as mentioned by Andrew Welburn. Zarathustra has been mentioned many times throughout this journey.

In this search of Judaism, Muslim, Christian roots, Zarathustra is the key to many enigmas, so being again in this part of the world is very exciting and heart-warming.

After visiting the temple, we then drove a bit farther in soft, desert, rolling hills and found another little building dedicated to Zarathustra, and facing it was a wall of fire coming out of the side of the hill. It was mesmerizing. Here there are no gas pipes. Sheep were grazing and to the east towards the Caspian Sea was the Abseron Peninsula, one of the most polluted areas in the world, a gift of the former Soviet regime who left major oil pollution.

Before the modern age, fire worshippers came to these distant shores from faraway India and Iran to worship.

On the far eastern part of this very polluted area lives a more conservative center of Islam, in stark contrast to the rest of the country which is quite westernized. From Baku, a short ferry ride and one lands in northern Iran at Bandar-e Anzali, where progress has gone backwards and the fundamentalists are having a heyday with cultural-social experiments gone wrong, resembling Soviet Russia's ignoble acts.

Zarathustra in Iran is buried under mountains of Islamic propaganda, ignoring its glorious past to favor their vision of God in the most narrow-minded way possible. Azerbaijan, being a close neighbor (historically it was part of Iran), must watch its neighbor closely so as not to import such desolate, non-progressive abuse of the masses.

We live in an amazing world from one end of the planet to the other, and to be a witness to it all is often heart wrenching!

Azerbaijan is a small country with powerful neighbors and lots and lots of oil! No weakling government would survive, they would be gobbled up in no time! Thereby a desperate need to show off power, money, influence, western ideas, lifestyle, and a powerful army.

Many Iranians come shopping in Azerbaijan by car, I was told. Cars filled with hungry Iranians, hungry for freedom, hungry for a regular life. As soon as they cross the border the women leave their cover-up clothes and put on miniskirts, lovely dresses, and so forth for a weekend of shopping and freedom, ready to go back to their forced prison lifestyle.

We left early the next morning for our excursion deep into the interior of Azerbaijan. The road went north, towards the Russian border, and we could watch the blue Caspian Sea whose level is rising ever higher, creating problems for the countries involved. The countryside was dotted with chemical plants, old ones, new ones, ecological disasters one after another, and was very dirty. Then we headed west towards the Caucasian Mountains separating Azerbaijan from the Russian provinces of Chechnya and Dagestan to the north, which are becoming ever more problematic with Muslim fundamentalists.

We arrived in Quba, a city next to a large flowing river, home to an old Jewish community. This new community was growing and it had enormous houses, palaces throughout the city, a synagogue, and a beautiful, well-kept cemetery. Ladies wearing scarves watched us as we were walking around its streets. I read that the local people were not very happy about the enormous amount of money coming from Israel into this village, thereby these incredible houses which were being built with money from relatives living elsewhere. The locals, in stark contrast, were living in small homes. Interesting phenomena, not conducive to love between neighbors.

The Israelis do not need visas to visit, as the westerners do, so some close ties with Israel are formed perhaps to deter the Muslim fundamentalists surrounding the area, especially the few Iranian fundamentalists. Geopolitics... Our world is immensely complex!

After our walk we headed up the river and noticed more sumptuous, castle-like homes being built along the beautiful scenery of forests and meadows with hilly backgrounds. These were palaces and there were many of them. Our guide said that these are the wealthy people from Baku who come here when it is hot in the summer, so the money is trickling down somehow. Our guide explained that the government only works with an illegal system of giving gifts and bribes to its elected officials, known as corruption in high places. Rampant in Russia, friends of friends having access to opening of trades, business with Europe. (It is a system rampant worldwide.) Since it is a small country the funds will somehow be distributed, we hope! The hopeful sign is that these wealthy people could have chosen to spend their funds in foreign countries, but they did not! Instead they chose landholdings, palaces, villas, estates which bring in jobs, etc., which is the positive side of such a corrupt system, as it is still in Russia. As our guide told us, "No one can open a business unless he knows someone." He had tried himself and failed.

We drove farther, reached the limit of the road, and traveled on a dirt road in between canyons, mountains streams, amazing scenery where a new super ski area was being built with hundreds of condos, hotels, and apartments. It was a real worksite! Our guide said that this is owned by the wife of the president's father. Then we went on to the Laza valley, with scattered tiny villages on mountainsides, men on horseback, shepherds with their flocks, and old, beaten-up cars going to these villages high up in the mountains. We stopped at the end of the road where a smart local businessman had started a little restaurant on the higher mountainside for the tourists who come here to walk, such as us. It is stunning scenery in this remote valley of the Caucasian Mountains.

We walked up a steep path towards a lovely waterfall, and then on to another hotel for tourists, which was now closed. They open in the summer when the heat is too much for the Baku citizens. They flock up here for relief. It was beautiful, serene, bare, and full of spring flowers. After a few hours of walking, we walked back to the little restaurant. The hillside was dotted with little, private, open-air, covered platforms for the tourists, like a small yurt with huge windows overlooking the splendid scenery, valley mountains. The table was set as if for royalty and we had a delightful lunch, as did a few Azeri tourists. Plates full of homemade bread, olives, tomatoes, feta cheese, etc.

A view of the Caucasian Mountains

Then we headed back to the next town called Qusar, which is home to the Lezgin people, another tribal people, so we stopped to enjoy the local market full of fruits, vegetables, dry goods, nuts, meats, herbs, and sweets which are totally delicious. Then we stopped at a local cheap hotel where we had a delightful supper outside. Many travelers were dining as well, some coming from Russia. The border is not that far, and there is a lot of exchange between the two countries. Many still have Lezgin relatives in Dagestan, the Russian province north of here, and vice versa.

The next stop would be another remote valley for a homestay. So we headed west, once again following a large river with forested hills, and many large, wealthy estates dotting the riverside. Then we started climbing in canyons on a small road which became a dirt road. I was a bit worried because the car did not have four-wheel drive, and this road was hardly passable. Huge rocks, precipices on the side, cliffs rising ever higher. I knew this was a remote place, but remote in the West is not the same as remote in the East!

We stopped to take in the fantastic scenery, rocks, mountains, cliffs, with no sign of life. This went on for a few hours, and then suddenly the scenery became softer, the mountains more rounded and green, and some villages on top of these softer mountains came into view with the great Caucasian snowy peaks in the background. This is the last stronghold of a very old people who have their own language and customs. They call themselves Lezgin, as mentioned before, neighboring Dagestan, a Russian province which has an equal amount of Lezgin people living in their territories, and they live here in these very demanding surroundings. I thought I was in Tibet or Nepal or Sikkim in the Himalayas. Here you can see the fabulous Caucasian Mountains reaching up to more than thirteen thousand feet, stretching to infinity on the horizon.

The small city at the end of the road is called Xinalig, and after that we reach Russia. It sits on top of a massive soft mountain overlooking the whole area, with a 360-degree view. The town is an old stone village with many tall cow manure bricks in neat piles next to all the houses, for fuel. No more trees here. There is no indoor plumbing except in a few more modern homes built a bit lower in the valley. The women have access to icy cold water from different fountains which bring water from the frigid slopes in long pipes. They do their washing there in large stone basins, and have red, red hands from the icy cold. Life is very strenuous up here, and this was spring, not winter. Flocks of sheep are on the mountains, and small enclosures and tiny rooms keep the flock safe next to their homes. One has to climb in between small winding paths to reach the village homes built on terraces, one on top of the other, with beautiful dry stonework. Electricity does come up to these homes, but it is not working all the time. They have constant power shortages. In a country that exports oil it is shameful. I felt that this lifestyle will not always be there. The women will move to the local cities and abandon this very hard lifestyle. The Baku crowd seems to have abandoned these people. Only the hardy ones come here. Although there are a few tourists who sleep here, there is not much money coming in!

We arrived at our destination and were shown our room. We stayed with a local family which had a large comfortable but primitive home. No bathroom, but an outside toilet (a typical hole in the ground) next to the tiny stone barn. Water was available in an adjoining building where people did the dishes and washed with warmed water heated in the main house. The owner was in the process of installing hot water, and a bath house.

The family was very hospitable. The son was living with his older mother and father, and his older sister came to help out with the cooking. His wife had just had a baby after ten years of marriage, and the baby was a preemie, a tiny one, which I got a glimpse of in the family room.

Our room was very similar to what I experienced in Iran in the mountain villages: rolled up mattresses with heavy blankets on the floor, very comfortable. We had our supper of rice, a meat–dry fruit stew, and some welcomed black tea. After a wonderful chat we went to sleep.

The next morning, we had a great breakfast of homemade bread, cheese, and tea, and then we were off with a local young man for hiking in the mountains. We hiked up through the village and headed up towards the snowy peaks. The shepherds were already up high on the mountainside with their flocks eagerly eating the spring young grass. Some of the locals had gone up with their ancient gardening tools to plant potatoes, which is one of their harvests. I climbed and climbed and the village became a dot in this immense scenery. Truly a beautiful area which speaks of ancient times when people chose these hidden valleys to hide from invading armies, and they have survived to this day.

The next day, more of the same hiking, and a visit to the local tiny Lezgin museum, and we came back for a hearty lunch with a local visitor, one of the young teachers taking care of education in this large village. Every day we saw the little ones, and the bigger children dressed in their clean uniforms going to school. The young man was very unusual, very bright, aware, friendly. He had learned that I was French and he wanted to practice it. He also wanted to go to France and study French literature. He said he read it in translation but was fascinated by its history and was quite knowledgeable. It was surprising! Where was he in his former incarnation? He was set on moving to Paris and studying there. He was going to be married in the summer to a young Lezgin lady living in Dagestan, as he was also from the Lezgin community. Our host then explained to us how difficult it was to live with older parents. His mom needed assistance to go to the outdoor bathroom, and she was slowly losing her conscious mind.

He was the only son living here and was solely responsible for taking care of them, and now he had a tiny preemie baby with obvious health problems. He owned a truck and tried to make a living trucking stones, food, and provisions between this remote village and the local city. So between planting potatoes in the higher arid ground in the meadows, a small flock of sheep, and building his own home, he was a very busy young man.

After spending these few days in a warm and friendly atmosphere, sharing their very difficult life, we headed back to Baku for the night. On the way I saw an interesting mountain which was standing out oddly in the landscape, facing the Caspian Sea, so I asked the driver to drive to its foot which he did reluctantly, and we headed straight up that funny-looking, rocky mountain. The path was well trodden, and I calculated a two- to three-hour walk to reach the top and back.

A few more local young men were also climbing it. It climbed steadily until we reached the back of the mountain which was a sort of hidden meadow with a large area for picnics, and some horses for rent and a dirty road ending in a large parking lot. Then we ascended the steep steps leading to the top. It is a pilgrimage site for women, called Besbarmaq Dagi. It is a *pir* or holy site. A group of women speaking Persian were climbing it, young and old, and it looked as if they were from Iran, all clad in their black chador clasped in between their teeth (as I had seen many of them hiking in northern Tehran), and regular shoes, climbing the steep stairs to the top while praying, chanting Islamic Koranic verses. They came here to ask for favors, or to heal sick ones. Here one could feel a mixture of Islam, former ancient animist beliefs (which I could also feel in the Lezgin village), and a bit of Tibet. How they got here is a mystery!

At the top, there was more climbing into the five very rocky mountain tops, where we could glimpse at the Caspian from fifteen hundred feet high. It was a beautiful sight. Then we had to run down so that our driver would not be so upset with us, but we were paying the bill! I found that in these organized trips if you do not tell *them* what you want, then they *tell you* what to do, or what is suitable for them, so I wanted to let him know that we would not be bossed around according to his schedule!

We had another hearty breakfast at our little hotel in the old city, and a chat with the only foreigners we saw: a couple of English women who were fluent in Azeri, a language close to Turkish, with the same root (one of them had written an English-Azeri dictionary and had spent several years in Istanbul). Then we were off.

We got caught in the Baku traffic and headed west into barren, desert-like scenery, and visited several Muslim sites hidden among rocks, a mausoleum devoted to saints, a pir. Then we stopped at a very ancient cemetery with a dome building looking like a beehive, and passed by a city which had a very large minaret by the mosque sticking out into the sky. The first minaret I had noticed, unlike in Morocco and Egypt where there are hundreds of them.

We slowly headed towards luscious forested mountains, then into another river valley. The road climbed slowly into more remote areas, looking very forbidden, and I wondered: *How did people ever find these places and live here?* The road was very narrow, by a river, winding its way through small poor villages by the side, all with small tended gardens, stone barns with enclosures next to the stone houses, fruit trees, and rocky walls. As we crossed a wide river coming from the high Caucasian Mountains we headed into more shrubby mountains and smaller villages hanging onto the sides. More flowering trees, apple trees (since it was spring), dotted the mountainsides and gave it a happy, clean face along with small green meadows for animals to graze.

Then higher up we climbed into no man's land for many miles with the road clutching the canyons, rocky mountainsides, an unpaved road. I thought for sure we would have a punctured tire. More lovely villages with the same architecture, bungalow-like, with the central rooms surrounded by large-bay-window rooms on all sides. In winter they live in the central heated room protected by the other verandah rooms which they use in the summer for the cool weather.

Now the scenery was more drastic, with cliffs coming down straight onto the road, and a dry river bed. No villages here or human habitation, just this twenty-kilometer-long, tortuous road suddenly arriving in this large valley with a large river bed, which is the home to Lahic and several other villages up the river on the side of the mountains which encircled this

A large valley and river bed in Lahic

large valley. I learned later that I could have hiked here in a few days from Laza valley where we were. Perhaps for future hikes!

In the distance there was a large bridge over this very wide river. The bridge was not finished, it dated from the Soviet era, still standing there. It was supposed to link up to the city of Quba.

We had to park the car at the entrance of the village, as one could not go any farther. One had to walk through this ancient village with cobblestone paths, and amazingly restored houses. I was very enthusiastic about visiting this famous village because here they speak Persian-Farsi which I can speak, unlike Azeri, the Turkic language which I am not familiar with, whose roots are totally different. Here I could converse with the locals.

This Persian village is said to have been founded by a Persian king more than a millennium ago. This was his retreat and as all former Persian kings he traveled with his craftsmen and entourage which numbered in the hundreds. This village has beautiful coppersmiths just like the ones I used to visit in the Tehran bazaar, and carpet weavers. A few centuries ago, the craftsmen sold their wares as far as Baghdad. Now only a few remain.

AZERBAIJAN

A woman weaving a carpet on a large loom

The houses have an ingenious building system. They are built of stone and in between the stones at certain intervals, they insert small wooden beams. They explained that it is to make provisions for movement during the frequent earthquakes that visit the region. The houses all have beautiful woodwork on their windows, overhanging balconies with ornate woodwork, and beautiful designs on carved doors and locks. Many of the mountain villages throughout the Eastern world like Nepal, Sikkim, etc., have such architecture. The small pathways are all paved with stones with a small trench in the middle to allow for the water to run down, making the village very clean.

I kept thinking about the long trip from Persia to this village, with the king and his long retinue, and this passage reminded me of such travels, taken from *The Odyssey of Ibn Battuta*. Ibn Battuta (1304–1369) traveled throughout the Arab world. This passage refers to territory north of here.

> Wheeled vehicles played an important role in the lives of the steppe and plain peoples at the time of the Mongol Empire. Ibn Battuta describes them having four large wheels, pulled by two or more horses, or by oxen or camels depending upon the wagon's weight, and guided

The village with its stone pathways and ornate woodwork

by a driver mounted on one of the animals. The wagons also carried people's living and sleeping quarters. This consisted of:

> A kind of cupola of wooden laths tied together with thin strips of hide. This is light to carry and is covered with felt or blanket cloth and in it are grilled windows. The person inside the tent can see others without their seeing him, and he can employ himself in it as he pleases, sleeping, eating, or reading or writing while he is journeying.

Other wagons carried equipment and provisions that were covered by a similar kind of structure bearing a lock. Ibn Battuta brought wagons of different sizes, one for himself and a slave girl, a smaller one for his travel companion al-Tuzari, and a larger one for his other companions drawn by three camels with a driver mounted on one of them.... It has been estimated that a wagon train traveling between ten to twelve hours a day at about four kilometers an hour might cover an average of forty to forty-eight kilometers a day. When Ibn Battuta at last encountered the sultan's residence it was as a vast city on the move, its inhabitants, mosques, shops, and kitchens—for cooking on the march was commonplace—all borne on hundreds of wagons, accompanied by thousands more on horseback, ranging from slaves to troops in the sultan's service.

Sultan Uzbek's entire family, his wives, sons and daughters, and their respective retinue, formed part of the massive mobile *ordu*. One of the wives, Bayalun, was the pregnant daughter of the "king of the Greeks," the Byzantine emperor. She sought the sultan's permission to travel to Constantinople (Istanbul), visit her father, to give birth to her child and then return. Not one to overlook such an opportunity, Ibn Battuta pleaded to be allowed to join the princess' company. After an initial refusal, consent was granted. Her departure meant grants of gifts from the ruler and his family which in total amounted to a "large collection of horses, robes, and furs of ermine," in addition to fifteen hundred gold dinars and silver ingots. This more modest mobile party comprised, in Ibn Battuta's estimation, about four hundred wagons, two thousand horses to draw them and for riding, as well as some three hundred oxens and two hundred camels as draft animals. Protection was provided by an army commander of five thousand troops in addition to the princess' own escort of five hundred Greek and Turkish troops. The journey to Constantinople was uneventful although the final third of the nine- to ten-week trip was covered by horse and mule owing to the rough and mountainous terrain; the wagons were left behind at a fortress on the edge of Byzantine territory.*

The truth might be quite different, but in any case, such was travel in those days for the caliphs, shahs, sultans, etc.

As for us, we carried our meager belonging, our small rolling suitcase, up to our guest home which was located north of the village. Horses with old colorful saddles, donkeys, children coming home from school, young women going home in western clothing. The women were not covered up as in the traditional Islamic villagers but were more in the style of former Russian women with handkerchiefs on their heads and skirts with sweaters. This was a mountain village but not as forgotten and poor as Xenalig, thanks to the Persian shah who adopted this idyllic valley as his "second home."

---

*   Waines, *The Odyssey of Ibn Battuta: Uncommon Tales of a Medieval Adventurer*, p. 52.

Young children returning home from school

We were welcomed by a local teacher at the high school who would rent us a room to make ends meet. His wife was also a teacher. He had built his own home and was still doing major renovations depending on funds. His children were older, and he enjoyed our company, and looking at the old small television in the warm living room.

The usual round of tea was served with sweets and then we took off to wander around the lovely restored village which seemed to be receiving some funds from the wealthier crowd in Baku. It is a great place to hike far into the mountains with guides and horses.

We went to a small museum in a former mosque which was quite interesting with guns, tools, and clothes from former times. Our host's younger brother took us there. He had suffered a head injury during his military service. He looked as Persian as can be and was a Shia Muslim but not a fundamentalist. He would be our walking, trekking guide for a couple of days.

Supper was served in the communal room with other visitors coming to meet us. We had homemade bread with feta cheese, cucumbers, radishes, grape leaves stuffed with meat, yogurt from local sheep, and black tea.

A woman bringing her cows into the stable for milking

After a nice sleep in the guest room with two tiny single beds (not the usual mattress on the floor of the poorer villages) and a large breakfast, we headed towards the mountains with our guide. I had told him that I wanted to hike to other villages in the vicinity.

We climbed away from the wide river bed into the mountains where lovely spring flowers were growing; sweet-scented violets, yellow cowslip, lilac-colored primrose, and apple trees were in full bloom. We could see horses in the distance, happy in their meadows, some cows, and of course sheep. After a couple of hours of steady climbing we stopped for tea from our large thermos. A lady at the next village was bringing in her cows so that she could milk them. She was dressed in blue jeans, a warm jacket, and a head scarf. The homes were scattered on the mountainside with enclosures for animals. Donkeys are used for transportation, and work. Small plots of land were made ready for planting by women working the soil. A very old tractor was on its way to working a distant plot. Stone walls with thorn brush on top of them kept the animals in. Houses were still being built by their owner with plenty of room in the opened basement for wood.

There were still some trees here and there. Hardly any foreigners come here, so we had fun visiting with the local people.

Then we climbed higher and we could see Lahic from the distance with its very wide river winding down into the canyon where we had come from.

The next village, with dry stone masonry homes, had the usual chickens running around, and water coming from a fountain. Then our guide said that we would go and visit one of his friends living farther up the mountain in his own homestead. We climbed up, his friend met us (thanks to cell phones) and invited us inside his large stone home where his ninety-year-old father was a beekeeper. The numerous hives were in the back of the house. The house had a great terrace paved with large stones overlooking the whole area, with wood stored and enclosures for the animals. He was self-sufficient. He served us tea and a copious omelet made from his hens' eggs and some greens, as it is usually served in Iran (*gurmeh sabzi*), again with yogurt, homemade bread, and apple candies. Then he took out his old Persian musical instrument and played some lovely ballads as we were eating. His wife was very hospitable and kind but they complained that it was very difficult making a living up here where everything had to be brought up, and the children went to school way down below in Lahic.

We walked to the next valley, to another small village, in the lower elevation. Here the ancient tractors were getting ready to plow the lower fields. We stopped by a lovely stone bench to admire the scenery and catch our breath for the long way home.

A man on horseback came to say hello and we visited another acquaintance of our guide. We climbed up to his house and we visited an old, old woman who looked ancient lying in her bed. The family again welcomed us with more tea warmed up on a small stove and more conversation. Our guide was very caring towards the old woman and we could see that he truly cared for others. He was a kind religious man who, because of his grave head injury, had had some kind of religious experience. He had been spared. So he was ever thankful to God for being alive! He told me he really wanted to visit Meshad, the sacred city of the Shia Muslims in northwest Iran, to give thanks.

Then we said our good-byes and headed down the riverbed, and by this time the weather looked ominous, grey, with dark clouds. More women were working in the gardens, and some lovely goats were coming out of their winter home: a small stone room with hay on the ground. Again we stopped for another visit with locals at a large farm with more beehives, chickens, gardens, and goats. An older woman and her daughter and grandson came to meet our guide and invited us in for more tea! It seemed our guide was making the grand tour of all his friends in the surrounding villages for our benefit.

It was getting late, so now we had to walk on the wide riverbed which had some very fast-moving water, icy cold, which we had to cross several times. I took my boots off, rolled up my pants, put on my Teva sandals brought for that purpose, and was treading the fast-moving water for a while. Then we headed up towards our mountain village. Some beautiful horses were running in their enclosed meadow and a man was feeding them. As the Sun was setting we arrived at our home along with the cows who were coming back to their little stone barns to get milked. The orange colors of sunset were bathing the surrounding mountains in its magical light amidst some dark indigo clouds.

There was still time to walk around the village so we went discovering again and were invited to the beautifully restored home of a very wealthy man from Baku. He had lived in Toronto, and his wife did not like it so they moved into this beautiful village and built a fantastic-looking home out of posts, beams, and stones, with beautiful art pieces, paintings, and furniture. It was also a small hotel for wealthy people from Baku or for foreigners, or for CEOs of oil companies to hold their meetings, he told me. It was truly a gem. It looked more like it belonged to Aspen or Vail, Colorado than to Lahic.

The stores were opened and offered fruits, vegetables, beans, lentils, and many herbal remedies, spices. Here they use herbal medicine and bush medicine. Lots of great-flavored honey, sweets, and breads. They are not lacking in anything except some help with plumbing, electricity, and road building. They manage to build their own homes with their meager earnings. The richer neighbors are building themselves very large homes with extensive fruit gardens and all the luxuries of the West. Many of them come and retire here, thereby bringing some funds into these remote villages. But life is hard and the Baku oil money does not include these local villagers, although their school is taken very seriously and they said that many of their graduates have made a name for themselves in the artistic field. Many writers, poets come from this particular region, and they are proud of them, very proud of their Persian heritage. Might this glorious setting be a remnant of the shah court with rich culture and artistic activities?

This area was once the home of illustrious people which in a way formed the bedrock of our own civilization.

But now more about Zarathustra.

> Let us turn back for a moment to the first civilization that followed upon a great catastrophe, to the ancient Indian civilization. There we find seven great and holy teachers known as the Holy Rishis. They point upwards to a higher being of whom they said, Our wisdom can divine this lofty being, but it cannot perceive it. The vision of the Holy Rishis is great, but the exalted being they called Vishva Karman is beyond their sphere. Vishva Karman, though permeating the spiritual world, is a being beyond what the clairvoyant eye of that time could teach.
>
> Then followed the civilization called after its great leader Zarathustra, and Zarathustra spoke as follows to those whom it was his mission to guide: "When the clairvoyant eye contemplates the things of this world—minerals, plants, animals, men—it perceives behind these things all sorts of spiritual beings. The being, however, to whom man is indebted for his very existence, who in the future is destined to dwell in man's deepest self, remains hidden as yet from the physical eye and the clairvoyant eye when one contemplates the things of this Earth." But when Zarathustra raised his clairvoyant sight to the Sun, then—so he said—more than the Sun is seen; as an aura is perceived surrounding man, so, in contemplating the Sun, the great Sun aura is discerned—Ahura Mazdao. And it is the great Sun aura that once brought forth man.... Man is the reflection of the Sun spirit, of Ahura Mazdao; but as yet Ahura Mazdao did not dwell on Earth.*

---

* Steiner, *The Gospel of St. John and Its Relation to the Other Gospels*, p. 14.

There were leaders of a different type altogether, of whom Zarathustra was one. I am not speaking now of the *individuality* of Zarathustra but of the "personality" of the original Zarathustra, the herald of Ahura Mazdao. If we study such a personality at the point where he stands in world history, we realize that this is not a human being who has risen through his own intrinsic merits. On the contrary, he is a personality who has been chosen to be the bearer, the sheath, who can only send his illumination into and work within a human sheath....

I have indicated how at a certain point of time, when it is necessary for world evolution, a human being is inspired by a higher spiritual being....

The personality of Zarathustra was chosen to be the abode of a higher Being and was filled with living spirituality. Such personalities were chiefly to be found in the early, pre-Christian civilizations which had arisen throughout Europe, in northwestern and mid-western Asia but not in other civilizations which spread through Africa, Arabia, and Asia Minor into Asia....

The personality of Zarathustra was chosen in somewhat the following way to be the bearer of a higher Being who was not himself actually to incarnate. It was decreed by the higher worlds that into this child there was to descend a divine-spiritual Being who when the child matured could work in him, make use of his brain, his faculties, and his will.... It will be clear to anyone with finer powers of observation that from the very beginning there is evidence of conflict between the soul forces of such a child and the external world; that in this child there is a will and an inner driving power at variance with what goes on in his environment. But such is the destiny of a personality thus filled with a divine-spiritual Being. He grows up a stranger, for those around him have no insight of feelings which would help them to understand him. Generally there are only very few—perhaps only one—with any inkling of what is developing in such a child. On the other hand, conflicts with the world around will easily arise....

When a child such as Zarathustra is observed clairvoyantly he will be found to have feelings, faculties, and forces of thought which will be quite different from those developing around him. Above all, it will be evident—that those around such a child know nothing about his real nature; on the contrary they feel an instinctual hatred of him....

BEYOND THE BLOOD

There is no sharper conflict visible to clairvoyance than that between a child born to be a saviour of mankind and the storm of hatred that is unleashed around him. This is inevitable, for it is just because such a child is different that the great impulses can be given to humanity....

The story is told that as soon as he was born, Zarathustra could smile—something that is usually not possible for several weeks. We are told that Zarathustra's smile came from his consciousness of the harmony of the world....

There is a second story, to the effect that an enemy, as it were another Herod, named Duransarun, lived in the region where Zarathustra was born and that when the birth of the child was divulged to him by Chaldean Magi, he tried to kill the infant with his own hands. The legend tells that as he raised the sword his arm was paralyzed and he was obliged to give up the attempt—these pictures of spiritual realities which could have been revealed only to supersensible consciousness. We are further told how this enemy of the infant Zarathustra, then caused him to be carried by a servant out into the desert to become the prey of wild beasts. But when a search was made it was found that no wild beast had touched the child and that he was sleeping peacefully. This attempt having also failed, the child's enemy caused him to be laid where a herd of cows and oxen would pass and trample him to death. Instead, so the legend tells, the first beast took the child between her legs, carried him off, and set him down when the whole herd had passed by. The same thing was repeated with a herd of horses. And the enemy's final attempt was to expose the child to wild animals robbed of their young. But when the parents sought news of the child they found that again the animals had done him no harm....

These indications are to be understood as showing that through the presence of the spiritual Being, of the Individuality who passes into such a soul, very special forces are called into play. Such a child is brought into disharmony with his environment. This is necessary in order that evolution may be given an upward impetus. Disharmonies are always inevitable if there is to be real progress towards perfection. It must also be realized that these forces help to bring such a child into his destined relationship with the spiritual world....

When an infant such as the Zarathustra-child is filled by a higher Being the little body is naturally immature and has to develop to maturity. The organic system of intellect and sensory activity is also disturbed. Such a child is in a world in which he may truly be said to be "among wild beasts.".... The happenings take place in such a way that when the spiritual forces work from outside in the form of hostility, as in the case of the Zarathustra-child, they are personified in the figure of King Duransarun. Everything also exists in archetype in the spiritual world and the external events correspond to what is taking place in that world.... If we say that the events occurring around Zarathustra have significance in the spiritual world, people think that they cannot be real. If we show that the events are authentic history, we then incline to regard the personality concerned as being no more highly developed than anyone else....

The soul of the infant Zarathustra was actually exposed to great dangers; but at the same time, as the legend relates, the "heavenly cows" stood at his side to succour him and give him strength.

Similar stories can be found over the whole area from the Caspian Sea, through our own region, and into western Europe, in connection with all great founders of world conceptions. Such personalities, without having risen to lofty heights through their own development, are indwelt by a spiritual Being in order to become leaders of men.[*]

We said good-bye to our host, and headed back to the main road away from this hidden valley and its many remote villages.

We stopped in Ismayili and walked around the marketplace. It was busy, as this is where the villagers come to sell their goods and buy what they need in their villages.

Then we headed towards other valleys in the heavily forested mountains, a very lush area by many fast-flowing streams and rivers coming from high snowy peaks of the nearby Caucasian Mountains. There were many gardens and homes with large gardens, and we stopped for another homestay. The home was large and housed several members of a family: married daughters, grandparents, and grandchildren. Our room was again a place where they stored things. We slept on a mattress on the floor with piles of blankets because it was not heated, and the gusty spring wind blew

---

[*] Steiner, *Background to the Gospel of St. Mark*, pp. 86–92.

in from the large windows. The village is called Galaciq and showed a more Russian influence since the Georgia and Dagestan borders are not far. We had a lovely communal dinner with a wonderful stew, salad, desert, tea, etc.

The next day we met our guide who was the husband of one of the daughters. Now unemployed, he used to be an accountant when Azerbaijan was part of the Soviet Muslim republics, and now he was forced to go into the woods and collect mushrooms and herbs to make a living. He knew the whole mountainous area. This side of the Caucasian Mountains is almost tropical, not the desert-like scenery of Xenalig which is a three- to four-day hike from here through the mountains. But here it was a beautiful hardwood forest of sycamore, beech, oak, and very large sweet chestnuts, as we were not so high up. So he took us for another long trek into the low mountains, forests, streams, high meadows, ravines, and fast moving water.

The forest floor was covered with leaves through which the spring flowers were raising their colorful heads. We had a tea break on this happy carpet.

We climbed higher, the weather was intensely foggy, and I had to make sure I would not lose our guide. We arrived in a surreal atmosphere with very large beech trees which might take two to four men to surround their enormous trunks. Some lonely cows and yaks were seen in the distance grazing. Our guide told us this eerie setting had been the site of much fighting between Muslims, invaders, and so forth, where thousands were killed. We saw their century-old, moss-covered tombs with signs carved in beautiful Arabic. A very large area with hundreds of tombs lay there as if abandoned, it was forgotten, but there were signs of picnics and gatherings where the dead were honored and celebrated and not forgotten!

This atmosphere, with hundreds of tombs scattered everywhere, reminded me that all these mountains, these passes where we had walked on, these mountain villages were invaded by the Mongol herds in 1220s when they were pursuing a defeated king out of Samarkand. They reached all the way to Tsibili through northern Iran, where they were defeated by the Georgian army, and when returning north via Russia they asked for local guides to take them through these very mountain passes, through the Caucasian Mountains to Russian soil for more pillage until they were stopped at the doors of Europe. So even though these remote places look inaccessible, they have been treaded by armies, on foot and horseback for millennia, as this excerpt shows:

> After getting permission from Genghis Khan they (Jebe and Subedei, his two generals) left the country south of the Caucasus. There was no fear that it presented any threat to them, after they had destroyed and plundered Irak-Ajemi, Azerbaijan, Georgia, and massacred so many of the inhabitants. With typical ingenuity and boldness they forced their way along the difficult passes through the Caucasus. When Derbent refused to surrender, they promised to leave them alone if they were given the services of ten guides to lead the way through the mountains. With typical brutality the Mongols warned the guides not to play any tricks; they beheaded one of them to show what fate awaited the rest if they did not point the right way. North of the Caucasus the Mongols set foot for the first time on European soil.... It is unlikely that their maximum numbers ever exceeded twenty thousand. A larger force would not have been able to carry out the long marches in the Caucasus, where the deep valleys, bad roads, and narrow passes were unsuitable for the maneuvering of larger units. As it was, Jebe and Subedei were able to mount unexpected operations in the mountainous terrain.[*]

The tall branches of the beech trees seemed to want to touch you. We spent quite a while honoring the past, the fallen human beings.

Then we climbed higher up, still among the fallen leaves, moss beds, stones, and lilac primroses bunched up announcing spring, after crossing beautiful mountain meadows home to cows, sheep, and horses. We climbed down to a raging mountain river while our guide was searching and foraging for herbs and spring onions to bring home.

Down below, we sat on cold rocks and had a lunch of boiled potatoes, bread, cheese, dry fruit, feta cheese, sugar, local walnuts, and radishes, prepared by our host! And hot tea with sugar cubes.

It was time to get back up, this time to the peaceful, beautiful mountain meadows where some signs of old buildings lay there, and later the clouds and fog were starting to evaporate. As we left the higher mountain

---

[*] de Hartog, *Genghis Khan: Conqueror of the World*, p. 118.

Wild horses and a foal foraging in the sunshine

meadows, heading back to the village, we could see the higher Caucasian peaks full of snow, high up amidst the opening clouds. I was glad that it was not all foggy, but was also happy to have experienced this area on a foggy day, giving it its almost unreal character.

As we arrived in the village through a different route, we saw many wild horses running around, beautiful animals which are still part of this scenery. I thought I might have been in the European Alps. Many large castle-like homes were being built by wealthy Baku Azeris for their second homes, all with beautiful gardens, orchards, and farm animals. Many of the horses had just given birth to beautiful foals.

We left after a couple of days and proceeded west on the main road. Here one could still see the influence of the Christians, many old Albanian churches in ruins but still standing there. We stopped in a lovely church which had been totally renovated and painted with large frescoes from top to bottom. The people inside said that they come from Georgia to keep up the building and to take care of the small Christian community living in the area as volunteers. Georgia is within an hour's drive.

The ruins of a small Christian church

The tall candles were lit throughout the small beautiful church, clean and very much alive. In the town one could see the Georgian women in their traditional black skirts, black sweaters, and black handkerchief clothing.

We stopped for a lunch of typical Persian food: feta cheese, homemade flat bread, greens such as green onions and parsley, tomatoes, radishes, and tea. My favorite foods, which I still eat in the summer at home.

Then we drove farther into the city of Illisu, and another valley called the Qaracay Valley, following a riverbed and more mountains.

There we left our guide and went walking around this old scenic village, where some of the locals were getting ready for a massive wedding. The village was a center for much hiking and mountaineering in the nearby high peaks during the summer months.

We hiked up the side of a mountain overlooking the river, and watched from afar a local shepherd bringing his large sheep herd home. It was not far from where we had been booked in a tourist hotel, where we had our first shower in a week and a lovely dinner where we were the only ones eating.

Breakfast was great in this lovely setting, large bay windows overlooking the mountains and valley.

The road to Seki was surrounded on both sides by very large orchards of nut trees. I never knew that this area was so rich in hazelnuts, I think they could supply the whole world with hazelnuts! The small trees were growing everywhere in endless gardens, orchards, one after another.

Then we entered the old city of Seki, which was on the way back to Baku. We were booked in a lovely old restored caravanserai. The town is picturesque, and one could see that this was a tourist spot, unlike the other cities we had visited. Some of the khans used to live in this city, so we toured the small modest palace at a higher elevation. The city seems to encompass many different mountaintops, so it is long walks to reach everywhere.

This was an important trade route between Baku and Dagestan in the north, leading to the Far East, and then on from here to Georgia, Armenia, and Turkey. This city was famous for its silk and embroidery, but since independence, the silk factories have closed.

We climbed up to another little village, not far from the city center, and saw a small chapel. At the entrance of this small complex, carved in stone, were the following words:

> Scandinavian mythology describes a god called Odin that came to northern Europe from a place called *Azer*.... I have studied these writings and concluded that it is not mythology, it is real history and geography.
> —Thor Heyerdahl

He wanted to acknowledge that we have roots here in these very old mountains. The Azeri people from Azerbaijan are in fact our ancestors. This was a place where a small ancient temple used to exist during the second or first centuries BC.

It is said that Odin came from this area and moved north towards Scandinavia, which would make these people their ancestors. The small chapel was dedicated to this acknowledgment. We headed back to our guide who took us for a lunch we will not forget!

The entrance to the caravanserai

Our guide, we found out, was a foodie, so we benefited from his findings. We stopped at *all* his favorite places. We lucked out, this became a foodie expedition in Azerbaijan instead of my scholarly search for Zarathustra!

We went to an outdoor restaurant with a garden, roses, and lovely table sets with a fountain in the middle, and he ordered the food for us. It was cooked on charcoal and was simply delicious—a mixture of stewed meats with eggplant, zucchini, tomatoes, potatoes, and lemon, accompanied by Persian salad greens and warm bread.

Then we went to town for dessert: their famous honey and nut sweets like the Greek baklava.

Then it was time to get back to our great lodging, the sumptuous caravanserai, meaning a hot shower and two single beds in a small monastery-like tiny room, but a beautifully restored complex.

We toured the city, and had more tea in a local teahouse with a lovely old man serving us. We could feel the influence of Georgia here, entering more into the west, rather than the Persian villages, or old tribal mountain homes.

Men were sitting down drinking tea and chatting as they can be seen throughout Turkey, Greece, etc.

Here many of the ancient sites were being renovated.

The young girls and women were not covered at all, except for the Russian-style head scarves. This is mostly a very western country and Islam does not appear to have much importance.

The next day we left, going southeast towards Baku, and stopped in Ganca, the second largest city. There we had problems because the president was visiting the area and roads were blocked. We finally arrived there and toured the city: markets, old mosques, a new church, and a very large Russian-style square, remnant of Stalin. Then back on the road to visit Qobustan, an archeological site south of Baku, our last stop.

As we drove towards the east, one could see a lot of building going on. Large homes, at least ten thousand square feet. Our guide explained that many Azeris work in Russia in Moscow in the food markets and other areas, and come home to build their dream homes.

So we passed many such homes in the process of being built.

We arrived in Qobustan, at a Stone Age cave drawing complex overlooking a large prison down below (I wondered who was in there, because it was a very big complex), and farther up some mud volcanoes, an arid, rounded jumble of rocks and low mountains.

Twelve thousand years ago it was the site of cave dwellers and hunting people, a walk from the Caspian Sea. It was strange to be thrown back into such remote times and enjoy the images carved on the rocks, of animals, people, old boats, stick figures with head sets, a fascinating journey. I took many photos of these remarkable petroglyphs. Especially amazing were the bowls carved out on the granite ground which filled with water when it rained, and since it was raining that day, it was quite extraordinary. I expected people to come out and start cooking!

After this rainy afternoon, with a glimpse into our very ancient past, we drove through miles of huge oil-drilling compounds by the side of the road and the Caspian Sea. Taking the black gold out towards its world markets, and deforming the scenery. We entered into the grey modern city, Baku, for another couple of days.

My last picture is of a very tall, needle-like building seen through a building housing the eternal flame.

AZERBAIJAN

The eternal flame

This small country is holding its own, between its powerful neighbors, thanks to its oil. But the Azeri people, living in the mountains in their own villages, live as they have for thousands of years: a life still steeped in tradition, farming, husbandry, agriculture, and mountain living which somehow ignores its artificial borders to the north, west, and south with people traveling back and forth for weddings, shopping, trading, and visiting family members in other countries (Iran, Russia, Georgia), the Persian speaking going to northern Iran, the Lezjin people going to Dagestan, Russia, and the educated Soviet Russia Azeris (like our guide) going to visit their former student colleagues in Georgia or Russia.

> Azerbaijan, a comparatively small country populated by a peace-loving people, has been the subject of repeated invasions by aggressive neighboring states and empires.

BEYOND THE BLOOD

In 1828, Iran and Russia concluded the Turkmenchai Peace Treaty and since that time ancient Azerbaijan was effectively split into two: southern Azerbaijan became part of Iranian territory and northern Azerbaijan—the territory of modern-day Azerbaijan—became a colony of the Russian empire.

In May 1818, as the Bolshevik Revolution swept Russia, the people of Azerbaijan who had hitherto been under Russian control declared their independence and formed the Azerbaijan Democratic Republic. It lasted for about two years, until in 1920 the eleventh Red Army invaded. Later the same year Azerbaijan became a Soviet republic within the Soviet Union. In the meantime, efforts by inhabitants of southern Azerbaijan to gain independence from their Iranian rulers failed.

Though during the more than seventy years that Azerbaijan was a part of the Soviet Union, industry, agriculture, and levels of education all developed. It remained a colony in the sense that its occupiers, in the name of the Soviet brotherhood of nations, stripped it of much of its riches and used them for their own enrichment.

Finally, as the Soviet Union collapsed, came the 1991 revolution which enabled the Azeri people to establish an independent republic of Azerbaijan.*

Like many other small countries around the world, gobbled up by hungry neighbors, it is maintaining its strong traditions which are rooted in their soil, thanks to its hard-working people living as they did long ago. It was a real pleasure to meet the Azeri people. Their age-old traditions of Zoroastrian culture, Muslim faith, Christian worship, and nature worship seem to have blended together during the Soviet atheistic materialistic violent regime. Now they have time to decide who they are and the West needs to acknowledge their needs rather than plundering their enormous resources.

---

*   Khudazarov, *Teach Yourself Azeri: An Easy-to-Use Azeri Language Course Specially Designed for English Speakers.*

Part X

Uzbekistan

It is important to note one thing. This exploration of the mysterious, sacred Avesta is intended to awaken a tender and loving feeling for this sacred ground in the hearts of the younger generation, an understanding of the messages from the distant past in every square inch of our homeland frontiers, of the mysteries hidden in this sacred soil, of the need to care for it well.

Truly, we must not forget that Central Asia, and especially Uzbekistan, has spun the wheel of human history, and is the home of historical events that are possessed of a mysterious power. Learning the history of the homeland begins with every person learning the history of the place where he lives.

Recognizing that our ancestor Zarathustra's teachings and the sacred Avesta are intimately related to one stage of the evolution of human cultural development, our duty today is to provide a thorough explanation of the nature of the evolutionary change. What's more, before the emergence of the teachings of the Avesta, people worshipped gods only as terrible, brutal forces. The distinctive writings of the sacred Avesta in the development of human society is that they taught people to worship not evil forces, but good, to counter coarse physical strength with spiritual perfection....

BEYOND THE BLOOD

> The shape of the doctrine of the sacred Avesta provides one more inclination that nothing but the fullness of education of an era can stand in opposition to the ignorance of that era. These sacred writings have yet another worldwide importance: they serve to strengthen the spirit of belief that human goodness must fight relentlessly against evil and darkness and a belief in the inevitable victory of good in that struggle.*

We left the busy Baku airport and headed for Istanbul. There my friend went back to the West and I headed to Tashkent, the modern capital of Uzbekistan, after a five-hour flight departing at midnight.

Uzbekistan is where other incarnations of Zarathustra occurred and, as quoted previously, where a reawakening of the importance of Zoroaster, and the Avesta, its sacred text, is happening. Uzbekistan, being on the eastern side of the Caspian, was logical to see after its western-side sister, Azerbaijan. The Caspian Sea is one very important body of salt water, separating east from west where the Soviet Republic had left its mark, both positive and negative! What happens here in the future will carry consequences for all of us. The diverse approaches of the political structures to lead modern people into living together as Muslims, Christians, Jews, Buddhists, and materialistic scientists shows signs of very creative approaches. At the southern part of the Caspian, the Iranians have opted for a backwards approach leading to enslavement, imprisonment, and lack of freedom in all fields. The Russians, a Christian nation, are struggling for power in an increasingly difficult world competing in various fields with China, and the European block. But this is getting into the political domain which is not what my intent is. More relevant is how all these people are going to live together in peace, and *what can we learn* on the North American continent from their creativity in facing their global problems of religious freedom. And for a change, we must face the fact that we don't have all the answers!

The airplane arrived in the early morning, loaded with businessmen and a few tourists such as myself, and women coming from a shopping trip. During some major delays I spent time chatting with people, one of whom was an engineer and businessman from Algeria. He was about seventy years

---

* Karim, *Traces of the Sacred Avesta*, p. 216.

old, and he said he had been educated in a Moscow university, and then had become a businessman, who spoke perfect English, French, Arabic, and had an Uzbek wife. He was complaining that the French had done nothing (of course there were many French tourists in the line) and that Russia had been great for Algeria and that now he was doing all sorts of business with the central Asian countries, and not Europe, because France had done them wrong! Interesting! Algerians via Moscow, now into Uzbekistan.

Finally I was awarded a visa (which I thought I already had) for a substantial amount of money, and a guide came to take me to my accommodation in the center of Tashkent, a very modern hotel where most of the foreigners are housed. Another guide came to explain my stay. As with Azerbaijan, I had to travel with a driver, and my Tashkent travel agent, an attractive young Uzbeki woman of Russian-Mongol blood, had done a very nice job of including all of my requests. Trips to distant places, visits to remote villages, homestays, yurt stays, hiking in the high mountains, and, of course, visiting the extraordinary cities of Khiva, Samarkand, and Bukhara. I would have drivers taking me everywhere except for one flight and one train ride on the fast bullet train from Bukhara to Tashkent. I would spend almost four weeks here.

After a deluxe breakfast in the modern large Hotel Uzbekistan, with busloads of French, German, English, and Chinese tourists doing the Silk Road trip, and various businessmen from India, China, Pakistan, and Europe, I went about visiting Tashkent.

The hotel faced the large meydune (circle) with the statue of Amir Timur, or Tamerlane, on horseback in the center. From there, very large avenues branch off, Soviet style. I just picked avenues and walked endlessly. I reached the large monument, "Crying Mothers," facing monumental marble buildings, fountains, then I walked on more very broad avenues lined with trees but almost empty of people. I walked through a large park and garden where women were working, weeding, cleaning. I stopped by a flowing stream which had a large restaurant, called Sharshara, full of hungry Uzbeks—young couples, families, working men—heartily eating traditional meals. I was served by a lovely young waitress dressed in modern clothes, and then went to the gigantic dome-like structure which housed the markets, like a covered football field. An abundant array of the usual eastern markets, but this was incredible. Mountains of food, piles of everything you can imagine. No one is starving here! I had to sample dates, walnuts, etc. Everyone was busy buying and selling.

Then I walked through the modern souk where there was much activity and I was stunned by the proportion of the market. Mountains of fresh strawberries, money changers, large soup and kabab restaurants serving many hungry shoppers. Then I headed through an old section of Tashkent, Chorsu, with old-style homes, mud walls. But I know that behind these sad-looking walls and homes are oases with gardens and lovely homes. I got lost in the winding streets and somehow finally arrived within sight of the Juma Mosque, after about twenty miles of walking. My legs were getting tired, and then I reached the large, newly renovated mosque complex: a museum, the large mosque, minarets, and a madrese building converted into arts and crafts studios where tourists could come and buy the beautiful articles from the local artists, which I promptly proceeded to visit, and then chatted with all the painters, textiles weavers, wood sculptors, clothing designers, etc. I must say that I love the East because of its ancient arts traditions which are still kept alive.

This was a very busy city, lively, full of activity, and I was definitely in Asia. The Uzbeks call themselves Asian, and they are Asian. The women's clothes were of their own style, no copy of Paris, London, or Rome like in Baku, its western sister. But their own very attractive style for the women comes from the villages and the Russian outfit of skirt and sweater jacket with small heels. Young women have the global outfit of jeans and a T-shirt. I loved the different mixture of people: Russians, Uzbeks, Tajiks, Chinese, Persian, many with mixed blood, and extremely handsome men and women. One corner of the world where so many different cultures have intersected over millennia make this part of the world very youthful and lively. Of course I am not even approaching the subject of "soul wanderings." Where were these people in former incarnations? Perhaps from Europe? This puts a different twist on my thinking.

Here is an account of a Chinese Buddhist master monk and traveler who came through this area in AD 639 from the north, and western China.

I chose this passage because it reveals the character of this part of the world, which was not always a Muslim territory, but open to many different trends in religions, a trait which I think still remains in the people.

> It was the early spring of the year 639, and the Master was obliged to wait two months at Kucha until the passes (north of Tashkent-Kyrgyzstan) of the Celestial Mountains were open. But at last it was considered safe for the caravan to leave, though events would seem to show that they left too soon. On the second day they came upon a large band of Turkish robbers; but the men were so busy fighting like vultures over the division of recently captured spoil that the caravan was able to slip past unmolested. Now they began to climb in earnest into the Tien Shan Mountains, at this point about forty miles wide.
>
> "These mountains," wrote the master, "are steep and treacherous. They reach to the skies and ever since the beginning of the world snow has been accumulating on them—snow that has been converted into ice which never melts either in the spring or in the summer and whose glare is blinding...."
>
> Passing now along the southern shore of Lake Issik-Ku... they found the khan of the Western Turks and his army was engaged in a hunting expedition....
>
> Hsuan-tsang was conducted to the khan quarters—"a large pavilion adorned with golden flowers whose glitter dazzled the eyes. Officials, dressed in shining garments of embroidered silks, had spread two rows of mats on which they were sitting, while the khan's body guards stood behind him. Although the khan was a barbarian prince who lived in a tent of felt, one could not look at him without a certain feeling of admiration and respect." Thus patronizingly did the civilized Chinese admit that these half-savages were not quite beyond the pale as he had imagined.
>
> Some of these Turks were Zoroastrians. "They worship fire, and do not use wooden seats because wood contains fire.... But for the Master's sake they brought in an iron warming-pan covered with thick padding and invited him to sit on it." Then the presents were fetched and duly admired, after which came music and feasting and a good deal of heavy drinking; "and although the music was of a rather barbaric kind, yet it charmed the ear and warmed the heart." The thoughtful

host had provided his guest with a non-alcoholic drink, and instead of mutton and veal he was offered a fattening meal of sweetmeats such as "rice cakes, cream, sugar candy, honey sticks, raisins, etc."

The master was made to earn his supper by delivering a sermon. He chose for his theme the Ten Precepts of Buddhism, which roughly correspond to the Ten Commandments of Christianity. The khan, we are told, was quite overwhelmed, "prostrating himself humbly to the ground and joyously accepting the teaching of the master." Indeed he too begged Hsuan-tsang to remain permanently at his court. "There is no point in your going to India," he said. "It is very hot there...."

The master probably passed through Tashkent to reach "Sa-mo-kien" (Samarkand). Here the king and his subjects were also Zoroastrians, and though there were two Buddhist monasteries they had long stood empty. "If visiting priests seek shelter in them, the barbarians pursue them with fire and drive them out." The king, too, was at first pointedly unfriendly; but on the second day he allowed Hsuan-tsang to preach to him, and to such effect that he immediately asked to receive the vows of abstinence. Thus overnight he became the master's staunch ally.*

To get back to the hotel, I took a private car which acts as a taxi to make extra money, and then enjoyed the evening watching Uzbek television shows and the international news.

The next day I met my travel agent for a coffee and I gave her the rest of the funds for the trip. I had another day of exploring the city. I walked again in different directions on broad avenues, visiting museums and the large-scale modern marble buildings which were everywhere. This leader is definitely Soviet: everything is monumental, and looks a bit useless. We might as well be next to Moscow instead of next to Mongolia. I guess the funds coming from the rich oil and gas fields are beautifying the city in a Soviet manner! Perhaps better than some countries where the money is spent on endless numbers of palaces, like in former Iraq. At least these are public buildings and spaces, as grandiose as they are. And it does attract many world conferences on various subjects. One of the last ones which

---

* Blunt, *The Golden Road to Samarkand*, pp. 39–40.

was spoken about was a world conference on religions with people attending from around the world! A good sign and effort.

The Uzbek people seem happy to have such a great western-style city. They are proud of it. On Friday (our Sunday), the huge park with the "Crying Mothers" monument was full of well-dressed village families with numerous children, grandfathers, sisters, etc., visiting and enjoying the site. In all, the city did not have the feeling of being run by a dictatorship. The military policemen were always courteous when I asked for directions.

I decided to enjoy the subway and not walk all the way to the Chorsu market. It was spotless and beautiful, like the subway in Moscow. The place was packed because it was the weekend. Restaurants were full, shoppers were everywhere, and the village women were selling their vegetables and nuts.

I was very surprised to see a booming, very alive city here, in a place which was inaccessible not so many years ago.

I searched for bookstores, but like Azerbaijan, bookstores, books, and magazines are not available. This is not a place where one goes to a café to browse for the latest books on the latest subject. The country is still trying to consolidate, unify as a people, and the café's open forum is not here yet. But I am sure it will come. When one exits one form of government such as the former Soviet regime, it is not the most simple thing to achieve freedom. Uzbekistan has powerful neighbors: China, Iran, Russia, and all the rest of the "Stan Countries" in the high mountains, Afghanistan. How to be modern, what a task! We have plenty of examples: former Yugoslavia, Iran, Palestine, Chechnya, etc.

So for the café, that will have to wait. I can get all the books I want back in Europe or the United States. Television is bringing in the outside world, and the youth will demand more freedom. As long as the extremists do not have access to power as in Iran and start dictating how to live!

The great challenge of our century is seen in this brand new country. How much freedom? How soon?

As in Azerbaijan, the strong government keeps the outsiders (the Muslim extremists) in their place by having a dictator-type secular government.

I had a lovely lunch by the Chorsu market, a wonderful soup cooked in an enormous pot to feed hundreds. I sat next to a Russian-looking woman with her daughter who looked half-Russian, half-Asian. I must say the people are extremely handsome, both men and women. We chatted as best we could, while eating this wonderful warm broth with bread.

By the evening I had a copious supper at the hotel packed with businessmen of all sorts and some tourists, and I retired for more Uzbek television watching. The Uzbek speak a Turkik language except in the southern part where they speak more of a Persian language, Tajik, but Russian is the main language as well. Amazingly, they have had to switch back and forth for the last two hundred years between reading arabic script, then changing to the Russian script, and now once again they are in the process of changing to the western script. And two thousand years ago it was Aramaic and Greek (Alexander the Great) and other scripts, with Chinese in the north. Amazingly versatile. Being able in the end to read in three very different and difficult scripts, this makes the mind more agile, intelligent. I have noticed that the young people are very quick minded! And they will become more so, beating their counterparts in the Western world who are becoming quite lazy, mentally lazier. I know, I used to be a teacher! And that is the reason why I mentioned earlier that what happens here will have an enormous effect for all of us in the world.

In the West one cannot fathom having to learn three different scripts. It is only one of the challenges facing this large country.

Islam Karimov, the president of Uzbekistan, wrote an amazing book, *Uzbekistan on the Threshold of the Twenty-First Century*, a remarkably frank research on the problems faced by his country and how to solve some of them. But implementing them is, of course, a totally different story!

Here is a sample from the chapter, "The Revival of Spiritual Values and National Self-Awareness":

> No society can progress without developing and strengthening spiritual and moral values in the consciousness of its people. Inherited cultural values have been a powerful source of spirituality for the peoples of the East for millennia. In spite of rigid ideological pressure over a long period, the people of Uzbekistan have managed to preserve their cultural values and their local traditions, which have been carefully transferred from generation to generation....

The revival of the spiritual-religious foundations of our society, the Islamic culture that contains the centuries-old experience of the moral consolidation of its people, is an important step on the path to self-identification and the restitution of historical memory and cultural-historical integrity. Old mosques are being reconstructed and new ones are built; educational centers are being expanded; religious literature is being published. However, the process of the revival of the national traditions of Islam and culture has been a vindication of the decision not to "import" Islam from outside, not to politicize Islam and not to Islamize our politics. The Muslim culture of our region Transoxiana showed a spirit of ethnic tolerance and openness. Its ideal described in the works of Farabi and Ibn Sina, was the Ideal City—a community of people united not only by religion, but also by culture and morals. The upholding of freedom of belief in our constitution not only dispelled fears of the possible overall "Islamization" of Uzbekistan, but also contributed to the revival of development of other religions. An understanding of the spiritual originality of Islam in Central Asia requires a profound study of the pre-Islamic culture that is a part of our cultural wealth.[*]

I stepped on the airplane on my flight to Khiva, the beginning of my Uzbek journey, and enjoyed the scenery below. The airplane was made in Uzbekistan (the Soviets had an airplane factory here), and was very noisy, I thought I would not survive the flight! And the weather was a bit stormy! I had been apprehensive about flying internal local flights, but I had agreed to one flight. We landed and I waited for my small suitcase. Everyone got theirs, but I did not!

I started to complain, "Where is my suitcase?" Thirty minutes went by and I got angrier and angrier, knowing that they had kept my suitcase on purpose. I screamed at the workers to get back in there and get my suitcase, that I would not leave the airport without it! Finally they got tired of my screaming and hollering and brought it out, saying some nonsense about it having been hidden. I had never had this kind of problem. They thought they could get some money out of an older stranded tourist.

---

[*] Karimov, *Uzbekistan on the Threshold of the Twenty-First Century: Challenges to Stability and Progress*, p. 89.

The unfinished Kalta-Minor minaret (at left) in Khiva

My driver was waiting, and took me to my guest house without delay, seeing I was all worked up! He had a set of beautiful gold teeth that captivated me and drove off my hot temper. He dropped me off and I would be on my own for several days in this museum city.

I swiftly left my room at Islambek Inn, owned by a Russian Uzbek, after chatting with their son who spoke perfect English and told me he was flying to Singapore for university study in a few days. I walked around this intact old fortress city. Many other foreign tourists were doing the same. It was raining, but I was mesmerized by this jewel as was everyone else. There was so much to experience, see, and take in. The exquisite tilework held my attention, and my camera was clicking nonstop to capture some of this beauty. The fat, unfinished Kalta-Minor minaret, which a khan wanted to build so that it could be seen from far away, is a good place to

One of the wood-carvers in his workshop in Khiva

find one's bearing (he died before its completion in 1858). No one lives in this museum city, but close by, outside. A few artisans such as woodworkers and wood-carvers had their workshops within the city, where little boys were lovingly imitating their father's art and where apprentices were learning their ancient traditional arts.

I walked the paths of this city from morning until evening, never tiring of discovering new palaces, new madreses, beautiful carved doors, ancient stairs to climb and look at the city from high above, the sumptuous old mosque with its dozens of tall carved pillars, some of them thousands of years old, large open spaces. I expected men on horseback to come in and complete the scenery. One gets transplanted into another time, it is quiet and peaceful. Children ride around on their bikes, especially in the evening when it is time to go home. Along some of the paths, the locals would sell their beautifully crafted fur hats, jackets, tablecloths, scarves, gloves, socks, etc.

Khiva is part of the ancient Khorezm Region. There are other cities close by to Khiva, such as Urgench, and Turkmenistan is just around the corner.

BEYOND THE BLOOD

In the Avestan language, *otar* means fire. In actuality, in the oldest... it would have been pronounced *khvar*, then *khodar*, then after that *otar*. One can imagine that the etymology of the word *khorezm* comes from a combination of the words *khvar* (fire) and *zam* (earth). This means it was recognized as the place where the fire-worshippers' holy fire was first lit, the holy land of the Aryan people. *Ahura Mazdao* himself embodies *otar* (fire) and it is worshipped as the child born of the light of his heart (sun). Fire is considered the chief means of distinguishing truth from falsehood.

There is no denying the significant role of Zarathustra during the time of transition from the worship of many gods (polytheism) to the worship of one (monotheism). But even during Zarathustra's lifetime, only some of the tribes living in the Aryan lands followed him. The gods of these tribes, too, were divided into two groups: the followers of Ahura Mazdao and those who acted in the name of Ahriman.*

Khiva, like Bukhara, used to have one of the largest slave markets in central Asia during the golden age of the Silk Road, and the girls were sold as far as Arabia or Baghdad to fill the harems of the caliphs. Many of these slaves were from all religions, but many from Christian countries became the mothers and favorites of caliphs and khans. During centuries of raids by the various Turkik and Mongol tribes, into all the countries of Europe, women and men were taken as prisoners and brought back to be sold as slaves. It was a common practice in those days, everywhere, in the ancient world. And as we know, Egypt and Greece would not have become what they were if it had not been for slaves, but those were different times.

Here is a glimpse of the importance of caravans and commerce during the Mongol Empire during the Pax Tatarica.

> Civilizations that had once been separate worlds unto themselves and largely unknown to one another, had become part of a single intercontinental system of communication, commerce, technology, and politics.
>
> Instead of sending mounted warriors and fearsome siege engines, the Mongols now dispatched humble priests, scholars....

---

*   Karim, *Traces of the Sacred Avesta*, p. 178.

The commercial influence of the Mongols spread much farther than their army, and the transition from Mongol Empire to the Mongol corporation occurred during the reign of Khubilai Khan. Throughout the thirteenth and early fourteenth centuries, the Mongols maintained trade routes across the empires and stocked shelters with provisions interspersed every twenty to thirty miles. The stations provided transport animals as well as guides to lead the merchants through difficult terrain.... To promote trade along these routes, Mongol authorities distributed an early type of combined passport and credit card. The Mongol *paiza* was a tablet of gold, silver, or wood larger than a man's hand, and it would be worn on a chain around the neck or attached to the clothing. Depending on which metal was used and the symbols such as tigers, or gyr-falcons, illiterate people could ascertain the importance of the traveler and thereby render the appropriate level of service....

Khubilai owned farms in Persia and Iraq, as well as herds of camels, horses, sheep, and goats. An army of clerics traveled through the empire checking on the goods in one place and verifying accounts in another. The Mongols in Persia supplied their kinsmen in China with spices, steel, jewels, pearls, and textiles while the Mongol court in China sent porcelain and medicines to Persia. In return for collecting and shipping the goods the Mongols in China kept about three-quarters of this output for themselves, they exported a considerable amount to their relatives in other areas....

The constant movement of shares gradually transformed the Mongol war routes into commercial arteries. Through the constantly expanding *ortoo* or *yam*, messages, people, and goods could be sent by horse, or camel caravan from Mongolia to Vietnam, or from Korea to Persia. As the movement of goods increased, Mongol authorities sought out faster and easier routes than the older traditional routes.*

Khiva was used as a stop point for these large caravans traveling between east and west. It grew, then fell, and grew again. Its history is so complex that one is amazed that this city is still standing! It has been invaded, changed hands, so many times. Now it is getting a bit of well-earned peace and an admiration well-deserved from an invasion by tourists from around the world.

---

* Weatherford, *Genghis Khan and the Making of the Modern World*, pp. 220–222.

But to come back to one of the most illustrious prophets in man's history, Zarathustra. Some of the legends tied to the Avesta even mention Khiva, and its famous well. The city lies close to the Amu Darya River (or Oxus River) which flows between the mountains of northern Afghanistan and the Aral Sea in the north. The other river is called Syr Darya, and flows farther north of the Aral Sea and the mountains and area of Tashkent.

Zarathustra, in one of his reincarnations, is claimed to have lived on the banks of the Amu Darya River.

Millennia ago, the Turanians and Aryans had multiple wars in that large area between these two rivers, and far beyond. The Turanians, according to Rudolf Steiner, were the fourth sub-race of the Atlanteans.*

> In Gumilev's opinion (a Russian scientist), Persia is the monotheistic land that had accepted the teachings of Zarathustra, while the Turanians were the polytheistic people of central Asia, believing in many gods, and opposed to Zarathustra's teachings....
>
> In our opinion, Zarathustra first preached his worship of one god (Ahura Mazdao) on the territory of the banks of the Amu Darya, to the tribes and people living there, referred to in the Avesta.... In these lands, especially in the capital city and the surrounding villages, Zarathustra's teachings must have started to spread widely before the Khorezm area was conquered by Turanians (Afrasiab). This could not have been very compatible with the ancient and staunch polytheism of the tribes living on the banks of the Syr Darya (the other river in the north).... The conflicts and contests then between the tribes on the banks of the two rivers, Amu Darya and Syr Darya, were expressed skillfully in the *Shahnameh* (the Persian "Book of Kings") of Ferdowsi (famous Persian poet).**

The clean, large, cobblestone paths led me from one madrese to another, from one palace to another, to old mosques, minarets, and watchtowers. I found a lovely restaurant housed within the city where I took my lunch. It was cooked by local ladies who made fresh noodle-like soup, salad, and

---

* For more on this topic, see Steiner, *Cosmic Memory: The Story of Atlantis, Lemuria, and the Division of the Sexes.*

** Karim, *Traces of the Sacred Avesta*, p. 196.

bread in the tiny kitchen. I sat on soft colorful cushions, with other tourists coming from around the world. Then I discovered another lovely restaurant, where I ate outside. More great dishes and smiling waiters. I found a place for great coffee and internet access to keep in touch with friends at a small converted hotel.

And then I would go on, wandering the paths, sitting on walls, chatting with ladies selling their beautiful crafts.

The magical time was at sundown when the orange-colored, soft light would hit the turquoise domes and the red mud walls throughout the city. All the photographers were out running from one site to another, catching that special framed picture, because it only lasts about forty-five minutes. And furthermore, the Moon was full, so more pictures with minarets and the full Moon from all sorts of angles to add to the beauty of the place.

On market day, outside the city, it was very busy, noisy, full of locals selling and buying mountains of goods, veggies, fruits, animals, and cheese. I found delicious honey to sweeten my tea.

Early the next morning, my driver came and we were off for a yurt stay. Khiva is in the Khorezm Region, part of the Amu Darya River reaching to the infamous Aral Sea. This area has many two-thousand-year-old fortresses and castles buried in the sand. Some of these forts were old observatories, pagan temples, also some remnants of Zoroastrian ruins. It was a rainy, muddy day to hike amidst these old ruins which just sat there, ghosts towns, wind-blown remnants of past civilizations.

I enjoyed climbing through these ruins which at one time must have been very prosperous with rivers running close by, farming settlements, and a wealthy and intricate society.

We then drove farther to the yurt complex called Ayaz-Qala, which sits in a very deserted, dry, hilly land.

I had an entire large yurt to myself, with bedding rolled out on the dirt floor covered with many colorful carpets. Another large yurt accommodating at least fifty people or more was used as a restaurant. There was only one French couple, so I would be the only one here spending the night, with my driver in the other yurt. We had some bathrooms outside, with icy water. The local workers were assembling another large yurt.

Some of the family members alongside their van

The cook was preparing food in an adjacent brick building. She served me some lunch of old bread and old tomato salad, then I hiked up the surrounding hills which had another old fortress. The wind was blowing hard, and it was rather cold. The desert sand was blowing in my face, and some lonely plants were growing amidst this desolate terrain. I could see an old truck trying to get started in order to get some water for the yurt camp.

Some women were climbing up to the fort, many of them with scarves, drudging through the sands. I spoke to the very friendly gang back at the yurt camp. They had come here for good luck. We had a photo session with me and grandma, grandpa, ma, daughters, and then they left in an old beaten-up van, at least fifteen of them. They invited me to their village, which would have been a lot more fun than this artificial yurt village. This area was poor and this settlement had been created for tourists with the help of UNESCO.

During the night, we had a major rain and wind storm which blew up some of the roof on my yurt and rain was pouring in on my mattress and blankets. The restaurant yurt was badly damaged by the wind storm, so me and the driver ate more old bread and tea in the little cooking area. I was happy to leave this made-for-tourists encampment. Not what I had in mind!

UZBEKISTAN

We then drove on to Bukhara, crossing part of Uzbekistan. The area had been used for growing cotton for many years, an industry developed during the Soviet era. It had drained the Aral Sea of its water because cotton is a very thirsty crop, and caused much damage to the land. One could see cotton on the side of the road caught in between bushes. We were not far from the Turkmenistan border, just a bridge over the Amu Darya River which was going to Turkmenistan.

We drove through poor towns and arid, dreary territory—not very attractive land. It must have seen better days. This was a major highway into Persia, south and Russia, north. It was a wealthy oasis at one time, part of the Persian Empire, Mongol, Turkik, then the Soviet regime, and so many others that I can't keep track of!

We stopped for lunch in a lovely restaurant for people on the road. We were served a large plate of roasted lamb meat, rice, and salad with tea. Better than what I had eaten back at the yurt, which gave me another bout of intestinal disorder! (Traveling is not always a piece of cake.) Truckers and families were enjoying their lunch as well.

Finally we entered Bukhara and my driver left me at Chor Minor Hotel, by the entrance to the city, and said that another driver would pick me up for my next journey. He returned to Khiva. Meanwhile, my host, an older gentleman with a young wife and two lively children, made me feel very comfortable in this renovated hotel. He brought me tea and sweets, and turned the television on. We spoke in Tajik, a language close to Farsi, which I speak. The people of this area have Persian origin, and therefore speak a tongue similar to Persian, as do the Afhan people just south of here.

I would spend several days in this very old, ancient city which I had heard so much of in my readings!

This city was certainly not a museum city, but lively and full of tourists coming from around the world to enjoy its cultural wealth.

With over 140 old buildings, to visit it was a daunting enterprise! In its heyday, it had 120 madreses, educating more than ten thousand Koran theology students. It is no wonder this was where Avicenna (Ibn Sina) was born and educated, he was one of Bukhara's illustrious citizens. Now I saw only one functioning madrese.

BEYOND THE BLOOD

Avicenna was born near Bukhara in AD 980 into a family devoted to learning. By the age of ten he had mastered the religious sciences, by sixteen was a well-known physician, and by eighteen, thanks to the commentary of Farabi had overcome all the difficulties in understanding the Metaphysics of Aristotle. His precocity is proverbial in the East even today. From the age of twenty-one until his death at fifty-seven, he wandered from one court in Persia to another as physician and even vizier, spending most of this period in Esfahan and Hamadan, where he finally died. During this turbulent life his intellectual activity continued unabated. Sometimes he even wrote on horseback while going to a battle. The result was over 220 works, which include the *Kitāb al-shifā'* (*Book of Healing*), the largest encyclopedia of knowledge ever written by one man, and the *Canon* [*of Medicine*] which became the best-known medical work in East and West and gained him the title of "Prince of Physicians."

The universal genius of Ibn Sina (Avicenna), the greatest of the philosopher-scientists in Islam, left hardly any field untouched....

Avicenna towards the end of his life wrote a series of works intended for the "elite" in which he sought to expound what he called the "Oriental Philosophy" or rather *al-hikmah* (theosophy, wisdom of god). In this "Oriental Philosophy" the role of the intellectual intuition and illumination (*ishraq*) becomes paramount; philosophy turns from the attempt to describe a rational system to explaining the structure of reality with the aim of providing a plan of the cosmos with the help of which man can escape from this world considered as a cosmic script. Henceforth, in the East, the primary role of philosophy became to provide the possibility of a vision of the spiritual universe. Philosophy thus became closely wedded to gnosis as we see in the Illuminationist (*ishraq*) theosophy.*

Bukhara is by the Zarafshon River, and until one hundred years ago, thanks to the river, it had a very complex irrigation system of hundreds of stone pools and canals to provide refreshing water to the inhabitants. So I stopped by one of the few remaining pools which has a beautiful central plaza with tall, very old mulberry trees for shade, green grass, and

---

* Nasr, *Islamic Life and Thought*, pp. 66–67.

One of the local artists doing embroidery

a bronze statue of Mullah Nasruddin on his donkey. Mullah Nasruddin is the *Grimm's Fairy Tales* of the Muslim world, and one of my favorites.

The main plaza is perfect for visitors to sit, chat, eat, stroll, etc., with a large outdoor restaurant where one can sit on colorful cotton pillows, benches, and tables, and eat local food. The place was full of locals, elder bearded men and their families, and young couples enjoying the atmosphere. It was also a place where brides and grooms in western attire would take pictures. I ordered some food and proceeded to enjoy the square, the food, the people wandering around, the kids fishing in the pond, the ducks swimming, and the great view of the entrance to a newly renovated madrese with its geometric designs in blue and turquoise arabesques.

There are three madreses facing the large pool. I started by visiting one of the madreses, whose little cells facing the spacious, large, enclosed garden were occupied by many artists. The open space was full of tourists who were sitting down, at least sixty of them, ready to be entertained by local dancers, music, and a fashion show of young beautiful Russian-Uzbek women showing their own haute couture. I joined the crowd, sat, and ordered tea. A large group of Israelis were sitting down to dinner, coming

The Kalon Minaret and Mosque

direct from Tel Aviv for rest and relaxation away from their daily problems. They were very loud and enjoying themselves in their bright orange T-shirts.

Then I went out to many other madreses, chatting with local artists. Farther down I walked to the oldest surviving mosque, called Maghoki-Attar, which sits on remnants of an old Zoroastrian temple, next to old Buddhist ruins, all being excavated. The avenue led to a covered souk with more carpets, embroidery, miniature paintings, handmade clothes, weavings, jewelry, etc. I crossed this busy area and entered the Kalon Mosque, with the 140-foot-tall Kalon Minaret dating back to 1127, spared by Genghis Khan one hundred years later during his assault on Bukhara in 1220. The very large courtyard can house ten thousand believers, and has been restored to its original splendor. Two turquoise domes shine in the sunlight. The onion-shaped tall openings facing the courtyard with exquisite blue and turquoise tilework give it an atmosphere of clarity, openness, and peaceful union with the wide open blue sky. Opposite the Kalon Mosque is a famous madrese dating back to the sixteenth century. I entered the madrese, but one cannot go past the large door, as it is a functioning school.

I snuck into the sacred tombs of Mir-i-Arab and Ubaidullah Khan with a few Uzbek men on a pilgrimage, while some foreigners were forbidden to enter. I am glad they accepted me as a pilgrim.

While looking at old instruments in a little shop in the bazaar, the wife of the merchant came in and was delighted to play some old tunes. She was a very gifted musician. Later her husband said there might be a concert nearby. I showed up and their teenage son took me to the local university. We went into a small theater where several women and men were assembled to play and sing. I had to explain that I loved music and appreciated their culture. They began a lovely ballad and concert full of warmth, and sorrow. I thanked them and returned to the old city.

I found a lovely coffee shop and had some real cappuccino served by a handsome young Uzbek couple with their little one-year-old baby.

I spent more time in the large bazaar looking at women weaving carpets in former large madreses, caravanserais, and palaces. They were also weaving their beautifully designed cotton fibers. Then I passed the gold market where women were arguing over prices. They were very fond of rubies set in gold, but not real rubies. Much in demand were gold ruby earrings. They must have had one hundred women selling their gold. Gold is better than a bank account!

The embroidery was exquisite. Unfortunately, my budget did not allow for much spending, it had gone to the travel agents!

By the evening I returned to my room facing the busy street and went to sleep, ready for another day.

These sumptuous settings had been the home of many illustrious poets, shahs, travelers, and astronomers, Avicenna, of course, being one of them. It was the Florence of the Arab world. But one conqueror stopped in the city in 1220 and changed it forever, spreading chaos, pandemonium, and death.

> Meanwhile, Genghis Khan and Tolui were laying siege to Bukhara, which had become under the Iranian Samanid Dynasty in the tenth century, the greatest Muslim religious center in that part of Asia.... There was an old proverb which ran, "In all other parts of the world light descends upon Earth; from holy Bukhara it ascends." Lord Curzon wrote in his *Russia in Central Asia*: "Students flocked to its universities,

where the most learned *mullahs* lectured; pilgrims crowded its shrines.... Well-built canals carried streams of water through the city; luxuriant fruit trees cast a shadow in its gardens; its silkworms spun the finest silk in Asia; its warehouses overflowed with carpets and brocades; the commerce of the East and West met and changed hands in its caravanserais; and the fluctuations of its market determined the exchange of the East."

Within the besieged city the will to resist soon weakened. One night a body of soldiers and their officers, believing their situation hopeless, broke out and attempted to slip through the Mongol line under cover of darkness; they were detected, pursued, and virtually annihilated on the banks of the Oxus. Soon afterwards—it was in March 1220—the leading citizens of Bukhara, seeing themselves betrayed and receiving a promise that their lives would be spared, opened the city gates....

Curiosity overcame fear, we are told, as the Mongol horsemen with Genghis Khan at their head surged into the city. The khan reined his horse before a fine building which he understandingly mistook for the royal palace. On being informed that it was the house, not of the shah, but of God, he entered it—some accounts say that he did not dismount until he was inside the building—and ascending to the reader's desk, introduced himself, through his interpreter, to the worshippers as the "Scourge of God" and ordered them to open their storehouses for his men. The order came a little late: soldiers were already breaking in everywhere, ransacking the granaries, looting the houses, and stabling their horses in the libraries where, "by an unexampled profanation [wrote a Muslim historian], the leaves of the glorious *Alcoran* served for litter to their horses and were trod under foot."*

That year, 1221, the great poet Attar (one of my favorite Persian poets), almost one hundred years old, lost his life when he was killed by Genghis Khan's troops a few hundred miles south of Bukhara, not far from Herat, on their way to Azerbaijan. He was a very refined wise man, a Sufi, perfumist, physician, and poet. A perfumist in the Arab world was almost a magician. He knew the atar of roses, essences of frankincense, myrrh, orange, cedar, and hundreds of others, and used them to cure illnesses, but mostly he was

---

*   Blunt, *The Golden Road to Samarkand*, pp. 75–76.

a healer of the soul. The Mongols were the antithesis of such refinement. The two clashes of different civilizations could not have been more powerful.

Here is a poem already mentioned:

The Newborn
Muhammad spoke to his friends
about a newborn baby, "This child
may cry out in its helplessness,
but it doesn't want to go back
to the darkness of the womb.

And so it is with your soul
when it finally leaves the nest
and flies out into the sky
over the wide plain of a new life.
Your soul would not trade that freedom
for the warmth of where it was.

Let loving lead your soul.
Make it a place to retire to,
a kind of monastery cave, a retreat
for the deepest core of being.

Then build a road
from there to God.

Let every action be in harmony with your soul
and its soul-place, but don't parade
those doings down the street
on the end of a stick!

Keep quiet and secret with soul-work.
Don't worry so much about your body.
God sewed that robe. Leave it as it is.

Be more deeply courageous.
Change your soul."*

---
* Attar, in Barks (trans.) and Khan, *The Hand of Poetry: Five Mystic Poets of Persia*, p. 58.

BEYOND THE BLOOD

Another famous Sufi, Bahauddin, the father of Rumi who was from the Samarkand-Bukhara-Balk region, left Samarkand in 1219, headed for Baghdad, and settled in Konya with his twelve-year-old son, Rumi. If they had remained we would not have had this more than famous Sufi poet.

At the time of Rumi's birth in 1207, Bahauddin was engaged in a powerful debate in Balkh (south of Bukhara), a controversy that had been raging for a hundred years at least. Simply put, it was an argument between mystics and philosophers, between those who rely on spiritual experiences and those who accept and follow a received doctrine.

Ghazzali began the debate with his attacks on Greek-based, rational philosophy. Bahauddin was a student of Ghazzali's work. The philosopher Fakhruddin Razi was his grand antagonist. Both were friends of the king. Razi accused Bahauddin of wanting to appropriate some of the king's power. The story is that the king sent Bahauddin the keys to his treasury and his crown. Bahauddin responded that he was not interested in any material realm of power and that he would gladly leave the country to dispel any rumor about his intentions. Probably it was at this time when Rumi was five, that Bahauddin took his family into voluntary exile in Samarkand. They returned to Balkh later and in 1219 they began the journey that took them through Nishapur, Baghdad, Mecca, Damascus, Laranda, and finally Konya. Before they left Balkh, Bahauddin gave a sermon before the king and a large assembly in which he predicted the destruction of Balkh by Mongol armies and the abolition of the monarchy, all of which happened in the next year, 1220.

Allaudin Kayqubad, the enlightened Seljuk ruler of the region known as Rum, invited Bahauddin to Konya, where a school was built for him. After only two years as the spiritual head of the Konya community, Bahauddin died, at nearly eighty years old. His son, Jalaluddin, was appointed to the position of Sultan. Rumi was twenty-four.*

A Bridge Called Saraat
They asked me what constitutes blasphemy. How can one be unfaithful to God? I say it is when there is perfect light and yet you still see

---

*   Barks and Moyne (translators), *The Drowned Book: Ecstatic and Earthy Reflections of Bahauddin, the Father of Rumi*, p. xviii.

darkness; when you are surrounded by miracles and yet claim partial responsibilities and reserve final judgment; when you refuse the vision and insight given you.

There is a bridge called Saraat reaching from the seen to the unseen, less than a hairsbreadth wide, yet every living thing could pass over it. Some people cross quickly and happily, laughing. Others are quiet and take their time. The unfaithful are those who consider they might actually *be* the bridge.

As mortal suffering and delight are true, so too are the joys and afflictions that come to spirit. Imagine in the ground the place where the Earth's progeny get torn apart and reduced to particles. From there one can see pure color, worlds of being and nonbeing diving into each other, small scenes that open like morning glories into the light of the kingdom, which is many times brighter than the Sun. I know this because it has appeared to my eyes.

Remember how Muhammad's soul flew out through his lips. Souls *do* leave like arrows from the body's bow. Some go true, some careless, and unintentional.*

By riding against Khorezm, Genghis Khan attacked a newly formed kingdom only twelve years older than his own Mongol nation, but he attacked not just an empire, but an entire ancient civilization. The Muslim lands of the thirteenth century, combining Arabic, Turkic, and Persian civilizations, were the richest countries in the world and the most sophisticated in virtually every branch of learning from astronomy and mathematics to agronomy and linguistics, and possessed the world's highest levels of literacy among the general population. Compared with Europe and India, where only priests could read, or China, where only government bureaucrats could, nearly every village in the Muslim world had at least some men who could read the Koran and interpret Muslim law. While Europe, China, and India had only attained the level of regional civilizations, the Muslims came closest to having a world-class civilization with more sophisticated commerce, technology, and general learning, but because they ranked so high above the rest of the world, they had the farthest to fall. The

---

*   Bahauddin, in Barks and Moyne (translators), *The Drowned Book: Ecstatic and Earthy Reflections of Bahauddin, the Father of Rumi*, p. 54.

BEYOND THE BLOOD

Mongol invasion caused more damage here than anywhere else their horses would tread.*

By the year 1220, by some stroke of destiny, Bahauddin and his son escaped the turmoil and went on to establish the greatest spiritual order stemming from Islam, the *Sufi* order, active worldwide to this day, but Attar, the great, talented, and peaceful Persian poet, perished in the bloodbath.

> When the Huns (Mongols) poured over from Asia into the countries of Europe during the early Middle Ages, causing alarming wars, there was a significant spiritual aspect to this. The Huns were the last surviving remnants of ancient Atlantean people; they were in an advanced stage of decadence which expressed itself in a certain process of decay in their astral and ether bodies. These products of decay found good soil in the fear and terror the Huns caused among the people. The result was that these products of decay were inoculated into the astral bodies of the people and in a later generation this was carried over into their physical bodies. The skin absorbed the astral elements and the outcome was a disease prevalent in the Middle Ages: leprosy. An ordinary doctor would of course attribute leprosy to physical causes.... Their line of reasoning is as follows: in a fight, someone wounds another with a knife; he has harbored an old feeling of revenge against him. One person will say that the cause of the wound was the feeling of revenge, another that the knife was the cause. Both are right. The knife was the physical cause, but behind it there is the spiritual cause. Those who seek for spiritual causes will always also admit the validity of physical causes.
>
> We see historical events have a significant effect upon whole generations and we learn how even in such fundamental conditions as health, we can bring about improvements over long periods of time.... Only by working for the improvement of the common karma can we also help the individual. It should not be our aim to promote the well-being of the single, egotistical self, but to work in such a way that we serve the well-being of humanity as a whole.**

---

*   Weatherford, *Genghis Khan and the Making of the Modern World*, p. 109.
**   Steiner, *Rosicrucian Wisdom: An Introduction*, p. 52.

After a great breakfast of eggs, homemade bread, yogurt, homemade jam, butter, cereal, and chatting with the lady of the house, a guide came to show me more of the city. We toured more old palaces, parks, old mosques, museums, large medunes (squares), old remparts still standing, and the mausoleum outside the city. He was a Russian Uzbek, and his mother was also a guide. He spoke several languages and enjoyed his work.

Buses touring the Silk Road, full of tourists, were parked by the luxury hotel in the center, unloading the older boomer generation. After many centuries of not being able to visit this area, they came from France, Italy, Israel, China, Japan, etc., and enjoyed buying exquisite paintings, handmade colorful flowery embroidered tablecloths, jackets, hats, carpets, old instruments, hand-painted wood lacquer boxes, and many other articles lovingly made in their studios. The government was helping the artisans and artists by providing beautiful spaces, rehabilitating the former ancient madreses, universities, and palaces into studios to work in. The whole city was a beehive of activity and foreigners were flocking to visit these distant lands, but not so foreign anymore. Young women were sewing exquisite embroidered jackets. They would look up from their work when you entered their tiny workshop and, with a smile, welcome you and chat about their lives. They were happy; no one made them wear the hejab. They were free, and this was a Muslim country. No one bothered me as I walked along its winding roads within the old living quarters, or the broad avenues or the old Jewish district with a lovely old synagogue. When travelers are welcome, the country survives.

Close by the synagogue, I spent much time with a puppet maker who had a stunning collection of homemade puppets: princes, princesses, an old wise man, children, etc. He sent his work worldwide to entertain children with a millennium-old artform. I bought four of them for my new grandsons. I made sure one puppet had very curly hair and a long beard, and the princess was beautiful for my two grandsons who have some of the same Persian-Mongol blood from these faraway lands.

After a long day of walking I found a lovely terraced restaurant overlooking the city, and ate the usual rice dish. Uzbek food is not the most tasty, unlike in Azerbaijan, Iran, or Turkey. The food here is bland and always the same, but one does not starve.

A view of the Nuratau Mountains

I spent much time at the stunning great Kalon Mosque at different times of the day—morning, midday, evening—to catch the light reflected on the beautiful colored tilework. Sometimes when a group of women came to visit they would fit perfectly with their colorful turquoise scarves and flowing black dresses with flower designs. Sometimes the immense space would be empty and it would be me, and the sky, and the sacred space.

And my head swirling with all the history.

At 8:00 AM a young man came by in his private car, with his wife and child, to drive me north of Bukhara towards the Nuratau Mountains, in the Pamir-Alay range, which are under seven thousand feet. We stopped in Nuratau, which had the lovely clean Chashma Spring flowing into a channel where many beautiful fish were living, and then into a large pool next to an old sixteenth-century mausoleum. On top of the little hill was the fortress of Alexander the Great. We walked up on the beaten paths and enjoyed the view of the area. Then we drove on through beautiful flat land covered with red poppies as far as the eye could see. We stopped and took photos of these classic beauties. The sky was sparkling blue, and the lively red meadows were inviting us to stop. Then we drove towards the lower mountains, and herds of sheep were eating in the empty spaces.

Then quiet villages at the foot of the mountains in the distance started to show up, little oases with green trees, and rocky mountains in the background. After asking a few trucks and cars for directions, because the driver was a bit lost, we turned off into an old dirt road. It winded its way through the rocky mountains, by a beautiful clear river, and into more desert-like land with silver-green bushes, brush, and some poppies on the rocky sandy soil. The dirt road climbed up and finally we found the little homestay farm and this area's villages, called Asraf.

We climbed down on a footpath into the little idyllic oasis. It had several buildings scattered on the mountainside with great stately walnut trees shading the homes. The water flowed down the mountain and a little bridge had been built. Next to the bridge was a lovely platform over the fast-moving stream, shaded by the walnut trees, where we could sit on colored pillows and drink tea while listening to the sound of the clear water running through the vegetable gardens, fruit trees, and walnut trees growing in profusion.

A Beautifully Planted Park
He made the earth submissive to you. Walk in those regions knowing that.

You should expect grace, that which makes life more than manageable, but you look elsewhere, wanting some delight other than that.

Your conscious being, with what you've been given, should be like a beautifully laid-out park with wildflowers and cultivated wonders, a swift stream with secluded places to sit and rest beside it.

When a grieving person sees you, he or she should recognize a refuge, refreshment, a generous house where one need not bring bread and cheese. There will be plenty.*

---

*   Bahauddin, in Barks and Moyne (translators), *The Drowned Book: Ecstatic and Earthy Reflections of Bahauddin, the Father of Rumi*, p. 102.

I was shown into a room with a rolled mattress on the floor and several cotton quilts. Other rooms adjacent to mine were occupied. We had a shower room with hot water and bathrooms on the opposite side of the river. Tables were scattered in the gardens for us to eat our meals. On the upper part of the farm there was an enclosure for the family cow which gave them milk for yogurt and cheese. Next to the kitchen, but separate, was the oven where the bread was cooked every day. This family had an enterprising father who started this homestay venture, and a lovely wife, with three children, two of them married and living at the home, with two lovely toddlers. All of them were working hard to maintain life on the land. They also had sheep, and on the way I saw many wild horses running around the large empty spaces in the valleys between these mountains. The daughter was getting ready to be married. The grandfather, who kept the vegetable gardens, was taking a nap in the grass while the chickens ran around.

The homestay is getting very popular in these parts of the world where the locals can make some well-needed money and the foreigners can have a meaningful stay sharing the lives of the locals. This one was called Yahshigul Guesthouse, owned by Babajan Kozokov. He was born in 1965 and they speak Tajik, but also Uzbek and Russian. Tajik is related to Persian as Uzbek is related to Turkish, as I mentioned before. Different races of people mingling, one older than the other. The Uzbeks are a Turk-Mongol race and the Persians are an Aryan root race. The features are noticeably different.

After leaving my belongings in my large room, I hiked up away from the farm towards the mountain on a steep path. It was beautiful, quiet, and I wondered if these areas had been left alone during the many transitions, wars, invasion, occupation, etc. It was tucked away from the busy roads. I could see many other little farms snuggling against the hillside next to the spring water. I had been told that some of them were summer homes, where people came to avoid the heat of Tashkent.

When I got back from my walk I was stunned to see three English women, sisters, ranging from twenty-eight to thirty-six years old. I had thought I would be alone. They all had traveled extensively in faraway places and were hardy souls. I enjoyed their company for the next few days, hiking in the surrounding mountains and eating communal meals.

We could help milk the cow, bake bread, peel vegetables, or simply enjoy the oasis after strenuous walks.

I, of course, could have stayed here for a year and observed the life throughout the seasons as I had done many years ago in the Elborz Mountain villages of Iran, north of Tehran.

Taken from the brochure about Asraf:

> Like all the villages along the Nuratau mountain range, Asraf has a long history.
>
> Ancient rock paintings in the mountains prove that people have lived here for more than two thousand years. Elements of the Sogd language can still be found in the Tajik spoken today. In the fourth century BC, Sogds who originated from the Zarafshan and Istrafshan valleys settled in the Nuratau Mountains to escape the troops of Alexander the Great. Until today many of the customs practiced here are more closely related to the ones in the Zarafshan area than the ones of the Samarkand or Bukhara Tajiks.
>
> For many centuries some of the caravan routes between Bukhara and Tashkent passed the Nuratau region. The trade route was used until the nineteenth century. During the long, hard, and dangerous trips, fortresses and wells situated in the Nuratau mountain valleys and the Kyzylkum plains were used as stopover points by the traders.

The next morning, after a refreshing breakfast, I sat in my now favorite place: the platform with pillows, on top of the flowing stream, shaded by majestic, very old walnut trees.

The three sisters, teenage guide, and I took off for a day of trekking in the surrounding mountains. All these mountains had lost their trees, they were bare and rocky with a few bushes here and there. The snow had all melted, and as we climbed farther up we could see other little villages tucked away in distant valleys with herds of wild horses, and sheep and goats grazing on the mountaintops and meadows. To the west we could see a red carpet of wild poppies before the desert, and some kind of lake extending to infinity.

BEYOND THE BLOOD

Here is a poem by Rumi:

The Lame Goat
You've seen a herd of goats
going down to the water.

The lame and dreamy goat
brings up the rear.

There are worried faces about that one,
but now they're laughing,

because look, as they return,
that goat is leading!

There are many different kinds of knowing.
The lame goat's kind is a branch
that traces back to the roots of presence.

Learn from the lame goat,
and lead the herd home.[*]

Small spring flowers—blue, yellow, red, and white—were growing in the cracks of rocky grounds and here I would have enjoyed riding, but I had not arranged it, next time!

A man was coming our way on the steep path, sitting on his small, white, furry, sweet-looking donkey. We walked farther and farther up into the mountain, looking at distant villages, and then as it was getting later we headed back for a lovely quiet lunch by the river. Freshly baked flat breads, sweets, tea, and butter. The evening was spent lounging around the farm, talking, reading, journaling, sharing travel stories, and taking a warm shower.

The next day we hiked following the flowing river on its rich banks into the lower village, where homes are scattered. We stopped and chatted with an ancient-looking woman and her grandchildren on her terrace, then

---

[*] Rumi, in Barks (trans.) and Khan, *The Hand of Poetry: Five Mystic Poets of Persia*, p. 106.

UZBEKISTAN

Flat-roofed mud homes and a garden at the foot of the mountains

crossed more tended gardens into the dirt road where men were busy building a new home with stones, mud, and sticks, as they had done ages ago. Turkeys with their young ones were playing in the gardens where women were planting vegetables, and young girls were bringing water in buckets from the flowing spring. Then we left the small river valley where mud walls were enclosing the flat-roofed mud homes, where colorful clothes were hanging on the lines, and gentle cows were grazing in their enclosure waiting to be milked. There were orchards, small plots where women were kneeling down tending to the young plants, and we walked up into the mountains where a large herd of sheep and goats were slowly moving. A young boy was galloping on his donkey having a wonderful time. Wild horses with colts were happily eating the fresh grass.

Then we headed home once again for our refreshing meal, and the three sisters left for England.

The next day, I was off again trekking with the guide in the other direction. A herd of cows were quietly chewing their cud in this alpine setting, we walked farther and saw more distant villages and followed steep paths in between rocky mountainsides until we could see our village as tiny dots. We slowly walked down, leisurely looking at the fantastic scenery. We trekked to the lower valley and saw a lady in a bright red dress gathering her large goat herd home to milk. A young boy was playing with his donkey and wanted to give me a ride. A viper was slithering in the tall grass next to the rocky stream. (He did not look too inviting.) I walked back, the grandfather was taking his nap on the platform by the stately walnut trees and I sat down to enjoy this restful shaded garden full of spring flowers. I was in Persia! The toddler was ready for his nap, the ladies were milking the cow, and I sat some more, daydreaming, wishing I could stay here listening to the stream tumbling from the mountains. Then a group from Prague came. They were camping, using the showers, all the hot water, using the picnic area, not buying anything, not paying much, and arguing about prices (pennies). Meanwhile, they had top-of-the-line equipment: backpacks, hiking shoes, etc. I was disgusted by their horrible, cheap behavior, as they used what little these people had, with no remorse. I was glad that I would be leaving the next day. They were brutes, uncivilized, and I wondered what they were doing here, walking through these mountains by themselves, spending a couple of dollars a day or less. What a world!

I forced myself to chat with one of them, a burly fellow, who said he owned a factory back home in Prague.

Teaching Schoolboys
You don't distinguish between
what is health and what is torture.

You can't tell the difference between
the hidden world and this one.

You are not traveling the path.
You are a boy playing,
and proud of your independence.

If the glamour of a mistress is enough
to satisfy, why do you need God?

If you *know* what delights,
how can you be drawn toward eternity?

But be sometimes flexible teaching schoolboys.
If one of them has difficulty learning
a particular lesson, be gentle.
Don't discourage any child
with harsh criticism.

Put sweet dried fruit in his lap.
Rub his head. Help him to try again.

If, though, your student refuses
to concentrate on the page,
if he won't read, send for the strap.

Threaten to take him to authorities.
Say that he will be shut up in a rat-house
and that the Head Rat will eat him!

This is how we keep moving on the way.
Little tastes encourage us.

And there are books which we must attempt
to read, the prophets. Be friendly
with those, and grow like schoolchildren
into understanding, remembering though,

that this world is full of people
who never read, and remain
in a dim, undeveloped stupor.*

My driver arrived on time and we headed towards Samarkand, past oil rigs at the foot of the lower mountains, and more endless poppy fields and vineyards growing by the road. The railroad to Tashkent was parallel to the road now, and finally the great mountains of Tajikistan, a wall of tall rocky mountains covered with eternal snow, came into view, and the plain of Samarkand, home of Amir Timur, or Tamerlane.

---

* Sanai, in Barks (trans.) and Khan, *The Hand of Poetry: Five Mystic Poets of Persia*, pp. 14–15.

BEYOND THE BLOOD

Tamerlane, a petty Turko-Mongol prince who claimed direct descent from Genghis Khan through the house of Chagatai his son, was born at Kesh about fifty miles south of Samarkand in 1336. When in his middle twenties he received an arrow wound which left him lame in the right leg and with a stiff right arm for the rest of his life. Tamerlane is the English corruption of "Timur-i-leng," timur the lame, Timur means Iron, the Iron Limper. But Tamerlane made light of these disabilities: by 1369, he had possessed himself of all the lands which had formed the heritage of Chagatai, and after being proclaimed sovereign at Balkh, made Samarkand his capital....

Ahead stretched a green sea topped by turquoise domes and glittering minarets: Samarkand, the chosen city of Tamerlane. Thirty-five years earlier he had found it still ruinous from the destruction wrought by the armies of Genghis Khan: he had resolved to make it once again the finest city in central Asia....

Samarkand, with its population of one hundred and fifty thousand, had under his direction become a thriving city which netted half the commerce of Asia; Clavijo (Spanish writer) estimated that even without its large suburbs it was bigger than Seville. In its markets were bartered leathers and linen from Russia and Tartary; nutmegs, cloves, cinnamon, and ginger from India; silks, musk, and diamonds from China, and the rich produce of her own orchards, melon-beds, and vineyards. Under the cool arches of its bazaars, merchants fingered rubies from Badakhsahn or haggled over rare pearls from Ormuz and turquoise from the mines of Nishapur (Iran).... If with one hand he had laid waste to the great cities of Asia which had stood in the path of his ambition, with the other he had fashioned in Samarkand his enduring memorial. Craftsmen, painters, and scholars had been sent to his capital, from cities he had destroyed, to be the instruments of his grand design. There were sculptors, stone-masons, and stucco-workers from Azerbaijan, Isfahan (Persia), and Dehli; mosaic-workers from Shiraz; weavers, glass-blowers, and potters from Damascus—in such numbers that "the city was not big enough to hold them, and it was wonderful what a number lived under trees and in caves outside." Elephants, brought from India with the plunder of Dehli, dragged the huge blocks of stone into position. Princes of the royal blood had been ordered to superintend the workshops so that no time might be lost; and Tamerlane himself, in the brief intervals of leisure between campaigns had seldom been long absent from the building yards.*

Tamerlane died in 1405 on his last campaign, trying to conquer China. He almost conquered the world, but death he could not conquer.

There is an interesting legendary account of a meeting between Hafiz and the most sinister figure of the era, the ferocious conqueror, Tamerlane, who swept south through Persia, killing seventy thousand people in Isfahan and entering Shiraz in December 1387. He summoned the aging Hafiz, then sixty-seven, and confronted him with lines from one of his poems,

If the young Turkish girl would accept my hand,
I'd give Bukhara for the mole on her cheek,
or Samarkand.

"With my bright sword," Tamerlane raged, "I have subjugated most of the known world, and yet you, a miserable wretch of a poet, would sell my native town and the seat of my government for the mole on a girl's cheek!"

"You're right," replied Hafiz bowing quickly. "It's by just such extravagant spending that I've come to the sorry position you find me in now."

The emperor was so delighted with Hafiz that he not only didn't punish him, but sent him away with a gift. Hafiz died and was buried in Shiraz in 1389.**

Whether or not the story is true, he adds some levity to history!

The meeting of two such powerful conquerors, two men of such different paths, is a powerful drama.

Hafiz, one of the greatest poets of the Persian-Islamic world, a conqueror of the soul, who never left Shiraz yet is still known throughout the world today, master of his spirit, and the wild, Mongol emperor of the

---

* Blunt, *The Golden Road to Samarkand*, pp. 138, 145–146.
** Barks (trans.) and Khan, *The Hand of Poetry: Five Mystic Poets of Persia*, p. 147.

physical world whose conquests have been forgotten. Two different currents meeting in such a simple story!

Here Rudolf Steiner's insights into the evolution of mankind are immensely helpful.

> One will be able to detect the radical difference between the condition of mind and soul prevalent among the Eastern peoples of prehistoric times and that of a later civilization. It was another mankind that could call Asia the last or lowest heaven and understand by that their own land, the nature that was round about them. They knew where the lowest heaven was.
>
> Compare this with the conception men have today. How far is the man of the present time from regarding all he sees around him as the lowest heaven! Most people cannot think of it as the "lowest" heaven for the simple reason that they have no knowledge of any heaven at all!
>
> Thus we see how in that ancient Eastern time the spiritual entered deeply into nature, into all natural existence. But now we find also among these people something which to most of us in the present day may easily appear extremely barbarous. To a man of that time it would have appeared terribly barbarous if someone had been able to write in the feeling and attitude of mind in which we today are able to write; it would have seemed devilish to him. But when we today on the other hand see how it was accepted in those times as something quite natural and as a matter of course that a people should remove them West to East, should conquer—often with great cruelty—another people already in occupation and make slaves of them, then such a thing is bound to appear barbarous to very many of us.
>
> This is broadly speaking, the substance of oriental history over the whole of Asia. While men had a high spiritual conception of things, their external history ran its course in a series of conquests and enslavements. Undoubtedly that appears to many people as extremely barbarous. Today, although wars of aggression do still sometimes occur, men have an uneasy conscience about them. And this is true even of those who support and defend such wars. They are not quite easy in their conscience.
>
> In those times however, man had a perfectly clear conscience as regards these wars of aggression, he felt that such conquest was willed

by the Gods. The longing for peace, the love of peace, that arose later and spread over a large part of Asia is really the product of a much later civilization. The acquisition of land by conquest and the enslavement of its population is a salient feature of the early civilization of Asia. The farther we go back into prehistoric times, the more do we find this kind of conquest going on....

Now there is a quite definite principle underlying these conquests. As a result of the states of consciousness, man stood in an altogether different relation to this fellow man and also to the world around him. Certain differences between different parts of the inhabited Earth have today lost their chief meaning. At that time these differences made themselves felt in quite another way....

Suppose a conquering people has made its way from the north of Asia, spread itself out over some other region of Asia and made the population subject to it. What has really happened?

In characteristic instances that are a true expression of the trend of historical evolution, we find that the aggressors were—as a people or as a race—young, full of youth-forces. Now what does it mean today to be young? What does it mean for men of our present epoch of evolution? It means to bear within one in every moment of life sufficient of the forces of death to provide for those soul-forces that need the dying processes in man. For as you know, we have within us, the sprouting, germinating forces of life, but these life forces are not the forces that make us reflective, thoughtful beings; on the contrary, the forces of destruction, which are also continually active within us—and are overcome again and again during sleep by the life forces, so that not until the end of life do we gather together all the death forces in us in the one final event of death—these forces it is that induce reflection, self consciousness. This is how it is with present-day humanity. Now a young race, a young people, suffered from its own over-strong life forces, and continually had the feeling: I feel my blood beating perpetually against the walls of my body. I cannot endure it. My consciousness will not become reflective consciousness. Because of my very youthfulness I cannot develop my full humanity.

An ordinary man would not have spoken thus, but the initiates spoke in this way in the Mysteries, and it was the initiates who guided and directed the whole course of history.

Here was then a people who had too much youth, too much life forces, too little in them of that which would bring about reflection and thought. They left their land and conquered a region where an older people lived, a people which had in some way or other taken into itself the forces of death, because it had already become decadent. The younger nation went out against an older and brought it into subjection. It was not necessary that a blood-bond should be established between the conquerors and enslaved. That which worked unconsciously in the soul between them worked in a rejuvenating way; it worked on the reflective faculties. What the conqueror required from the slaves whom he now had in his court was influence upon his consciousness. He had only to turn his attention to these slaves and the longing for unconsciousness was quenched in his soul, reflective consciousness began to dawn.

What we have to attain today as individuals was attained at that time by living together with others. A people who faced the world as world conquerors and lords, a young people, not possessed of full powers of reflection, needed around it, so to say, a people that had in it more forces of death. In overcoming another people, it won through to what it needed for its evolution.

And so we find that these Oriental conflicts, often so terrible and presenting to us such a barbarous aspect, are in reality nothing else than the impulses of human evolution. They had to take place. Mankind would not have been able to develop on the Earth, had it not been for these terrible wars and struggles that seem to us so barbarous.*

Tamerlane's youthful forces were in full force, as we can see from history.

> Tamerlane's conquests were in Afghanistan and Persia, where he captured Isfahan and feasted his eyes on the spectacle of a pyramid of seventy thousand skulls. He sacked Baghdad, massacred most of the inhabitants, and took what treasures he could—not very much treasure for Baghdad had never recovered from the wounds inflicted by Hulagu. He overran Mesopotamia, swung north to Moscow, which he held for over one year, and three years later he was outside the walls of Dehli, admiring a still more extravagant pyramid of skulls. In 1401 he

---

* Steiner, *World History in the Light of Anthroposophy*, pp. 29–32.

swept over Syria pausing three days in Aleppo to build a comparatively small tower of skulls: according to an Arab chronicler it was thirty feet high.... It was the turn of Damascus, which held out for a month. The city was sacked and the Great Umayyad mosque was left an empty shell.... He returned to Baghdad to avenge the deaths of his officers.... During the following year he prepared for the invasion of Asia Minor.*

It is interesting to notice how, as explained by Rudolf Steiner, this man born in the Mongol-Turk race came to build one of the most beautiful cities in the ancient world from the rampages of his conquests. He encountered the older forces in the architects, artists, poets, and artisans of the Muslim world, not youthful forces, and thereby tamed somewhat his own wild forces in administering the building of his new city, Samarkand.

We entered Samarkand and drove through the small streets of the old city lined with old, flat-roofed houses with electric lines dangling from everywhere, and I found my hotel tucked away in a small alley, the caravanserai. It was a medium-sized, pleasant hotel with a courtyard, large restaurant, and two floors of spacious, clean rooms with baths. It had many tourists from around the world: Australians, Russians, French, English, etc.

I dropped my bag and went discovering my new home. No need for a map here. The Bibi-Khanym Mosque, named after Tamerlane's beloved Chinese wife, could be seen from very far away. I only had to walk towards its dominant turquoise dome which sparkled in the sunlight at the very end of my street. By the side of the gigantic mosque was a very large covered market for food of all kinds, and many restaurants serving workers and shoppers where I stopped for lunch. Older opulent women served me soup and bread and we chatted. They were curious that I was alone!

Then I headed for the Bibi-Khanym Mosque and was surprised at the size of this city. It was expansive, vast, and I would need to walk around for many kilometers to visit all of its rich treasures, not so contained and intimate as Bukhara and Khiva. But Tamerlane had designed this city with his imported architects and laborers. Many pilgrims were visiting the mosque, especially women, as it was a sacred site. The tale says that a woman will

---

* Payne, *The History of Islam*, p. 260.

The Bibi-Khanym Mosque in Samarkand

be bringing lots of children into the world if she crawls under the gigantic marble Koran which sits in the center of the courtyard. The gigantic mosque was crumbling under the weight of its enormous, tall domes, beyond repair after numerous earthquakes.

It was evening time, and I walked towards the old city to my hotel while glancing backwards at the Bibi-Khanym's turquoise dome with the setting Sun's orange glow on the beige, brick towers.

After a hearty breakfast, I strolled through the markets, past the Bibi-Khanym Mosque, and I headed towards the large avenues after savoring a coffee while sitting by the great mosque, a perfect spot to enjoy the city.

The large avenue, filled with large arts and crafts stores, led to the most famous, awesome site in the ancient world: the Registan. It was surrounded by extensive green lawns, gardens with small restaurants for ice cream or refreshments, fountains, formal flower gardens, trees, and wide marble paths leading to immense stairs descending into the majestic ensemble of three gigantic madreses. It is vast, opulent, and sparkling, with turquoise and tilework. One walked on large flowery mosaic tile scenes or cobblestones on which sat various fountains, flower gardens, and benches where

The Registan in Samarkand

one could rest. The madreses were all built after Genghis Khan's destruction in 1220, and they have survived the many earthquakes and invasions of the last eight hundred years. The Soviets did much to preserve the buildings, and the present government has restored them to their present magnificence. Tamerlane's grandson, Ulugbek, the mathematician, scientist, and philosopher, added much to the ensemble of madreses.

I walked through all three majestic towering madreses, just to get a feeling for this space. The proportions are pleasing to the eyes, and the vastness fits with this part of the world. The tallest mountains are at the foot of the city, the vast desert plains stretch to the Caspian Sea. It is no wonder Tamerlane made this city his chosen one, which was later abandoned for Bukhara by other shahs.

Many women with colorful scarves, red brocade dresses, and colorful skirts were visiting from their villages, as well as men with their favorite hats, children with families, young girls, teenagers in various attires, and a handful of tourists. People were enjoying their beautiful cities and heading back to their villages to talk about the richness of their culture.

BEYOND THE BLOOD

The former madreses which housed the students were transformed into many cells for arts and crafts studios like in the other ancient cities. Everyone was visiting the cells and conversing loudly with the artists. I thoroughly enjoyed the musicians, instrument makers, embroideries, jewels, miniature painters, etc. Everywhere was a delight for the eyes, sitting in an alcove looking at the domes or the tall minarets, or on a bench looking at the passersby.

I walked away from the Registan to look for some lunch. As I mentioned before, the food here is not the best! But following my nose, meandering here and there, after quite a while I saw an interesting restaurant and went in. The owner, assisted by his wife and sons, was presiding over a gigantic cauldron sitting on a bed of coal, cooking a most wonderful meal of rice and stew—just what I was looking for. They prepared a table for me in an open-garden space where many Uzbeks were eating. It was delicious, not a tourist place. I enjoyed the atmosphere, the food, and the warmth of the owners. It was more of a family meal than a restaurant!

But here is a rendering of one of Tamerlane's famed gargantuan meals:

> Passing through a high gateway the ambassadors entered the garden, from which wardens armed with maces were vigorously excluding an inquisitive crowd. After paying their respects to several members of the royal family and handing to the appropriate officials the gifts destined for the Amir, the guests were conducted to the palace, where they found Tamerlane seated on a high dais placed under a richly embroidered canopy. In front of the dais played a fountain in whose basin red apples were floating; no doubt it was the creation of Syrian craftsmen, who were past masters in the art of designing fountains "whose beauty they enhanced by an endless variety of sprays and jets":
>
> > *His highness had taken his place on what appeared to be small mattresses stuffed thick and covered with embroidered silk cloth, and he was leaning on his elbow against some round cushions that were heaped up behind him. He was dressed in a cloak of plain silk without any embroidery, and he wore on his head a tall white hat on the crown of which was displayed a balas ruby, the same being further ornamented with pearls and precious stones. As soon as we came in sight of his Highness we made him our reverence, bowing and putting*

the right knee to the ground and crossing our arms over the breast. Then we advanced a step and again bowed, and a third time we did the same, but on this occasion kneeling on the ground and remaining in that posture. Then Tamerlane gave command that we should rise to come nearer before him, and the various lords who up to this point had been holding us under the arms now left us, for they dared not advance any nearer to his Highness.

....

Now came the serious business of eating. First, gigantic leather platters piled high with mutton and horse-meat, roasted, boiled, and stewed, were dragged into the banqueting hall. The croupe of the horse, with the saddle-meat attached but the leg disjointed off, was considered the most succulent; but sheep's saddle and buttock, with the ham removed, was also a delicacy. When Tamerlane called for any particular dish, the platter was pulled along the ground—it was impossible to lift it—to within about twenty paces of where he sat. Here the carvers, dressed in aprons with leather sleeves, knelt and cut it up. The slices were placed in huge bowls of gold, silver, or porcelain, laid out in rows. To each bowl were now added knots of horse-tripe in balls the size of a fist, and a whole sheep's head. Lastly, the cooks came forward with gravy and folded slices of bread. The bowls were then distributed by some of the more privileged courtiers, two or even three men being needed to life each bowl. "The amount of meat that was placed before us," wrote the astonished Clavijo, "was a wonder to behold."...

Dessert followed, consisting of melons, peaches, and grapes on the same lavish scale, washed down with draughts of mares' milk sweetened with sugar and served in goblets of gold and silver—"an excellent drink that it is their custom to use during the summer season."*

After *my* meal, I headed towards the most magnificent site I have ever seen! I had been told by a French couple with whom I had chatted by the Bibi-Khanym Mosque, while having my daily dose of café, and she had told me that her favorite site was the cemetery. Surprised, I headed down another avenue, past the old Jewish quarters, across the busy highway, and up one of the entrances to the cemetery.

---

* Blunt, *The Golden Road to Samarkand*, pp. 148–149.

Shah-i-Zinda in Samarkand

I walked through fields of tombs, scattered throughout the hill facing Samarkand, with irises blooming on many of them, wild poppies, and roses, and several women were weeding the area. On top I could see the Bibi-Khanym Mosque in the distance as well as all the other domes on the horizon, and facing the other side I could see the tall majestic snowy peaks of Kyrgyzstan, and then from the top I walked down the avenue lined with mausoleums and holy shrines which have been here for over a millennium.

This complex is called Shah-i-Zinda, or "the Living King," which is supposed to be the shrine of Kusam Ibn Abbas, a cousin and close fellow fighter of the prophet Muhammad who is said to have brought Islam to these distant lands. Tamerlane and his grandson, Ulugbek, then chose this site to bury their own family and favorites near the Living King.

This is a famous place of pilgrimage, and it was full of pilgrims, visitors, families, men and women, children, babies, and old men, all visiting, admiring, and paying homage to the dead.

I was speechless, stunned by the intricate, brilliant tilework exhibited throughout the many mausoleums lining the avenue. Amazing that it lasted all these hundreds of years (of course it has been renovated), showing

An entrance to a mausoleum at Shah-i-Zinda

Islamic arabesque tilework in its most magnificent forms. The bright lapus lazuli color, the turquoise domes, the terracotta brick work, and beautiful colors all give this complex a sumptuous aura.

The tilework is beyond anything imaginable, and is a stunning accomplishment from the Muslim world. It is a celebration of arabesques, geometric patterns, stars, squares, triangles, polygons, circles, all in a dancing pattern of shapes and forms in various colors from light turquoise, dark turquoise to brilliant lapuz lazuli, black, and white. Mathematics and forms, frozen in time. A feast for the eyes of the westerners not accustomed to this display of brilliant colors. I took many pictures, and sat there until the end of the day, again when the setting Sun gave its orange magical quality to the mausoleum's red terracotta tones, adding to its splendor.

The dazzling geometric figures have a cooling effect on the person and restrict the exuberance and enthusiasm of passionate souls. The strict forms and palette of cold colors bring clarity, peace, and harmony to the cacophony of feelings. The fabulous designs bring order into the soul, and order in the soul means health. The calculated, cold forms confine the soul's unlimited passions and give peace to the onlooker. And amidst these forms devoid of human images, the theologian, the mullahs argued the finer points of the hadīth, sacred sayings, the sacred Koran. By contrast, the Sufis plunged into the world of forbidden music and free-flowing poetry coming from inspired realms reaching up to God.

And here I will make an interlude, inspired by these graceful arabesques, their architects and designers, and make some remarkable discoveries, thanks to the spiritual research of Rudolf Steiner. We know that nothing that has been made by man, created by man, is lost to mankind. Even though it disappears from our view, it is still there, to come back at some later time. More insight about karma.

Steiner, through his spiritual-scientific research, made some discoveries about certain nineteenth-century individuals, one of them Schubert, in his eight volumes devoted to karmic relationships. Here he states that Schubert and Vischer, in a former lifetime, were born and raised under the background of Arabism in the eighth and ninth centuries.

> It seems to me that just as the earlier life of Friedrich Theodor Vischer can be understood only when one can view it against the background of Arabism, so the essence of Schubert's music, especially the undertone of many of his songs, can be discerned only when one perceives... that there is something spiritual in this music, something Asiatic which was shone upon for a time by the desert sun, took on greater definition in Europe, was carried through the spiritual world between death and rebirth and as something essentially human, removed from all the artificialities of society, came to birth again in a penniless schoolteacher....
>
> In Franz Schubert we have a reincarnated Moorish personality, one who had little opportunity of cultivating musical talent in his life among the Moors, but who, on the other hand, steeped himself with

impassioned longing in whatever was to be found in the way of art and, I will not say of subtle "thinking" but rather of subtle "reasoning," which in the train of Arabic culture had come from Asia, passed across Africa, and finally reached Spain.*

And further on, Steiner states that many of the nineteenth-century individuals had an incarnation during the eighth and ninth centuries of Arabic culture.

> What takes place on Earth is lived through in advance by the beings of the highest hierarchies, by the Seraphim, Cherubim, and Thrones, and that a human being who is passing through the life between death and a new birth looks *down* to a heaven of soul and spirit as we look *up* to the heavens. There, in that heaven of soul and spirit, the Seraphim, Cherubim, and Thrones live through what subsequently becomes our destiny, what is brought to realization as our destiny when we descend again to the Earth.
>
>   Now...it was foreseen by the souls belonging to the community into which the individuality we are studying had been drawn, that through the coming centuries it would be their destiny to preserve a line of progress that would be quite uninfluenced by Christianity.... The ordering of the world is by no means so simple. While on the one hand the mightiest of all impulses poured from the Mystery of Golgotha into the whole of the Earth evolution, on the other hand it was necessary that what had been contained in earthly evolution *before* the Mystery of Golgotha should not be allowed at once to perish; it was necessary that what was...non-Christian should be allowed to stream on through the centuries.
>
>   And the task of sustaining this stream of culture for Europe— as it were of enabling a phase of culture not yet Christian to continue on into the Christian centuries—fell to a number of individuals who were born into Arabism in the seventh and eighth centuries AD. Arabism was not, of course, directly Christian, but neither had it remained as backward as the old heathen religions. In a certain direction it had made steady progress through the centuries. A number of souls born into this stream were to carry forward in the spiritual world,

---

* Steiner, *Karmic Relationships: Esoteric Studies, Volume One*, p. 137.

untouched by the conditions prevailing on Earth, that which the spirit of man, separated from Christianity, can know, feel, and experience. They were to encounter Christianity only later, in later epochs of earthly evolution. And it is in truth an experience of shattering grandeur, full of deep significance, to see how a large community lived on in the spiritual world removed from the development of Christianity, until in the nineteenth century the majority of these souls came down to incarnation on Earth. As you may suppose, they were very different individualities, with every variety of talent and disposition.

Friedrich Theodor Vischer was one of the first souls from this community to descend in the nineteenth century.[*]

In these very complex lectures, Steiner explains that it was the task of these individuals ("a large number of bearers of non-Christian culture, particularly, too, of Cabbalistic culture") to bring in our materialistic culture, Darwin's natural sciences.

But what I wanted to bring is this: that the mathematics and geometry of the arabesques are perhaps being transformed in a later stage into music, the line in space becoming line in time or music.

The frozen beauty of the material world in the arabesques and sacred geometric forms seen throughout the world of Islam come back to life, awaken to life in music, sound, and poetry in the work of the Sufi masters throughout the ages.

Hazrat Inayat Khan, the great Sufi, musician master:

> My aim is to direct the attention of those who search for truth towards the law of music that is working throughout the universe, and that in other words may be called the law of life: the sense of proportion, the law of harmony, the law that brings about balance, the law that is hidden behind all aspects of life, which holds this universe intact and works out the destiny of the whole universe, fulfilling its purpose....
>
> All the religions have taught that the origin of the whole of creation is sound....
>
> The music of the universe is the background of the small picture we call music. Our sense of music, attraction to music, shows that

---

[*] Ibid., pp. 130–132.

there is music in the depth of our being. Music is behind the working of the universe. Music is not only life's greatest object, but it is life itself. Hafiz, the great and wonderful Sufi poet of Persia, says "Many say that life entered the human body by the help of music, but the truth is that life itself is music...."

Music is a miniature of the harmony of the whole universe, for the harmony of the universe is life itself. Man, being a miniature of the universe, shows harmonious and inharmonious chords in his pulsation, in the beat of his heart, and in his vibration, rhythm, and tone. His health and illness, his joy and discomfort, all show the music or lack of music in his life.

What does music teach us? Music helps us to train ourselves in harmony, and it is this that is the magic or the secret behind music. When you hear music that you enjoy, it tunes you and puts you in harmony with life. Therefore man needs music; he longs for music. Many say that they do not care for music, but these had not heard music. If they really heard music, it would touch their souls, and then certainly they could not help loving it. If not, it would only mean that they had not heard music sufficiently, and had not made their hearts calm and quiet in order to listen to it and to enjoy and appreciate it. Besides, music develops that faculty by which one learns to appreciate all that is good and beautiful in the form of art and science, and in the form of music and poetry one can then appreciate every aspect of beauty.

What deprives man of all the beauty around him is his heaviness of body and heaviness of heart. He is pulled down to Earth, and by that everything becomes limited. But when he shakes off that heaviness and joy comes, he feels light. All good tendencies such as gentleness, tolerance, forgiveness, love, and appreciation, all these beautiful qualities come by being light—light in the mind, in the soul, and in the body.*

The beautiful words of this Sufi, master musician, make one realize the depths of the chaos which is living in the souls of the Muslim extremists who are traveling the world trying to impose their absolutism, the deadly interpretation of the Koran and nihilistic approach to the sacredness of life, and their forbidding of the sacred art of music, as well as the enslavement

---

* Khan, *The Music of Life: The Inner Nature and Effects of Sound*, pp. 71, 132.

of women, and brainwashing of innocent children. Many of these fundamentalists claim to have studied under Sufi brotherhood, but how far this is from the truth can be seen from the words of a true Sufi master.

Seeing the glorious, majestic masterpieces of the past inspired me to look for these correspondences, of space, time, past karma, past lives, past and future. At the end of the day, after having many thoughts dancing in my head, I walked back to my hotel for a well-earned rest.

I revisited the avenue of mausoleums before I left this ancient city. With a guide, I visited several other sites, parks, former palaces, the simple crypt of Tamerlane and his descendents, and, finally, the Ulugbek Observatory. In this funny-looking structure, like a curved underground metro cylinder, Ulugbek, more an astronomer than a king, measured the distance between Earth and Moon, and came extremely close to our own calculations.

We also drove outside of the city to a little village complex called Khoni Ghil Meros (clay pit) where they were making paper the old way. It was fascinating to observe these ancient methods of making paper out of wood, all by natural means. From cutting the wood into long thin branches, then slicing them in thin layers, boiling them in large cauldrons, and then, by very ingenious means, beating boiled mush with large logs moved up and down by a water-wheel system. The little compound was sitting amidst gardens and a stream where kids were diving in. They offered tea for the tourists, and I bought a couple of little books of handmade paper. I had run out of money and my bankcards were not working!

The Samarkand area has been well-known since the eighth and ninth centuries for mill papermaking. Papermaking originated in China, and, of course, Papyrus in Egypt, then Samarkand in the middle as part of the Silk Road imported vast amounts of paper to the ancient world, and up to the nineteenth century to Russia. This is a revitalization of this ancient papermaking technique.

Here is more about the heritage of the Mongol invasion:

> Something as simple as preparing a single-page document on vellum or parchment required the labor of a long line of skilled workers. Aside from the herder who raised the sheep, the slaughtering and skinning

were so important to make quality writing material that it required a skilled craft of skinners. Over several weeks, the skin had to be cleaned and scraped of hair on the outside and flesh on the inside, soaked in a sequence of chemical baths, stretched on a frequently readjusted frame, sunned, alternately wet and dried in a precise sequence, shaved, and finally cut into pages of the appropriate size. To make the pages into a book, a whole new sequence of trades were drawn on to make the ink, copy the text, illustrate it, color it, and bind it with leather that had already been through its own sequence of workshops.

The replacement of parchment by paper, a Chinese innovation already known but only rarely used in Europe prior to the Mongol era, required more skill in one worker, but far fewer steps and thus, in the overall process, less energy and labor. The papermaker cooked down shredded rags and other fibrous materials, dipped a frame into a vat to coat it with a layer of the fibers, treated it with chemicals, and dried it.*

After several more walks through the Registan, the Bibi-Khanym Mosque, the markets, the museums, and the café, on a sunny morning I boarded the Afrosiyob, the bullet train to Tashkent. It was a plush train with all the comforts needed, including the Internet. It was full of businessmen with laptops, young women and men, families. We passed green valleys, snow-clad mountains in the distance, shepherds guiding their flocks, and poor villages. Then I was in my hotel room watching Uzbek television. I had made a new arrangement with my travel agent. I had complained that I did not want to stay in Tashkent for another three days, so she scheduled, to my delight (to keep me quiet since I can be a pest when I need to), a stay in the mountains north of Tashkent, called the Ugam Chatkal National Park, close to the Kazakhstan-Tajikistan borders.

Early the next day my guide arrived in a jeep, and I was ready for my last journey in Uzbekistan. We drove through busy Tashkent, full of morning traffic, and arrived on the empty highway, due north past lovely villages in the surrounding mountains, with gardens, fruit orchards, and more mountains with modern homes tucked on the verdant low mountainsides.

---

*   Weatherford, *Genghis Khan and the Making of the Modern World*, p. 237.

A view of the Chorvok Reservoir

We climbed higher and reached the Chorvok Reservoir, a pristine, crystal-clear, turquoise, immense lake. We overlooked the town of Chimcan and climbed up, crossing the large river being fed by snow from the mountains of Kyrgyzstan which was nearby. We took a small winding dirt road, and had to stop at an army post to show my passport because we were close to the borders. Then after a few miles on the mountain dirt road, we stopped at a posh resort for the wealthy of Tashkent, with beautiful bungalows with all the comforts of the Western world, including a cook and a cleaner. The gardens, water fountains, little lakes with fish, formal flower gardens, were all on the side of the mountain overlooking the very powerful, large Pskem River flowing down from the mountain, several hundred feet down. But it was empty, it was not the busy season yet. We left the car with the very pleasant caretaker and we started walking on a footpath towards the higher elevation, with the higher, rocky, snowy peaks as our guide. The path was strewn with lovely spring flowers—yellow, blue, white, pink—growing by the riverside which we were following. Poppies were showing up as we climbed higher into the small valleys. The views of the villages below were breathtaking and I could have stayed here another

Inside Ugam Chatkal National Park

week. Beautiful carpets of light yellow anemone types of plants filled the side of the path. We reached a forest of birch and met a local young man working. We hiked up a canyon ending in a tall powerful waterfall, then we escalated the other side of the canyon which was not so easy as I did not have my hiking sticks! But being part goat, thanks to my childhood, I made it without an incident!

On top we reached another lovely path and went into another valley, higher up, from which we could see the tiny waterfall we had just left. The same incredible mountain scenery: large open meadows in the mountains, flower carpets, ten-foot-tall mullein spires everywhere, onion types of plants, other tall flowers coming out of cactuses, and the forbidding icy snowy peaks were now closer and closer. We reached a quiet meadow lined with birch trees after crossing a small stream on shiny rocks. We met some folks who were working in the meadows, getting a portion of it ready for planting potatoes. A small home was in the distance. The guide said that people moved up here during the summer, but I did not have time to go to their villages farther up.

Two children on a path in Ugam Chatkal National Park

We headed back, and on the path a strange looking flower, a kind of calla plant, almost black, was coming out of the rocky soil, saying hello. Then we followed the opposite side of the mountain, looking down at the mountain stream path we had climbed up. It was beautiful, and I was glad to have visited this small section of the world's mountains, not as tall as the ones next door, the Pamir Mountains, but tall and majestic enough.

Farther down, a young man was harvesting some honey from the hives scattered throughout the lower mountains. He brought some very rich tasting honey. Then we walked farther down the mountain and reached a mountain farm with a little family sitting in the meadow. A very large flock of black and brown sheep were grazing up above. The three young children had red rosy cheeks and were very friendly (about five or six years old) and walked us down the path. We passed an archeological site being excavated by Europeans in the summer, deep caves dating back to many thousands of years ago when ancient man lived in the surrounding caves. This area was under the sea, when we were not man yet, but jellyfish!

We arrived back at the resort and my guide said that we would have lunch. So I went walking around the lovely estate, looking at the fast-moving river and the enchanting mountain scenery. Then it was time to have lunch. The table was set with a white linen table cloth and some great-looking lamb kababs on skewers, with dried fruits, walnuts, tea, candies, fresh baked bread, potatoes, and yogurt. It was a feast, and I was quite hungry. The Sun was setting, and I took a few more pictures of the vermillion and indigo clouds with tall rocky peaks showing through them. We drove back to the dam, and the guide left me at a lovely resort by the turquoise lake to spend the night. He drove back to Tashkent. I had a lovely room facing the water and enjoyed walking around the gardens which had a profusion of blooming irises in all colors. Then I sat on the large terrace and drank my tea, taking in the beauty of the sumptuous setting before retiring to sleep. The area had many very large hotels by the shore to accommodate the Tashkent crowd during the summer months. My stay was coming to an end.

In the morning, the taxi arrived and we drove to Tashkent, but not without being stopped by the police because the driver had made a U-turn where he was not supposed to. In the glove compartment, I had noticed he had a large envelope full of cash. He said not to worry, grabbed a handful of the paper money, left, and came back. He said all was fine, he just had to give the policeman plenty of money!

Then he told me this is the way it is in Uzbekistan. You have to pay everyone, it is a way to make a living for a large number of people.

The hotel was full of people who were celebrating a sumptuous wedding feast. The women's clothes were like the Arabian tales of *One Thousand and One Nights*, one richer than the other. Splendid and colorful Muslim outfits, modern risqué gowns, deer-like lovely almond eyes, colorful lipstick on lovely faces, very young and very old. Everything was there: high, high heels, flowing hair, hidden hair. It was a beautiful party. Only the central Asian people give such a grand feast!

My Uzbekistan journey ended and the long way home began.

Part XI

Fes, Morocco

SIX MONTHS LATER

I arrived at the Rabat airport from Madrid and met my sister (a year-and-a-half younger, but five inches taller!) who had flown from Boston to spend some time with me because since our having had children, and my extensive traveling throughout my life, we had not had much time to connect.

We had lived part of our childhood in Rabat and had many fond memories. Because we were young, we had no bias towards the French or Arabs, we did not go to church, and did not know anything about the Muslim religion. We were blissfully unaware of everything! We just lived here in a Muslim world, and enjoyed it even though it was being occupied by the French (us). We heard tales of unpleasant things, such as, *We need to hide here if they come*, but that went in one ear and out the other like a game, and we went to school with the local children, many of them coming from the Magreb Mountains. And we adored our house helper, Fatima. When she left us because her father married her to an old man, we were heartbroken and so was she.

We remembered the powerful sunlight and the new sunglasses we were given, and watching with fascination the women walk around in black tents, different from the beautiful colorful clothes of the modern Moroccan women.

Fortunately I had delayed my coming to Fes by one year as I felt I was not ready to *be* here. I had to prepare myself so that I would live here and stop the endless chatter of criticism and be a blank page for life in a Muslim city, and accept it all. I did not want to be a hypocrite and pretend to accept Allah, but wanted to truly be here as a free human being meeting other free human beings who happened to have chosen to *be* Muslims. Thanks to this one-year delay my sister was able to join me and I had a chance to practice some of the most difficult practices to be ready for *being* here.

> The Christian Church chose this "practice of pure love" as its favorite saying. To be sure, this saying is used a lot by Christians, however, seldom are actions guided by it. Furthermore, it is also not easy when we consider the consequences. Let us consider for a moment what it means to love all human beings: to bestow love without expectation of love in return, without recognition, without demand for reward—for our ideal should be that we love a human being because he or she is a human being! How far must we be in our development in order to be capable of such love? Can we educate ourselves to this selflessness that we love all others as we love ourselves by means of commandments and dogmas of the church or through the coercion of a moral law? Is it not much more fruitful for our souls if we bring this lofty virtue to blossom within us without any coercion whatsoever?
>
> In practicing this teaching of Christ, a Hindu, a Muslim, a Parsi, a Catholic, a Protestant, a Jew—indeed, even a heretic—could be a true Christian without even belonging to the Christian Church.[*]

We stayed in the medina, just north of Rabat, on the other side of the river flowing into the Atlantic Ocean. It was an older, poorer section where I rented a room for several nights in a renovated antique ryad for a bargain price (as usual), in a small fortress town typical of the ancient world. Our room was reminiscent of the Arabian nights, with a beautiful alcove, arabesque woodwork, fancy metal lights, luxurious bedding and brocade curtains, large colorful tiles in bathrooms, a fountain in the central courtyard, and a wall fountain with floating rose petals. This was another world. My sister was in awe, which was good because the outside was full of dirty streets, mud, donkeys in the alleys, outdoor markets, and lots of people

---

[*] Steiner, *Esoteric Lessons 1910–1912: From the Esoteric School, Volume Two*, p. 62.

walking about screaming and talking, which she was not used to! And, of course, the very early morning call to prayer.

We walked out of the older medina, followed the fortressed walls for a few kilometers, and crossed the large bridge over the river flowing into the Atlantic Ocean to the other side, into the real Rabat Medina where we wandered about just breathing in the Moroccan life. We stopped at a bakery and enjoyed homemade flat bread with mint tea, sitting and chatting with lady bakers, and had plenty of time to chat ourselves about our lives which had been very different. She married a Greek Orthodox–Russian, and I married a Muslim-Persian. She learned Greek-Russian, and I learned Farsi. She learned Greek cooking, and I learned Persian.

For lunch we found a lovely restaurant by the side of the river, a new marina with kayakers, families, and courting lovers in beautiful, colorful clothes. We had a sumptuous meal of fish tagine, with a shrimp and avocado appetizer, fresh bread, butter, and olives. Our server was a most pleasant young man who had a lovely beautiful wife, he said, and two children. (He was not just looking for a tip!) By the end of our meal, he called us sisters, especially my sister who is all heart, and I am more head, as the reader notices from my heady writings! I am reminded of the words:

wisdom + love = action
light (thought) + darkness (warmth) = movement

We walked through to another older part of the city sitting on the hill overlooking the ocean, where no cars have access. The lower walls are painted blue, giving it a Mediterranean look. The cobblestone alleyways are spotless, with large terraces overlooking the sea and river. A lady invited us inside her home, onto her large terrace to have some mint tea and sweets and look at the great scenery. She said this was her ancestral home. Then we walked to another beautiful garden and museum, and settled more into our new surroundings. Many wealthy people live here in sumptuously renovated ryads—Moroccans as well as foreigners—including writers, artists, government officials, etc., as evidenced by the number of guards outside the doors. It is just a skip and a jump from southern Spain. We found another grand café and teahouse with lots of locals, young couples, tourists, young girls, and women having tea and looking at the outstanding scenery from its many nook and cranny terraces. Fig trees were overhanging on the cliffs going straight to the river and ocean.

Then we walked through the modern city to the site of the grand old mosques where only the tall wood pillars are standing, with the very richly decorated mausoleum in marble and gold decorations, and magnificent colored-tile designs for the king's father's tomb, with guards in sumptuous uniforms sitting on superb king's horses posted by each gate.

At the end of the day, we took a taxi to where we used to live, which was not far from the ocean, south of Rabat, but it was all built-up, and we could only faintly recognize the powerful waves hitting the rocky shoreline.

I could not see the little garden where we had played and eaten its golden and red-ripe figs, and where I started my gardening debut by planting my first tulip bulbs, all enclosed within a whitewashed wall. I used to do the shopping for my mother, so I became very adept at talking to the merchants. This was my first training in traveling, shopping, and enjoying different lifestyles without feeling fear or discomfort because I was only six or seven years old. I remember trying to figure out how to speak the language, Arabic! In my mind, I thought that I only had to replace the letters by a different script, then I could speak it. That is what I was thinking about at an early age. I always felt badly that my parents did not hire someone to teach us Arabic.

We boarded the train to Fes on a bright sunny morning. The train was comfortable and full of families, young students, businessmen and businesswomen, old ladies, and a concerned man who told us to watch our suitcases!

We watched the Moroccan landscape change from dry, plastic-ridden fields and poor small towns to lovely farms with olive trees, fruit trees, lonely mud farms in the distance, poor towns with dilapidated buildings with clothes hanging on balconies, donkeys loaded with fruit, bricks, and wood, men working in the fields, children playing in the streets, arid, softer mountains in the background, and gentle hills. As a man had told me on a previous trip, we are in a third world country!

We arrived in the early afternoon and our guide greeted us. Another taxi took us to the old medina, at R'Cif square. From here no cars are able to go through the labyrinth of its narrow, tiny, complex alleys of which there are hundreds! A man came and loaded our things on a cart and we walked up the narrow cobblestone alleys, stairs, turning right, then left, then right, full of people, to our little dar (a small old traditional home), which I had rented for a month from a French family.

My sister was a bit taken aback by the garbage and detritus, and we finally arrived in a dark alley, under another building bridged over our new home and multiple buildings several stories high and made of sandstone, preventing the sunlight from reaching down below, like an ancient fortress. A very old lady of a city!

Our guide gave us the keys, took the remainder of the money for the rent, and he was off. We walked up the tiny, very narrow, blue ceramic-tiled staircase and were welcomed into the lovely renovated dar. It was three stories high, with a large covered opening on the roof, a large dining alcove, sitting rooms, a kitchen, three bedrooms, a tiled bathroom, and a lovely terrace overlooking the city. The owners, like many other foreign owners of these renovated dars and ryads, take delight in renovating the old dars and ryads to their former glory, full of beautifully carved woodwork, tall carved doors, delicate forged ironwork, tilework, great beautiful handwoven pillows, curtains, and bedspreads, bathrooms with exquisite tiles, a lovely kitchen, colorful Moroccan pottery, and lots of space for the two of us. The people who renovate these fantastic, fallen-down places spend years shopping and talking to architects and historians, which is why they are doing it! Many come from England, Spain, the United States, Australia, France, etc. They bring much money into the old city of Fes, and keep the artisans busy, and alive! Every June, Fes is home to one of the most amazing music festivals of ancient sacred music (Sufi music being an important one), when thousands of music enthusiasts flock to the city, which is booked up months in advance!

In her lovely book, *A House in Fez: Building a Life in the Ancient Heart of Morocco*, Australian Suzanna Clarke describes this love at first sight for Fes.

> Maybe it was a fit of madness, but on just our second visit to the old Moroccan capital of Fes, my husband and I decided to buy a house

there.... We responded to Morocco in a way we had to no other country. We found it as multi-layered and intriguing as the patterns in the tilework adorning the buildings, each of which has its own hidden meaning. Morocco has the mystique of a land from the Old Testament yet appears to be coming comfortably with modernization. Internet cafés rub shoulders with artisans' workshops; peasants on donkeys trot beneath billboards advertising the latest mobile phone. Outside mosques, running shoes are lined up next to pointed-toed babouches.... Back at home in Brisbane after that first trip, our far-too-expensive Berber carpet lay on the floor of our living room reminding us of the sensual beauty of Morocco, and of our ignorance of the traps of that enormously different and distant culture.... The advertising that bombarded us daily seemed more intense, the supermarkets soulless. Most of the food sold there was so far from its origins as to be unrecognizable, obscured by packaging designed to conceal the contents....

Where were the lively, crowded markets that echoed the way humans traded for centuries? Where was the produce pile high in the open, direct from the farm, allowed to ripen on the vine or on the tree, or in the earth? In Moroccan markets you could smell, handle, and often taste things before buying. You looked at the farmer or the stall-holder in the eye as you quibbled in a good-natured way about the quality or the price.*

I could not agree with her more. A great read, as they say!

Fes was constructed on a hilly terrain stretching over 350 hectares which allowed it to develop and excel in various domains: architecture, hydraulics, handicrafts, technological creativity, landscapes, gardening, culinary art, culture, and science. Fes is distinguished by its history, the oldest in the Kingdom of Morocco, and also by its capacity to erect beautiful and long-lasting buildings and monuments.

Fes is generally believed to have been founded around 808 by Moulay Idriss II and later became the capital of the Idrissid dynasty (788–956). The name is attributed to a pickaxe (fa'as in Arabic) that was dug up during the first phase of the construction of the city. This foretells the ability of the Fassis (people from Fes) as master builders.

---

* Clarke, *A House in Fez: Building a Life in the Ancient Heart of Morocco*, pp. 3–4.

FES, MOROCCO

The site of Fes was chosen for its proximity to the river named Oued Al Jawahir (river of pearls) which flows through the medina. It is quite rare to find an example of urban life so intimately linked to the hydraulic system of a water source. This Idrissid city owes much to its river, which is fed by sixty springs, not only determining its location, but also the development of its characteristic landscapes: houses with courtyard-gardens, ryads, enclosed gardens, orchards surrounding the ramparts, and an abundance of both still and flowing water. From the earliest foundations, two walled cities emerged on the banks of the Oued: "Adwat al Andalus" (the Andalusian bank) is located on the right side and "Adwat al Qaraouiyine" (the left side). These twin cities formed what is now called "Fes el Bali" (ancient Fes). The chroniclers of this period recorded the legacy of two women, Fatima al-Fihri and her sister Meryem, daughters of immigrants from Kairouan (Tunisia). In the ninth century, they gave Fes two religious monuments considered to be the oldest and most prestigious: the Qaraouiyine University-Mosque and the Andalusian Mosque. However, it was under the rule of the Almoravid (1061–1147) and the Almohad (1147–1269) dynasties that Fes underwent unprecedented urban development and economic growth. In addition to the unification and integration of the medina within the ramparts, Fes witnessed a dynamic "urban revolution" that prompted the realization of architectural, hydraulic, and commercial productions. A twelfth-century survey testified to the opulence of Fes, which had become not only a crossroad of international commerce, but also one of the greatest centers of cultural and spiritual influence of the Middle Ages.*

Fes was the capital of the grandson of Hassan Idris-ibn-Abdullah (the prophet's daughter Fatima married Ali, and Hassan was their son). Now it is home to more than 300,000 people.

We settled down and quickly changed to get a bite to eat, and to look at our new home, at least one-thousand-year-old Fes. It had not changed for centuries, which is one of the reasons I wanted to stay here for a month. To get into the rhythm of living in a Muslim world with no pressure to conform! Meaning, I do not wear the hejab, but I love the Moroccan clothes,

---

*   *Fes Medina Tourist Circuits.*

unlike living in Iran where one *has* to wear the hejab, and one gets punished for not doing so by a special branch of the police force.

Fes was a center of Islamic culture and spiritual life hundreds of years ago, almost a millennium. Many well-known writers, philosophers, poets, and caliphs lived here, passed by here, served here, and studied in their famous theological madrese, which is another reason for choosing this ancient city to end my pilgrimage for this journey. It is also a museum city, but thoroughly lived in within its thick fortress, red sandstone walls. I would have the time here to ponder, meditate, and see what comes!

> Almighty God, make of it a house of science and wisdom, so that in it Your Book (the Koran) may always be read and Your Laws always observed. Let its inhabitants hold fast to the Koran and the Sunna as long as You shall preserve it.
> —Moulay Idris, the founder of Fes

We locked our door with three separate locks, which took forever since I am not good with keys!

Then came the daunting task of finding our way in this maze of cobbled alleys going under buildings, archways, and tiny narrow alleyways where you can't see the sunlight. So I would proceed using mathematics: *One right, two lefts, then a sharp turn...* Well, that did not last too long. After a while there is no more to count! And we of course would got lost, then a band of urchins would come and rescue us, or a young teenager, or an old man, and try to lead us in the correct direction. A young man took us to a restaurant, just ten minutes from the house. My sister had some reservations about following him into the very dark and narrow alleys, up some stairs in an old unlit building. It looked like the perfect spot for getting robbed, or worse! But there we entered, as if by magic, a lovely, large, four-story building that had been converted into a restaurant, and it was full of teenagers on a trip from Europe enjoying Moroccan cuisine! The food was great—couscous (our favorite), salad, bread, and tea—and we sat on beds of pillows in brocades and colorful designs, in small alcoves for privacy.

FES, MOROCCO

One of the cobblestone alleyways

Before going home we had to buy a few things, so we headed back to the mosque by the R'Cif square. I had memorized the way to a shopping area in the medina for that section of town. We found some freshly baked bread from one of the many local bakers, pomegranates, oranges, vegetables, and fresh mint tea. The merchants are always fun and ready to joke and share information about their relatives scattered around the world. We passed by the butcher with freshly cut meat, chickens in cages, eggs, colorful mountains of spices, herbs in enormous bags, pre-soaked chickpeas, etc. It was the usual wealth of the Middle Eastern world, unlike the wrapped items of our Western world, which don't smell like food anymore, or look like it, either!

The next few days were spent discovering this incredibly rich city by, of course, getting thoroughly lost, and trying to find our way back, and getting lost some more! We usually tried to get back before dark, for safety, but that did not always work.

We also had to deal with the shoemaker's shop below our home because the glue used to make the colorful leather slippers gave off fumes that were invading our living room, and giving us headaches! So we opened our windows and hoped for the best.

One day we met our neighbor, a young lady in her late teens and from a large family. She said she would accompany us to the local hammam at around 5:30 PM. So we were off—with our soap, towels, brushes, and shampoo—and went into a long, dark, tunnel-like alley. She said this was our "Fes metro." Then I noticed two old men crouching by the entrance. They were the keepers of the fire, which was constantly burning to keep the water warm for the hammam. Piles of wood were delivered here on donkeys' backs.

This was a Wednesday, so it was busy. We entered the steamy rooms and proceeded to take our clothes off, just underwear is worn here. The rooms were full of women with children, women of all ages from light skin to very dark skin, getting ready for the weekend (Thursday is our Saturday). My sister again did not feel very comfortable, but the heavyset massage lady was already at work, peeling off the dirty layers from her skin. We chatted with young and old women, and left feeling renewed, rejuvenated. It was a real community feeling as I had experienced before. It is here that many things are discussed openly and warmly, and children are lovingly massaged, washed, bathed, and well cared for and loved by mothers, aunts, sisters, and cousins. Sometimes I wonder how these children feel when they emigrate to such cold countries like the United States, or those of northern Europe. Where is the warmth they received from their grandmothers, mothers, aunts? Here the women are proud of their sexuality, which in the Koran is not ignored. The prophet said he enjoyed perfumes and women! So it is not a society which is prudish. Even though the women cover themselves up more here, in their homes they are much freer. But with television, phones, and the Internet, the younger female generation is demanding more than being a man's pleasure object. They want to know about love, falling in love. Times are changing, but it will not be easy. Here we have a more definite distinction between man and woman! In Europe, sometimes we have a unisex, but not here, which brings me to quote this passage from Rudolf Steiner:

> Let us suppose that a woman lives in a certain incarnation. It cannot be denied that this woman, by reason of her sex, will undergo experiences which differ from those of a man, and that these are not merely dependent on her inner soul life, but are connected predominantly with external happenings, with circumstances in which she will find herself simply because she is a woman, and which will in turn react upon the whole state and disposition of her soul. It is reasonable to say that women are led to act in ways which are intimately connected with the fact of being a woman. After all, it is only in the realm of spiritual companionship that the male and the female are balanced. The further we penetrate into the pure soul nature and the outer aspect of the human being, the more accentuated we find the differences between men and women in relation to their lives. We can say that women differ from men also in certain soul qualities, that they have a greater inclination to those qualities of soul which lead to impulses that can only be termed emotional. Women are more disposed to soul experience, than men. Intellectuality and materialism—in other words, that which has come about through men—are more natural to men's lives, and this deeply affects their soul life. A closer connection with the soul and the feelings in the case of the woman, and with the intellectual and materialistic in the case of the man—this is how it is actually determined by their respective natures. This is why women display certain nuances in their soul life by virtue of being female.
>
> I have already described to you how that which we experience as qualities in the soul between death and a new birth forces its way into our next bodily organization. That which is related more strongly to the psyche, to the emotions, and tends more towards the inner soul between birth and death will have a greater tendency to enter more profoundly into the organism, and to impregnate it far more intensely. And women, through their aptitude to absorb impressions related to the psyche, to the emotions, will take the experiences of life, too, into great depths of soul. Men may have richer and also more scientific experiences, but these do not penetrate the man's soul life as deeply as they do in the case of a woman. The whole of the world of her experiences is

deeply graven in a woman's soul. Therefore those experiences will have a stronger tendency to work into the organism, to embrace the organism more closely in the future. In this way a woman will through her experiences in one incarnation develop a tendency towards a deeper intervention in the organization and thereby towards the formation of the organism itself in the next incarnation. A deep working into and working through the organism will bring forth a male organism. A male organism appears when the forces of the soul desire to be more deeply graven into matter. You can see from this that the woman's experiences in one incarnation result in a male organism in the next incarnation. Occult teaching here shows that there is a connection which lies outside the bounds of morality. For this reason occultism states: man is woman's karma. The male organism of a later incarnation is the result of the experiences and events of a preceding female incarnation. Even at the risk of giving discomfort to some of those present here—after all, many men today are horrified at the thought of incarnating as women—I must state the facts entirely objectively.*

Well, there is no doubt about it, I will be a male in my next incarnation. It is too bad, because by then women will begin being more important, and men less so! This brings the male-female discussion under a very different light.

Now we were getting acclimatized, and were going farther and farther into the medina. We found the two main cobblestone paths, Tala'a Sghira (the small rise) and Tala'a Kbira (the big rise), which go up the hill towards Bab Boujloud, a monumental gateway. From those two main arteries, multiple cobblestone paths go in all directions, full of shops, one after another, and invariably we would go into a store never to come out without buying something! Every day we would come home with a bag. The shopkeepers are experts!

From that main avenue we would try and branch out to other small alleys, and, of course, we would get lost!

One of my favorites was close to Bab Boujloud on one of the leading arteries of the medina. There were a few cafés, restaurants where the

---

* Steiner, *Manifestations of Karma*, pp. 173–174.

A man doing embroidery in his shop

tourists, visitors, or locals would sit and chat and drink delicious moroccan coffee or mint tea, eat pastries made with almonds, sugar, dates, walnuts, honey, etc., or rest from walking. We could observe the life of the city: women going to the hammam with their plastic buckets, men with donkeys laden with goods going to the shops to deliver everything, some motorcyclist teen braving the pedestrians, a few begging souls, girls going to school, men going food shopping for supper, mothers and daughters going shopping, musicians, and French lady tourists with weary husbands who were tired of shopping. Life had not changed here for millennia, and we would just sit there and enjoy the life in the East.

Then we would plunge once again into the heart of the medina where some of the shop attendants would say hello, noticing that we were still here. We would stop by a favorite cloth shop, looking at the fabulous array

A street musician

of goods from all colors of the rainbow. Our path always went the same way which I had memorized, by the huge Qaraouiyine Mosque which was always busy with believers going in to pray, then the library, Madrese Meshahia, Madrese Attarine, and all the souks surrounding the mosque. It is a maze, an incredibly rich maze. And this is only one little section of the old city.

On this long main artery of the souk, which have numerous alleys leading to tall residential old buildings, blind alleys, and forgotten small palaces, we would go by many beautiful fountains decorated in lavish ceramic styles, small mosques, madreses (teaching the Koran), hammams, and every single inch of the main path is lined with numerous shops. We entered the area of the woodworkers, then some magic squares filled with beautiful, colorful pottery, then perfumes, then silver jewelry, etc.

FES, MOROCCO

A ceramic-tiled fountain

By late afternoon, we would be exhausted by this cacophony of goods, sounds, smells, and human activity. Our legs needed some rest, and the shopping bags were accumulating!

The next day would come. We would start the day with perhaps trying to find a famous palace, and then spend most of the morning not finding it, or perhaps it was closed for renovations. But then we would discover something else which was breathtaking, some amazing garden with orange trees and a lovely fountain with dazzling geometric tiles in the middle, and some magical woodwork on a door, or an archway painted in stunning colors with woodwork so intricate and delicate that it looked like embroidery.

Then we would find a restaurant perched up on some terraces, after climbing four or five floors. We would rest and look at the old medina from the rooftops. Tall minarets and palaces to the horizon, looking no different than they had one thousand years ago. Then the sound of the noon prayer would come, immersing the city in a cacophony of mournful voices calling the believers to prayers, reminding them that God is present. *Allah Akbar! God is great!*

An ablution fountain

We thought God was great too! And we would enjoy our meal and start heading into the beehive of Fes once more.

The morning was always a challenge. Before dawn, all the mosques which surrounded our home began chanting the morning prayers, the muezzins not all in unison from their tall minarets, all starting within four or five minutes of each other from all directions at around 5:00 AM, making sleep impossible unless you slept through it. But it was part of the charm of being woken up to the sound of holy prayers. Don't forget, now it is time to pray, get up, and be disciplined! But I would plunge once more into the dream world.

Later after our breakfast of homemade bread, honey, butter, cheese, and eggs, we would plan our day once more. After several days in the congested medina, we decided to go to modern Fes. So we found our way to the R'Cif square to take a shared taxi to the new city with large avenues lined with tall

A tree-lined avenue in modern Fes

trees, immense water fountains, and a regular wealthy western city. We found a lovely garden restaurant for teachers and students, but we sat there anyway amidst traditional, covered-up Muslim women wearing the ugly grey or dark clothing and working at their computers, and bearded men who were more traditional than the rest of the people I had seen. The devoted, religious-looking crowd was not warm to us foreigners, but rather cold and distant. I was a bit taken aback by this behavior coming from people who were obviously educated, and of the younger generation. The Fessi of the medina who were not formally educated, but trade people, artists, much more sophisticated, were not in any circumstances cold and distant. They always invited us for couscous on Fridays at their homes, or to come in to have tea. Here, I found perhaps the kind of atmosphere one would find in Iran, where if you do not wear the hejab, you are considered a bad Muslim. They are becoming fanatics, fanaticism has come. How sad! The younger people who should be more tolerant are becoming less tolerant, but this was not the usual behavior in Morocco, I only encountered it in this particular restaurant. They seem to want to distinguish themselves with their clothing and arrogant attitude! Somber, intolerant, lifeless! But they are in the minority.

These words by Rudolf Steiner bring some much needed insight:

A sequence of three earthly lives may take its course in yet another way. The following may occur. We observe a soul, who, gripped by a certain fanaticism, satisfies its own strivings, a soul who reveals a religious, egoistic element. We find such souls today. There have always been such souls in the evolution of humanity on the Earth, souls who are instinctively endowed with a certain faith because of an inner egoism that awaits a kind of retribution or compensation for earthly life in the world beyond. Such an expectation may be thoroughly egoistic and connected with a fanatic narrow-mindedness in relation to what is imparted to humanity by spiritual science or the Mysteries. There are many people today who hold fast to the possibility of insight into the spiritual world, but who reject fanatically, in a narrow-minded way, anything that is contrary to the confession in which they were born and brought up. Such souls are usually too easy-going to learn to know anything about the spiritual world and although they believe in a beyond, they harbor a profound egoism.

 A configuration of this nature indicates again that the soul cannot find the correct path between death and rebirth. The gifts of the beings of the higher hierarchies cannot be received rightly. They work in such a way that, although he can fashion his bodily constitution and partly participate in the formation of his karma, nothing fits properly. He becomes, for example, a hypochondriac, a hypersensitive person who is destined by his mere physical organization to be so affected by his surroundings that he goes through life with a morose, dissatisfied, discontented disposition. Life impinges upon him and he feels continually wounded. The reason a person is a hypochondriac, a pathologically melancholic individual, may be found in what has been described. It is prepared and predestined through the physical organization. When such a soul again goes through the portal of death, supersensible investigation reveals that he falls strongly under the influence of the ahrimanic forces. These forces now color what a man gathers between death and a new birth and in the next incarnation without his intervention he is so predisposed in his thoughts and feelings as to be narrow-minded. He is incapable of looking at the world in an open, unbiased way. Souls in our environment who display narrow-mindedness, who are incapable in their thinking of going beyond certain limits, who are as if equipped with blinders, who in spite of genuine efforts are limited, owe their karma to the conditions described above....

There are many people like that today. Indeed they appear to have a highly developed soul activity but as soon as they have to go beyond a certain field that they have worked out for themselves, everything collapses. They are utterly incapable of going beyond their rigid boundaries. If we look back into previous embodiments of such people, we find two incarnations as described earlier. This can also shed light on the future of the many souls who, because of love of ease and egoism, lock themselves up in a faith the foundations of which they never inquire about. Is it not so that many people today adhere to a faith because they were born into it and are too easy-going to question it? They are equally as good Protestants, or Catholics as they would have been Muslims had their karma arranged for them to be born in Islam! We have reached the point in the evolution of mankind when souls will lag behind, in a sense, and will be handicapped in a future incarnation unless they are prepared to open their eyes to what can stream from the spiritual worlds in a variety of ways.*

After chatting in the morose atmosphere of the garden restaurant, we walked on the various large avenues, and found a beautiful pastry shop full of happy, lively Africans. We also found a delightful, upper-class restaurant filled with employees from banks and government offices, where we enjoyed a fantastic meal. And then it was time to return to our old medina.

Here is a typical Moroccan story:

Jeha was known for his sense of humor and his fondness of tricks, especially towards his close friends, who sometimes wanted to get even.

One day, his friends heard that he was having some financial problems, going through hard times. They could not find a better time to bother him and get even, so one of his friends called him: "Hey listen, Jeha! You remember my brother who went on a trip? Well he is back, and he wants to pay you a visit! We agreed to come to your house tomorrow night."

---

*   Steiner, *Life Between Death and Rebirth*, pp. 228–230.

Jeha, a bit confused, answered: "Well, all right! I would really like to see him! But—"

His friend interrupted him and added: "I am afraid that you are a bit embarrassed, Jeha! You do not have to invite us to dinner. Just a little bit of tea and some cookies will do, we just want to visit with you!"

Jeha accepted regretfully, and was forced to borrow some money from his neighbor to buy the necessary goods for his friend's visit. He bought some cakes, and prepared the tea. His friends arrived, but without the brother who had returned from his travels.

Jeha saw that the brother—who was the main guest—was not there, and he wanted to know why. He was immediately reassured that he was coming any minute now. Jeha welcomed his guests and they started gossiping about one thing or another. Then the brother arrived with two of his friends. Jeha, seeing three more guests, welcomed them as well.

A few minutes later, there was another knock on the door. Three more friends appeared, laughing and joking. They wanted to see the brother and his friends who had come back from a trip abroad and wanted to wish a good party for Jeha.

A few minutes later, more and more friends arrived. His house was now full of people. They were laughing, joking, gossiping, and all sorts of frivolous things. It was a joyful party, and everyone was having a grand old time.

Jeha was obliged to enjoy the grand party. He was completely tied up with this cacophony—to which he was a stranger—and could not figure out how to get out of this miserable forced party, to what saints he could send his prayers. They must have something to eat! And he had to honor all his guests with some food.

He went to his wife, and asked if she could cook something or go borrow some money from the neighbors. But she became livid with anger and said it was his fault to invite all these friends of his.

Jeha, embarrassed and beside himself with this predicament, started to think about how to solve this problem. He noticed that by the door there were lots and lots of shoes which his guests had taken off before entering his living room. He took all the shoes and put them in a very large basket, and went out without being seen.

Jeha sold all the shoes and bought everything he needed to make a sumptuous meal. His wife was in charge of cooking, and he went back to his guests who were happy and laughing louder and louder. Jeha started to share in their laughter, their funny anecdotes, and their jokes.

When the meal was ready, Jeha began to share all the different special dishes with his guests, one better than the next, with pride. Jeha said: "This is your house! You are at home! The food is also yours! Help yourselves, and don't leave anything since it is all yours! Enjoy *your* belongings!"

Everyone thanked Jeha, while laughing and joking, thinking they had made fun of him, and had played a great joke on him!

After ending the feast with large glasses of delicious mint tea with lots of cakes, they said their good-byes. Great was their surprise when they could not find their slippers and shoes. "Where are our slippers? Where are our shoes, Jeha?" And everyone was screaming and hollering about their shoes.

As soon as they had calmed themselves down, Jeha started to tell them: "You knew very well that these days I am having a very difficult time financially and you insisted on inviting yourselves even though I do not have the means to entertain you. You forced me to do whatever was necessary to satisfy you. Well, I could not find any way to buy what I needed to feed you, and not feel ashamed, so I used your shoes."

And when his friends started to argue, Jeha justified himself by saying: "In no way did I trick you! Besides, while you were eating this sumptuous meal, didn't I repeatedly tell you that you were enjoying your belongings?"

They could not find anything else to say, so the brother of the traveler said: "We wanted to make fun of you, Jeha! But now we are going home with bare feet!"*

Most of the residents of the old medina are people from the artisan families, the poorer section of Morocco. They have been in the trades for hundreds of years and are still preserving their art forms, which are handed down from generation to generation. The richer crowd lives in the modern cities, except for the few who own old ryads and renovate them into luxurious

---

*   Chakir, *Recueil de Contes du Folklore Marocain* (tr. M-L. Valandro).

restaurants. The others are the rich and artistic westerners who renovate the ancient ryads into sumptuous homes with much care and love! But they do not reside here full time, most of the homes get rented out and their owners come periodically to solve various problems.

Many of the old palaces have been restored through various foundations and are now museums, or places where the young can learn and preserve the old art forms.

Another day, we ventured outside Fes el Bali (old Fes) to Fes Jdid (new Fes), which was the site of the Mellah (the oldest Jewish quarters in Morocco). Many of these ancient parts of the city were peopled by refugees from Tunisia during the ninth century and Spain from the twelfth century onward.

Fes Jdid is close to the royal palace which covers many acres, and the area is more spacious and sunnier than Fes el Bali. The king has several palaces in all the major cities and comes to visit and stay there throughout the year. One of the taxi drivers said that when you see lots of things wrapped in blue plastic (gigantic walls of plastic), hiding building sites, ugly sites, that means the king is coming for a visit. He does not like to see garbage or unfinished projects, so they get hidden!

Walking through the souk, we met a Fessi man who was shopping and he invited us to his shop, which, of course, we entered, even though we had said that we would have a moratorium on buying! Well, that was the end of our visit. We laughed about it. We just can't win or walk away from the expertise of these merchants. We spent our time looking at carpets and tablecloths, drinking mint tea and eating dates. Of course we bought something, but we had fun in his shop where he sold herbs, oils, carpets, etc. He had lived in France and was happy to be home with his large extended family and children. Then we walked back through a lovely public garden with many fountains, situated on the side of the palace, which was heavily guarded all along the walls and entrances. Then we re-entered Fes el Bali through Bab Boujloud and again walked back down to our tiny dar.

One day we got so lost way down in the medina, where it goes in circles forever and ever, it seemed! I asked one young man to help us and he took us all the way to the house. He was a student at one of the most famous, oldest madreses, the Qaraouiyine University, built in 859 by Fatima al-Fihri, who had been a refugee from Tunisia (Kerouan) with her sister.

FES, MOROCCO

The young man wanted to be a Muslim cleric. He was clean shaven, upright, with a handsome face, and would make a wonderful mullah. We asked him to be our guide, so he showed up the next morning at 9:00 AM, but with his father who looked unwell, and took us all over the medina. We visited the herb, pharmaceutical, henna, perfume, and essences souk and entered a shop with a wall filled from top to bottom with jars of all kinds of flower and wood essences. The place had an aura of magic, old medicine, and alchemy. The atmosphere was thick, but not unpleasant. The owner and practitioner had a club foot, was an herbalist, and practiced medicine the old way. His son said in a matter of fact way that his father was a wise man, a healer. After spending some time there looking, we asked him if he had a remedy to deal with my sister's arm which retained fluids because the cancerous glands in her armpits were removed twenty years ago. She had no drainage from a nonfunctioning glandular system and had been under severe stress for a few years with family matters. So the doctor proceeded to have my sister sit down quietly and he lit some candles. Slowly he proceeded to drop in special herbs on the fire with a quick movement and recited verses from the Koran with his hand on his heart. I watched, not disturbing the atmosphere, and my sister took this very seriously. Then the herb doctor asked my sister to spit on the little flame covered with herbs, and with a brisk movement of his hand he removed some unseen thick clouds. Afterwards, he asked how she felt. She said she felt something coming out of her heart region and felt much better, as if a weight had been lifted off her shoulders. He showed us pictures of other people from foreign lands who had received his healing services. I bought some flower essences—rose, orange blossom, and jasmine. I thanked him and my sister gave him some money for his services.

The Muslims believe in angels and other invisible beings, they are a fact to them. Muhammad's visitations by the angel Gabriel is the basis of the Koran. So it is no surprise that the serious Muslim healer who wants to bring healing through plants always joins forces with famous sentences from the Koran to fight entities, evil spirits, which bring illnesses to mind and body.

The world holds something within it that goes beyond its physical aspects. The signs for this have no lips, however, and therefore meaning has to be given to them. A completely new world opens up in the Devachan (heavens) for someone able to read the writing of the plants. You can also think of every animal in the world as a letter, and you will gradually be able to decipher these letters. If you understand what comes to expression in animals' lives you will relate to them as someone able to read and not as someone who merely describes the letters, which is the way of modern conventional science. Learning to recognize the world that lies in the animal you are able to see another, completely different world behind the physical world—the astral world. Learning to see the plant world as letters you gain the ability to see into the mental world. This is not something divorced from reality. Quite on the contrary, it is something firmly based on reality that teaches us to see the abundant meaning of life....

So you see that man has a share in the higher worlds, that the astral body extends into those worlds, and that the devachanic world for its part casts a kind of shadow into this world. Someone who knows nothing of those higher worlds is subject to them like a slave, powerless against powers that control the chains. Just as the physical person can only be free if able to develop the will to face another person in freedom, so can the astral nature of man only be free if it recognizes its connection with the whole astral world. For as long as people live only in their ordinary inner feelings, their astral nature has them on leading strings, as it were. They are always possessed by it. They come free when they recognize it. Just as we perceive and know the physical world around us, so we must face those spirits, spiritual eye to spiritual eye, and know who we are dealing with. It is the same with the world of thoughts. This is the way to real freedom, seeing through the world around us. To gain the right measure of understanding we have to consider what lies behind the physical aspect.[*]

The Muslim healer knew that we have to deal with negative energies (bad spirits, elementals) and he dealt with them with special plants, fire, spit, and holy words from the Koran. My sister felt a relief from the negative energies (bad spirits) surrounding her and encroaching upon her freedom. He could not deal with her arm, but he could help her with her emotional state of being. In this more than thirteenth-century-old city, the people

---

[*] Steiner, *Original Impulses for the Science of the Spirit*, pp. 76–77.

turn to the holy man and plant medicine for their health. He knew that I knew what he was doing, but that I had my own way of dealing with such happenings, and he understood that as well!

On many of our walks along tiny hidden paths, I had the chance to glimpse into small rooms, with a door ajar, with a few people, perhaps outsiders, sitting on the ground with a cleric somberly sitting and facing them, doing a healing with the Koran in between them.

> What does the healer in such a case actually communicate to the one needing to be healed? It is, to use an expression of physics, an "exchange of tensions." What lives in the healer, namely certain processes in his etheric body, relates in a particular way to the one to be healed, creating a kind of polarity. Polarity arises just as it would in a more abstract sense when one kind of electricity, say positive, is produced and the corresponding other, the negative, appears. In this way polarities are created. This is a supreme deed of sacrifice. We are calling forth a process within ourselves which is not only intended to be meaningful to ourselves, for then one would call forth one process only. In this case, however, the process is intended to call forth in the other the polar opposite. This polarity will depend on the contact established between the healer and the person to be healed; when this is produced, when the opposite process is called forth in the other, this is, in the fullest sense of the word, the sacrifice of power, the transmuted power of love, a deed of love. We must be in no doubt therefore that any endeavor to heal must be carried by this power of love, or else it will fail. Nevertheless, processes of love need not necessarily enter our conscious awareness; they may well take place in the subconscious.... Even in the case of healing processes where the immediate connections are hidden from us, where we cannot observe what is being done, there is a deed of love involved, even if it has taken on the form of mere technique.*

Here it is explained in another way, in much more powerful images, leaving no room for vague ideas which is the gift of spiritual science, but it is not for faint-hearted human beings. Whenever we have to engage in a healing process, whether a gentle healing or a healing of major proportion,

---

* Steiner, *Manifestations of Karma*, p. 192.

it is the same process which has been spoken of here in different ways. We see that the more sage and selfless the healer, the more that person can handle and transform the forces which that individual faces. In Christ we have the ultimate Healer as spoken of in the New Testament, but within the Muslim world, throughout the ages, there have appeared Sufis, sages, and holy clerics who were powerful healers, and many of their mausoleums are scattered all over the Islamic world and are the destinations of major pilgrimages to this day, where individuals receive healing.

> You will realize, therefore, that your lives are guided by powers of which you yourself are not aware. The ether body is worked upon by forms that you yourself previously called into existence on the astral plane; beings and forces in the higher region of Devachan, inscribed by you in the Akashic record (where everything known to man is inscribed), work upon your destiny. These forces and beings are not unknown to the spiritual researcher; they have their own place in the ranks of similar beings. You must realize that in your astral body and in your ether body, as well as in your physical body, you feel the workings of other beings. All that you do involuntarily, everything to which you are impelled, is due to the working of other beings. It is not born from nothingness. The various members of the human being are all the time actually permeated and filled by other beings, and many of the exercises given by an initiated teacher are for the purpose of driving out these beings in order that an individual may become more and more free.
>
> The beings who permeate the astral body and make it unfree are known as "demons," and the beings you yourself generate through your true or false thoughts are of such a nature that they gradually grow into demons. There are good demons, generated by good thoughts; but bad thoughts, above all those that are untruthful, generate demoniacal forms of the most terrible and frightful kind, and these interlard the astral body. The ether body is also permeated by beings from which human beings must free themselves; these beings are called "specters," "ghosts." Finally, permeating the physical body there are beings known as "phantoms." Besides these three classes there are yet other beings, the "spirits," who drive the ego hither and thither—the ego itself also being a spirit. It is a fact that you generate such beings who then determine your inner and outer destiny when

FES, MOROCCO

Donkeys being used as taxis

you descend into reincarnation. These beings work in your life in such a way that you can feel the "demons" created by your astral body, the "ghosts" or "specters" created by your ether body, and the "phantoms" created by your physical body. All these beings are related to you and approach you when the time comes for incarnation.

It can be seen how religious scriptures express these truths. When the Bible tells of the driving-out of demons, this is not an abstraction but is to be taken literally. Christ Jesus healed those who were possessed by demons; he drove the demons out of the astral body. This is an actual process and the passage is to be taken literally.[*]

Our guide then took us to more hidden places. We saw where some of the donkeys were living, fed, and bedded, in an old dilapidated caravanserai. The donkeys are the taxis in Fes. In the vicinity of another old mosque we entered a cavernous building housing many weavers hard at work, and it was full of French tourists. We toured a beautifully renovated madrese where we could see the students' small cells, like monks, where the students memorized the

---

[*]   Steiner, *Rosicrucian Wisdom: An Introduction*, p. 64.

Koran and deliberated its finely arabesque thoughts. Then it was time to get back to the house, after arguing with our guide over the outrageous price he quoted us, which was more than what the professional guide had asked for!

The next day we walked to the old Andalusian quarters, one of the oldest parts of Fes dating from the ninth century when the first Andalusian refugees migrated here. This area was famous for its international students and the development of the rich decorative arts. Many of the Andalusians helped in the construction of Fes. At that time, Fes was the capital of arts and crafts. The town shows a distinct character in its buildings which reminds one of the Alhambra. We walked through old ryads, palaces, decorated with flowery, geometric motifs and Arabic scripts on tiles, wood, and marble. And, of course, the marble fountains were there to bring in the sound of fresh water.

This part of the city was different from Fes el Bali. It had bigger ryads, some of them preserved by the government in their original state, untouched but sadly decrepit! They had palatial doors with exquisite carvings, forged ironwork, tiles, large courtyards. We walked through countless old tiny paths, with a young man who volunteered as our guide in this other maze. Families still live in these quarters, from different parts of the country. The guide said in some areas here they speak Berber and consider themselves distinct from other Moroccans. Much has been written about the Arabs and the Berbers.

All this incredible richness of the arts is baffling. How did this come about? How did this highly artistic Muslim culture become what it is, stemming out of the Muslim world, from Muhammad's vision announced by the angel Gabriel, the sacred book the Koran, in just a few hundred years?

Here Rudolf Steiner has some of the most outstanding insights, which bring help towards understanding the evolution of humankind, and all the streams which originated together and then became separate, such as the Judaic, Christian, and Muslim world.

> The Athenian philosophers who were cast out by Justinian (AD 529) were welcomed by Khosrau I (531–579) at his Academy of Gondishapur in Persia, which he had modeled on the great Academy of Alexandria. The same curriculum was followed, and a vast body of knowledge was gradually accumulated. Teachers were gathered from the Syriac-speaking schools of the Nestorian Church, Edessa, and Nisiblis, and

learning from the Monophysite Church, which was in close touch with Alexandria, was also bestowed.

In the eighth century, the wealth and power of Harun al-Rashid procured Greek manuscripts, many of which were medical, from the Roman Empire, and these were translated into Syriac and Arabic. An association had been formed with the Academy by the Abbasid court when it was established nearly at Baghdad, and when Harun al-Rashid and his ardently pro-Greek minister, Ja'far ibn Barmak, a Persian from Merv in Khurasan (by the Uzbekistan border with Turkmenistan), sought for scholars to aid in their mission of Hellenizing Persian and Arab subjects, they drew many from this rich source. The luster of the court itself was also enhanced by the presence of learned men from Gondishapur. So strong was the Abbasid desire for a brilliant culture that the victor at the poetic contests received one hundred pieces of gold, a horse, an embroidered caftan, and a lovely slave. It was in the scientific realm, however, that Gondishapur excelled, and it was mainly from this center that Greek science passed to the Arabs.

The school of medicine was much to the fore at Gondishapur, and had been established before the time of Khosrau. Medical knowledge was derived through many different channels, notably Alexandria and India. Greek medical science passed through Alexandria to India, and returned after being worked upon by Indian students. Gondishapur had an observatory, where Indian material also appears to have been received. Translators of astronomical works came from Merv, where Harun al-Rashid had been educated, and which was a city of Buddhist and Mazdean connection; Khurasan (Uzbekistan-Iran) in all probability furnished further mathematical and astronomical lore.

In the magnificent structure of knowledge built up by the Muslim world, Neo-Platonism had considerable influence, but Aristotle held the central place.*

And then in an amazing lecture cycle called *Three Streams in the Evolution of Mankind* comes some amazing insights:

---

*   Steiner, *The Redemption of Thinking: A Study in the Philosophy of St. Thomas Aquinas*, p. 166.

Whoever has any inkling of the wisdom of Gondishapur will indeed regard it as in the highest sense dangerous for mankind, but also as a phenomenon of great power. And the intention was to deluge with this learning not only the immediate vicinity but the whole of the then-known civilized world—Asia, Europe, and everywhere....

The preliminaries for this were prepared. But the influence that was to have gone out from Gondishapur was deadened, held back by retarded spiritual forces, which were nevertheless connected—although they form a kind of opposition—with the outflow of the Christ Impulse. Through the appearance of Muhammad and his visionary religious teaching, there was a deadening of the influence that was meant to go out from Gondishapur. Above all in those regions where it was wished to spread the Gnostic wisdom of Gondishapur, Muhammad took the ground from under its feet. He skimmed the cream off it, and so the Gondishapur influence was left to trail behind and could accomplish nothing in face of what Muhammad had done. Here you can see the wisdom in world history; we come to know the truth about the Muhammadans only when, in addition to other things, we know that Muhammadanism was destined to deaden the Gnostic wisdom of Gondishapur, to take from it the strong ahrimanically seductive force which would otherwise have been exercised upon mankind....

This spiritual life of the Middle Ages is studied very one-sidedly. But go and look at the pictures which were painted about the way in which the Schoolmen behaved towards the Arabian philosophers; see how in the sense of western Christian tradition the Schoolman is shown standing there with his Christian doctrine and preparing to tread the Arabian men of learning under foot.*

In this next lecture, Rudolf Steiner explains what was at stake, what forces were behind the shaping of the Academy of Gondishapur.

The mystery of Golgotha preceded the middle point of the fourth epoch by 333 years, by just as many years prior to this point, as years after it, certain spiritual powers intended to direct the evolution of mankind into quite different channels from those into which it was

---

*   Steiner, *Three Streams in the Evolution of Mankind: The Connection of the Luciferic-Ahrimanic Impulses with the Christ-Jahve Impulse*, pp. 88–89, 91.

ultimately led by the Mystery of Golgotha. Now 333 years after the year of AD 333, is the year AD 666. This is the year of which the writer of the Apocalypse speaks with such great fervor. Just read the chapters where the writer of the Apocalypse refers to the year AD 666. Therein, according to the intentions of certain spiritual powers, something should have happened to mankind, and it would have happened had the Mystery of Golgotha not taken place. If the Mystery of Golgotha had not occurred, the descending path upon which mankind was destined to travel after AD 333, and which would have been the climax in the culture of the intellect or mind soul, would have been used in order to lead mankind in a direction quite different from the one intended by those Divine Beings who have been connected with mankind since the beginning, since the Saturn evolution. This was to take place through bestowing upon mankind, by means of a kind of revelation, something which only at a later period should enter human evolution—the consciousness soul and its content....

If this had been achieved, if the intentions of certain beings had been fulfilled—certain beings who are opposing the evolution of mankind, but who wish to seize upon this evolution—then mankind in the year AD 666 would have been caught in a surprise and would have been endowed with the consciousness soul to such a degree of intensity as will occur normally only in the distant future....

Although events did not follow this peculiar, phenomenal pattern, although they did not assume the magnificent, but diabolic form which was intended, traces of these intentions may be found in history. They took place through deeds of which we may only say, that human beings perform these deeds on Earth, but perform them actually as the "handymen" of certain beings, when in AD 529, as an enemy of the traditions of the sublime wisdom of the Greek culture, he (the Emperor Justinian) closed the Schools of Philosophy in Athens. Thus the last representatives of Greek learning, with the sublime Aristotelian-Platonic knowledge, were exiled; they fled to Persia, where already in earlier periods Syrian scholars had found refuge, when Leo Isauricus in the fifth century had banished the Greek scholars from Edessa. Thus in the Persian Academy of Gondishapur, at about the year AD 666, was gathered all the choicest learning brought over from ancient Greece which had not paid heed to the Mystery of Golgotha. And the teachers within the Academy of Gondishapur were inspired by luciferic-ahrimanic powers....

If what was intended to come over mankind in AD 666 which, had it taken place, would have lead to the cutting off of the subsequent evolution and to the elevation of humanity to the consciousness soul as early as the year AD 666—if what was intended by the Academy of Gondishapur had been fully successful, then in the seventh century AD here and there, highly learned human beings would have arisen, who would have had the task of traveling through northern Africa, through western Asia, through southern Europe, through Europe in general, spreading everywhere the culture of AD 666 as it was intended by the Academy of Gondishapur. The aim of this culture was especially to make the human being dependent entirely upon his own personality, to fully bestow upon him the consciousness soul....

There was no possibility, however for this to occur. The world already had taken on a form different from the one which would have permitted this to occur. Therefore, the entire blow which occidental culture was to receive from the Academy of Gondishapur was weakened. And instead of the wisdom which might have resulted from the academy, a wisdom in comparison with which everything we know today in the outer world would be a mere trifle, instead of the result of a spiritually inspired wisdom attained from brilliant and magnificent learning, a wisdom about all that which will be gradually mastered through natural scientific experimentation up to the year AD 2493, instead of all this, mere remnants remained in what Arabian scholars brought to Spain. But even this wisdom was weakened, it did not come out in the way it was intended; it became vitiated. In its place remained Muhammadanism, Muhammad with his teaching. Instead of all that was intended to originate from the Academy of Gondishapur, Islam arose. Through the Mystery of Golgotha the world was diverted from this fatal direction.*

---

*   Steiner, *How Do I Find the Christ?*

These are mighty insights into the evolution of our consciousness, our history. Just think of the disaster which would have happened to mankind if we had had the amazing knowledge given to us almost two thousand years before we were supposed to receive it. Considering how savage we were, how unconcerned for others, how blood thirsty and selfish, where would we be now? Completely annihilated by our lack of respect, lack of concern, selfishness, with no chance of survival. We can only thank the higher spiritual powers who have averted such a fall. The Islamic revolution took all the great scientists, writers, and poets far away from the diabolical forces of knowledge and led them to the dedication of their fantastic knowledge, to Allah, the One God. The result is all the culture which spread from southern Spain through to Asia with its incredible Islamic architecture, arts, calligraphy, medicine, astronomy, and mathematics, all dedicated to serving, praising the One God, Allah. Instead of having been dedicated to a knowledge mankind was not ready for!

Now that man is ready for such knowledge as we see it today in the various domains—gene manipulation, the discoveries of the computers, going to the stars, telepathy, fast trains and machines, armaments, nuclear power, artificial insemination, and more to come—how are we to face the dilemma of modern inventions, and man's selfishness? Are we ready to face up to the responsibility of all this knowledge? A resurgence in the Islamic religions perhaps is a reminder that we might not be ready. The Muslims feel they are not ready for the West and its advancing and sometimes diabolical inventions (nuclear bombs, armaments, sexual and gender revolution) and they put the break on by adopting an ancient lifestyle which wants to go back and remain in the past. But when the Islamic discontented souls begin by dictating, through forceful and drastic draconian laws, how to dress, live, pray, work, raise children, and eat, then they have joined hands with the negative forces of evolution, the ones that forge ahead without concern for anyone but their own selfish motives of power and monetary gain. The middle has always been the path of progress, not ruled by the past or the future, but the present where we think of the other human being as deserving as much as we have ourselves.

A donkey laden with sheepskins

For what else is love than widening one's consciousness to encompass other beings? It is love when we are willing to deprive ourselves, to sacrifice ourselves to whatever extent for the sake of another. Like the skin that received the beam of light, and out of the pain became able to create a higher entity: the eye; so will we, through widening our life to encompass the lives of others, become able to attain a higher life. There will then, out of what we have given away to others, be born within us love and compassion for all creatures.*

We ended the tour of the Andalusian quarters by arriving at the large Chouara Tannery which is by the river at the edge of the medina, so as not to pollute the medina center. The center in all of the medinas is always occupied by the mosque, the madreses. The polluting crafts—such as tanning, ceramics, and pottery—are always on the outskirts of the medina. The donkeys were arriving with loads of sheep, goat, cow, and camel skins, and workers were unloading them to be brought inside the tannery for the difficult job of treating, pounding, scraping, dyeing, processing, and drying.

---

* Steiner, *Supersensible Knowledge*, p. 63.

FES, MOROCCO

A view of the Chouara Tannery

A guide brought us up several sets of stairs to a large terrace where we could view the tannery. He gave us some fresh mint to put under our noses, so that the odors would not bother us. This traditional tannery is the largest of four still functioning in the medina. It was a most amazing sight. A beehive of activity was happening several stories below. Men in rubber boots were stepping inside large earthen vats. I was told that pigeons' very acidic droppings and pee from goats are used to soften and dye the leather. That is why so many pigeons are kept, to obtain their droppings. The tanners were dressed in shorts and many of them barefooted, going from one vat to another, working the precious skins. Then the skins were bathed in vats of various colors made from synthetic or organic dyes from plants, flowers, tree bark, etc. Then the skins—bright pink, orange, sienna, indigo, yellow, red—were ready to dry out in the sunshine on the terraces covered with straw, to become beautiful articles: shoes, purses, exquisite jackets, etc. I had a renewed appreciation of leatherwork after visiting these very hard-working tanners, as I had when visiting Marrakesh's tanners two years prior to my trip to Fes. The guide said there are 150 families working here in this large tannery and they each take turns in welcoming the tourists, and

The ruins of the ancient Roman city of Volubilis

thereby share in the selling of their work in a communal way. He explained that not all the children are interested in keeping this work. If they desire to study or do something else, they are able to do so. But it is gruesome work, and not easy to watch the men sitting with piles of skins by their sides, scratching away, softening the leather in their many tiny cells in the medina.

Another day we took the fast train to Meknes, one hour away, for a relief from the intensity of Fes and our surroundings. We arrived early in the morning and took a rented taxi to Volubilis, a very well-preserved Roman archeological site, where we walked around the very large and well-preserved ancient city. A totally different area—gone, lost, forgotten—and so different from the present Muslim atmosphere that it jolts one's inner being. There was the sunlight, the baths, the open spaces, the beautiful images of the zodiac, Gods, plants, flowers, African animals depicted in immense mosaics on floors, fountains, living with the elements, skin exposed to the Sun, the cosmos.

The taxi was waiting and we then headed to a village sitting on top of a mountain which is the home of the mausoleum of Sidi Abdellah el Hajjam, a saintly man and healer. There a young man offered to guide us around this lovely mountain town. We climbed up ancient stairs and paths with beautiful old homes and gardens. At the top we were rewarded with a fantastic scenery of the small city, the mountains behind, and the enormous mausoleum-mosque compound, with its large green domes, full of pilgrims down below. Women had brought their picnics and were lounging, sitting on large tablecloths, eating and drinking by the mausoleum. We had a lovely lunch in the center of town, after a small visit to an olive press where we tasted the golden oil with fresh bread. The young man was a student of literature and his parents were teachers. He was very well-informed, and open to the modern world.

Then we headed for Meknes to walk around the old city, and on to the fast train back to Fes where I caught a terrible flu to keep me in bed for a couple of days!

One morning, we decided to go up to the ancient ruins above Fes, sitting on top of the hill in the north, dating back to thousands of years ago. We took a taxi and walked around, looking at the beautiful panorama of the city below us. I chatted with a man dressed in a traditional handwoven djellabah who was selling knitted hats made by his daughters. He lived in the hills. He said that his father had fought in World War II and that the French did not do much for his father! I bought several hats and thought: *How sad history is!* Then we walked back because it was close to the large former Jamai Palace which had been converted into a five-star hotel. We went inside and sat on a lovely terrace and ordered some café, while admiring the lovely gardens and the sumptuous setting, with the city of Fes below us. Then we started our walk back to the southern part of the city, hoping not to get lost!

We saw a lovely shop selling beautiful tablecloths and we went in. It was filled with young men at work, weaving the tablecloths. Three small floors of weavers were patiently weaving beautifully colored striped cloths and, of course, we bought a couple of them. By now our small suitcases were so full, we did not know how we were going to close them. And besides, the suitcases had to be dragged down the alleys, stairs, etc., in order to get to the taxi!

Somehow we got back to the usual familiar area of the large mosque and then home.

One of the tablecloth weavers at work

We had explored the shops selling cloths, textiles, shoes, pottery, ceramics, some books in French, perfumes, essences, oil of argan, spices, and herbs. We just could not buy everything, which was a pity. The small carved wooden shelves were precious but too heavy, the carved trays too large, the ceramics too fragile.

One day we decided to try on the gorgeous djellabahs. We tried on dozens—green ones, red ones, pink ones, white with embroidery, yellow, orange, bright green—you name it, we tried it. And we bought a couple each so that we could wear them at home and think we were back in Fes. I must say that our western fashion is no match for Moroccan clothes. They are comfortable, attractive, and pleasing to the eye! The Moroccan women love to wear colors, bright colors, unlike the Muslim women in Iran who wear dreary colors, but not by choice. They are not allowed to wear bright colors in Iran. It's against Islam over there. Only grey, black, and dark brown are allowed! Reasoning: if you are a woman, mourn!

This reminds me of a story about a beautifully dressed man in blue. He was a handsome Persian man, full of dignity, and he was walking in a section of north Tehran, called old Shemiran, during a very dreary day, a

One of the pottery shops

rainy and muddy winter afternoon in 1979 during the revolution when the city was in a crisis. Many were being thrown in dark prison cells and the women were made to wear the hejab. Here was this flowing figure, dressed in exquisite blue, with a beard. He made my day. But I cannot finish this story without mentioning something written by the famous Henry Corbin, professor of Islamic studies at the Sorbonne (1954–1974).

> *Kabud-pushan*, "dressed in dark blue," is the way the Persians designate the Sufis, referring to their custom of wearing blue-colored clothing; many different explanations have been given. Here wearing blue means something precise.... Wearing blue clothing means that the Sufi is only on the elementary stage of his mystical life....
>
> But another great master (Najm Kobra) says ... one will wear black clothing and dark blue when the inward spiritual battle has won over the lower forces or psyche (*nafs ammara*), as if to mourn the death of the lower self! The meaning is thereby not the same as for Lahiji; here it is not a lower stage.... Here in the higher spiritual domain or consciousness, where due to concentration of one's spiritual energy, the mystic has access to different states of consciousness, Najm Kobra

mentions that one can wear light blue clothing. In any case, one must take into consideration the differences between masters when speaking about the symbols of wearing colors.*

Perhaps forbidding the use of colors was a blow against the Sufis in Iran where the regular establishment is not fond of them. They have free access to God, without the mingling, power-hungry theologians, like Rome in our Western world.

In any case, here colors are a part of life. Whether man or woman, everyone is wearing bright-colored clothing to express their exuberance, their moods, their sorrows. It is one sign that the soul is very much alive! The whole souk is nothing but colors, which is heaven for a painter.

One day we decided that it was pajama day. I needed some pajamas, so we wandered around trying to find the clothing section, but we got lost somehow, I could not remember where it was. So we must have looked very disoriented because two very muscular, clean-shaven, handsome men dressed in western clothes asked if we were in trouble. I said no, that we were just a bit lost. He said he was a police officer and offered us his help. I declined his offer, telling him that we were fine, we were just looking for pajamas!

I was surprised to see that the souk has undercover policemen. I thought it was very wise! I never saw a police officer. This is a Muslim, old city, and they take care of their business! Another guide told me, while touring the Andalusian quarters, that there are cameras all over the old city, so that one can assure that there is some safety in old Fes. That also surprised me!

Anyway, we did find the clothing section after all, and we bought some sumptuous pajamas for home, after spending at least a couple of hours looking at the large inventory.

In our small alley and branching from there, we always pass many tiny cell-like shops where the tailors are sitting cross-legged, bent over, working on embroideries on their laps, sewing tiny colorful beads on sumptuous garments used in weddings or for special occasions. Sometimes they will work together, chatting, three or four in a tiny cell, working from daybreak

---

*   Corbin, *L'Homme de Lumière dans le Soufisme Iranien*, p. 166 (tr. M-L. Valandro).

until night, drinking tea under a small dangling lightbulb, sometimes with a radio playing chantings from the Koran. They work for years, dutifully making a living for their extended family, and we see the fabulous clothes that are sometimes hanging in the shop. After their job is done, the marvelous, colorful pieces are sent to the regular shops on the busy arteries. Many Moroccans come to the tailors and order custom-made clothes.

One morning I looked at the map and noticed that we could go to a famous spa town. So we went to the outskirts and used a shared taxi with three others to go to Sidi Harazem for some bathing in warm mineral water. It took quite a while to travel the twenty odd kilometers, but I love hot springs! We brought our bikinis, towels, etc., and finally arrived in a rocky, hilly terrain with some trees and a bit of an oasis. We looked for the pools, but there weren't any! The large pool was farther down and it was a luxury hotel which was closed!

It was not a spa town but a place where sick people come to drink its famous water. They come to cure kidney diseases, liver diseases, etc. We had come for hanging out in bikinis in hot springs. Well, we can't win all the time. I don't know what I was thinking! So we headed back after a lovely ride in the southeastern countryside.

I needed to find a bookstore, so we went up to the entrance of Bab Boujloud and stopped, of course, to have some of my sister's favorite, hot-fried dough. Then we went where I had noticed an old bookstore selling French, German, and English books. I spoke to an old man and told him I wanted a book with the ninety-nine names of Allah written in Arabic, so I could study them and practice my Arabic. Sufis have adopted this practice. But he had none! Then I noticed a calendar that had just that, so he promptly gave me his calendar.

We adapted ourselves to the rhythm of Fes el Bali. On Friday mornings, shops were always closed until the afternoon. After breakfast, the call to prayer by the muezzins at all Fes el Bali mosques was at noon, and many of the residents attend. Then they go home to eat couscous for a traditional family gathering. Wednesdays and Mondays are usually days to go to the hammam, to get ready for the weekend of Thursday and Friday. It is a duty for the Muslim man to make children on Thursday night (our Saturday night).

So I have noticed that all the women attend the hammam on Wednesday evenings, making themselves beautiful for their husbands, even the ones who are past childbearing age! Henna, washing hair, getting rid of unwanted hair, etc., and, of course, the men do the same, the barbershops are full! Men here like to have their hair spotless, with great haircuts, and the hammam is full as well with the men doing the same! Hammams are called spas in the Western world. Well, the Muslims know a lot about spas.

During the week, early mornings are busy with merchants setting up. There is quiet for the noon prayer and lunch, and also during the three o'clock prayer. Then it all wakes up again after four o'clock when families are out for more shopping until they all go home for supper, prayer, and rest. It is a nice rhythm which is dictated by the call to prayer, which people observe or not!

Every day we passed by several mosques with many believers going in to do their daily prayers, whether it was a small mosque along one of the main arteries, or a famous mosque complex, or the mosque by R'Cif square. The shoes are neatly arranged outside, the proverbial old men sitting at the entrance, the women fixing their scarves before entering, others coming out of the designated ablution washroom next to the mosque for the sacred washing rituals.

> Every prayer begins with the *niyya*, the formulation of the intention, for instance, to perform the evening prayer with its three cycles or *rak'a*. During one *rak'a* the praying person stands upright, uttering the words *Allāhu akbar*, "God is greater [than anything else]" and the Fātiha. Then one bends from the hips, straightens one's posture, prostrates, sits, and then performs another prostration. In the first two *rak'a*, another chapter or some verses from the Koran are also recited. Each prayer consists of a prescribed number of *rak'a* (daybreak prayer, two; noon, four; afternoon, four; sunset, three; and night prayer, four). The various movements and positions are accompanied by special formulae. At the prayer's end one utters the profession of faith while sitting, as well as a formula of blessing on the Prophet and the believers.
>
> When prayer time begins, the muezzin calls from the minaret of the mosque or, in some areas, from its roof. The call to prayer, *adhān*, consists of the profession of faith and some additional short phrases and is sung in long cadences.... Once the *adhān* is over, the believer

undertakes the ablution. He or she can perform the prayer alone in any clean place or else in the mosque with the community; in both cases absolute ritual purity is the first condition. After each minor pollution (caused by solid, liquid, or gaseous matters leaving the lower part of the body, as well as sleep or fainting), the minor ablution, *wudū'*, is required: the face, part of the head, the arms to the elbows, the feet to the ankles have to be washed in running water that has not been touched by anyone. The details of the ablutions, elaborated exactly in the course of time, have to be observed minutely, from the intaking of the water in the nostrils to the movement of the fingers when cleansing the ears; each movement should be accompanied by a specific prayer formula.... After major pollutions such as sex, menstruation, and childbirth, a full bath, *ghusl*, is required in which no place in the whole body, including the hair, can remain dry. Only then may the prayer be performed and the Koran touched and recited....

The belief in the purifying power of ritual prayer is intense; the Prophet compared it to a stream of water that washes off sins five times a day.*

Mosque comes from the word *masjid* in Arabic, meaning "the place where one prostrates." When one realizes how many believers prostrate in this reverent manner, I must quote a few passages from Rudolf Steiner where he gives us insight into the importance of kneeling, and what it means.

> Let us look at the way we express reverence, at the very gestures themselves.
>
> We bend our knees, put our hands together, and incline our heads towards the object of our reverence. These are the human organs through which the ego and especially our higher soul faculties come to expression most intensely. In physical life human beings stand upright by keeping their legs straight; their ego radiates out through their hands in acts of blessing, and by moving their head they can observe the heavens and the Earth. By studying human nature, however, we learn that when our straight legs are stretched in strong, conscious action they do their best if they have first learnt to bend the

---

*   Schimmel, *Islam: An Introduction*, pp. 39–41.

knee where reverence is really due. For this genu-flexion opens the way for a force which seeks to find its way into our organism. Knees which stretch without ever having learnt to bend in reverence convey only their own triviality to which they have added nothing. But legs which have deigned to bend receive, when they stretch, a new force, and now it is this and not their triviality which they can spread around them. Hands that would gladly bring blessing and comfort, without having been clasped in reverent devotion, have not much love and blessing to give out of their triviality. But hands which have learnt to fold in reverence have received a force which can flow forth from the hand, for it is a hand that is now powerfully permeated by the ego. For the force received through folded hands passes through the heart, enkindling love, and when it flows again into the hands it becomes blessing. And the head, too, however much it beholds of the world, confronts it only with its own triviality unless it has bent in reverence, when a new force enters it and the feeling this engenders is given back to the world....

What we acquire through reverence in youth returns to us in old age as strength for living, and if we turn in reverence to the divine it flows back to us as an experience of the Almighty. That is what we feel, whether we look up to the starry heavens in their infinite glory, and our reverence glows for all that surrounds us on all sides and is beyond our comprehension, or whether we look up to our invisible God, in whatever form, living and moving throughout the universe.

We look up in reverence to the Almighty, and we come to feel with certainty that we cannot advance towards a union with what is above us unless we first of all approach it from below with reverence. We draw nearer to the Almighty when we immerse ourselves in reverence.[*]

As believers feel God's presence in their mind's eye, heart, they go beyond themselves.

A man must not take an egoistic view of his existence; he must realize that while he stands in the world as a thinking being, his thoughts do not belong to himself alone; for after his death they must pass out into the whole cosmos and become forces which continue to work therein. If we think good thoughts we give over our good thoughts to

---

[*]   Steiner, *Transforming the Soul, Volume One*, pp. 91–94.

the Cosmos at our death. If we think evil thoughts, we give over our evil thoughts to the Cosmos at our death. For man is not only put into Earth-existence to develop simply as a free being. That he certainly must do.... But there is yet another reason why he must become a free and independent being: he is put into the world that he may become a being through whom the gods themselves work, to guide the Cosmos from epoch to epoch.

I might say that what the gods have to weave as thought into the Cosmos, they must prepare in what can be thought and pondered over in the lives of individual human beings. These lives are the Sanctuaries in which the gods must cultivate those thoughts which they continually require in the development of the world, so that they may embody them in their Cosmos, as actual impulses of force.*

Walking by the many mosques within the old city, one is surrounded by a feeling of piety, simplicity, and closeness to the spiritual world. Individuals stand naked before the "other world," beyond the "mountain of Qāf," as many of the Arab poets and mystics have sung and written for centuries. So here is a tale by Sohravardī, a famous Persian poet and initiate:

At the beginning of the tale that Sohravardī entitles "The Crimson Archangel," the captive, who has just escaped the surveillance of his jailers, that is, has temporarily left the world of sensory experience, finds himself in the desert in the presence of a being whom he asks, since he sees in him all the charms of adolescence, "O youth! Where do you come from?" He receives this reply: "What? I am the first-born of the children of the Creator and you call me a youth?" There, in this origin, is the mystery of the crimson color that clothes his appearance: that of a being of pure light whose splendor the sensory world reduces to the crimson twilight. "I come from beyond the mountain of Qāf.... It is there that you were yourself at the beginning, and it is there that you will return when you are finally rid of your bonds."**

---

*   Steiner, *The Evolution of the World and of Humanity*, p. 137.
** Corbin, *Swedenborg and Esoteric Islam*, p. 3.

We had not bought enough flower essences so we wandered along one of the quiet side streets and entered a small shop full of colorful oils in beautiful glass jars. The man was helpful, and we smelled all sorts of lovely scents. One bottle after another, and we got to chatting. He was a diabetic and had to be careful about his health. We purchased some more jasmine, cedar, and gardenia essences so that back home I could make my own mixtures of oil mixed with flower essences and give them as gifts or use them in my daily "spa." His wife came and was thankful for the purchases. She was a beautiful lady and they had several children, and making a living was not so easy for a family man. Moroccan men and women all use flower essences, it is part of their customs. The men openly go to the herbalist and essence doctor and discuss what they need, and the doctor gives them a mixture of what he thinks they will like. Some come because they are getting married, or have a girlfriend, and it is important to them. The women also have their favorite perfume mixtures, and they explain which perfume they enjoy for themselves. It is fascinating. Some of the most famous perfumists live in Morocco in a grandiose style. Many of the plants come from Morocco, from trees and roots which grow in the Atlas Mountains and are shipped elsewhere for drying and processing. We left with our gifts. My favorite is still rose, lavender, and orange blossoms. We also purchased some argan oil for the face and for making creams. We often entered some of the shops and watched the women pound the argan nut and make the oil.

Rose water is the essence of Islam and is used within the vicinity of the mosque. The rose and apple family has a five-pointed star. The five-pointed star is the image of man, as seen in Michelangelo's famous drawing.

Many shopkeepers are seen daily sweeping their small shops, sprinkling some water scented with rose oil outside, or sprinkling orange blossom flower essence inside their shops, as well as burning some incense nearby. Inns, hotels, and homes all use orange-scented water to bring a healing, relaxing, comforting atmosphere for their guests.

I cannot omit a few paragraphs from the fantastic book by Celia Lyttelton, *The Scent Trail*, which is a must read by a master storyteller who *lives* for perfumes and essences. This excerpt takes place in Marrakesh.

FES, MOROCCO

As I passed the spice souk I breathed in the smells of yellow-ocher cumin and deep red cinnamon, of nutmeg, henna, cloves, garlic, and ginger as I passed the rows of sacks they were stored in. I found the souk el Attarin sign (*attar* is Persian for perfume) on a blue tile on a street corner.... I almost got lost in a convoluted web of alleyways, but my nose did not let me down. Following it, I eventually found myself in a lane of perfume sellers who sat behind white cloth curtains that shielded hundreds of vials of perfume from the heat and sunlight. As soon as I showed a glimmer of interest, the perfumers grabbed my arms and hands and dabbed me with scents, and because oriental scents are not diluted with alcohol, their potent, oily perfumes lingered on my skin.

I was anointed with jasmine, rose from Kelaa Mgouna, musk, sandalwood, patchouli, flower of the night, neroli, and narcissus. Then I explained I wanted to try all the different petit-grains; there are several major oils distilled from the unripe fruits, twigs, and leaves of the citron tribe. The golden apples of the sun, the perfumer told me expansively, give off the odor of angels. And it's true, the golden "apples" of the Hesperides do give off a heavenly aura....

We entered the medina by way of the herb souk, where we bought a bouquet of mint, absinthe, sage, marjoram, scented geranium, and clary sage....

We threaded our way along tiny lanes and, behind a mosque where the ablutions fountain had run dry, came to a courtyard where, Professor Martin explained, the dead are embalmed in cloth soaked with musk before they are buried. Now, as in ancient times, Muslims go into the next world perfumed. A wizened old man walked past us swinging a censer of smoldering frankincense to cleanse and purify the air; I watched him walk away in a cloud of incense. Turning into a square where shops sold spices and perfumes, we stopped at one which must have had several hundred jars of ingredients for perfume, for cooking, and for healing potions. In Morocco scent is used as much for cooking and for medicine as it is for perfume.[*]

---

[*] Lyttelton, *The Scent Trail: How One Woman's Quest for the Perfect Perfume Took Her Around the World*, p. 60.

In the very early morning before everyone is up, there is plenty of activity. People put their refuse by their doors in plastic bags. Some of the leftover food is dropped by as well for all the cats to feed on. There are thousands of cats in the city, all hanging out, trying to keep warm in the winter and cool in the summer. Some live in the shops and are well-fed, we see them in cardboard boxes on top of piles of books in small bookstores taking naps, or in large bowls in ceramic shops, or kittens huddling together on some refuse. Then come the donkeys who are sometimes let free to go through the garbage and eat some, and then the hard work comes. The donkeys with their saddlebags are led throughout the old city to pick up all the garbage and exit through the main doors to drop the refuse in massive containers to be taken out later by dump trucks. The cobblestone paths are swept with straw brooms, and in the early morning, like an army, the collectors move across the city to keep it clean before everyone gets up. The numerous cats keep the city free of rats and mice. I never saw any, but it is quite a job.

Of course there is donkey poop, as well as cat poop, so when you walk it is better not to wear sandals, but shoes with socks, and to watch where you step. When it rains, the whole city is washed clean, as the water pours on the stones and flows down to the river running at the bottom of Fes el Bali.

Throughout the city, the government authorities are trying to salvage this very old city which shows signs of age everywhere, with old homes that are dragging, falling down, too expensive to repair. So they have tried to support these very old ryads by fortressing them with enormous cedar log buttresses and scaffoldings. But the ancient red stone material is wearing down, cracking, and showing dangerous signs of crashing down on other buildings, tunnels, etc., or simply disintegrating. The city needs billions of dollars to renovate them, and only a few foreigners can afford to remodel the fantastic museum-like ryads. Many squatters live in these old ryads and make do with the way things are: lack of toilets and water, rain falling in, etc. The Parthenon in Athens has received many billions for their ongoing renovations. This city is a *living* museum and no one (local or foreign) seems to want to give funds to keep it as a living relic of past ages for future generations to enjoy.

One of the most intriguing thoughts and truths for me is reincarnation, which I have mentioned many, many times on this journey. The fact that we have had more than one life, and will have more in the future. *Where do I come from?* is a question which leads us to past ages, long ages ago. *Where am I going?* The work of Rudolf Steiner brings some insight into these questions. He states that bringing knowledge about reincarnation was his *karma*. After probing, reading, searching, and meditating on his many lecture cycles, I am still enthralled by the formidable input he gives us concerning these matters, most of all with regard to the three religions in which I am deeply involved in this journey. What does it mean to be born a Muslim, to perform these ablutions every day for thirty years or more, to say these prayers to Allah? What does it mean to go to a church service, now that most people do not, or to pray to some religious symbol such as the Madonna, or some saint, or martyrs? What are we achieving? And what if we do not pray, if we are simply a shopper, someone who does not care at all about God, and his saints? All these questions over the years pile up and up and many times, as I am studying a page, an answer just jumps out at me. There it is! That's it!

And that is why I am writing. I am writing about all these moments of light, of understanding, of making some sense of what life is about, which I have tried to share with the reader in the many passages which I have quoted throughout this book.

How can I travel in a warm, lovely country with people who believe other than I do? How can I keep my beliefs and allow others to have theirs, even if they do not respect mine? I always manage with what I call my "universal" language.

It takes much practice, and it does not come from anywhere! It comes from other lifetimes, from other lives, lived in other periods of time. And what strikes me is this: This lifetime this individual needs to be just the way he is. This individual has chosen this particular faith, gender, country, family, and language because of his former life, karma. So this person *needs* to be a devout Muslim, Christian, Atheist, African, Chinese, etc. If I have a "holier-than-thou" attitude which the Christian settlers had, *My God is better than yours, my abstract God up there only shines on me, me the*

Christian, me the Muslim, me the Jew, etc., then I am not respecting what others have chosen for this lifetime.

But to understand this very deeply, we need the help of the knowledge of karma, its laws, its enlightening truths.

The following gem is a truth which helps a human being when faced with dilemmas.

> The imperfections of an earlier epoch are still more important for the following epoch than its perfections. The perfections are there to be studied, but what has been elaborated to a certain degree of perfection on the Earth has, as it were, reached an end, has come to a conclusion in evolution. What has not been perfected is the seed of the following divine evolutionary process. Here we come to a remarkable, magnificent paradox. The greatest blessing for a subsequent period is the fruitful imperfections, the fruitful, justifiable imperfections of an earlier period. What has been perfected in an earlier epoch is there to be enjoyed. Imperfection, however, imperfection originating in great men whose influences have remained for posterity, helps to promote creativity in the following period. Hence, there is obviously tremendous wisdom in the fact that imperfections remain in the neighborhood of the Earth, inscribed in the records of the Akasha Chronicle between Earth and Moon.
>
> This brings us to the point where we can begin to understand the principle that perfection signifies for the different epochs the end of a stream of evolution. For imperfection in this sense men should actually be thankful to the gods.... If a man were deliberately to ignore his imperfections, he would, it is true, inscribe them as described, but they would have no light nor would they be capable of having any effect. Only those imperfections that are inscribed because they were due to necessity and not the result of laziness can work in the way that has been described.*

Meaning that we are far from perfect, but that allows for movement towards perfection.

---

* Steiner, *Life Between Death and Rebirth*, pp. 260–261.

In that respect, Rudolf Steiner mentions that the Chinese were a race which had developed to perfection. They are the remnant, the best example of Atlantean people. An epoch which covered millennia, and which had seven races. Out of the fifth root race the Semite race came. They were highly imperfect, but because of these imperfections they could learn, change, and metamorphose. The sixth and seventh root race, out of which the Chinese-Mongol race came, was a race that had gone to perfection as we know from their highly developed culture to this day. But they could not develop further, that was left to the fifth root race, the Semites, the white race, the race which escaped Atlantean disaster and went to settle in the Gobi desert and from there peopled India, Persia, Egypt, Europe, and Greece while mingling with the others. Here we see how imperfection has a function. It is the same with our own life. Our imperfections bring us back. Rudolf Steiner mentioned an exercise for getting to know our past incarnation, one of very many. It is excruciatingly difficult (for me, that is), and in this exercise one has to focus on what it is that makes us do the wrong thing (apparent wrong thing), that leads us to disaster, to what it is we strongly dislike in our life, all of it, our weaknesses, our stupidity, everything negative. And he says if you concentrate on that, then that is the being that stands there, who led you before you were born to this incarnation. You needed to go through all these painful experiences, not the good ones, to learn something. Daunting!

Georg Kühlewind put it in another way: "You are always wrong! No matter what! Don't blame anyone else, but yourself, then you might get some answers!"

Here are more words of wisdom from Rudolf Steiner:

> We have had these sorrows, these sufferings. Being what we are in this incarnation, with normal life running its course, our sorrows and sufferings are dire misfortunes, something we would gladly avoid. By way of a test, let us *not* take this attitude but assume that for a certain reason we ourselves brought about these sorrows, sufferings, and obstacles, realizing that owing to our earlier lives—if there have actually been such lives—we have become in a sense more imperfect because of what we have done. After all, we do not only become more perfect through

the successive incarnations but also, in a certain respect, more imperfect. When we have affronted or injured some human being, are we not more imperfect than we were before? We have not only affronted him, we have taken something away from ourselves; as a personality, taken as a whole, our worth would be greater if we had not done this thing.... We must make compensation for the affront, we must place into the world a counterbalancing deed, we must discover some means of compelling ourselves to overcome something. And if we think in this way about our sufferings and sorrows, we shall be able in many instances to say: these sufferings and sorrows, if we surmount them, give us strength to overcome our imperfections. Through suffering we can make progress.

In normal life we do not think in this way; we set our face against suffering. But we can also say the following: every sorrow, every suffering, every obstacle in life should be an indication of the fact that we have within us a man who is cleverer than we ourselves are. Although the man we ourselves are is the one of whom we are conscious, we regard him for a time as being the less clever; within us we have a cleverer man who slumbers in the depths of our soul. With our ordinary consciousness we resist sorrow and sufferings, but the cleverer man leads us towards these sufferings in defiance of our consciousness because by overcoming them we can strip off something. He guides our sorrows and sufferings, directs us to undergo them. This may, to begin with, be an oppressive thought but it carries with it no obligations.... We can say: within us there is a cleverer man who guides us to sufferings and sorrows, to something that in our conscious life we should like most of all to have avoided. We think of him as the cleverer man. In this way we are led to the realization which many find disturbing, namely that his cleverer man guides us always towards what we do not like. This, then, we will take as an assumption: there is a cleverer man within us who guides us to what we do not like in order that we may make progress.*

It is good to look back on one's life in a certain way, and above all to envisage clearly those things that one did not like. All this leads to

---

*   Steiner, *Reincarnation and Karma: Their Significance in Modern Culture*, p. 46.

a more intimate knowledge of the inner kernel of our being.... It is well to know clearly what we really wanted to be, and what we have become against our will, to visualize what would have suited us in the time of our youth but was not our lot, and then, again, what we would have liked to avoid....

We must therefore be quite clear as to what a retrospect into the past means; it tells us what we did not want, what we would have liked to avoid. When we have made that clear to ourselves, we really have a picture of those things in our life which have pleased us least. That is the essential point. And we must now try to live into a very remarkable conception: we must desire and will everything that we have *not* desired or willed.... The most important thing is that we should ardently wish or picture ourselves wishing for the things we have *not* desired, or concerning which we have not been able to carry out our wishes, so that we create for ourselves, in feeling and thought, a being hitherto unfamiliar to us. We must picture ourselves as this being with great intensity. If we can do this, if we can identify ourselves with the being we have ourselves built up in this way, we have made some real progress towards becoming acquainted with the inner soul-kernel of our being; for in the picture we have thus been able to make of our own personality there will arise something that we have not been in the present incarnation but which we have introduced into it. Our deeper being will emerge from the picture built up in this way.... Then there develops the perception that this picture is derived from an earlier life.*

As I travel through many different countries, I meet lots of young people who wish they were living in the West. They do not like where their karma has brought them, and they want to leave. One young man I remember in Cairo said he could not stand it, he wanted to be in Tel Aviv so that he could go clubbing, dancing, have fun, and live a normal life, as he put it. He did not care about being a Muslim or a Jew, he just wanted to live his life as a free being, making his own choices. *My God is better than yours*, is not an issue with this young man, but his freedom is, as it is for millions of people like him. The abstract God dictates what is right. One God is right

---

* Ibid., p. 13.

over here on the planet, and another God is right on the other side, and the individual is forced to chose, so wants to leave. The home countries which do not allow one's personal freedom to develop are losing some of their best individuals. A knowledge of what stands behind the forces preventing the freedom of individuals is the only way out of these perpetual wars among nations, tribes, and people. These insights are what spiritual science brings.

> What takes place on the plane of world history can be grasped only when it is grasped in the light of the supersensible realities behind it. We can then perceive the concrete impulse given to world-historical events by spiritual powers, whereas by speaking only of an abstract Divinity no true vision is possible.
>
> Those who speak only of an abstract Divinity must actually—since they are bound to think of this Divinity as operative everywhere—seek it, let us say, in a Turkish battle of the Middle Ages, both on the side of the Turks and also on the side of those against whom the Turks were fighting! Thus the abstract Divinity is there at war with itself, engaged in a self-conflict.
>
> When spiritual Beings whose mutual relationships arise... from the fact that certain tasks pass over from one group to another, but also that certain groups lag behind, others reach normal stages, others again storm forward—when we realize that in the spiritual world there is a multiplicity of Beings struggling against each other yet able to be mutually helpful, only then does it become possible, without being guilty of inconsistencies, to apply human concepts to happenings taking place behind the scenes of world history in the supersensible world....
>
> It is particularly important for men of the present day to perceive in detail how man is a reflection of the supersensible, and how historical events are also reflections of the supersensible. This is the only path by which man can find his way back again to the divine-spiritual world. Purely abstract ideas of a Divinity are still able to influence those who have not yet begun to perceive and think in the sense of the modern spiritual life. But the number of the latter constantly diminishes and the number of those who are willing to perceive and think will increase all the time. Those people must be led back once again to the religious life. This can succeed only if the concretely real operations of the

spiritual world are placed before the eyes of their souls, if they are not prevented by abstract, generalized thought of a Divinity about which nothing is truly conveyed but is referred to merely by an all-embracing word, with the details not understood.*

The Arab Spring which ignited in Tunisia is an example of what stands behind people's yearning for freedom. The Iranian revolution is another example of how a short-lived, free impulse was squashed by a take-over government of abstractions, the Ayatollas. Human beings in all these countries *want* their freedom, because they are part of the world evolution of humankind, where the Earth's destiny is to have free-thinking individual who are no longer under the yoke of a foreign power, religion, dictatorial government or monarchy, etc.

> In earlier times men did not unfold their thoughts as they have today. They did not unfold their thoughts by inner activity, inner effort. They unfolded thoughts by devoting themselves to contemplation of external nature and just as we perceive colors, and sounds today, they simultaneously perceived the thoughts. But in still earlier ages, when men gave themselves up to instinctive, unconscious clairvoyance, they received, together with the clairvoyant pictures, *thoughts* as gifts from the divine-spiritual worlds. Men did not work out their thoughts; they received them....
>
> The basic condition of human freedom is precisely that man shall unfold his thoughts himself in inner activity, and that out of these self-evolved thoughts which I have called *pure thoughts*, he shall also draw his moral impulses....
>
> Such moral impulses springing from the soil of man's own being, did not and could not exist in the earlier epochs of the evolution of humanity. Moral impulses had then to be imparted together with the thoughts, which were, so to speak, God-given, like commandments that were unconditionally binding and made a man unfree....
>
> It was from outside, therefore, that there came to man what he then laid hold of in his inmost soul. Hence in those olden times man's feeling for his Gods was such that he turned primarily to them when seeking to

---

* Steiner, *The Driving Force of Spiritual Powers in World History*, pp. 50–51.

find the causes of world-happenings and of his own life. When a man spoke of the Gods he spoke as though he was seeking to find in them the causes of his own existence on Earth, and of the manifestations of nature on Earth. He always looked back to the Gods as the primary causes of things. Whence came the world? Whence came I myself? These were the great religious questions of an earlier humanity.

Since that period things have changed.... We humans have all passed through a number of lives on Earth.... And if only we have the necessary will for it—for it depends upon the will—we can find in ourselves the force to produce our own world of thoughts, an individual world of thoughts....

Today man has acquired the freedom to work out his own thoughts but these thoughts would all remain hermits in the cosmos if they have not been taken from and brought back again into the cosmic harmony....

An older humanity felt that its moral ideas came from the Gods....

But now, if we turn to the moral aspect of these thoughts we shall say to ourselves: when we enter the spiritual world—either through the gate of death or in the Earth's future or whenever it may be—when we enter the spiritual world we shall meet the Spirits of Personality, the Archai. We shall then be able to perceive what it has been possible for them to do with our thoughts which, to begin with, for the sake of our freedom were isolated within ourselves. We shall recognize our worth and dignity as men from what the Spirits of Personality have been able to do with our thoughts. And cosmic thought turns directly into moral sensibility, moral impulsion....

What is important in our age is that man should have the resolute will to be a free being. In most cases he still does not will it and so has to accommodate himself to the idea. It is still difficult today for a man to wish to be a free being. What would please him most would be to wish what he likes and that the right Spirits would be there to carry out his wishes in an invisible way, supersensible way....

Today man does exactly this—he confuses freedom and indulgence of benevolent Gods with his love of ease and his wishes for comfort. There are still many people today who wish that there were benevolent Gods to carry out their wishes without much assistance from themselves.*

---

*   Ibid., pp. 53–59.

These thoughts and insights are not easy to grasp, but with some effort we can understand them.

Walking through the old city, one does not go one hour without hearing, or using oneself, the *Basmalah* (in the name of God), *in shā'a 'Llāh* (if God wills it), *al-hamdu li 'Llāh* (praise be to God), *salām alaikum* (peace be upon you), or *mā shā'a 'Llāh* (what God has willed, has come). We will be walking by a shop and all of a sudden be taken out of our reverie by a strong *Allāhu akbar* (God is greater), to which I just say, "Thank you," for lack of anything else to say. These formulas are part of life in the old city or in any Muslim country.

> Formulas run through the life of the Muslim like weft through warp. The *Basmalah*... inaugurates and sanctifies every undertaking, it ritualizes the regular actions of life such as the ablutions and meals; the formula *al-hamdu li 'Llāh* (praise be to God) brings them to a close.... The *Basmalah* evokes the Divine Cause—and therefore the presence of God—in transitory things and the *Hamdalah*—the praise—in a sense dissolves these things by reducing them to their Cause.
>
> The formulas "glory be to God" (*subhāna 'Llāh*) and "God is greater" (*Allāhu akbar*) are often associated with the *Hamdalah*, in accordance with a *hadīth*, and recited with it. "Glory be to God" is said to nullify a heresy that is contrary to the Divine Majesty....
>
> According to tradition, all these formulas, when recited a certain number of times, miraculously wipe out sins, be they as numberless of the drops of water in the sea....
>
> Another formula of quasi-organic importance in the life of a Muslim is the following: "if God wills it" (*in shā'a 'Llāh*); in saying this the Muslim recognizes his dependence, his weakness, and his ignorance in the face of God and at the same time abdicates all passional pretention; this is essentially the formula of serenity. It is also an affirmation that the end of all things is God, that it is He alone who is the absolutely certain outcome of our existence; there is no future outside Him....
>
> The Muslim—and especially he who observes the *Sunnah* right down to its minutest ramifications—lives in a fabric of symbols, participating in their weaving, since he lives them, and thus benefits from

all these means of remembering God and the next world, even if only indirectly. For the Christian... this situation of the Muslim appears to be a superficial formalism or even Pharisaism, but such an impression fails to take account of the fact that for Islam the will is not a matter of "improvisation," the will is determined or channeled for the contemplative peace of the mind.... To pronounce formulas for each and every occasion may amount to nothing, and seems like nothing to one who conceives only of moral heroism, but from another point of view—that of virtual union with God through the constant "remembrance" of things divine—this verbal way of introducing into life spiritual "points of reference" is on the contrary a means of purification and of grace about which no doubt can be entertained.*

These formulas, magic words, are always present and part of the life here. People use them, not as a monotonous, robotic movements of the lips, but truly meaning them. It's a way to meet the other, to *be* with the other human being, who becomes open to who we are, and gives us a blessing, a warm word, to say, "Yes, we are both human." I found myself using *in shā'a 'Llāh* and *Basmalah* to show kindness and understanding. I always remember my father-in-law, in Tehran, beaming and saying to me *mā shā'a 'Llāh* when he was pleased about something, or when we were sitting in his beautiful garden in Karaj, outside Tehran, sitting on the ground having a great lunch under the cherry trees, before everyone retired to a siesta, or when reading in this magical setting within the protection of the red earthen walls, again beaming *mā shā'a 'Llāh*. Or the waves of *Allāhu akbar* shouted from all the rooftops of Tehran at sunset, wave after wave, for hours, for many nights during the Iranian Revolution in 1979.

Here I want to mention a passage from Rudolf Steiner about "Not my will, but thy will be done," which is one of my favorites, the *in shā'a 'Llāh* of Islam.

> When we look back over the past we realize that although we sense a divine element shining into us, we have not utilized all the forces it could have made available to us, and it is our shortcoming which

---

* Schuon, *Understanding Islam: A New Translation with Selected Letters*, pp. 57–59.

make us unequal to this divine gleam that leads to the mood of prayer directed to the past. What, then, is the influence coming from the future that in a similar way impedes our ascent to the spirit? We need only to think of the feelings of fear and anxiety that gnaw at our soul life in the face of the unknown future. Is there a force that can give us a sense of security in this situation? Yes, there is. It is what we may call a feeling of humble dedication to whatever comes to us out of the dark womb of the future. But this feeling will be effective only if it becomes a mood of prayer. Let us avoid misunderstanding; we are not singing the praises of any kind of submissiveness. We are describing a definite form of it—submission in the face of whatever the future may bring. Those who harbour anxiety and fear for what the future might bring hinder their development, hamper the free unfolding of their soul forces. In fact nothing obstructs this development more than fear and anxiety in the face of the unknown future. However, the results of submitting reverently to the future can only be judged by experience. What does this submission to future events signify?

Ideally it would mean saying to oneself: "Whatever is coming my way, whether it be in the next hour or tomorrow, it is not going to be altered by any amount of fear and anxiety, because right now I do not know what is coming. I will therefore await it with complete inner calm, without the slightest emotional tremor!" All those who can meet the future in this relaxed and humble way, without losing any of their energy in the process, will be able to apply their soul forces in the most intense and free manner. It is as though one hindrance after another were to fall away as the soul is filled more and more strongly by this feeling of openness towards approaching events. This feeling, however, neither comes of itself nor comes by our being commanded to feel it. It is the result of what we can call the other prayerful mood, the one directed towards the future and its wisdom-filled course of events. To dedicate ourselves to this divine wisdom means that we call up again and again the thought, feeling, and soul impulse that what will come has to come, and that it will in some way have its good effects. To call forth this frame of mind and to give it expression in words, feelings, and ideas—this is the second prayerful mood, the mood of humble submission....

The mood of prayer brings us on the one hand to look at our strictly limited ego, which has worked its way from the past into the present, and shows us clearly how very much more there is in us than we have put to use; and on the other hand it brings us to look towards the future and shows us how much more can flow from the future into our ego than it has grasped so far. Any prayer belongs to one or other of these categories. If we realize what our soul is expressing, then in the very prayer itself we shall find the strength that brings us beyond ourselves. For what else is prayer than the lighting up in us of the very force that seeks to transcend what our ego is at the moment? And if the ego is gripped by this striving, it already has within it the strength for progress. If the past has taught us that we have more within us than we have ever put to use, then prayer is a cry to the divine that it may fill us with its presence. When we have found our way to this knowledge with the feelings of our heart, we can count prayer among the forces that will aid the development of the ego. We can do the same with prayer directed towards the future. If we are anxious or afraid of the approaching future, we lack the attitude of submission that prayer can bring. We must never forget that our destiny is ordered by the wisdom of the world. A sincerely submissive mood works quite differently from anxiety and fear; for whereas these hinder our development, submission enables us to approach the future with life-enhancing hope and an openness to receive it. So that submission, although it may seem to diminish us, is a powerful force carrying us towards the future so that the future enriches our soul and raises our development to ever new heights. We have now grasped what an effective force prayer is. And realizing that this has the effect of promoting ego development, we shall not need to expect any particular external effects, for we now know that prayer is itself a source of light and warmth: of light, because we set the soul free in its relation to the future and dispose it to accept whatever may emerge from that unknown realm; or of warmth, because we recognize that although we failed in the past to bring the divine element to fruition in our ego we have now brought it into our feelings so that it can be an effective force in us. Prayer that springs from looking back over the past gives rise to the inner warmth which is spoken of by all who understand prayer in its true nature. And the inner light comes to those who understand the submissive mood of prayer.*

---

* Steiner, *Transforming the Soul, Volume Two*, pp. 72–75.

FES, MOROCCO

A sentence that we can so often hear people say today, which is abused on its application as few others is: "I am a Christian." Esotericists should be clear that "being a Christian" is a distant ideal toward which they must constantly strive. To live as a Christian means, above all, to accept with serenity whatever destiny may bring us; to never complain about the work of the gods; to accept with joy whatever they may send. It means that the saying, "Look at the birds in the sky, they do not sow, they do not reap, they do not gather into barns, and yet they receive what they need," becomes second nature in us. Accept with gratitude what is given to us. Then we are living according to this verse. If we do not do this, then the verse becomes blasphemy in our mouths.*

So indeed we can agree that all the formulas which the Muslim use daily have a magical strength, and sometimes act like a balm on the soul.

The beautiful *salām alaikum* (peace be upon you), with the simple gesture of the hand on the heart, is a powerful one used many times a day in Fes el Bali, to welcome everyone, believers as well as non-believers.

[Here are] the beautiful lines of the Indo-Muslim poet-philosopher Muhammad Iqbal, who in one of his last poems tells a praying person that even though his prayer might not change his destiny, yet it can change his spiritual attitude by bringing him into touch with the Absolute Reality:

> *Your prayer is that your destiny be changed.*
> *My prayer is that you yourself be changed.*

This means that you accept willingly and lovingly whatever God has decreed.**

I met Annemarie Schimmel in Boston for a luncheon next to Harvard University, where she taught. She had graciously accepted to meet me to discuss Islamic calligraphy's powerful sacredness. I am reminded of this

---

*   Steiner, *Esoteric Lessons 1910–1912: From the Esoteric School, Volume Two*, p. 101.

**   Schuon, *Understanding Islam: A New Translation with Selected Letters* (from the foreword by Annemarie Schimmel), p. vii.

amazing woman who was in her late seventies in the late 1980s, and as we walked to her class, in between the lovely buildings of the university, I was awed by the love which poured towards her from her "Muslim students" as she walked by them. They were from Pakistan, India, Egypt, etc., and were getting a degree in Islamic studies from Harvard Divinity School. The warmth going towards this great Islamist and believer was something I had not experienced before. They truly venerated her because she was a real scholar on Islam and a devout Muslim, but of German birth. She was repeatedly invited and celebrated all throughout the Islamic world for her amazing scholarship. Yet she was a woman, and did not wear the hejab. You could feel that she was treated like the famous women saints in the history of Islam. Her books are used worldwide and are translated in many languages.

When she spoke, it was a strong language, with clear-cut sentences and no frivolous talking of any kind. When she spoke the name of Muhammad it was with a warmth and respect that I have seldom seen. She had become what she had studied and lived by during her whole life. My son who came along, who was about ten or eleven years old at the time, was being his usual very mischievous self, and she did not appreciate that at all!

She wanted children to be submissive, obey their elders, and keep quiet! Far from that, here I saw the clash of civilization. This child was a promethean individual who had come down to Earth to question, improvise, be creative and active, and not be told what to do. A young man of the West, with a different destiny, according to a different karma!

This child had chosen a mother from the West, and a father from the East. Annemarie had chosen parents from Germany for a life of profound scholarship on the Koran.

I have no doubt that she was a great Muslim scholar in a past life!

So what happens if we chose to believe in a monotheistic religion, the Old Testament, as opposed to a threefold one? To get back to this question:

> In considering karmic relationships we shall be concerned chiefly with how causes and effects are connected with the four different bodies (physical, etheric, astral, and ego)....

Our external destiny in a later life depends upon what we do in this physical life. Our external destiny is the environment into which we are born. Anyone who has done bad deeds prepares for himself a bad environment and vice versa. That is the first important karmic law: what we did in a former life determines our external destiny....

There is a second fundamental law. If we look at the way a person develops, we see that in the course of his life he learns an extraordinary amount. He absorbs concepts, ideas, experiences, feelings, and all this produces great changes in him.... All this has produced a corresponding change in the astral body for it is the most subtle and delicate and responds most quickly to change....

The ideas, feelings, and so on which transform the astral body during a long life will produce a marked change in the etheric body only in the next life. Thus if someone wants to be born in his next life with good habits and inclinations, he must try to prepare these as much as possible in his astral body. If he makes the effort to do good, he will be born in his next life with the tendency to do good and that will be a characteristic of his etheric body.... A person who simply hurries through the world will find in his next life that he cannot stick at anything....

We can trace the various temperaments, also, back to a previous life, for they are qualities of the etheric body.

The choleric person has a strong will, is bold, courageous, with an urge for action....

The melancholic person is very much occupied with himself and hence apt to keep himself to himself. He does a lot of thinking, particularly about the way in which his environment affects him....

The phlegmatic person has no real interest in anything; he is dreamy, inactive, lazy, and seeks sensuous enjoyment.

The sanguine person on the other hand, gets easily interested in anything, but he does not stick to it; his interest quickly fades....

The four temperaments express themselves in the etheric body, and so there are four main types of etheric body. They have differing currents and movements and these impart a particular basic color to the astral body....

The melancholic temperament is karmically determined if a person in his previous life was compelled to lead a narrow, restricted existence and to be alone much; if he was always preoccupied only with himself and unable to take much interest in anything else. If, however, a person has learned a great deal from experiences but has also had something of a hard struggle, if he has encountered many things and has not merely looked on at them, he will become a choleric. If again, he has had a pleasant life without much struggle or toil, or if he saw and passed by many things, but only as an onlooker, all this will work karmically into his etheric body of his next life: he will become a phlegmatic or a sanguine type....

How then, should we try to influence our etheric body for the next life? Everything done to develop the etheric body produces a result, however slowly, and education can take pains to instill quite specific habits. Whatever the etheric body acquires during one life comes to expression in the physical body in the next life. All the habits and inclinations of the present etheric body will create a predisposition to good or bad health. Good habits will produce good health; bad ones will create a tendency to some specific illness in the next life. A strong determination to rid oneself of a bad habit will work down into the physical body and produce a tendency to good health.... Infectious diseases, strangely enough, can be traced back to a highly developed selfish acquisitiveness in a previous life....

From what has been said you will realize that habits and feelings, which first belong to the spiritual life, can later express themselves in physical life. There is an important principle here: if care is taken to inculcate good habits, not only will the moral life of subsequent generations be improved, but also the health of a whole people, and vice versa. This is then their collective karma....

Another interesting karmic connection is between an habitually selfish attitude and a loving sympathy with others. Some people are hardened egoists—not only in their acquisitiveness—and others are unselfish and sympathetic. Both attitudes depend on the etheric body and may even find expression in the physical body. People who in one life have been habitually selfish will age quickly in their next life; they seem to shrivel up. On the other hand, if in one life you have been ready to make sacrifices and have loved others, you will remain young and healthy. In this way you can prepare even the physical body for the next life.*

---

*   Steiner, *Founding a Science of the Spirit*, pp. 55–59.

I had to quote this long passage because of the extreme difficulty of the subject. But it helps in finding an answer to some of my questions on karma. What kind of body will a Muslim and the Muslim people inherit for their next life? (The Muslim extremists and fundamentalists are not included.) Their spiritual, religious practice will develop certain characteristics within their astral bodies, which again will show up in the etheric bodies of their next lives. Good habits, a strong etheric body, meaning a healthier body which is spoken of in the Koran, a resistance to illness. On the other hand, in our Western world such as the United States, etc., what are we developing with our materialistic attitude? Or pseudo-Christian religions?

> There is a form of illness very widespread today—nervousness or neurosis—which was hardly known a hundred years ago. This is not because it was unrecognized, but because it was so uncommon. This characteristic illness springs from the materialistic outlook of the eighteenth century. Without that, such an illness would never have appeared. The occult teacher knows that if this materialism were to continue for a few decades more, it would have a devastating effect on the general health of mankind. If these materialistic habits of thoughts were to remain unchecked, people would not only be neurotic in the ordinary sense but children would be born trembling; they would not merely be sensitive to their environment but be hypersensitive, receiving from everything around them a sensation of pain. Above all, mental ailments would spread rapidly; epidemics of insanity would occur during following decades. This was the danger—epidemic insanity—that faced mankind, and the possibility of it in the future was why the leaders of humanity, the Masters of Wisdom, saw the necessity of allowing some spiritual wisdom to be diffused among mankind at large. Nothing short of a spiritual picture of the world could restore to coming generations a tendency to good health.*

It is a daunting task! We are already in a world of epidemic psychological disorder and insanity, and it is only through the insights that spiritual science can bring to us that we can face the future, and even have a future.

---

* Ibid., p. 59.

Whether it is a Muslim country, a Christian one, a Buddhist one, a Jewish one, etc., the problems we are faced with can only be resolved by paying attention to our spiritual legacy, to spiritual science.

In most Muslim countries people have a more difficult life compared to the western countries, but a life of comfort and luxury is not always such a good thing for future incarnations.

> When life becomes physically more comfortable due to improved health conditions, the soul is affected in the opposite way; in the course of time the soul experiences a certain emptiness, a sense of dissatisfaction, a lack of fulfillment. If the trend towards ever greater physical comfort and health continued along the lines envisaged in the context of a purely materialistic outlook on life, such souls would feel less and less incentive to progress inwardly. The whole thing would be accompanied by a stultification of the soul.
>
> If you take a closer look at life you will see signs of this already. There has hardly been an age before ours in which so many people live in such pleasant outer conditions and yet go about with their souls barren and unoccupied. That is why such people rush from sensation to sensation; if they have enough money they travel from town to town in order to see something; if not, they rush from pleasure to pleasure every night. Yet for all this the soul remains empty, and ends up at a complete loss about what to look for in the world to fill the void. Especially when life is exclusively geared to outer, physical comfort, the inclination to think solely in terms of the physical will be strong.... In this way human souls are becoming more sick as physical life is rendered more healthy....
>
> A materialistic approach to life may well ease things on the physical side but will at the same time create inner difficulties, which may then lead the individual concerned to seek for the content of a spiritual view of life out of his soul's sufferings.*

The future lies like an enormous question before us—not like a vague, abstract question, but as a concrete question. How do we approach what has wanted to enter our earthly world ever more and more as a question to humanity, even as a spiritual revelation, ever since the

---

*   Steiner, *Manifestations of Karma*, p. 170.

last third of the nineteenth century? And how should we relate this to what has been revealed in the past?...

The fact is, that when one turns to the spirit on the one hand, then, on the other, those people who want only to worship what was in the past are drawn towards the spirit of contradiction or opposition. And the more we attempt to take hold of the spirit of what is to be the future of humanity, the more will the people looking to the past be obsessed by the spirit of opposition.

In humanity today it is noticeable how religious feeling is trying to imbue new life into itself. It consists mostly of fumbling attempts. Spiritual-scientific attempts should not be fumbling ones. Through them the real, concrete spirit world should be taken hold of.... The mere religious tradition is not enough for us, we want to have an inner religious experience.*

As everyone knows, throughout the Islamic world there has been an awakening of the believers who willingly took to the streets to try and implement some changes, as the Arab Spring of 2010 has shown. This is a sign of the times, something new is trying to emerge which will allow more freedom. Many are dying in this process, many have died trying to bring to birth new freedom, a new spirit is trying to be born out of the ashes. But as quoted above, the many forces which want to remain in power and behind the times are very much active and will fight to keep to the past. But the only way to get stronger is to have hindrances, like our imperfections. They lead us to overcome them, and become better in the process.

I had left the leather shopping for last. While walking on the main artery of the medina I noticed a beautiful handmade pair of boots, with a lovely design on the leather. So I followed the man to his shop through various alleys and entered an enormous store where several men were making beautiful boots with different designs. I watched them as they sat cross-legged and worked all day. They passed around the hookah, they were smoking, but not tobacco, as I could see from their very yellow complexions. It was

---

*   Steiner, *Cosmic New Year: Thoughts for New Year 1920*, pp. 46–47.

sad for me to realize that many of the people working in the medina were addicted to different substances. The job is tedious, demanding, and for many smoking was a way to stand the difficult work, year after year.

I looked at the enormous inventory of beautiful handmade leather bags in all different shapes, forms, and colors, and I appreciated the work involved in making these treasures. Fes is truly a beehive of artistic activity. I was happy to purchase a few gifts for friends and family; the shopkeepers were very thankful and glad we were there to admire their beautiful articles. I will always treasure my pocketbook, which I can give away as a family heirloom.

The Fessi have not lost their artistic way of life. But very close by was the market where one could buy all the machine-made articles shipped directly from China!

I wondered how long the artists will be able to maintain their lifestyle, their art, their traditions.

My stay in Fes was coming to an end, and I felt that I had made the right decision in wanting to be part of a very old city, an ancient way of life.

One rainy morning, with a suitcase and a huge bag filled to the max, I dragged my belongings down the narrow stairs and alleys with difficulty. A lovely old man who was cleaning the street with his broom, with his donkey waiting, took my bags and brought them to the taxi stand as a gesture of goodwill. He was ancient, content, and doing his job of keeping the city clean as he has been doing for years.

I thanked him, gave him a good tip, and took the taxi to the train station. As I was getting ready to travel back to the Western world, I thought about these words:

> Materialistic people, no matter how well-educated, how scientific, or prominent, when they enter the spiritual world unprepared, they stand far below the simplest primitive people, who through their prayer are already in touch with forces in the spiritual world. In our scientific materialistic age, whose scientific accomplishments are so boundlessly amazing, human beings have more and more forgotten how to pray. They fall asleep and awaken with their everyday thoughts. But what are they doing in this way? For something is happening through this

omission. Every time, they kill something of their spiritual life, of their spiritual forces on the physical plane.*

I had accomplished, but not finished, my long journey into trying to decipher the mysteries behind Muslims, Christians, and Jews. But as usual, when I finish one journey, another one comes, because more questions have turned up and a new path seems to have appeared out of nowhere. There is no end, just beginnings!

> When no longer numbers and figures
> Are keys to all creatures,
> When those who sing or kiss
> Know more than all the learned scholars,
> When the world returns to itself
> In a life of freedom,
> When once again the light and shadow wed
> And these united give the real clarity,
> When man can know the true world story
> In myths and in the form of poems,
> Then will the whole deformed being
> Vanish before one single secret word.**

A man must not take an egoistic view of his existence; he must realize that while he stands in the world as a thinking being, his thoughts do not belong to himself alone; for after his death they must pass out into the whole cosmos and become forces which continue to work therein. If we think good thoughts we give over our good thoughts to the Cosmos at our death. If we think evil thoughts, we give over our evil thoughts to the Cosmos at our death. For man is not only put into Earth-existence to develop simply as a free being.... But there is another reason why he must become a free and independent being: he is put into the world that he may become a being through whom the gods themselves work, to guide the Cosmos from epoch to epoch.

---

* Steiner, *Esoteric Lessons 1910–1912: From the Esoteric School, Volume Two*, p. 38.

** Novalis, *Heinrich von Ofterdingen*, part II, in Stein, *The Ninth Century and the Holy Grail*, p. 90.

BEYOND THE BLOOD

I might say that what the gods have to weave as thought into the Cosmos, they must prepare in what can be thought and pondered over in the lives of individual beings. These lives are the sanctuaries in which the gods must cultivate those thoughts which they continually require in the development of the world, so that they may embody them in their Cosmos, as actual impulses of force.[*]

I must thank the reader for going on this long journey because the reader has become a sanctuary, as has been quoted above. A sanctuary, a sacred place for all these thoughts to be pondered and meditated on, thereby helping the gods fulfill the Earth's destiny.

---

[*] Steiner, *The Evolution of the World and of Humanity*, p. 137.

Bibliography

Al-Gazzali. *La Alquimia de la Felicidad*. Madrid: Editorial Sufi, 2002.

Armstrong, Karen. *The Battle for God*. New York: Ballantine Books, 2000.

Barks, Coleman, and John Moyne, translators. *The Drowned Book: Ecstatic and Earthy Reflections of Bahauddin, the Father of Rumi*. New York: HarperCollins, 2004.

Barks, Coleman, trans., and Inayat Khan. *The Hand of Poetry: Five Mystic Poets of Persia*. New Lebanon, NY: Omega Publications, 1993.

Béji, Hélé. *Islam Pride: Derrière le Voile*. Paris: Éditions Gallimard, 2011.

Blunt, Wilfrid. *The Golden Road to Samarkand*. New York: The Viking Press, 1973.

Bock, Emil. *The Apocalypse of Saint John*. Edinburgh: Floris Books, 1986.

———. *The Childhood of Jesus: The Unknown Years*. Edinburgh: Floris Books, 1997.

———. *Saint Paul: Life, Epistles and Teaching*. Edinburgh: Floris Books, 1993.

Boyce, Mary. *Zoroastrians: Their Religious Beliefs and Practices*. London: Routledge and Kegan Paul, 1979.

Chakir, Yousri. *Recueil de Contes du Folklore Marocain*. Translated by Mohamed Adghoghi. Casablanca: Edisoft, 2007.

Clarke, Suzanna. *A House in Fez: Building a Life in the Ancient Heart of Morocco*. New York: Pocket Books, 2007.

Corbin, Henry. *L'Homme de Lumière dans le Soufisme Iranien*. Paris: Éditions Présence, 1987.

———. *Swedenborg and Esoteric Islam*. Translated by Leonard Fox. West Chester, PA: Swedenborg Foundation, 1995.

———. *The Voyage and the Messenger: Iran and Philosophy*. Berkeley, CA: North Atlantic Books, 1998.

de Hartog, Leo. *Genghis Khan: Conqueror of the World*. New York: Barnes and Noble, 1989.

Fes Medina Tourist Circuits. Fes: ADER-Fes, 2005.

Ibn 'Arabî, Muhyiddin. *Traité de L'Amour*. Translated by Maurice Gloton. Paris: Albin Michel, 1986.

Jîlî, 'Abd al-Karîm al-. *De l'Homme Universel: Extraits du Livre al-Insân al-Kâmil*. Translated by Titus Burckhardt. Paris: Dervy-Livres, 1975.

John of the Cross. *Ascent of Mount Carmel*. Translated by E. Allison Peers. Tunbridge Wells, UK: Burns and Oates, 1983.

Karim, Tohir. *Traces of the Sacred Avesta*. Tashkent: Gafur Guliam, 2007.

Karimov, Islam. *Uzbekistan on the Threshold of the Twenty-First Century: Challenges to Stability and Progress*. New York: St. Martin's Press, 1998.

Khan, Hazrat Inayat. *The Art of Being and Becoming*. New Lebanon, NY: Omega Publications, 2012.

———. *The Music of Life: The Inner Nature and Effects of Sound*. New Lebanon, NY: Omega Publications, 2005.

Khudazarov, Telman M. *Teach Yourself Azeri: An Easy-to-Use Azeri Language Course Specially Designed for English Speakers*. Baku: Nargiz, 2009.

Kühlewind, Georg. *Wilt Thou Be Made Whole? Healing in the Gospels*. Great Barrington, MA: Lindisfarne Books, 2008.

Lyttelton, Celia. *The Scent Trail: How One Woman's Quest for the Perfect Perfume Took Her Around the World*. New York: New American Library, 2007.

Munk, Rabbi Michael L. *The Wisdom in the Hebrew Alphabet*. Brooklyn, NY: Mesorah Publications, 2010.

Nasr, Seyyed Hossein. *Islam: Religion, History, and Civilization*. San Francisco: HarperSanFrancisco, 2003.

———. *Islamic Life and Thought*. Albany, NY: State University of New York Press, 1981.

Ozak, Muzaffer. *Love is the Wine: Talks of a Sufi Master in America*. Putney, VT: Threshold Books, 1987.

Payne, Robert. *The History of Islam*. New York: Dorset Press, 1987.

Prokofieff, Sergei O. *Eternal Individuality: Towards a Karmic Biography of Novalis*. London: Temple Lodge, 1992.

Roché, Déodat. *Les Cathares, Précurseurs des Temps Modernes: Extrait des Cahiers d'Etudes Cathares*. Aude: Arques Par Couiza, 1963.

Rumi, Jalaluddin. *Words of Paradise: Selected Poems of Rumi*. Translated by Raficq Abdulla. New York: Viking Studio, 2000.

Sáenz-Badillos, Angel, and Judit Targarona Borrás. *Poetas Hebreos de Al-Andalus, Siglos X–XII: Antología*. Córdoba: Ediciones El Almendro, 2003.

Schimmel, Annemarie. *Islam: An Introduction*. Albany, NY: State University of New York Press, 1992.

Schuon, Frithjof. *Understanding Islam: A New Translation with Selected Letters*. Bloomington, IN: World Wisdom, 2011.

Schuré, Édouard. *The Great Initiates: A Study of the Secret History of Religions*. Hudson, NY: SteinerBooks, 1989.

Stein, Walter Johannes. *The Ninth Century and the Holy Grail*. London: Temple Lodge, 2001.

Steiner, Rudolf. *At the Gates of Spiritual Science*. London: Rudolf Steiner Press, 1970.

———. *Background to the Gospel of St. Mark*. London: Rudolf Steiner Press, 1985.

———. *The Christian Mystery: Early Lectures*. Great Barrington, MA: Anthroposophic Press, 1998.

———. *Christianity as Mystical Fact: And the Mysteries of Antiquity*. Great Barrington, MA: SteinerBooks, 2006.

———. *Cosmic Memory: The Story of Atlantis, Lemuria, and the Division of the Sexes*. Great Barrington, MA: SteinerBooks, 1987.

———. *Cosmic New Year: Thoughts for New Year 1920*. Great Barrington, MA: SteinerBooks, 2007.

———. *Cosmosophy, Volume One*. Spring Valley, NY: Anthroposophic Press, 1985.

———. *Deeper Secrets of Human History in the Light of the Gospel of St. Matthew*. London: Rudolf Steiner Press, 1985.

———. *The Driving Force of Spiritual Powers in World History*. North Vancouver, Canada: Steiner Book Centre, 1972.

———. *Egyptian Myths and Mysteries*. Hudson, NY: Anthroposophic Press, 1971.

———. *Esoteric Christianity and the Mission of Christian Rosenkreutz*. London: Rudolf Steiner Press, 2001.

———. *Esoteric Lessons 1904–1909: From the Esoteric School, Volume One*. Great Barrington, MA: SteinerBooks, 2007.

———. *Esoteric Lessons 1910–1912: From the Esoteric School, Volume Two*. Great Barrington, MA: SteinerBooks, 2012.

———. *The Evolution of the World and of Humanity*. Blauvelt, NY: Garber Communications, 1989.

———. *The Fall of the Spirits of Darkness*. London: Rudolf Steiner Press, 2008.

———. *Founding a Science of the Spirit*. London: Rudolf Steiner Press, 1999.

———. *Freedom of Thought and Societal Forces: Implementing the Demands of Modern Society*. Great Barrington, MA: SteinerBooks, 2008.

———. *From Beetroot to Buddhism…: Answers to Questions*. London: Rudolf Steiner Press, 1999.

———. *The Gospel of St. John and Its Relation to the Other Gospels*. Spring Valley, NY: Anthroposophic Press, 1982.

———. *The Gospel of St. Mark*. Hudson, NY: Anthroposophic Press, 1986.

———. *How Can Mankind Find the Christ Again?* Hudson, NY: Anthroposophic Press, 1984.

———. *How Do I Find the Christ?* London: Rudolf Steiner Press, 1968.

———. *Karmic Relationships: Esoteric Studies, Volume One*. London: Rudolf Steiner Press, 1972.

———. *Karmic Relationships: Esoteric Studies, Volume Three*. London: Rudolf Steiner Press, 1977.

———. *Karmic Relationships: Esoteric Studies, Volume Five*. London: Rudolf Steiner Press, 1966.

———. *Karmic Relationships: Esoteric Studies, Volume Six*. London: Rudolf Steiner Press, 1971.

———. *Life Between Death and Rebirth*. Hudson, NY: Anthroposophic Press, 1968.

———. *Manifestations of Karma*. London: Rudolf Steiner Press, 1995.

———. *Mystery Knowledge and Mystery Centres*. London: Rudolf Steiner Press, 1997.

———. *Original Impulses for the Science of the Spirit*. Australia: Completion Press, 2001.

———. *An Outline of Esoteric Science*. Hudson, NY: Anthroposophic Press, 1997.

———. *The Principle of Spiritual Economy: In Connection with Questions of Reincarnation: An Aspect of the Spiritual Guidance of Man.* Hudson, NY: Anthroposophic Press, 1986.

———. *The Redemption of Thinking: A Study in the Philosophy of St. Thomas Aquinas.* Spring Valley, NY: Anthroposophic Press, 1956.

———. *Reincarnation and Karma: Their Significance in Modern Culture.* New York: Anthroposophic Press, 1960.

———. *Rosicrucian Wisdom: An Introduction.* London: Rudolf Steiner Press, 2000.

———. *Rudolf Steiner Speaks to the British: Lectures and Addresses in England and Wales.* London: Rudolf Steiner Press, 1998.

———. *Staying Connected: How to Continue Your Relationships with Those Who Have Died.* Great Barrington, MA: Anthroposophic Press, 1999.

———. *The Sun Mystery and the Mystery of Death and Resurrection: Exoteric and Esoteric Christianity.* Great Barrington, MA: SteinerBooks, 2006.

———. *Supersensible Knowledge.* Hudson, NY: Anthroposophic Press, 1987.

———. *The Temple Legend: Freemasonry and Related Occult Movements.* London: Rudolf Steiner Press, 1997.

———. *Three Streams in the Evolution of Mankind: The Connection of the Luciferic-Ahrimanic Impulses with the Christ-Jahve Impulse.* London: Rudolf Steiner Press, 1965.

———. *Transforming the Soul, Volume One.* London: Rudolf Steiner Press, 2005.

———. *Transforming the Soul, Volume Two.* London: Rudolf Steiner Press, 2006.

———. *Unifying Humanity Spiritually: Through the Christ Impulse.* London: Rudolf Steiner Press, 2014.

———. *Universal Spirituality and Human Physicality: Bridging the Divide.* London: Rudolf Steiner Press, 2014.

———. *What is Necessary in These Urgent Times.* Great Barrington, MA: SteinerBooks, 2010.

———. *World History in the Light of Anthroposophy.* London: Rudolf Steiner Press, 1977.

Talbi, Mohamed. *Ma Religion c'est la Liberté: L'Islam et les Défis de la Contemporanéité.* Translated by Dr. Mohamed Salah Barbouche. Tunis: Éditions Nirvana, 2011.

Teresa of Ávila. *The Life of Saint Teresa of Ávila By Herself.* Translated by J. M. Cohen. London: Penguin Books, 1987.

Vitray-Meyerovitch, Eva de. *Rûmî and Sufism.* Translated by Simone Fattal. Sausalito, CA: Post-Apollo Press, 1987.

Waines, David. *The Odyssey of Ibn Battuta: Uncommon Tales of a Medieval Adventurer.* London: I.B. Tauris, 2010.

Washington, Peter (ed.). *Persian Poets.* New York: Knopf, 2000.

Weatherford, Jack. *Genghis Khan and the Making of the Modern World.* New York: Three Rivers Press, 2004.

Welburn, Andrew J. *The Book with Fourteen Seals: The Prophet Zarathustra and the Christ-Revelation.* London: Rudolf Steiner Press, 1991.

———. *Mani, the Angel and the Column of Glory: An Anthology of Manichean Texts.* Edinburgh: Floris Books, 1998.

www.ingramcontent.com/pod-product-compliance
Lightning Source LLC
Chambersburg PA
CBHW021813300426
44114CB00009BA/157